Political Islam

Nazih Ayubi studies the Islamic movements of six countries in detail and traces both the intellectual sources and the socio-economic bases of political Islam, arguing that as a belief system and a way of life, it is a modern phenomenon, dating back only to the inter-war period. He describes the major proponents as urban, educated and relatively young people, whose energies were mobilised, but whose expectations were not fulfilled by the post-independence 'populist' regimes in the Arab World.

Ayubi stresses the traditional concern in Islam for the collective enforcement of morals, but argues that there is no case for the commonly held misconception that politics in the Arab world begins from theological principles: the historical connection between Islam and politics can be explained as an attempt by the rulers to legitimise their actions. He suggests that radical Muslims are reversing this position by subjecting politics to their specific religious views, and argues that their movement is in some senses an anti-state one. He concludes by discussing possible intellectual responses to fundamentalism, drawing on the thinking of contemporary Muslim liberals.

Nazih Ayubi is Reader in Politics and Director of the Middle East Politics Programme at the University of Exeter. He has written widely on politics in the Middle East and the developing world.

Political Islam

Religion and Politics
in the Arab World

Nazih N. Ayubi

London and New York

First published 1991
by Routledge
11 New Fetter Lane, London EC4P 4EE

Simultaneously published in the USA and Canada
by Routledge
29 West 35th Street, New York, NY 10001

New in paperback 1993

Typeset from author's disks by
Witwell Ltd, Southport
Printed and bound in Great Britain by
Biddles Ltd, Guildford and King's Lynn

British Library Cataloguing in Publication Data
A catalogue record for this book is available from the British Library

Library of Congress Cataloging in Publication Data
Ayubi, Nazih N.
    Political Islam : religion and politics in the Arab world /
Nazih N. Ayubi.
        p.   cm.
    Includes bibliographical references and index.
    1. Islam and state.   I. Title
JC49.A928   1991
297'.1977—dc20   90–42326
                                                  CIP

ISBN 0-415-05442-7
ISBN 0-415-10385-1 (pbk)

To Lindy

Contents

Preface

The subject of this book is 'political Islam', or the doctrine and/or movement which contends that Islam possesses a theory of politics and the State. Political Islam represents only one of several intellectual and political manifestations of the interplay between religion and politics. Although as a theory it is a modern improvisation which started to emerge after the First World War, political Islam does indeed invoke the traditional sources and precedents; hence the necessity in a work such as this to delve briefly into the theory and practice of the historical Islamic State.

Our study is mainly, but not exclusively, confined to the Arab world, where the discourse of political Islam has manifested itself most vigorously in recent years. The book is based in large measure on a presentation of the political theses of the fundamentalists and neo-fundamentalists in the Arab world, and also on an examination of the response, critique and analysis to which these theses have given rise among Arab intellectuals. Literature in the Arabic language, from a dozen Arab countries, is invoked whenever possible to highlight the character of the 'internal' debate and inquiry, even when such literature may not necessarily offer the most sophisticated level of philosophical discourse or socio-political analysis.

This book is also concerned with an attempt to relate ideas to their political and socio-economic context. The sources on this aspect are neither as abundant nor as methodologically advanced as the sources pertaining to the intellectual discourse. This 'political sociology' type of study is often regarded by the authorities in Muslim countries as more 'dangerous' than studying the Islamic, or even the Islamist, texts. All the more so, as the Islamist movement has developed over the last few years into a basically anti-State movement – a subject that will receive a great deal of our attention. The relations between religion and politics are complex and contextual: the current Islamic revival is not simply a means for retreating into a nostalgic past but also a device for coping – in one way or another – with the present and the future. By the same token, it would be naive to regard Islamism simply as part of an 'American-Saudi design' to consolidate the rule of a native, but dependent, bourgeoisie; or else to regard Islamism simply as the battle cry of the oppressed and exploited masses in their revolt against internal despotism and foreign hegemony. The Islamic revival is potentially all these things, and much more, depending on the specific contingency of every social and political situation – as we set out to illustrate in this book. The 'cut-off' point for material dealt with in the book is Summer 1989.

In undertaking the research for this book, I was greatly helped by a grant from the Economic and Social Research Council, received jointly by Tim Niblock and myself; within that project I have undertaken this comparative study of Arab countries, while he is concentrating on a Sudanese case study to be published later on. I would like to express my gratitude to the ESRC for funding this project. The writing of the book was facilitated as a result of a six months' sabbatical leave from my university in the academic year 1988–1989. Although six weeks of this period were taken up by a lecture tour in China and Japan (which was thought-provoking in its own right), the leave did provide a much-needed – albeit rather brief – space in which to pull some of the strings of this work together. I would like to thank the University of Exeter for this opportunity, as well as my colleagues in the Department of Politics for their help and support.

I would also like to acknowledge that some passages included in this book have appeared previously, in different form, in *Inquiry* (Vol. 2, no. 1, December 1981, pp. 18–23), and in *The Journal of International Affairs* (Vol. 36, no. 2, Fall/Winter 1982/83, pp. 271–283); they have been used here with permission from the publishers.

This book fits within a broader interest of mine, developed over the last few years, in the socio-economic as well as the cultural bases of the Arab State. Another book of mine on the political economy of the Arab State is nearing completion (and in some ways the two books should complement each other). During these years I have accumulated a number of debts and I am pleased now to acknowledge some of this indebtedness. I am grateful to Abd al-Malik Awda who has, over the years, convinced me – in word and in deed – that secularism has roots in Egyptian society and in Muslim culture. I am also grateful to Roger Owen and P. J. Vatikiotis for their long-standing support and encouragement. Alas, Malcolm Kerr is no longer with us to be thanked personally for his help and support, but all those who had the chance to cooperate with him remember him with gratitude and affection. Ali Hilal Dessouki, my friend for three decades, has always helped with exchange of ideas and provision of sources. Saad Eddin Ibrahim I have known for half that period, but his help and support have been continuous. Sayyid Yasin has been generous with the suggesting of ideas and sources. Bahgat Korany has provided unfailing help and encouragement, and Sami Zubaida has also helped on several occasions. I would also like to thank Fred Halliday for his comments on the manuscript. Paul Auchterlonie's bibliographical help and his indexing of the book are gratefully acknowledged. Lindy has given me the most generous and continuous support, and has done the initial word-processing and copy-editing of the book – it is difficult for me to express the full measure of my gratitude to her.

All translations from the Arabic language throughout this work are mine unless otherwise indicated. The transliteration system followed in the book is basically that used by the *International Journal of Middle East Studies* (IJMES), except in the case of words or names that have become familiar in a certain romanised form (e.g. Quran, Nasser, Khomeini).

Nazih N. Ayubi
Exeter

1 The theory and practice of the Islamic State

It is often suggested that contemporary attempts at 'Islamic revival' are seeking to retrieve and to reinstall a type of religious state that had existed at some point in the history of Muslim societies. Implicit in this suggestion is the view that Islam has a specific theory on politics and the State, and that the Islamic revivalists are attempting to implement anew this existing theory of the State. The impression that such a theory exists is usually reinforced by the fact that the contemporary Islamists repeatedly invoke the religious and the juridic texts, as well as certain historical precedents of 'Islamic government', in their attempt to prove the 'obligatoriness' of an Islamic State. It is therefore necessary for any work on the contemporary discourse of 'political Islam' to delve to some extent into the juridic text and into historical precedence in order to trace some of the origins of the Islamists' argument. I should hasten at this point, however, to warn the reader that I am not setting out here to offer a potted history of the Muslim State or a concise review of the history of Islamic thought. Readers unfamiliar with this material would do better to refer first to some of the more systematic treatments available in some of the books which are mentioned in this chapter (e.g. Rosenthal, Watt, Lambton, etc.).[1] Rather, the purpose of this chapter is to deal with some of the concepts and the precedents which would shed light on our subsequent treatment of the subject of political Islam. It is therefore highly eclectic and interpretive, as well as structurally rather complex, since it deals with several loosely related themes rather than with one integrated thesis. For these reasons, it would perhaps be convenient to highlight in advance some of the main pursuits of this chapter.

IS ISLAM A 'POLITICAL' RELIGION?

It will be argued in this chapter that the original Islamic sources (the Quran and the Hadith) have very little to say on matters of government and the State. However, the first issue to confront the Muslim community immediately after the death of its formative leader, Prophet Muhammad, was in fact the problem of government, and Muslims had therefore to innovate and to improvise with regard to the form and nature of government. Indeed, the first disagreements that emerged within the Muslim community (and which led to the eventual division into Sunnis, Kharijites, Shi'is and other sects) were concerned with politics. But theorising about politics was very much delayed, and most of the Islamic political literature available to us seems to have emerged when the political realities that it addressed were on the decline. Furthermore, most of what emerged, at least within the Sunni tradition, was also produced 'in the shadow of the State'. The State had sanctioned a certain 'methodology' of writing, based on linguistic explanation (*bayan*) and on reasoning by analogy (*qiyas*), and had also sponsored the juridic elite that wrote on political subjects. The result was an elegant and elaborate body of jurisprudence, and a formal theory of the caliphate that, through monopoly and repetition, had become altogether entrenched in the 'Arab mind'.

With the passage of time, subsequent generations have found it extremely difficult to distinguish between what was meant as description and what was meant as prescription within this literature. Furthermore the elegant body of jurisprudence has been elevated almost to the level of the *Shari'a* (religious law) itself. Today, when most *salafis* and some fundamentalists (for definitions see Chapter 3 and the Glossary) call for the implementation of shari'a, what they really have in mind is the implementation of the jurisprudence formulated by the early jurists. This jurisprudence has now been extracted from its historical and political context, and endowed with essentialist, everlasting qualities. The point is thus overlooked that this jurisprudence was in the first place a human improvisation meant to address certain political and social issues in a certain historical, geographical and social context. What is also often overlooked is that the main body of the official jurisprudence fulfilled a certain political function by imparting religious legitimacy to the government of the day, which had usually come to rule by force or intrigue and which, in its daily conduct, was not generally living up to the Islamic ideal.

A point not elaborated upon in this chapter, but for which the material in this chapter provides the necessary background, is that the neo-fundamentalists, or the proponents of political Islam, have actually introduced some novel, and radical, changes in the way the Islamic political tradition is understood. While they want to preserve the close link between religion and politics that the traditional jurisprudence had developed, they want to reverse the order within this link. The traditional jurists had forged a link between politics and religion by giving a religious legitimacy to political power. The political Islamists maintain that religion and politics cannot be separated, but because they are now in the position of resisting the existing State, not of legitimising it, they are seeking the politicisation of a particular vision of religion that they have in mind. To achieve this purpose, the contemporary Islamists are often inclined to be more innovative and less textual in their approach. They do, of course, invoke the text and quote the source, but in doing so they are highly selective and remarkably innovative. Political precedence is of practically no interest to them, neither is the main body of official jurisprudence, apart from a few exceptions such as Ibn Taimiya. Indeed, in spite of being Sunnis, they seem to have no qualms about borrowing concepts and practices from the anti-Sunni sects: their major concept of *hakimiyya* seems to be of kharijite inspiration, and their frequently practised *taqiyya* seems to be of Shi'i inspiration.

We shall argue throughout this book that political Islam is a new invention – it does not represent a 'going back' to any situation that existed in the past or to any theory that was formulated in the past. What it keeps from the past is the juridic tradition of linking politics and religion. But even then, it seeks to transform the formalistic and symbolic link that the jurists had forged between politics and religion into a *real* bond. Furthermore, political Islamists want to reverse the traditional relationship between the two spheres so that politics becomes subservient to religion, and not the other way round, as was the case historically.

One of the themes that this chapter also explores concerns precisely this last point: i.e. why was there a certain fusion between religion and politics throughout the history of the Islamic State? One familiar answer to this question is that Islam is by its very nature a 'political' religion. This is a proposition – widely held in both Western and Muslim circles – that we endeavour to refute throughout this book. It is about time that this Orientalist/fundamentalist myth was dispelled once and for all. Even the common interpretation of the term *umma*, familiar in Western and Muslim circles alike, as a specifically Islamic community, should be subjected to serious scrutiny, for neither in the Quran itself nor in subsequent writings by Muslim authors was this term given such an unequivocally religious connotation. The impression in Western circles that Islam is a political religion may be an extension of the view that Islam was a religion that established itself by military conquest. The now widely held opinion among Muslims that Islam is both 'a religion and a State' (*din wa dawla*) is a measure of the extraordinary intellectual influence of the modern fundamentalist thesis on mainstream Muslim opinion. Far from being a conventional piece of wisdom, this thesis is indeed quite new, dating, as we illustrate in this book, to the third decade of this century at the earliest.

Islam is indeed a religion of collective morals (as we argue in Chapter 2), but there is very little in it that is specifically political – i.e. there is very little in the original Islamic sources on how to form states, run governments and manage organisations. If the rulers of the historical Islamic states were also spiritual leaders of their community, this was not because Islam required the religious leader (*imam*) to be also a political ruler. Indeed, quite the reverse – Islam had spread in regions where the modes of production tended to be control-based, and where the State had always played a crucial economic and social role. The 'monopoly' of a certain religion has always been one of the State's usual instruments for ensuring ideological hegemony. The historical 'Islamic' State inherited this tradition.

In the earlier phases of the Islamic State the mere fact of being Muslim was rewarding enough from an economic and political point of view: for initially the expanding conquests and the imposition of poll taxes (*jizya*) on the non-Muslims of the conquered lands had guaranteed financial incomes and military/administrative positions for the Muslims, who were still a minority in these newly opened-up regions. However, at a subsequent point, during the time of 'Umar, the influx of Muslims from Arabia to the *amsar* (conquered lands) had become so rapid and so extensive that not all the newcomers could be put on the register (*diwan*) for regular payment. It was these frustrated groups, usually from the minor or peripheral Arabian tribes, which were to form the first religio-political opposition movement against the State, that of the *Khawarij*. Eventually, too, extensive territories were conquered in and around Persia, where large populations embraced Islam but did not become Arabised. It was the social and political exclusion of such communities that eventually led to the emergence of the second major religio-political opposition movement against the State, that of the Shi'is. Both the Khawarij and the Shi'is attempted to use religious arguments to shed doubt on the legitimacy of the government and the rulers. It was precisely at this stage, and by way of a counter-argument against the claims of the protest movements, that the official juridic theory of the State was to emerge.

By now, the State incorporated large Muslim but non-Arabic-speaking communities, as well as ever-increasing numbers of

Arabic-speaking Muslim converts. Thus it had to confront not only a problem of security and order (represented by the protest movements) but also a growing financial crisis. Gone were the days when being Muslim involved receiving a regular income, gone even were the days when being Muslim exempted one from paying tax to the State. The *jizya* imposed on the dwindling numbers of non-Muslims was no longer sufficient to support a State that was both larger and more complex and that was also threatened by various protest groups. The new official theory had to justify and legitimise, in religious terms, the increasing necessity for imposing various types of tax on the Muslims themselves. This was the historical origin of the convergence between religion and politics. Ideologically, it was expressed in a body of writing that was produced by the State-employed jurists with the implicit intention of conferring religious legitimacy on the political rulers. This was not only part of the 'traditions' of the region, required by the nature of the dominant modes of production, but was also, more urgently, a response to a growing political and financial crisis of the State.

Religion and politics were thus brought together in the historical Islamic State by way of the State appropriating religion. This is, of course, the reverse of the European experience where, historically, it was the Church which appropriated (or at least interfered in) politics. Secularism in the West has involved a gradual exclusion of the Church from the domain of politics. It was a relatively 'easy' process because religion was institutionalised; once you removed the Church, you had also removed religion from politics. In the modern Arab State, secularism was introduced by 'emulation', and it could not in any case exclude religion simply by excluding the Church, because there is no Church as such in Islam (with the partial exception of Shi'ism). Such factors have given the contemporary movement for political Islam its distinctive features. As we shall see later in the book, the fact that the contemporary State lays claim to secularism has enabled some forces of political protest to appropriate Islam as their own weapon. Because the State does not embrace Islam (except in a 'defensive' reactive way), it cannot describe its opponents as easily as the traditional State could as being simply heretic cults. Political Islam now reverses the historical process – it claims 'generic' Islam for the protest movements, leaving to the State the more difficult task of qualifying and justifying its own 'version' of Islam.

Without anticipating the full content of the book any further, I think that it would be possible now to consider in more detail the various aspects of the theory and practice of the historical Islamic

State that might prove useful to our eventual understanding of the contemporary movements of political Islam.

The most important elementary point to remember is that the Quran did not stipulate a specific form for the State or the government, nor did the Prophet Muhammad appoint a successor for himself even though he knew his demise was imminent (cf. e.g. Shalabi, 1983: 151ff; cf. also the authors quoted in Chapter 9). The fact that Islam had emerged in a 'stateless tribal society' led Muhammad to establish a politico-religious community, which was based on faith as the main criterion for membership, although it nevertheless subjected the believers to the authority of a certain political leadership (Rodinson, 1971: Ch. 6). Unfortunately, hardly any political or administrative correspondence pertaining to internal affairs was recorded in the time of the Prophet. It is believed that inscription was confined to covenants and agreements that concerned the propagation of the religion and the organisation of external relations; it is reported that for this purpose the Prophet – being illiterate – had to use the services of more than thirty literate scribes (al-Harawi, 1986: 349ff).

The main piece of political literature inherited from the Muhammadan period is the document (*al-sahifa*) often known as the 'Constitution' of Madina, the text of which is attributed mostly to the *hijra* episode from AD 622 to 624 (Watt, 1968: 4-5, 130-134). The 'Constitution' speaks of the believers as forming one community (*umma*) which also includes the Jews of Madina. Although composed of tribes, each of which is responsible for the conduct of its members, the umma as a whole is to act collectively in enforcing social order and security, and in confronting enemies in times of war and peace. The document is very interesting because, although it establishes the foundations for a trans-tribal and basically religious community, it does not negate sub-units completely, nor does it exclude non-Muslims from the envisaged political dominion (cf. Baydun, 1983: 106-108). It is in fact the source of a 'corporatist' tradition based on 'unity in diversity' which, with its multiple religious communities (*milal*) and varied functional associations (*asnaf*), was to characterise the Islamic state for centuries to come.

Given the limited nature of political stipulations in the Quran and *Hadith* (sayings of the Prophet), Muslims have had from the start to borrow and to improvise in the developing of their political systems, inspired (i) by the shari'a as represented in the Quran and the *Sunna* (traditions of the Prophet including his Hadith); (ii) by Arabian tribal traditions and (iii) by the political heritage of the lands they conquered, especially Persian and Byzantine traditions. The influence of the first source was more noticeable during the era of the first four *Rashidun* (wisely-guided) caliphs, the second during the Umayyad dynasty, and the third during the Abbasid and Ottoman dynasties.

Muslims had indeed been state builders, in the practical sense, in fields such as military expansion, government arrangements and administrative techniques – in this respect they probably preceded Europeans (Tachau, 1985: 3). But these were not really 'states' in the modern sense of the term: they were 'externally' imperial systems, and 'internally' dynastic systems, akin to many other ancient and mediaeval systems that are normally distinguished from the modern state (compare Eisenstadt, 1969). In our opinion, therefore, it is of little use to try, as some Arab constitutional lawyers have done, to survey the elements recognised in contemporary constitutional theory as defining a state, and then to attempt to prove that if these elements were present in the Islamic system, it was thus, theoretically and legally speaking, a 'state' (cf. e.g. Basyuni, 1985: 14ff; 'A.'Abdalla, 1986: esp. Chs 1 and 2). Nor is it useful to identify key issues pertaining to the subject of the state in Western political thought and then to try to locate similar ideas in the writings of Muslim thinkers in the hope that they will be helpful in pinning down a concept of the Islamic State (cf. e.g. Nasr, 1963: 15-66).

Since the 'State' is a Western concept, representing a European phenomenon that developed between the sixteenth and twentieth centuries in relation to such phenomena as the Renaissance and the growth of capitalism and individualism, it is natural not to find such a concept in Islamic thought prior to the modern era. However, Islamic political thought did have much to say about the body-politic and, of course, about rulers and governments; this, when examined and reconstructed, can give us an understanding of what is the closest thing to the concept of the State in traditional Islamic thinking. If it can be argued that the concept of the State in Europe cannot be understood in isolation from the concepts of individualism, liberty and law, I shall be endeavouring in this chapter to illustrate that the Islamic concept of the body-politic cannot be understood in isolation from the concepts of the group (*jama'a* or *umma*), justice (*'adl* or *'adala*) and leadership (*qiyada* or *imama*).

Many writers, both in Arabic and in European languages, speak about the 'Islamic theory of the State'. On close examination, however, one finds that in reality they are addressing themselves specifically to the problem of government and especially to the conduct of the ruler, and not to the state as a generic category or to the body-politic as a social reality and a legal abstraction. For the category of 'politics' in traditional Islamic thought is a classification of types of statesmanship, not of types of state. If the 'State' is to enter into such literature it appears at a lower point of the 'royal hierarchy': it will be as a ministry or chamberlainship or judiciary attached to the chief ruler, and the monarchy (*mulk*) in turn will appear only as a specific practice of a specific individual, that is, as a 'personal monarchy' and not as a total abstracted State (al-'Azmah, 1987: 48–49). Even when the Islamic bureaucracy developed and became quite complex, officials and other 'public' personnel appointed to certain jobs or dismissed from them, never signed a contract with the 'State' or any other 'moral personality', but simply with a certain individual employer (*al-muwalli*) (cf. Tabliyya, 1985: 161–162).

Thus the jurists, classical philosophers and men of letters speak of the community, or of government, or of the rulers; the idea of classifying political units as states only starts to appear casually in the nineteenth century in Afghani's writing, and then more clearly in the twentieth century in the writing of secularist thinkers who were influenced by the West (Butterworth, 1987: 91–111). This is not to belittle traditional Islamic thought in any way, for neither did the concept of State appear in European writing earlier than the Renaissance – it is only to emphasise that we should not judge traditional Islamic writings by what we know and understand only now.

As just suggested, Muslims built their states and developed their government through innovation, improvisation and borrowing. As for Islamic political theory, it has on the whole taken shape subsequent to the historical development that it addressed, and indeed most major political concepts did not develop except during periods when the political institutions about which they were 'theorising' were in decline (cf. Rosenthal, 1958; Schacht, 1964; Enayat, 1982). Thus, for example, the 'caliphate theory' goes back to the period of the deterioration of the caliphate as an institution during the Abbasid dynasty, the appearance of more than one caliph in several Muslim cities, and the growth of opposition movements of *Shi'is, Kharijites, mu'tazilites, Ikhwan al-safa*, and others, against the Sunni rulers in Baghdad. Indeed the caliphate theory was mainly a Sunni refutation of the arguments put forward by the escalating opposition movements (including the Shi'a), and it represented a quest for the ideal, not a positive description of what was actually there (cf. Lambton, 1981).

In spite of this historical context for the emergence of the theory of the caliphate, it would be too simplistic just to speak of an official, conservative Sunni ideology and a liberal or radical ideology of the

Shi'a and other 'non-conformist' groups. More complex patterns, and sometimes indeed ironies, were involved, especially in the cultural and intellectual sphere, which will require some historical backtracking at this point.

In the early Rashidun period, nomadism was being fought as a force of pre-Islamic ignorance (*jahiliyya*); emphasis on Islamic integration and a clear preference for urbanism were the order of the day. Tribalism was never eradicated completely, however; in some ways it had gained added vigour. Because the system of financial 'distribution' during the conquests was based, among other things, on tribal lineage it was therefore functional for the Arabian fighters to establish and to elaborate systems for the verification and control of tribal lineages (*dabt al-ansab*). It was precisely the groups that could not complete this process early enough and well enough that were eventually left in the *amsar* without regular pay, or without adequate participation in the affairs of the community, and who eventually formed the backbone of the opposition movements of Khawarij, Shi'a and others (cf. al-Sayyid, 1984A: 45–76). The tribal issue was indeed quite prominent in the era of 'Uthman and was much invoked, in complex ways, in the conflict between 'Ali and Mu'awiya. A revived, if extended, tribal *'asabiyya* dominated the Umayyad era, giving rise to resentment among non-Arab communities which expressed itself in various 'nationalistic' anti-Arab claims (*shu'ubiyya*), and it is indeed significant that proponents of such claims were initially known as *ahl al-taswiya* (the proponents of equality).

Shi'ism developed in close proximity to such opposition movements and together they played an important religio-political role in bringing down the Umayyads and installing the Abbasids. The Abbasids, although ruling in the name of an Islamic and not an Arab state, maintained leadership in the hands of the Arabs. The socio-ethnic grievances of the underprivileged elements were now acquiring the form of a cultural conflict, striving to express its political content in certain intellectual styles. Whereas the socio-nationalistic movements indulged in glorifying their non-Arab heritage and belittling that of the Arabs, defence of the Arab past, especially its *jahili* period, had acquired for the latter the dimension of a struggle for national identity, even for survival.

The Arab rulers thus initiated a process of retrieving the jahili tradition. This was achieved through the *tadwin* (inscription and registration) movement, which was started by the Abbasid caliph Al-Mansur in AD 761 and lasted for about a century. This was a movement sponsored by the State to rewrite (or more accurately to write – oral tradition having prevailed until then) the history of the pre-Islamic and early Islamic periods from the perspective of the political and social concerns of the Abbasid period (al-Jabiri, 1985: 59–61). Knowledge was now being comprehensively recorded from an official, 'statist' point of view and the administration was also being 'Arabised' in language and culture. From now on, the 'text' was indeed to acquire a certain authority that was partly epistemological and partly political.

THE SANCTITY OF THE AUTHORITATIVE TEXT

Given this historical/political conjuncture surrounding the 'registration' of the Islamic literature, especially jurisprudence, our understanding of Islamic political thought could benefit considerably if that thought were to be subjected to a process of 'deconstruction', in the manner of Jacques Derrida. Although hermeneutic approaches have been used on a limited scale by Arab scholars to analyse the text, resorting to a deconstructionalist approach has been quite rare among Arab writers, with the possible exception of Muhammad 'Abid al-Jabiri (cf. Thamir, 1988: 92–98). Unfortunately, al-Jabiri's project for probing the Arab 'political mind' has not been completed yet, though some insights can be drawn from other works by him. In the following few pages, I will draw extensively on al-Jabiri's valuable contribution in this respect.

The traditional 'text' was quite specific in recording the so-called *'ilm* (knowledge based on oral tradition and 'transmitted' wisdom – *naqliyyat*) rather than on recording *ra'y* (knowledge based on rational thinking and logic). The official 'text' also maintained its silence with regard to many other spheres of knowledge: it did not record the Shi'i tradition, or the *kalam* (theological philosophy) or 'sciences of the early teachers' (mainly Greek thought), nor did it record discourses on politics (such as that of Ibn al-Muqaffa'; d. AD 756) which were based on pre-Islamic (mainly Persian) political concepts (al-Jabiri, 1985: 61–69).

The *tadwin* therefore fulfilled a certain historical (political) function at the time but it also exacted a powerful intellectual impact on most Arabic thought in subsequent periods. First, it has produced an obsession with the Arabic language ('miracle of the Arabs'), especially in its 'beduin' form, which by its very nature is believed to have a magical explanatory power (*bayan*). Yet this language, thinks 'Abid al-Jabiri, is a 'sensual' one, more musical than expressive. It is also an ahistorical language, a language rich in synonyms related to nomadic concerns and poor in terms related to urban life, even as it existed in the Muslim cities of Madina, Damascus, Baghdad, Cairo and elsewhere (ibid.: 75–93). Secondly there was the tremendous production of *fiqh* (jurisprudence); the Islamic civilisation can be defined as a civilisation of fiqh, in the same way that one can say that the Greek was one of philosophy and the European is one of science. In this fiqh, Islamic shari'a overrides all that precedes it, making fiqh a highly 'autonomous' body of knowledge. The methodology of fiqh is in turn strictly textual: analysing the relationship between words and their meaning, and applying opinion only by way of establishing analogy (*qiyas*) – it is basically an exercise in 'investing the text' (ibid.: 96–106).

Such intellectual tradition had in itself contributed to the very belated emergence of theoretical works on politics and the State in Islamic writing. There is an irony here, for whereas the problem of succession (the caliphate) was the first major intellectual issue to confront the Arab-Islamic society (i.e. immediately after Muhammad's death in AD 632), it was the last issue about which Arab-Islamic thought had tried to theorise. Even *kalam* which emerged initially in the 'political' context of condoning or refuting the *raison d'être* of Umayyad rule would not ultimately include politics into its theoretical concerns. If some may argue that despotism had prevented such theoretical elaborations on politics, that might be true concerning oppositional tendencies, but why was not the caliphate itself legitimised in any elaborate theoretical way until two centuries had passed with this institution in place? Al-Jabiri believes that such theorisation could not have been achieved before the logical 'rules' of thinking were codified in a way that would permit a justification and legitimisation of the status quo, a process that was only achieved with the jurist al-Shafi'i (d. AD 820), following whom every writer, philosopher or jurist proceeded to delve into the subject of the caliphate (ibid.: 106–107).

It was only with the process of *tadwin* in the middle of the ninth century AD that writings on the caliphate emerged, first among the Shi'is, then by way of reaction among the Sunnis, and most specifically after Al-Shafi'i had specified the 'methodological rules' of Sunni thought and had enumerated the four sanctioned sources of shari'a: the Quran, the Sunna, the *ijma'* (consensus), and the *qiyas* (analogy). From the ninth century AD on, the term *ijtihad* had been separated from its old link with the free use of personal opinion (*ra'y*), and restricted to the drawing of valid conclusions from the Quran, Sunna and the consensus, by way of analogy (*qiyas*) or systematic reasoning. By the beginning of the tenth century AD 'the gate of ijtihad was closed' and the rule of *taqlid* (emulation; imitation; tradition) was formulated so that doctrine may not be derived independently from the original sources but through the teachings of one of the recognised schools (Schacht, 1964: 70–71). In al-Jabiri's view, this kind of methodology has imparted to the Arabic-Islamic discourse since that era (political writings included) a certain timeless, ahistorical character (al-Jabiri, 1985: 111–137).

Yet such methodological constraints on the development of Arabic-Islamic thought imposed on it by its close association with the State and with Sunni ideology are not as serious in al-Jabiri's view as the constraints that were imposed on Arabic-Islamic thought through its indulgence in Hermetic, Gnostic and other 'anti-rationalist' pursuits. The opposition groups were the first to go in that direction, the Shi'ites, Sufis and Isma'ilis, to be followed later by certain segments of the Sunnis. The traditional jurists had since then made it one of their major concerns to combat such tendencies, and the Sunni Islamic state, under the Abbasid caliphs al-Ma'mun, al-Mu'tasim and al-Wathiq, had in some ways turned into the 'state of reason' (*dawlat al-'aql*). Al-Ma'mun had a 'political dream', for the realising of which he resorted to the 'universalist mind' (Greek logic) in order to support the religious statement on which his State was so ideologically dependent. Al-Kindi (*c.* mid-ninth century AD), the 'first Arab philosopher', who argued for the 'rational state' was one of his main intellectual supporters.

Eventually, however, this 'rational moment' in the history of Islamic thought, so dependent on the unity and prosperity of the centralised State, was gradually extinguished. Al-Farabi (d. AD 950), who lived in conditions of growing political and social disintegration, had to seek the integrity of society in a new system that would simulate the natural order of the universe. The metaphysics of Ibn Sina (Avicenna) (AD 980–1037), followed more specifically by the Gnosticism of al-Ghazali (d. AD 1111), would then relapse into a negation of the rules of logical 'evidence', into a denial of the concept of causality, and thence into a marginalisation of the once prosperous natural and mathematical sciences – not only epistemologically but also socially and historically. The crisis arising from the emergence of an artisanal counter-culture, in opposition to the orthodox 'madrasa' culture of the State, was now partly overcome by the integration of Sufism into orthodoxy on a certain basis by the theologian al-Ghazali (Gran, 1980: 523).

Be this as it may, what concerns us most here is the politics of ideas. What can be said with confidence is that after the political dispute between 'Ali and Mu'awiya had erupted, *kalam* had started in matters of politics, by way of religion: are things pre-determined for man, or has he a free choice with regard to them? When both the opposition and then the State resorted to the older cultural heritage to support their cause, they utilised these sources to suit their political concerns. The irony, however, is that the socially radical opposition movements had increasingly been supported, epistemologically speaking, by a 'non-rational' (Gnostic, mystic) ideology. On the other hand, the State, which was socially conservative, had been for much of the time more intellectually 'rationalistic'.[2] However, once the Arab-Islamic State – already witnessing a high degree of internal social conflict – was subjected to tremendous external pressures from the Crusaders, the Mongols and the Latins, the socially radical character of the opposition movement was to retreat somewhat and the non-rational character of its ideology to grow, whereas the rationalistic character of the State's ideology was to retreat and the conservatism of its social objectives was to strengthen. The age of decline in the Arab-Islamic civilisation had thus set in (al-Jabiri, 1985: 345-349; compare Gran, 1980: 522-523). Intellectually speaking, this process of decline, maintains al-Jabiri, has left the 'Arab mind' too dependent on *bayan* (linguistic and deductive logic) and on *'irfan* (Gnostic knowledge), and less versed in *burhan* (material and empirical evidence); and this has left its mark on all subsequent Arab-Islamic intellectual production but most particularly on jurisprudence. Furthermore, with the passage of time, the body of Sunni juridic writings on politics and the State was gradually divorced from its social and political context, and given an essentialist, ahistorical degree of reverence that elevated it almost to the level of shari'a itself. The text, as Michel Foucault would have suggested, has already become authority.

THE JURIDIC THEORY OF THE ISLAMIC STATE

Having established the historical, social and intellectual context in which the juristic theory of the caliphate had developed, it would now be useful to examine briefly its main propositions. We start with the issue of 'legitimacy'. Initially, Abu Bakr and 'Umar, the first two 'guided caliphs', had emphasised the aspect of 'legitimacy' by resorting as much as possible to the nomadic-inspired tri-partite principle of *shura* (inner consultation), *'aqd* (ruler-ruled contract), and *bay'a* (oath of allegiance). This method was used in the appointment of their successor 'Uthman. Gradually, however, *shura* was overlooked, then *'aqd* and *bay'a* were also dropped with the establishing by the Umayyads of a hereditary semi-aristocratic monarchy. The first religious issue to engage the scholars of *'ilm al-kalam* was indeed political in essence. This was over the issue of 'predetermination versus free choice' (*al-jabr wa al-ikhtiyar*), as the Umayyads had supported the concept of the Absolute Divine Will to legitimise their rule on the basis that it was a pre-determined Godly plan (al-Jabiri, 1986: 571–572). From the ninth century AD, during the Abbasid era, the contradiction between the 'legitimacy of government' and the 'unity of the umma' came to the fore. Ahmad ibn Hanbal (d. AD 855) established a precedent by opting for 'unity of the community' over 'legitimacy of government' in case the two were irreconcilable.

From now on the emphasis in the juridic theory was on the authority of the leader (caliph) as a political symbol, and the unity of the 'group' (*jama'a*) as a human base (al-Sayyid, 1984B: 122–141). The classical writings of al-Mawardi and Abu Ya'la al-Farra' are illustrative of such an emphasis. Later on, when the authority of the leader and the unity of the community ceased to be intact and absolute, the emphasis, as in Ibn Taimiya, was to shift to shari'a as a basis for ideological unity, since political and human unity were no longer obtainable.

When all disintegrated, and separate dynasties ruled over various parts of the Islamic dominion, the legitimacy not only of government but of the *State* itself was under question. From the twelfth century AD on, the main 'realistic' source of legitimacy for the regional dynasties might have become the defending of Muslim lands militarily against the invaders, whether Crusaders, Mongols or Latins (as was the case with the Ayyubids and the Mamluks in Egypt and Syria and the Murabits in North Africa). This might have given the regional sultanic dynasties a new type of legitimacy for as long as they could confront the foreign enemy and keep it at bay (Shalaq, 1988: 157–163).

What concept of the 'State' emerges from all of these developments? It could perhaps be argued that the emphasis on leadership in Islamic political thinking had been a constraint on the development and institutionalisation of a State concept. From quite early on, 'Umar was to declare: 'O Arabs: there is no Islam without a group, no group without leadership, and no leadership without obedience' (Khalil, 1985: 51 *et passim*). 'Umar indeed was the State: he considered a palm-seedling or a small lamb dying on the bank of the Euphrates to be his personal responsibility. When 'Umar on his deathbed appointed six persons for consultation (*shura*), this was simply so that they would choose one from among their number to become the next caliph, not to consider a method or an institution for consultation. Although 'Umar had trained some educated personnel for political and administrative roles in the new State, many of them eventually rebelled against the State over the issue of land distribution in the conquered territories, rebellions that continued under 'Uthman, 'Ali and Mu'aw-iyya, and acquired important socio-religious dimensions as Kharijite or Shi'ite opposition movements.

The Abbasid dynasty, now ruling a much more complex society and drawing extensively on the juristic treatises of its own paid scribes, was also to emphasise its own concept of leadership. Writings on the caliphate by jurists such as al-Mawardi, al-Muradi and Ibn Hazm are mainly concerned with the caliph – his qualifications and traits. Rights are mainly classified into those of the leader (*imam*) and those of the community. There is hardly any trace of rights of the individual (ibid.: 54–74). Even Ibn Taimiya, who subtitles one of his major works *Fi huquq al-ra'i wa al-ra'iyya* (on the rights of the ruler and the subjects) speaks only of civil individual rights over one's life and possessions, and does not mention public or political rights of any sort. The subject of individual rights and the related subject of liberty receive very little attention from the jurists (cf. Watt, 1968: 96ff).

The 'official' Sunni theory, which reached its peak under the Abbasids and subsequent dynasties, had thus ended up translating a proclaimed religious authority into a pure political authority. The original religious concept of *tawhid* (one-ness, unification, mono-theism) was gradually transformed into a concept of unique, supreme, and absolute power for the ruler. Hasan Hanafi describes this process thus:

> [The] religious authority is eventually transposed into political authority: the ruler is now unique in his power, with no sharer or opponent or competitor for this power; he owns everything, is capable of everything, and there can be no questioning of his decisions and orders. It was thus easy to move from religious authority to political authority, from thanks due to God to thanks due to the Sultan...and from asking help and forgiveness from God to asking for them from the Sultan. (Hanafi, 1988, I: 7–8).

The leadership concept in traditional Islamic writing is also so personalised that any delegation of power is normally seen as dim-inishing the position of the caliph. Al-Mawardi was actually displeased to see that the number of 'delegation ministers' (*tafwid*) was growing at the expense of 'execution ministers' (*tanfidh*) in the Abbasid period. The mere appearance of ministerial posts was not welcomed to start with, but the predominance of 'delegation ministers' was particularly lamented because they were considered to be encroaching on the one and only source of real political power – the caliph (cf. al-Sayyid, 1984B: 91). Such glorification of political leadership will remain a characteristic feature of Islamic political thought, even up to the modern period, as can be seen in the reference to concepts of the 'benevolent despot' in the writings of Afghani, 'Abdu and others (al-Jabiri, 1982B: 95–96).

The previous review should leave us in no doubt that the overall orientation of the Sunni juristic theory was pointing in the direction of condoning cooperation with the government of the day, even if it was 'usurped' (i.e. not legitimately assumed and/or conducted), because even though such a government might have fallen short of the ideal, it was still better than disorder and strife (*fitna*). The integrity of the community had thus taken precedence, in the final analysis of the Sunni jurists, over pious and just government. Not only should the Muslim tolerate such a government; it was in fact permissible for him to take office on behalf of an unjust sultan if refusal to do so caused him to fear for his person, his people or his possessions (Lambton, 1981: 250ff). It was even permissible to have commercial transactions with the tyrants if, by rejecting the ruler's offer, one feared for oneself or one's property (ibid.: 256–257). The Sunni jurists had thus ended by legitimising all government *per se*, both in its political and in its economic roles.

The Shi'i jurists were in a somewhat different position as many Shi'is had to take office under Sunni rulers. The Shi'a held that all government in the absence of the spiritual imam was usurped, and so they were not concerned to legitimise the authority of government either in its central or its delegated levels. Their concern was to justify dealings between their following and the government and to allow some degree of participation by them in public affairs (Lambton, 1981: 243ff). Unlike the Sunnis, Shi'a jurists did not strive to impart legitimacy to government in favour of stability; rather, by having recourse to *taqiyya* (concealment of belief in adverse conditions), they were able to cooperate for specific purposes with the holders of power while refusing to accept any responsibility for the existence of an unjust government. It was in other words a *de facto* recognition and compliance, rather than legitimisation. The Sunnis therefore ended up legitimising government power, while the Shi'is evaded the issue – but in both cases, the end result was to induce popular acquiescence and political quietism. (ibid.: 242–263).

Because the Shi'a were not politically dominant for much of the time and because they adopted the concept that all government in the absence of the imam was usurpous, their jurists had much more leeway in the condoning or condemning of specific rulers. In the Sunni tradition, however, which merged spiritual leadership (*imama*) with political leadership (*mulk* or *sultan*) in the institution of the caliphate, it was less easy to incite disobedience against the usurping or unjust ruler while remaining firmly within the tradition. To resist government one had to resort either to open militancy or to spiritualistic disdain. In the first case, the group was subjected to unrelenting war from the State; in the second case, the individual was often subjected to a tortuous ordeal.

On their part, the jurists were almost always state functionaries. It is hard to imagine that they would have wanted to wreck the State or even seriously to challenge its legitimisation myths. Those who appeared to cast some doubt on the legitimacy of government were tortured, as happened with the jurist Malik under the caliph al-Mansur. Others, such as Abu Hanifa, were persecuted simply for refusing to work as scholars or judges for the caliph, an attitude that might have implied a certain disapproval of what was taking place. Even that great justifier of the status quo, al-Mawardi (d. AD 1058) did not want his classic *Al-Ahkam al-Sultaniyya* (new edn 1985) to be published before his death, while the other great conservative jurist, Ibn Taimiya, was of course to die in prison (cf. Mutawalli, 1985: 46–51).

The juristic theory of the Islamic state, as we have seen, emerged mainly, and flourished particularly, when the caliphate as an historical and political reality was weakening and withering. This theory was therefore obsessed with an attempt at rescuing the community from its unhappy destiny by overemphasising its presumed religious character. It envisaged a Utopia of how things should be, far more than it described how things were in reality. The juridic theory of the Islamic state, trying as it did to incorporate the State into the shari'a, was based on fiction (since there is very little in the Quran and Sunna about politics and the State). The theory of the 'Islamic state' is little more than elaborate fiqh presented as though it were pure shari'a.

But as the fiction was elaborated upon, repeated and reiterated, in volume after volume, it came to represent to subsequent generations not simply an ideal that *should* be aspired to, but a reality that is believed to have existed – history is read into the fiqh (which was *prescribed* by the jurists), and is then taken to be a *description* of what things were like in reality. Hence the renewed political potential (and even power) of that *fiqh-cum-shari'a*.

Furthermore, with the passage of time, and as the gap continued to widen between the juristic theory and the social and political realities, the juristic theory which was elaborated 'in the shadow of the State' came ironically to represent in modern times one of the main intellectual tools used by the politico-religious opposition against the colonial-European and the national-secularist governments – a point that will be looked at later.

It should be remembered, however, that the political theory of the jurists was only one of a variety of genres of writing among the traditional Muslim authors. The orientation of historical, philosophical and literary writings was often quite different, not to mention the 'intellectual production' of various protest movements that have not reached us or else have reached us in a distorted form. An example of the different interpretations and treatments of a basic concept in Islamic thought – that of the umma – should illustrate this point satisfactorily.

THE CONCEPT OF UMMA AND THE BODY-POLITIC

The intellectual development of the concept of umma is illustrative of the way in which concepts have varied and altered, depending on time and on the social/intellectual group that espouses them (cf. al-Sayyid, 1984: 17–87; Bensaid, 1987: 149ff). Currently this term is taken simply to mean the Islamic community – it is believed to be purely religious rather than socio-historical in meaning. But this has not always been the case – the specifically religious connotation of the term umma makes its appearance relatively late, and is particularly related to the meaning attached to this term by the Islamic jurists.

The traditional concept of umma was not always religious in connotation and many of the traditional writers have indeed distinguished between a religious and a social meaning of the term. The multiple implications of the umma concept are in fact in the Quran itself where it is used to mean time/era, or method/pattern, or community. This community in turn is sometimes defined by a common religion (or part of a religion) whereas it sometimes applies to *any* community.

Muslim thinkers try to reconcile the difference in the two meanings by speaking about the umma of 'call' (*da'wa*) which is either Arabia in the narrowest sense or the whole of humanity in a broader sense, and the umma of 'response' (*ijabah*) which obviously encompasses those who have accepted Islam. It is clear that the two are not one and the same category, for not all have accepted the 'call' and *ummat al-da'wa* must be defined, therefore, by other criteria than common belief. The various Islamic writers alternated between the two meanings, with the theologians and jurists being more inclined to the religious concept and the thinkers and historians more inclined to the socio-historical (al-Duri, 1984: 103, 281).

A brief look at some examples may help at this juncture, and I shall rely a great deal on the valuable work of Nasif Nassar in this respect (Nassar, 1983). Al-Farabi (d. AD 950) related umma to the city and used two other synonyms for it: community, *jam'a*, or 'gathering', *jam'* (this latter including the tribe and the clan). He speaks of the Arabs and other 'ummas surrounding them' such as the Abyssinians, Indians, Persians, Syrians and Egyptians. He refers to several characteristics of an umma: physical character, natural traits, and a common tongue. Then he distinguishes the umma as a group from the *milla* as a set of views and deeds, ruling the life of a certain community (Nassar 1983: 39–51).

Al-Mas'udi (d. AD 956) did not use the term umma in the religious sense, nor did he speak of an Islamic umma. To him, Muslims were people of a creed (*ahl al-milla*). An umma may possess a milla or may not. He speaks of seven great ummas, including the Persians, Syrians, Greeks, Egyptians, Indians, Chinese and Turks. According to him, each umma has some physical characteristics as well as a common tongue and one king. This may imply a certain degree of confusion but it is certainly indicative of how he distinguishes between the concept of umma and that of milla (Nassar, 1983: 67–79).

By contrast, al-Baghdadi (d. AD 1037) and al-Mawardi (d. AD 1058) are more typical of the jurists' understanding of the concept. They lived during the time of the Buwaihid's domination over the Abbasid caliphate and the rise of the Fatimid dynasty in Egypt and Syria. Their most important concern was to support the Sunni creed and the Abbasid caliphate against the challenge represented by Imamite Shi'ism and Isma'ili Fatimism, and they were thus inclined to ascribe to the notion of umma a specifically religious connotation rather than a socio-historical one, and to argue for the unity of the community of believers in spite of the multiplicity of political leaderships. Theirs was, therefore, an ideological rather than a socio-historical discourse. Having unwillingly to acknowledge the possibility of having more than one imam, they found it necessary to insist on the unity of the one religious community. The reality of division within the Islamic state had to be compensated for by over-emphasising the spiritual unity and one-ness of the community. Al-Mawardi is therefore inclined to use umma and milla interchangeably – the integration of the community cannot now be achieved politically and has thus to be emphasised religiously. The growth in the power of ministers was sadly observed and the emergence of regional princely rule had reluctantly to be accepted as a reality, but every effort had to be exerted to subject such usurpous rule (*imarat al-istila'*) to the ultimate spiritual legitimacy of the religious imamate (cf. al-Hasab, 1984: 69–71).

Like Baghdadi, al-Mawardi was unable to comprehend that among the reasons behind the disintegration of the Islamic caliphate there might have been some reasons related to the socio-historical division of the community of Muslims into various ummas, in the ethno-cultural sense. He chose instead to seek a juristic formula, however unrealistic, that would reinvest the formal unity of the Sunni community in spite of the growing dispersion of the centres of government (cf. Nassar, 1983: 88–101).

Writing in the first half of the twelfth century, al-Shahristani (AD 1076–1153) produced a historical objective treatise on *al-milal wa al-nihal* (religions and sects). In it he distinguishes between ummas on the one hand, such as the Arabs, the Persians, the Greeks and the Indians, and on the other hand millas (or shari'as) and *nihlas* (which to him connote rather unorthodox trends or opinions). His writings, however, are not void of occasional confusion between the concept of umma and that of milla. This can probably be attributed to the power of the (non-Arab) Seljuks during his time, combined with the threat of the Crusaders. Both factors would have contributed in different ways to blurring the distinction between the two concepts (ibid.: 120).

From now on – with the only exception of Ibn Khaldun – the theologians will have the final say and the concepts of umma and of shari'a will go hand in hand – in an ideological attempt to cope with the disintegrating state of the Islamic dominion. The destruction of the old order by the Mongols' sacking of Baghdad in 1258 had disturbed the intellectual coherence of the jurists. Ibn Taimiya (d. AD 1328) would even go to the unusual extreme of emphasising the supremacy of the shari'a over the unity of the community. Politically and symbolically Ibn Taimiya placed his main emphasis on the shari'a itself, as the only means whereby a lasting, sound unity could be established for the umma. Rejecting *taqlid* as represented by the rather pragmatic-realistic jurisprudence of recent scholars, he starts again from the concept of *tawhid*, goes back into the Quran and Sunna, and reinterprets them, in line with the Hanbali position, in a much stricter way – arguing strongly both against Islamic pluralism (sects, mystics, etc.) and against juridic innovation and ploys (*bida'*, *hiyal*), and most emphatically urging higher religious standards for the ruler (Faruki, 1971: 60–64; Rosenthal, 1958: 51–61). His ideas represent, therefore, an unusual blend of militant rejectionism and *salafi* conservatism, a blend that a number of later Islamic movements were to draw upon in the future.

Ibn Khaldun (AD 1332–1406) deserves special attention among all Islamic thinkers because of his distinctly sociological approach. In spite of his emphasis on the concepts of *'asabiyya*, *'umran* and *dawla*, he has also dealt with the concept of *jil* by which he most probably meant group or community. His understanding of the term umma is certainly socio-historical, as he talks, for example, of the Greeks, Persians, Egyptians, etc., and he regards umma as a phenomenon that is of 'longer term' than that of dynasty/state (*dawla*). He usually speaks of the Islamic community as a milla, not an umma, for the meaning of the latter to him is more closely related to a concept of group, people or race (although he does not seem to attach too much importance to the factor of language). He further relates the concept of umma to that of *watan* – a term that expresses a certain relationship between a specific group and a specific territory, and which is different from the term *jiha* which he uses in a purely geographical sense.

Ibn Khaldun's socio-historical approach is different from that of the traditional jurists, not only with regard to the concept of umma but also with regard to his entire treatment of the subject of politics. Although still tied to the traditional concept of the caliphate he is inclined to attach more attention to description, not merely prescription. He thus presents us with examples and classifications capable of interesting analysis and comparison (cf. Qurban, 1984 and literature cited; and contrast with al-Azmeh, 1982: 27–40; for an abridged version see Ibn Khaldun, 1978).

More specifically, it is Ibn Khaldun who, among the traditional Islamic thinkers, places the State most positively in the centre of his intellectual concerns. He is consequently most often recalled by contemporary Arab writers in their political discourse, for they seem to regard Khaldunism 'as headings for a reality that we live, but cannot speak' (al-Jabiri, 1982A: 464ff).

The State in Ibn Khaldun's understanding is a 'mix' composed of a natural dynamic factor which is *'asabiyya* or group solidarity, to which are added elements that result from the very existence of the State itself. Some of these are material, such as the accumulation of finance through tax extraction and the mobilising of armies using these monies, and the appearances of royal grandeur and luxury. Others are psychological, derived from the people becoming used to submitting to its will and to believing in their duty to do so ('Abd al-Salam, 1985: section 2). However, it is this very *'asabiyya* of the Arabs (as well as of other nomadic peoples studied by Ibn Khaldun such as the Persians,

Kurds, Turks and Berbers) which is the main factor in the downfall of their states and the ups and downs of their government. For not only does this *'asabiyya* lose its vigour with the passage of time, but as it assumes power its appetite for consumption and luxury expands, and the victors' 'expenses will exceed their income', pushing people into more extraction and confiscation of wealth from the society, 'whereupon those who run factories and production get weaker, and with their weakness the head of the state weakens and his power wanes, and the state eventually falls' (al-Jabiri, 1982A: 404-405).

It can thus be seen that Ibn Khaldun's rather sociological approach distinguishes him from the main tradition of Islamic jurisprudence, and renders his analysis far more relevant to a political scientist interested in the subject of the State. Conventional Islamic political theory as developed by the jurists is, however, not without merit. Like all Islamic jurisprudence, its rather rigid final mould (inherited over the generations from the Abbasid period) had provided in real life a certain element of stability during the centuries which saw the decay of the political institutions of Islam (Schacht, 1964: 75). But quite apart from its apparent lasting impact on the 'Arab-Islamic mind', which is epistemologically and politically important by itself, that juristic body of writing has its own intellectual elegance as well as the ingredients of an interesting theory of politics that is worth studying both on its own terms as well as for the purposes of comparison with other intellectual traditions.

With regard to the body-politic in general, the community, *umma* (increasingly defined in religious terms), not the 'state' *dawla* (whether a dynasty or a territory), is the jurist's basic unit of analysis. The umma is given an 'ideological' definition by the jurists: its universal function is the propagation of the divine message (*da'wa*). Political authority is understood as the instrument through which the application of the main tenets of the divine message is overseen. Sovereignty is not, therefore, for the ruler or for the clergy, but for the Word of God as embodied in the shari'a. The Islamic State is not, therefore, an autocracy or a theocracy, but rather a nomocracy. The State is perceived merely as a vehicle for achieving security and order in ways conducive to Muslims attending to their religious duties, which are to enjoin good and to prevent evil (*al-amr b'il ma'ruf wa al-nahy 'an al-munkar*).

Legislation is not really a function of the State, for the (divine) law *precedes* the State and is not one of its products. The legal process is confined to deducing detailed rules and judgments from the broader tenets of the shari'a. A certain element of equilibrium and balance is presumed among three powers: the caliph as guardian of the community and the faith; the ulama or religious scholars involved in the function of rendering religio-legal advice (*ifta'*); and the judges who settle disputes according to religious laws (*qada'*). People are bound to the system through a concept of loyalty (*wala'*) – loyalty is meant to be to the umma rather than to the regime; to the idea rather than to the individual (Rabi', 1980: 132–149, 165–167).

'People of the Book' (*ahl al-kitab*) or resident non-Muslims belonging to other monotheistic religions recognised by Islam (mainly Jews and Christians) are also bound to the community by the same concept of loyalty. They are accorded their freedom of belief, security of life and possessions, and usually exemption from military service, in return for paying a sort of 'poll tax' (*jizya*). Unlike the Islamic sects (*nihal, firaq* or *tawa'if*) which were normally persecuted by the Sunni State and which struggled for their own group autonomy within or without the State, the non-Muslim religious minorities formed an integral (social and economic) part of the Islamic State. Whereas the Islamic sects opposed the dominant ideology and the central power and survived only by way of resisting or deceiving it, the religious minorities accepted the ideology of the State, however reluctantly, and conformed to its expectations of them; their survival was not as much a function of their resistance as it was of the tolerance of the Islamic state (cf. the excellent analysis in al-Khuri, 1988).

The social functions of the State are the subject of very little attention. The concept of *tadbir* (administration, management, possibly economy) is sometimes invoked, and the caliph is likened to a shepherd attending to his flock, but this is less typical of the juridic writings. The concept of politics (*siyasa*) itself was, of course, originally used in the sense of dealing with livestock; its usage with regard to humans implies having to persuade/coerce the presumably less wise and capable. The leader in such a case must possess a certain clout (literally a 'goad' – *shawka*) in order to secure obedience (cf. Lewis, 1988).

The main function of the State in juridic Islamic writings is really ideological: the State is an expression of a militant 'cultural mission' that is religious in character and universalist in orientation (Rabi', 1980: 165–174, 208–211; 1983: 268–288). The State has no cultural autonomy from the society; it has an emphasised moral content which does not recognise any separation between private and public ethics, and which accepts no physical or ethnic boundaries – its civilisational target is the entire universe. Michael Mann is basically right in his observation that in Islamdom 'the wider sense of community has possessed a technical infrastructure of language, literacy, education, law, and ritual in which the primary transmitters have been *culture* and the *family*' (Mann, 1986: 347 – emphasis added). We shall indeed come back to the subject of the family further on in this work (Chapter 2).

Domestically, the main values of this State are not freedom or equality, but justice (*'adl* or *'adala*) – a vague and apportionate concept close enough to the elusive English concept of 'fairness'. The connotation of *'adl* is very extensive indeed: it means 'giving to each his due' and it governs man's relations with his family, with his colleagues, and with his followers. It means that one 'should be honest and true in everything that is due' – a very 'enveloping cloak' indeed (Rabi', 1983: 292–297).

Since justice is such a relative, flexible concept that will be applied to each case according to its own merit, the effectiveness of its application is related not to the existence of general abstract rules to be applied by the State impersonally on individuals, but to the presence of a pious and wise ruler. Hence the emphasis in Islamic writings on the character and qualities of the leader (*imam* or *khalifa*).

The logical sequence of the major political concepts in Islamic writing can now be understood: if the 'group' (*jama'a*; *umma*) is the central political unit, then it is logical that 'justice' (*'adl*; *'adala*) as an apportionate notion of ranking people would become the highest political value. And since the application of justice is highly contingent and discretionary, it is natural that 'leadership' (*qiyada*; *imama*) would become the most important, even exclusive, political 'institution'. This is, of course, quite different from the logical sequence that eventually predominated in European political thought, and which can be schematically presented thus: the 'individual' → 'liberty' → law/state. This may perhaps explain some of the difficulties that the concept of the 'State' (and the related concept of the 'rule of law') have encountered in trying to entrench themselves, culturally and socially, in Muslim lands since the nineteenth century – but this is a somewhat different issue that we will touch upon later in the book.

There is no doubt that jurisprudence has represented the most significant contribution in Islamic thought, political thought included. But what can we make of Islamic jurisprudence from the point of view of political science? A number of points are suggested here.

First The declared message is almost always the same: that the ruler *should* be guided by the revealed word in everything that he does; that the integrity of the community should be maintained at all costs, preferably symbolised and guaranteed by one imam; and that this imam should apply the shari'a and should be fair and just to his God and to his people – justice being a flexible concept of 'apportionate' dealing, meaning giving everyone his due. Such a 'state', as emphasised by the theory of Islamic law, is, of course, a fiction which has hardly ever existed in reality (Schacht, 1964: 76–77). Increasingly, juridic attempts were undertaken to make the rulers' deeds appear to be in line with God's word; though these attempts were very rarely about making government more responsible to the people and their needs.

Second Islamic jurisprudence tells us a fair amount about what the Muslim State was not. By elaborating on the requirements and prescriptions, the juridic discourse is implying that what was happening in reality was very different. By advising the ruler to make sure that his officials were not resorting to cruelty to extract taxes, it was implying that they were in practice using cruel means. By reminding the ruler that non-Muslims should not be assigned posts of authority or that they should not be allowed to dress like Muslims, it implied that in reality these rules were not strictly adhered to (Sharara, 1981B: 179).

Third If the juristic message is so idealistic (and by implication this suggests that the reality was different), one wonders why much of the juridic literature was addressed apparently freely to the rulers, and often even requested by the rulers themselves? It seems to me that this relates to the complex role of the 'intellectual' in an authoritarian society. First the ruler wants to be seen as seeking advice from men of knowledge, and this act by itself – and regardless of the content of the advice – is desirable and imparts a certain degree of legitimacy. At the same time it may secure a mellowed attitude from the intellectual in practice, as he is commissioned by the ruler to do his job, and is often taken into the employ of the ruler. It matters less in this case that the prescription itself is idealistic – indeed it can be argued that the more unrealistic the better, for the more unattainable the Utopia appears to be, the greater the readiness on the part of the people to accept the reality as unavoidable.

Al-'Arawi (Laroui) maintains that as a Utopia the caliphate theory was 'the shadow of the real sultanate' in two different senses: it was the reversed, counterpart image of the status quo, expressing discontent with it, but it was also an instrument for consecrating the status quo – the more idealistic an ideology it is, the less likely it is to be applied, and the less likely to harm the sultan or to threaten his position (al-'Arawi, 1981: 114–125).

The whole complex process acts in the final analysis if not to legitimise the government at least to keep the ruler's position undisputed.

Occasionally, of course, some jurists get it really wrong by asking for 'immediate delivery'; they subsequently fall into disfavour with the ruler and suffer dearly for it. The specific rulers survive and prosper, but in the longer term this accumulation of juridic traditions builds up the myth that what the jurists call for is the natural, legitimate state of affairs. As the jurists tended to build in a repetitive manner on what their predecessors had said and sometimes copied at great length from each other, their writing came to be taken as real precedent, and not as wishful thinking. This ahistorical jurisprudence appears in retrospect, now that it is distilled and abstracted, to be an integral part of the shari'a. It seems to acquire an intellectual life and a moral value of its own, which appeals to subsequent generations, especially in times of difficulty. It inspires a kind of nostalgia for a 'just' past (that never really existed). Jurisprudence has thus acquired over time a role that in the heyday of its production it never actually played. It is now often regarded as *the* shari'a itself: indeed, when contemporary Islamists call for the application of shari'a, what they usually mean is the adoption of the mainstream juridic tradition as it appears in the major mediaeval texts.

According to 'Abid al-Jabiri, the 'Arab mind' seems to be domi- nated by an 'ancestral model' (*namudhaj al-salaf*), closely wedded to the methodology of juristic deduction by analogy: often dealing with intellectual possibilities as given realities, and inclined to use the ideological for glossing over deficiencies in the epistemological (al- Jabiri, 1982B: conclusion). The 'Arab mind' ends up being ahistorical: divorcing words and constructs from their meaning and context, meandering freely between the past and the present, and with a certain tendency to feel more at home when dwelling in the past (al-Jabiri, 1986: 565–573). Indeed, with the passage of time, Islamic political discourse has almost confined itself to the issue of *khilafa* and *imama* as elaborated by the mediaeval jurists, and this tradition has continued even to the present time among the *salafiyya* school (those who revere ancestral Islamic texts and personalities). As al-Jabiri has most aptly put it

> The salafiyya reads history into the *shar'* and reads *shar'* into history; just as it reads State in religion and religion in State – this is what in fact forms its identity . . . The 'bitter' fact [however] is that it is not only today that the State has parted company with Islam, but that the case has always been so [even] in the past. (Al-Jabiri, 1982B: 66)

WHY WAS POLITICS RELIGIONISED?

The question may now be asked: why did political thought (and political struggle) in the Arab-Islamic dominion express itself mainly in religious terms? It should be remembered, to start with, that this is by no means an 'Islamic' peculiarity – for the separation of philosophy (and social action) from religion is a fairly recent and specifically European practice. But are there possibly some additional social and historical factors more specific to the Middle East that might also have contributed to this phenomenon?

Marx had pondered as to: 'why the history of the East appeared as though it was a history of religions.' In considering the answer he seems to have endorsed the thesis of Bernier's work on Oriental cities: 'Bernier rightly considered the basis of all phenomena in the East (he refers to Turkey, Persia, Hindustan) to be the absence of private property in land. This is the real key, even to the Oriental heaven' (quoted in P. Anderson 1980: 473–474). The answer to the question may not really be as easy, but the issue of the 'modes of production' does have something to do with it (cf. al-Tawati, 1985: 31–42).

The pre-Islamic Arabian society, nomadic with a dominant pastoral sector but with important commercial and agrarian networks, was to change its largely 'communal' nature after the emergence of Islam and the establishment of the Arab-Islamic empire. That change from a 'communal' base was not in the direction of a comprehensive 'slavery' mode of production, as happened in many other ancient civilisations (although slavery was known extensively on a domestic level and sporadically on an economic level) (cf. Tizini, 1971: 137–193). Ecological factors, the bureaucratic traditions of several of the conquered peoples, as well as some strategic decisions taken by 'Umar and others in the early decades of the empire (regarding in particular the non-distribution of conquered lands and the maintenance of an ethnic division of labour), had all pointed in the direction of an 'etatist mode of production'. Eventually, this 'control-based' mode of production superimposed the State both on the agrarian sector (as a builder of the hydraulic works and an extractor of the agricultural surplus), and on the commercial sector (as the builder and protector of trade routes and of commercial and military shipping fleets).

The ruling class in the Umayyad dynasty had a distinctly Arab *'asabiyya* (i.e. an extended tribal solidarity), which allied itself with elements of the local semi-feudalist and urban aristocracy. With these elements integrating themselves into the State machinery, and with more Arab soldiers and officials involving themselves in land acquisition, a sort of 'bureaucratic feudalism' was increasingly becoming the dominant social form.

With the Abbasids, the dominant form of 'bureaucratic feudalism' (*iqta'*) was maintained and the cosmopolitan nature of the society was acknowledged, although the ruling dynasty was deriving its legitimacy from its Muhammadan lineage, and increasingly from an Islamic juristic apologia. The trading component of the etatist mode of production was expanded in the first Abbasid era, and so too was a flourishing scientific and intellectual movement. The expansion in trade and in science and learning stimulated an industrial and technological sector of notable significance. A 'commercial bourgeoisie' of sorts was in the making, but the continuation of state dominance, combined with the pull from increasingly autonomous semi-feudalistic regional leaderships had disrupted the process of accumulation, constrained the development of the forces of production and contracted the scope of the imperial market. The bourgeois element was still articulated, via the State, with the semi-feudalist formations and even with some remaining slavery components; none of these forces could impose its hegemony or impart on the society its dominant character (cf. Tizini, 1971: 192–193). The State thus continued to enjoy tremendous power over individuals and groups within society.

With the decline of the Abbasids in their second era, and although some semi-autonomous regions had prospered for some time on their own – notably Egypt and Spain where repair and development of the hydraulic systems stimulated foreign trade and led to a fairly prosperous economy (cf. Isma'il, 1980, I: 117) – if anything, the Arab-Islamic empire as such was to be gradually pulled back, under the influence of semi-nomadic armies, into an increasingly semi-feudalistic, if still significantly bureaucratic, mode of production. Arabia – the source and origin of the whole process – was to sink back into a semi-isolated nomadic mode of production, while North Africa was to undergo the seemingly endless alternations between the forces of urbanity and the forces of nomadism that were so eloquently described by Ibn Khaldun.

While the process of decay set in, not only was social exploitation and injustice growing, but the last source of the religious legitimacy of the Abbasid caliphate – i.e. its preservation of the unity of the umma – was also being eroded. That was precisely the time when not only were movements of social protest gathering momentum, but so was the ideological controversy over the caliphate theory itself: the jurists writing the strongest apologia for it, and the philosophers and historians, as well as the unorthodox sects, challenging its entire intellectual base.

Modes of production in the Middle East had always tended to be control-based and/or externally influenced. The process of accumulation was always too dependent on the power of the State and on the conditions of foreign trade, not to speak of its vulnerability *vis-à-vis* the constantly present 'nomadic factor'.[3] The process of accumulation was as a result never very cumulative – it had always been subject to interruptions, reversions and cyclical phases. Even in times of prosperity and progress no single mode of production was dominant. Social formations were never clearly differentiated and classes were not clearly self-conscious. The State did not appear to correspond for any lengthy period to any hegemonic class interest but was mainly the function of a consecutive series of scrambles for political power (al-Tawati, 1985: 42–44).

The lack of social 'representativeness' of the State was often compensated for by the State adopting religion in an attempt to impart an ideological or cultural cohesiveness on the society (a practice which was also known in the pre-Islamic period in Egypt, Mesopotamia and elsewhere). Opposition to the State in such circumstances is difficult to communicate in purely political terms. Opposition may therefore take the form of trying to remove the ruling group and to replace it altogether, usually militarily – i.e. to take over the 'control keys' of the society. Opposition may also take the form of social and ideological protest. Since the State has claimed for itself a religious *raison d'être*, protest movements may also feel tempted to express their opposition in religious terms. Feeling desperate, however, some of these movements may be driven either to 'extreme' ideological formulae (often completely 'rejectionist'), or else to deeply escapist – e.g. mystic or messianic – manifestations (for details see Muruwwa, 1981). Sporadic resistance may express itself in the activities of certain movements of social banditry (e.g. *al-shuttar, al-'ayyarun, al-futuwwa*, etc.) (al-Duri, 1982: 76–81) whose attacks are not only confined to the State but may also harm the social groups of artisans, merchants and peasants as well. Last but not least there is the age-old force of tribalism which, especially in Arabia and Barbary, continued to represent a force of decentralisation, often, if not always, opposed to the State (Rodinson, 1981: 166–167).

Such movements of opposition and protest often play into the hands of the State which claims (and often appears) to be the guardian of order against chaos and disintegration, of reason against irrationality and stupidity. For all the State is oppressive, it is not after all pure evil: it often attends to the hydraulic base of agriculture and safeguards the trade routes; it usually sponsors education and learning, albeit according to the 'Orthodox' schools. Also – at least initially – it guards the safety of the Islamic dominion and even expands its boundaries, bringing in more Muslim converts and more financial resources. Initially – that is, in the Rashidun and Umayyad eras – the Islamic expansion was mainly 'external', bringing more lands under the Islamic banner, even though the majority of their populations remained non-Muslims and their rulers remained strictly Arab. In the Abbasid period, external conquests had slowed down but the Islamic universalist ideal came nearer to realisation by opening up to the non-Arab communities through a process of 'internal Islamisation'. The state became less ethnically derived and more abstract and autonomous, through the creation of a regular army and differentiated administrative and financial institutions, while maintaining a cosmopolitan but broadly Islamic character (Shalaq, 1988: 152–157).

If the State is not abiding by the tenets of Islam domestically, if the ruler is no longer perceived to be just and pious, then he is at least maintaining the torch of the *da'wa* abroad, expanding *Dar al-Islam*, or at the very least maintaining the territorial unity and the 'ideological' character of the Islamic state. This explains why the 'legitimacy' of the caliphate had seriously declined when it was no longer able to continue and to sustain its conquests, and worse still when it became unable – in the later Abbasid period – even to maintain the integrity of *Dar al-Islam* itself.

Traditional Islamic politics was shaped less by Islam as a belief system (since, as already remarked, the Quran and Hadith contain very little indeed on politics) and more by the nature of the modes of production and the economic requirements and cultural traditions of the territories that eventually formed the Islamic dominion. Authoritarian and despotic rule formed part of the political traditions (Egyptian, Persian, Byzantine) of the territories that the Muslim Arabs incorporated in their new state. The hydraulic and semi-feudal modes of production of these countries were then subjected to the 'conquestal' ramifications of a nomadic mode of production, emanating from the Arabian desert but now becoming 'politicised', since it was now being applied to other countries and not merely to neighbouring tribes.

A controversy emerges with the early conquests, concerning the rules for the distribution of wealth, i.e. conquered land: should they be the 'nomadic' rules of sharing the booty, familiar to the conquerors from Arabia, or the 'Oriental' rule of public ownership prevalent in the more settled 'hydraulic' societies conquered by them? 'Umar made a strategic decision in ordering that the land would become public property, 'leased' to those who cultivated it in return for tribute (*kharaj*). The 'tributary' character of this mode of production was thus confirmed and was to last for many centuries to come (cf. on this concept, Samir Amin, 1978: 10–23). 'Umar took this important decision to avert squabbling and disunity, to provide for future generations and, most specifically, to avoid decay, decline and the destruction of the irrigation system (al-Sayyid, 1984B: 265). At the same time a *diwan* (administrative register) was established to regulate the payment of salaries to Arab soldiers and administrators (cf. al-Buraey, 1985: Ch. 5), thus laying the basis for the emergence of a Muslim state bureaucracy, with a distinctively 'circulationist' financial function.

The resulting constellation of modes of production (articulated with each other in different ways at different places) was largely control-based: the State had a fairly direct control over the producers (initially farmers but increasingly merchants and artisans and a few miners as well). The relations of production – but specifically the relations of distribution – were decided politically (and militarily) rather than 'technically' and economically.

Initially the main form in which the Islamic state extracted surplus was the *jizya* ('poll-tax') taken from non-Muslims. This was easily justified by the 'right of conquest'. Eventually, as the numbers of converts to Islam grew, a serious financial problem developed for the State. Sometimes the same amount of tribute continued to be taken from the converted but with difficulty and under a different name, and in a few cases when this was not possible, some rulers even tried to slow down the rate of conversion. Ultimately, however, an ideological justification was needed to legitimise the extraction of tribute from Muslims and to condone the pattern by which the State, almost exclusively, distributed the economic surplus. It was not a mere accident that one of the earliest *political* tracts in the history of the Muslim State was a book by Abu Yusuf (d. AD 795) on taxation. For it was now no longer sufficient to relate taxes merely to the stamped 'necks' of the non-Muslims; taxes had also to be related to water, land and trade (cf. Sa'd, 1988).

The intervention of ideology was required at this stage, and 'Islam' was ready to play the role – after all, it had been most functional in motivating the economically rewarding conquests in the first place. But now the task was harder – it was to define and legitimise not only the relationship between Muslim and infidel but mainly that between

Muslim and Muslim. Gradually an 'Islamic' political theory would be elaborated, premised in the main on the principle of obedience to the ruler and the necessity of avoiding civil strife. This theory would increasingly owe less and less to the nomadic egalitarian ethos (expressed in concepts such as *shura*, *'aqd* and *bay'a*), and would become more and more 'Orientalised'. From the Iranian culture in particular the concept was borrowed of a whole cosmology in which everything is arranged in a certain order, governed by a universal principle of hierarchy: a hierarchy of things, of 'organs' of individuals and groups (al-Sayyid, 1984B: 89–123). Everyone has his proper station and rank in a stable and happy order, with the caliph/king standing at the top of the social pyramid. His authority is made to sound almost divine (he is now the successor of God – not of Muhammad – on earth), and opposition to him, bringing strife to the Islamic community, is made to sound tantamount to downright blasphemy.

The point to be emphasised here is that the rulers did not become authoritarian because their rule was inspired by certain essential tenets of Islam; rather the Islamic theory of politics was developed gradually and piecemeal (and mainly in response to social and ideological opposition from various protest movements), by jurists who played the role of the ideologues of rulers. The rulers were in control of the producers and of the economic surplus in their society and were looking increasingly for an ideological rationale to legitimise their control of people and of resources. With the passage of time, the ideology needed to be more elaborate because the issue now at stake was not simply the territorial integrity of the new Islamic domain but also the exclusive right to charge rent-cum-tax from Muslims and the need to maintain the unity of the market and the security of the trade routes. The elaboration by the jurists of segregationist and demeaning policies towards the *dhimmis* also took place at this later stage. If the Muslim – now that there were no more new conquests or new conquered – was being charged financially nearly as much as the non-Muslim, then he needed instead to be assured of his 'ideological' superiority over the *dhimmi*, to be provided with the ritualistic means that 'enable him to celebrate his historical victory and allow the community to re-enforce its unity by renewing its agreement over a common victim' (paraphrased from Sharara, 1981B: 175–181).

The impotent caliph is increasingly presented as the one who is not able to become despotic (*yastabidd*). The proper Sultan is in charge of all political and social affairs, indeed representing 'the shadow of God over his devotees' (al-Sayyid, 1984B: 113). Such 'Persian influences' are not only to be found in the writings of people such as Ibn al-Muqaffa' and al-Jahiz, but even in the most 'standard' Arab-Islamic writer of the eleventh century AD, al-Mawardi. The cultural hegemony of the State reached such high and sophisticated levels under the Abbasids that they were paying monthly or annual salaries to proponents both of the 'rational' *kalam* school as well as of the 'textual' *hadith* school. Eventually it was the jurists and scribes who won the day, whose services became so important as the nature of the economy and the society increased in complexity and as difficult legal and administrative tasks had to be tackled on a daily basis.

With the growth in the power and autonomy of the peripheral parts of the Empire during the later Abbasid period, not only was the territorial integrity of the Islamic dominion threatened but so also was the symbolic unity of its leadership, as other imams/caliphs/amirs were to claim their autonomy in various parts of the land of Islam. The emphasis of the jurists was now having to be laid first on the unity of the community and later on the supremacy of the shari'a: even though the caliph was not maintaining the territorial integrity and the unity of leadership of the Islamic dominion, obedience to him was premised on the proposition that he was the one who oversaw the application of shari'a (the only remaining symbol of the unity of the community) in society. The fact that the caliph might not have lived up to his expected role mattered less. The 'utopian' elaborations of the jurists followed very easily from the type of learning that they possessed. Even if the message had sounded unrealistic and unattainable, it had helped to fulfil two major functions: to justify the government of the day, while also ensuring for the jurists (as judges, advisers, scribes, officials, etc.) a political and social role to be played. As members of a 'middle class' of intelligentsia, they often assumed a mediatory function between the caliph on the one hand and the various social forces (notably the merchants and the urban 'masses') on the other.

The ulama had thus carved out for themselves a certain 'space' as a moral authority and an intellectual elite, and at various times enjoyed a certain degree of autonomy *vis-à-vis* the ruler.[4] However, the autonomy of the ulama, who were in the main state employees, was bound in the final analysis to be limited, normally manifesting itself only in emergency situations. Ibn Taimiya was among the exceptional ones: by ranking the integrity of the shari'a higher than the unity of the umma, he was prepared to condemn the ruler if he did not live up to the ideological ideal (cf. Faruki, 1971: 60–64). It is little wonder that he spent most of his life (and died) in prison.

Other manoeuvres were also used by the rulers to contain or to constrain the autonomous function of the ulama, such as the tradition initiated by the Mamluks of appointing representatives of the four juristic Sunni schools: they disagree with each other and the rulers can always obtain a *fatwa* legitimising whatever they want to do. It is telling that the last of all the 'great' jurists, Jalal al-Din al-Suyuti (d. AD 1506) wrote a famous treatise on the importance of not running after the Sultan.

It is possible, therefore, to say that there was a very high degree of symbolic and organisational autonomy among the political elites of the historical Islamic state, and that there was a relatively high degree of symbolic autonomy, but only minimal organisational autonomy, for the religious elites. There was also a growing tendency for the separation of the two, although the religious groups and functionaries did not associate themselves as autonomous entities, nor did they constitute tightly organised bodies, except when, as in the Ottoman Empire, these were organised by the State (cf. Eisenstadt, 1986: 27–29).

One of the most interesting things is that the ideological elaborations of these traditional Islamic clerics, extracted from their historical and political context, have been systematised and distilled over time, thus to become a major source of an idealised inspiration for the contemporary Arab proponents of Islamic revival. As Maxime Rodinson expresses it

> Usually, allegiance to Islam . . . goes hand in hand with loyalty to a superior system of social values. These values are those of the traditional world, which is idealized as a world in which the pace of life was calm and tranquil. Other supreme social values are a will to justice and goodness, tempered by the firmness made necessary by human imperfections . . . If traditional Muslim society did not altogether exemplify these values, as is sometimes reluctantly acknowledged, the problem lay with the misfortunes of the time, with human nature, and above all with the perfidy of non-Muslims. (Rodinson, 1981: 161)

It is one of the ironies of Utopia that nostalgia can indeed be aroused for things that have never really existed.

2 The politics of sex and the family, or the 'collectivity' of Islamic morality

To say that Islam is not a particularly 'political' religion because the Quran and the Sunna have not stipulated the form of the State or the pattern of government is not to suggest, however, that Islam is a 'private' individualistic sort of religion. Quite the reverse: Islam is indeed a religion that stresses above all the *collective* enforcement of *public* morals. It is this 'collective' and 'public' nature of its conception of morality that has induced many people, especially in Orientalist and fundamentalist circles, mistakenly to attribute to Islam a specifically political nature. But a distinction between the two areas is absolutely basic to any understanding of the nature of Islam as a belief system.[1]

Islam is indeed very much a social religion, seeking to organise the practices of social life, and above all the minute details of family life. This purpose, moreover, is not regarded as a personal pursuit, but as a social (collective) one. If government is regarded as important, it is not really because of the inherent importance of the 'political' as such (i.e. the representation of interests, the working of institutions, etc.) but because of the crucial role expected from the ruler as a guardian of the moral code, who would oversee the adherence to its stipulations. Perceived as such, one is in a better position to understand why calls for the installation of an Islamic State or an Islamic government always seem to pay overwhelming attention to the family as a social unit and to issues such as veiling, segregation of the sexes and the imposition of extreme penalties for moral crimes such as adultery and drunkenness.[2]

In Islamic culture, family life (viewed from a strictly male point of view) is sacrosanct, and raised above everything else. Take this interesting case, for example. The jurists of the Islamic Liberation Party were consulted on the issue of *nushuz* (female religio-legal disobedience within the family). The answer was as follows: 'If the husband asked his wife to attend an election rally or a public conference, and she disobeyed him, she is not *nashiz* (see definition above); if he ordered her to shut a window, and she disobeyed, she is *nashiz*'. The distinction as explained by the jurists themselves is obviously between things pertaining to 'public life' and things pertaining to 'private life', and there is no doubt that the latter is seen as fitting more 'naturally' within the sphere of religion (in Haidar, 1987: 168).

The origins of much to do with sex, women and the family in the Islamic culture will probably have to be traced back to the nomadic realities of Arabia before and around the time of the emergence of Islam. The 'lineage mode of production' or the 'kin-ordered mode of production' characteristic of the nomadic society can be regarded as a 'particular way of establishing rights in people, and thus laying claims to shares of social labour' (Wolf, 1982: 91). In most such modes, people are allocated differently to positions of power, depending on certain criteria including, in particular, gender. In Middle Eastern nomadic society, women have always been important both for production and reproduction purposes. The reproduction function is particularly crucial in conditions of high mortality due both to environmental causes and to the frequency of tribal wars.

Frequent tribal wars presumably also led to a relative shortage of men. This was probably behind the practice of unrestricted polygamy in *jehiliyya* (pre-Islamic times), which Islam then restricted to four wives as the maximum allowed to one man (in addition to concubines).[3] The abundance of women, made even more substantial by the acquisition of female slaves as booty during the early Islamic conquests, might also have resulted in women becoming sexually active rather than passive creatures. Women would thus compete for the favours of men, and would have to excel in subtle allurements in order to attract men towards marriage, love and sex (el Saadawi, 1982: 135ff).

It should also be remembered that unlike some other cultures, the Arab-Islamic culture has come to regard sex as one of the desirable and legitimate pleasures of life (even of the 'after life'!). There is no sense of guilt surrounding sex in Islam, nor a call to torture the body or to scorn or suppress its desires (as in, say, Christianity and Hinduism) – only a need to ensure its 'hygiene' (thus the elaborate rituals for washing and cleanliness) and to regulate its requirements 'according to certain standards that would integrate it into the community' (Zai'ur, 1988B: 36–37). The difficulty, however, is that in the Muslim culture too, women are believed to be sexually active, if not aggressive – i.e. it is a concept of the *femme fatale* who makes men lose their self-control and succumb to temptation and disorder (*fitna*).

Furthermore, the Arab-Islamic culture lays more emphasis on 'external' rather than on 'internal' moral enforcement – on precautionary safeguards rather than on 'internalised' prohibitions.[4] The result is that rather than expecting the man to be socialised and trained into self-control, the solution would be to hide the woman's body and to seclude her as much as possible from men, except within the marriage relationship (cf. Zakariyya, 1987: 180–181).

From the beginning the tightly controlled patriarchal family was found to be a much more suitable unit of socialisation than, say, the tribe, towards achieving the objective of creating an integrated Islamic umma (Mernissi, 1985: 80–85). Marriage is strongly urged upon men in all Islamic treatises, classical and modern, not only for procreation but also for its sheer sexual pleasure. Unsatisfied male sexuality has always been considered a social danger in both Islamic and popular culture, and unshed semen has been regarded in both as medically harmful. Although some jurists tolerated masturbation in certain circumstances it was generally regarded with contempt (except – according to Shafi'i – when practised by the woman on her man) (Musallam, 1983: 31–34). Sodomy and homosexuality were also generally condemned. Furthermore, because the procreational and the pleasurable functions of sex were distinguished from each other and regarded as equally legitimate, contraception and birth control have been known both within the formal Islamic jurisprudence as well as in Arabic erotica (Musallam: 89ff).

Thus it can be seen that if sex is considered such a powerful urge for both man and woman to the extent that, when alone, the man cannot and the woman will not resist the temptation of the 'devil', who will always be the third partner (as per a popular Arab proverb), and, 'if, on top of this, the society where these two people live is a patrilineal one, as is the Muslim society, only one solution is possible: separate the two sexes by confirming the seclusion of the woman' (Salman *et al.*, 1987: 11). Of course, Arab women, especially working peasants, were not always veiled and secluded, nor were they without social and even political power (cf. Bill and Leiden, 1984: 98–110). But there is little doubt, historically speaking, that the 'established' classes in urban centres usually veiled the women, and that, socially speaking, a woman can acquire the highest freedom of movement in male surroundings only when she reaches an advanced age, i.e. when 'society considers her a-sexual' (Salman *et al.*, 1987: 11). So it is not really because the woman is regarded as inferior that she is segregated in Muslim society, but rather because she is regarded as a source of

sexual provocation (seduction) and therefore of social disarray (sedition) – the word *fitna* in Arabic has the two meanings.

The traditional 'ideal type' is thus, if you like, a male socialised into
the desirability and even the necessity of sexual gratification, and a
woman who is presumed to be equally, if not more, keen on sex. But
since she is also regarded as somewhat morally and mentally inferior
to man, her sexuality must be controlled and regulated by the husband
for his and the society's benefit, if the moral and the economic bases of
the patriarchal society are not to be completely wrecked. It should be
remembered at this point that whereas many aspects of social life have
changed significantly over the centuries in Muslim societies, the
character of the family has probably changed the least. Even legally,
the family law is the only one to remain more or less Islamically intact
in most Muslim societies, whereas laws and regulations governing
economic, political and even, to a large extent, educational and
cultural affairs have been 'modernised' and 'secularised'.

But the Muslim family has been subjected to economic and social
pressures in recent decades. Unfortunately, the psychological and
sexual anxieties resulting from this, and the tendency for such
anxieties to be religiously and politically transferred and/or projected,
have not received sufficient analysis.

The rapid and extensive rural–urban migration that has been taking
place throughout the Middle East in recent years has had some
profound psychological influences on the newly urbanised communities, especially in the newer, hurriedly assembled, non-traditional
quarters. A subsequent growth in the inclination towards verbal and
physical violence has been observed by many. In addition, heightened
sexual sensitivity usually follows the move to the city. Veiling had
traditionally represented one of the standard responses to such a new,
anxiety-provoking situation; as we have just noted, veiling in peasant
(as distinct from nomadic) societies had – historically speaking –
usually tended to increase with urbanisation. Contemporary migrants
to the city from the countryside do not usually take to veiling in the
traditional manner, although their sexual sensitivity is just as keen as
immigrants of earlier generations – if not even more so. Recent rural
migrants (as well as the lower urban classes among whom they live)
appear to be so preoccupied with sex in their daily conversation, and
so sensitive about it, that almost every word or gesture may have a
sexual connotation for which (for example, in Egypt) apology must be
made in advance by constant repeating of the words 'I beg your
forgiveness' (*la mu'akhadha*).

Recent migrations to the cities usually force the family to change its habitat from the cosy, enclosed courtyard life of the extended family in the rural village and the traditional country town, to the 'exposed' environment of apartments or rooms in larger buildings, where main facilities are frequently shared, and where female contact with the outside world is required for shopping and other necessary activities. The daughters eventually go to school, which means that they have to walk or to use public transport; indeed the wife or the daughters may have to go to work to enable the family to cope with the burdens of urban life and its higher consumerism. The patriarchal head of the family would thus feel his dignity eroded for being unable fully to support his family and for having to allow them to work for or with other males. The verbal semi-sexual abuse that these women may receive on the way to or from work, and the fondling of their bodies that may occur on public transport and in other crowded areas, will most probably injure his masculine dignity and impart the feeling that he has turned into a cuckold or a pimp (compare Mernissi, 1985: 163–164).

The urban experience is not necessarily more attractive for the female, who has to go through all these undignified happenings, who now has to compete with all the other working women in looking 'presentable' (which means higher expenditure on clothes and cosmetics, in crushing financial circumstances), and who very often has to hand over her earnings to her husband at the end of the day/month – for he often regards this as his right in return for allowing her to go to work in the first place!

Another familiar outcome of urbanisation is delayed marriage for most young men (and women). Longer periods of schooling and poor employment opportunities, combined with the severe housing crisis in most cities have pushed the marriage age for most urban Arab youths to the late twenties or beyond. As Fatima Mernissi observed, in Egypt and Tunisia the average age of marriage for men is currently 27 and for women 22. In Morocco, Libya and Sudan, men marry at around 25, women at around 19. Even the Gulf oil-exporting countries, known for their conservatism, have witnessed a marked increase of unmarried youth as age at marriage for men is now 27 and for women 20. Nuptiality patterns are particularly influenced by urbanisation: thus the male urbanised youth marry later. In 1980, in metropolitan areas of Egypt, the mean age at marriage was 29.7 years for males and 23.6 years for females. In the urban areas of Upper Egypt, where the fundamentalist movement is strong, the mean age at marriage was 28.3 years for men and 22.8 years for women (Mernissi, 1988: 11).

Sexual practices have not changed correspondingly to any great extent: sex remains highly desirable, but basically unobtainable outside marriage, and marriage now occurs later. In consequence, sexual anxiety and frustration represent a serious problem among young people. There is no guilt-consciousness attached to sex as such, as for example with traditional Christianity, but unlike the situation in contemporary Western industrial societies, sexual relations before marriage have not been liberalised. The sexual frustration of the youth in Muslim society as a result of delayed marriage is doubly painful because there is no high value attached to abstinence and non-indulgence. As Hisham Ju'ait (Djait) explains, partial release may be achieved for the unmarried male via purely 'physical' homosexuality, which may also carry with it shades of a transferred power desire directed at a new object (Ju'ait, 1984: 161-165). But even physical homosexuality is not always obtainable and is usually condemned; thus sexual frustration continues.

Frustration at work, or lack of social or educational achievement, accentuated by sexual anxiety and/or repression in the male, may then project itself into a kind of floating aggression, to be released against all female relatives, including the mother (although this is a very complex area since the attachment between son and mother is usually overwhelmingly strong – see Salman *et al.*, 1987: 8-9), and also against the children who may, in their turn, receive the wrath of their oppressed, angry mother as well (B. Yasin, 1985: 61-66). It has also been argued that the national sense of humiliation suffered by the Arab male as a result of the defeat by Israel, and the social sense of humiliation caused by the prospect of class demotion that may result from the reversal of certain socio-economic policies in a number of Arab countries – these two types of humiliation both leading to a sense of lost dignity – may have contributed to a process that turns women into 'an easy target for the "restoration" of dignity'.

> The removal of the veil, women's work outside the home, women's independence and the related stigma of 'promiscuity', are all seen as a principal cause of the evils of current life, intimately related to the loss of 'manhood', i.e. of personal dignity.
> (Shukrallah, 1989: 92-93).

Both the Moroccan writer Fatima Mernissi (1985: 160-164) and the Syrian writer Bu'Ali Yasin (1985: 66-70) corroborate the theory of Wilhelm Reich that sexually frustrated males do not normally externalise their feelings into a rebellion against *all* the manifestations of political, social and economic repression in society, but rather internalise the agony at the level of moral and religious defence. A sexually repressed man, as Mernissi explains, is preoccupied with symbols related to 'purity' because his only available experience of genital sexuality (e.g. sodomy, masturbation) is deemed 'dirty' by his society's standards and consequently felt to be so according to his own standards. The one and only 'Islamic' solution repeatedly being advised to the youth is early marriage – but in today's conditions this is more easily said than done. Some of the Islamists are indeed so out of touch with realities that they still speak – in the present tense – of the man's right to have intercourse with his female slaves (in Haidar, 1987: 28–30). Even the renowned contemporary Syrian Islamist Sa'id Hawwa is a subscriber to this fantasy: 'What would a man whose lust has been aroused do? He has no option of course except to marry or possess a female slave (*ama*)'! (Hawwa, *c.* 1980: 324).

Sex-related anxiety in Arab men is also likely to grow in modern conditions, given the persistence of the old concept of 'honour'. To have men's honour 'embodied in the sexual behaviour of their female relatives' was a much safer and easier system when women's space was 'strictly confined to the courtyard and ritual visits to the hammam or the local saint's tomb'. In the contemporary urban space women are much more 'exposed' (both in the sense of being unveiled as well as their movement not always being directly controlled) with more risks to the male honour involved. 'It is no wonder that women, who have such tremendous power to maintain or destroy a man's position in society, are going to be the focus of his frustration and aggression.' (Mernissi, 1985: 160–161). Frequent migration to the Gulf or to Europe has also produced some unsettling changes. Often it would be the man alone who could or would emigrate, leaving the family behind him 'exposed' and uncontrolled. In a few cases, only the woman could obtain a contract to work abroad, thus forcing the man to assume the 'feminine' (and rather despised) role of attending to domestic matters. The current 'conservative' wave that is hostile to women in the Muslim world is not simply a re-traditionalising regressive trend. More aptly it is 'a defence mechanism against profound changes in both sex roles and the touchy subject of sexual identity' brought about by rapid social transformations, and such relapses into 'archaic' types of behaviour should be regarded as 'anxiety-reducing mechanisms in a world of shifting, volatile sexual identity' (Mernissi, 1988: 11).

With the move from village to city, the individual is abruptly confronted with the repressive impact of a distorted type of peripheral capitalism and the alienating impact of a modernisation drive that is in many of its aspects little more than an enforced process of Westernisation. Such agonies become most alarming to the individual when their impact encroaches upon him within his own family – for the family is, after all, the last vestige of security and identity for him. The family as an institution has survived many modes of production, more or less intact, in most societies. It has survived particularly successfully and resiliently in Muslim societies, where it remains the major reservoir of socio-religious mores and, legally, the last bastion of Islamic values and jurisprudence. The Arab family is so intertwined with other social spheres, such as those of economics, politics, etc., that it is almost impossible to study any of these without reference to the family. The family itself is in turn very tightly regulated, at least in the legal sense, by the Islamic shari'a, which also to a large extent governs the wealth of the family (for example, restricting inheritance to the family and regulating its distribution within it) (Barakat, 1984: 219ff). Most aspects of legislation in most Muslim countries have been largely 'secularised' – except for family laws (*statut personnel*). This is the last area to be invaded by secularist European-inspired laws and it is also the first line of attack for any demand for the establishment of a so-called 'Islamic order'.

One may search the manifestos of the Muslim Brothers or the Iranian clerics for a detailed description of what an Islamic *state* or an Islamic *economy* should look like, but such a search will be in vain. The Islamic state, some will say, is based on consultancy (*shura*). Others will say that this is desirable but not actually required. Even those who do accept shura as an integral part of Islamic government will disagree about its definition and whether it is invested in the political leadership, in the religious scholars, or else in the people or community at large. One will be told that the Islamic economy is against usury – but this is merely defining something by what it is *not*. Nobody will say what an Islamic economy will actually look like. Yet any Islamic manifesto will include, *a priori*, a detailed account of the moral precepts that the public is to observe collectively and that are to be overseen authoritatively, especially in the area of sex, women and the family. For if Islam – as we argue repeatedly in this work – is not a particularly 'political' religion, this does not mean that it is a private, 'individualistic' religion. Very much the contrary: it is about *public ethics* and *collective morals* – and hence Islam's *apparently* 'political' character in the eyes of many people.

Maxime Rodinson has aptly observed that whereas Muslims may have different interpretations of the social, economic or political implications of Islam, their perception of the moral features of that religion is almost unchanging:

Muslims make themselves different images of Islam according to the social strata to which they belong, the sort of education they have received, their political affiliation, and even their individual temperament. But everywhere the dominant, almost unchanging image is of Islam as guardian, guarantor, surety, and protector of traditional morality . . . Fondness for the advantages of tradition is partly responsible for the male tribe's religious faith, which cuts across political beliefs and classes. As with Latin Catholicism in the past, for example, religious tradition can be exploited in order to dominate the sex which males unquestioningly consider weak and subordinate. (Rodinson, 1979: 8)

The concept that ethics in Islamic society are public and not private, collective and not individual, is partly related to the fact that in the 'original' solidarity-based Arab society, shame-related values have usually been more important than guilt-related values. This point should not be exaggerated out of all proportion, but I think that it is fairly valid, as the Arab is still usually more concerned about apparent, collective norms and behaviour, and the frightening likelihood of a scandal, *fadiha*, than he is with regard to private, discreet matters that nobody can see (compare Barakat, 1984: 350–352). In fact the fast shift, under modernisation, or more specifically Westernisation, from the community-based concept of shame to the individual-based (and/or legally formalised) concepts of guilt, without these last concepts becoming adequately internalised within the individual, is, in my view, one of the main causes of psychological and social agony (and corruption) in many contemporary Arab societies. Although his definitions may differ somewhat from mine, Ali Mazrui argues that both African and Islamic traditional law are more conscious of the imperative of shame as against guilt, than Western law has been in the modern period. In his view, the 'modern' shift of emphasis from the first to the second 'has not worked':

Shame . . . is a principle of wide social accountability . . . Guilt . . . is a principle of *individual* culpability . . . The substitution of cage for the villain to replace compensation for the victim . . . the focus on personal individual accountability as against collective responsibility have all resulted not only in escalating violence and criminality, especially in . . . cities, but also in the relentless decay of the police, judiciary, legal system and prison structures. (Mazrui, 1985: 9–10)

There is therefore a high degree of dissonance, and conflict, between the 'traditional' values to which the individual has been socialised, especially in the village community of the countryside or the desert, and the 'modern' values by which economic, administrative and legal organisations are supposed to be governed, especially in the urban, semi-industrialised and rather impersonal environment of the city.

To the ordinary citizen in a Muslim country, deprived for centuries of the means (and the skills) to express himself politically and to defend his own interests via political action, the pains and conflicts that go with urbanisation, industrialisation and modernisation may appear to him like a basically 'moral' problem: a problem of the bad new times that render a husband dependent on his wife's wage, that tempt his daughter with advertisements for expensive imported apparel and richer men in expensive flashy cars, etc. Economic and class considerations may therefore transpose themselves to the recently-urbanised person, with his various sexual anxieties, as moral issues pertaining to the erosion of values such as obedience, contentedness, modesty and piety. He may then join ranks with others who feel the same way to try to urge the authorities, in the name of Islam, to do something about it. When they do this it is not basically because Islam is a political religion – as many maintain – but because it is premised on the *collective* enforcement of *public* morals.

This implies several things. The traditional Arab-Islamic 'practical wisdom' has moved the responsibility for sin and error outside the human being and on to circumstances, fate and the outside world (Zai'ur, 1988B: 37). Thus, to avoid adultery, simply conceal the body of the tempting female; to avoid theft, simply chop away the hand that committed it! Furthermore, morality is not an individual, but a social, concern. It is not sufficient for you personally to be honest, proper and pious – *everyone* should be. Islam is about 'enforcing good, and prohibiting evil'. In doing these things you are expected to take an active stand. According to the Prophetic tradition (see 'Abd al-Qadir 'Awda, 1951: 10–12) wrong should be righted 'by the hand'; if this is not possible, then 'by the tongue'; and if this also proves to be impossible to attain, then 'by the heart', but this last 'is the weakest of faith'.[5]

This may help to explain why family-related matters seem to figure most highly in the programmes of practically all Islamic movements. Indeed, with a certain fringe of such movements, the obsession with sex, women and the human body is so strong that it borders on the pathological. Take this ruling issued by one contemporary Islamist, for example: 'It is religiously prohibited (*yahrum*) for a woman to look at the thigh of her daughter, sister, mother, neighbour or friend, in a bathroom or anywhere' (in Haidar, 1987: 167). Such may be an extreme personal opinion but I think it is still fair to say that sexuality remains, in general, a very significant *public* (and hence, by extension, political) issue in most Muslim societies. Val Moghadam is correct in observing that:

> [T]he view of woman as benevolent wife/mother and destructive sexual creature is present, in varying degrees, in the ideology, culture and symbolic systems of many societies. However, the preoccupation with female sexuality, and especially of its regulation and control, is striking in Islamic discourse. (Moghadam, 1988: 225)

'Until when', wonders Hisham Sharabi, 'will this suppressed subject of sex, which is no more than a natural biological function, remain the predominant factor in this [Arab] society, and in its social relations and political and intellectual activities?' (Sharabi, 1987: 10). Even the Islamic writer Hasan Hanafi admits that one of the characteristics of the Islamist approach is that it is dominated by

> a sexual perception of the world: they start with the veil, with segregation and turning the eye away and turning the voice down. [Yet] the larger the veil, the greater the desire to recognize what it hides! There is more to social and political life than such a sexual perception of social relations that classifies a citizen [only] into man and woman, male and female . . . Such a classification might not signify a virtue, but may indicate a repressed sexual desire and a sublimated sexual deprivation. (Hanafi, 1980: 42–43)

Fu'ad Zakariyya also expresses his puzzlement as to why the contemporary Islamic movements are obsessed in their religious 'struggle' with the issues of dress, segregation and the like, rather than with issues such as social justice, types of government or useful international alliances. He then offers a partial answer:

> The attaching of such an enormously great weight to sex, as though it was the greatest problem dwarfing all others such as bread, shelter, and the feeling of security and justice, is a type of excessive prohibition which is in fact another form of excessive interest in sex – it is the other side of the same coin of erotic deprivation. (Zakariyya, 1987: 20–21, with minor editing)

A persuasive analysis has been put forward by Muhammad Mahfuz, in which he explains how the 'family problem', as one may call it, might have encouraged the militant Islamic organisations in Egypt to think and act in a certain way (Mahfuz, 1988). He argues that in Egypt girls and boys mature sexually at an early age. But outside the village (where they normally marry around the age of puberty), they and their parents cannot afford an early marriage for them. Now many young people go on to higher education, graduate in their twenties, cannot find employment for several years, then cannot afford the exorbitant expenses of housing and furnishing – especially given the newly acquired taste for 'necessities' such as televisions, refrigerators, stoves and other such durables. The result of this, he interestingly suggests, is that:

> Monasticism was the innovation of Christian Egypt. But this was a political option by way of resisting Roman injustice. The modern involuntary monasticism is evidence of the bankruptcy of the system, and [it provides] a social justification for destroying it. (ibid.: 108–109)

Among the militant Islamic groups, *Al-Takfir w'al-Hijra* came up with the most radical solution. They pooled their financial resources (often acquired through work in oil-exporting countries), rented apartments collectively in peripheral areas of the city, and lived in a simple, semi-communal manner (without most modern electric and electronic equipment), relying on income from free (non-governmental) earnings in small trade, services and agriculture. Some men divorced their previous wives if they did not agree to joining the new communes, some wives deserted their previous husbands to live their new pious lives, and some girls absconded from the parental home to join the intense young men with the long dark beards and short white gowns. The authorities presented the movement as consisting of sexually lusty and depraved types who debauched under-age girls, under the leadership of a new long-haired Rasputin. Muhammad Mahfuz thinks that the authorities should have examined the real, and enormous, problem:

> Millions of young people of both sexes are suspended and deprived of their instinctual rights to home and marriage. The society is increasingly suppressing them, without solving their problems, or even discussing the solution presented by the *jama'a* [of *Takfir*] . . . [And this] at a time when Egypt was . . . replete with furnished apartments and with nightclubs providing prostitution on a large scale for the leading politicians and the fat cats. (ibid.: 112–113, with some editing)

Empirical evidence from Egypt (see Chapter 7) confirms that the highest percentage of members of the militant Islamic movements comes from the newly built and rapidly expanding periphery of the cities, especially Cairo, where such social problems and 'moral' issues reach critical levels. The enforcement of Islamic ethics may appeal to the young males as a way of ensuring 'coverage' (*satr*) for, and control over, their female folk. The enforcement of such ethics may also appeal to the student or working female who may *voluntarily* choose to veil herself (a phenomenon that has not been adequately analysed). In addition to this being a manifestation of social protest (especially in its extreme, ultra-Islamic forms), it may also help the female avoid the intrusions and molestations of males, and save her from a potentially rough competition for men based on physical beauty and expensive dressing up.[6] Pursuing their studies or their careers, 'women have to cross the street! Streets are spaces of sin and temptation, because they are both public and sex-mixed. And that is the definition of *fitna*: disorder!' (Mernissi, 1988: 11). In the crowded conditions of the market, street and public transport in a city such as Cairo, for example, women are most vulnerable. As Fadwa el Guindi put it:

[M]en harass women in public by the most demeaning and undignified words, gestures and touching. Because men define the public world (not including the workplace) as their space, women are treated as intruders. And while women are being physically harassed, they are also accused of bringing it upon themselves by being there.
Therefore, a woman in public has a choice between being secular, modern, feminine and frustratingly passive (hence very vulnerable), or becoming a *mitdayyinah* (religieuse), hence formidable, untouchable, and silently threatening. (el Guindi, 1981: 481)

There is evidence that similar manifestations exist in Muslim Beirut and that there, too, the 'Islamist' option seems to impart a certain sense of cohesion and equality and to ameliorate, at least psychologically, the difficulties of finding suitable housing and sufficient income for food *and* dress (cf. Sharara, 1985: 330–341).

Properly understood, the call for an 'Islamic order' may often turn out to be little more than a quest by the agonised, recently-urbanised communities for a collective enforcement of conventional public morals, at a time of major social dislocation.

3   The variety of modern Islam: intellectual expressions and political roles

From the time that the Christian capitalist West began to encroach economically, culturally and politico-strategically on the Muslim world (especially from the late eighteenth century), Muslims have not ceased to debate the cultural and political role that Islam should play in confronting, or in adapting to, the challenge of the West. Two issues have been particularly pressing: one concerns Western concepts (and values) such as secularism, modernisation, and development; the other concerns the Western concept (and institution) of the territorial, bureaucratic State.

In recent years, and several decades after the acquisition of formal independence, the debate has been given a more urgent, and sometimes even a violent character, by the fact that development endeavours seem to be faltering, and because the 'modern' State which championed these endeavours seems to be more interested in 'controlling' than in representing or in serving its society.

'Development' may be defined briefly as a process through which an entity can reach its maximum potential, both quantitatively and qualitatively. The major pursuit involved in any development process is over 'effectiveness', which revolves around man's better mastery of his physical and social environment. But for any development process to be capable of continuity and self-perpetuation the objectives of 'effectiveness' should be defined within one's own cultural frame of reference. The European industrial and technological revolution emerged from within the cultural renaissance and the religious reform. Development, in historical perspective, was never simply the outcome of technological know-how, but was the result of cultural pride and political determination as well. If the objectives of 'effectiveness' are not defined within one's own cultural frame of reference, as is the case with many of the 'imitative' developmental activities in the Third World, feelings of 'alienation' may intensify and the quest for 'authenticity' may acquire a special urgency. In the Middle East, 'modernisation' was not on the whole a 'natural' process corresponding to domestic social, intellectual and technological developments. It took place partly as an act of defence (i.e. 'defensive modernisation') against the pressures of the capitalist colonial powers and was then reinforced by the colonial powers in ways that served their own interests. Thus the secularisation and codification of laws, the installation of modern 'legal-rational' types of organisation, the expansion of modern European-style education and even the creation of territorial 'sovereign' states, were all processes that took place under the hegemony of an expanding capitalist/colonialist Europe.

In the debate over development, two cultural concepts frequently surface. The first is that of modernisation; the second that of secularisation. Modernisation is an extremely confusing concept, for it connotes aspiring to, or moving towards, whatever is possessed by 'modern' societies. The problem is that the 'things' possessed by modern societies may be the ways and means whereby man can better control and exploit his natural environment (hence, for example, industrialisation), or they may simply be the most recent fashions and trends or whatever happens to be a matter of particular taste or à la mode in the West (hence Europeanisation - *farnaja* in Arabic - and Westernisation).

Modernisation is a potentially misleading concept because it can easily be mistaken for Westernisation, itself simply no more than the borrowing of certain alien social and cultural habits that may not be superior in or by themselves. Obviously, a more liberated and enlightened attitude will not result automatically from casting off the Eastern veil and putting on a revealing super-mini frock. After all, the veil can possibly be regarded, from a socio-historical point of view, as the particular costume of a specific geographical-cultural region, developed at least partly in response to the harsh weather conditions of burning sunshine and dusty winds. (Hence, among some peoples – for example the Tuaregs – it is also worn by men.) It could perhaps be argued that the veil is a particular way of dressing, just as using chopsticks is a particular way of eating. None of these social customs is superior to another; they are simply culture-specific.[1]

Mustafa Kemal Ataturk was, of course, the epitome of this approach of mistaking Westernisation for development. His people were not going to think any better because their heads were covered by European hats, their bodies were not going to function better because they were inside Western clothes, nor was their literature going to advance because it was written down in the Latin alphabet! Now, more than half a century after Ataturk started his movement, Turkey is not in any notable way more advanced than a country like Egypt, whose revolution took place thirty years later, whose development was arrested by a not inconsiderable number of wars, and who did not have to deny her own culture in the same way. Yet this ridiculous approach, in which aspects of effectiveness in the Western civilisation are confused with certain of its cultural norms and habits, persists under the misleading slogan of modernisation. This is part of a process that one Arab writer has termed 'the modernisation of poverty' (G.Amin, 1974).

ISLAM AND SECULARISM

Another concept frequently related to development is that of secularisation. The concept again is very much part of modernisation in its Western context. Much of the stagnation of Christian Europe in mediaeval times was due to the domination of the Church over the State, especially through its control of learning and of land. The European Renaissance was therefore related to freeing both 'ideas' and 'capital' from the grip of the Church.

This phenomenon has no parallel in the history of Islam. First, Islam has no Church and no clergy in the sense of an elaborate ecclesiastical hierarchy. Since the time of Prophet Muhammad, the rulers in the Islamic State have never been 'men of religion', but were often assumed to be 'religious men', and there is a big difference between the two. Even in minority Shi'ism, with its more elaborate and slightly more hierarchical body of religious scholars, these scholars have never been summoned to take over power directly, until Khomeini – in a most unconventional manner – in his book *Wilayat-i-Faqih* (guardianship of the jurisconsult) called for this (and eventually managed to achieve it). However, it is not an idea that has been pursued by Islamic scholars in other countries, and it remains specifically Khomeini-ist in nature.

Secondly, Christianity is basically a *faith* while Islam is mainly a *shari'a* (*nomos* or 'religious law'). Christianity has very few regulations for organising the social and economic affairs of the individual and the community; for such rulings, Christian societies have delved into the Old Testament or relied on imperial and national traditions. Islam, on the other hand, contains principles that regulate man's relationship to God (*'ibadat*) and principles that regulate man's relationship to other men (*mu'amalat*). Many Muslims therefore believe in the holistic nature of Islam in the sense of its being a way of life and not simply a religion (*dunya wa din*). This fusion of matters of belief with matters of conduct in Islam makes it difficult to separate religion from politics. For there is no Church that, if it interferes in matters of government, can be asked to mind its own business or can be neatly excluded from politics. Islam is believed to be all-encompassing and all-pervasive; 'secularism' is therefore considered by many to be a concept not only alien to, but also incompatible with Islam.

In the West, separation of Church from State was considered 'necessary' (or desirable) because of the clergy's *interference* in scientific and socio-economic matters; and this separation turned out to be possible because the Church was embodied in an ecclesiastical hierarchy that could be neatly separated and isolated from politics. In Islam, separation of religion from politics (in this case the analogy of Church and State would be inaccurate) is, to say the least, extremely difficult; furthermore, there is a large question mark in many Muslim circles as to whether it would be either desirable or appropriate. From an Islamic perspective, the 'Golden Age' – whether viewed in terms of moral purity, of military conquest or of technological and cultural advancement – was lived according to a formula that made no effort to separate 'belief' from 'life'. On the other hand, in the Islamic memory the concept of secularism can be related only to periods of colonial hegemony, or, alternatively, to national attempts at experimenting with various Western 'developmental formulas' (such as capitalism, socialism, etc.) that appear not to have worked.

The contemporary resurgence of Islamic trends was a reaction to the perceived failure of these formulas, and it should not be looked upon only as a 'return to the past', but ought to be seen at least partly as a search for a new and effective social formula that, because it is not simply imported (and thus alien and ineffective), might stand a better chance of being authentic and of producing results as well. Islam also holds the added attraction of being basically an untried formula in modern times. The argument therefore runs along these lines: you have tried all possible 'secular' formulas and they did not work, so why not give Islam a try? All working political systems have certain shortcomings that lower them from the idealistic levels implied by their theoretical expressions. The 'truly Islamic society' is still all Utopia since, apart from the still evolving case of Iran, nobody has yet seen what this society looks like and how it feels in reality. In that context, the Iranian revolution must be regarded as a breakthrough: its fate has continued to have a tremendous impact on Islamic movements all over the world, either by tempting them even further into adopting the non-secular 'Islamic alternative', or else by dissuading them from the attempt altogether.

Another 'advantage' of secularism in the Western experience is the way it has facilitated the full integration of people from different religions and different sects into the community. Here again the Islamic experience reveals some differences. In comparative historical perspective, Muslims can be proud of the relative tolerance accorded by the Islamic state to its Christian and Jewish subjects. They rightly point to Islamic Iberia where prosperous communities of Christians and Jews flourished, and then to re-conquered Spain where, with no Muslims left, the cruelties of the Inquisition took hold and multiplied into appalling religious wars that disfigured the whole of Europe.

The problem is, of course, that non-Muslim groups living in modern Muslim societies may not find sufficient reassurance in a formula that was superior several centuries ago. Although Muslim rulers have often placed non-Muslims in quite superior posts, the ultra-orthodox attitude does not condone the appointment of non-Muslims to positions of leadership or high power. This, for example, explains why Egypt's Christian community (the Copts) have recently been so alarmed by the country's increasing tendency to adopt Islamic legislation. Their full citizenship, with equal rights and obligations, established for them under Muhammad 'Ali in the early nineteenth century, has now become threatened by a possible revival of the concept of *ahl al-dhimma* ('protected subjects' traditionally exposed to special 'religious' taxes – *jizya* – and forbidden to govern over or to judge between Muslims).

This formula, which was so noble in the Middle Ages, does not seem compatible with the egalitarian achievements of the latter part of the twentieth century. While a small number of contemporary Islamic writers have produced some interesting juridic arguments establishing the status of non-Muslims as full citizens rather than protected subjects (cf. Huwaidi, 1985; al-Bishri, 1980), the main orientation among the neo-fundamentalists, following in the path laid by Mawdudi and Qutb, has been extremely antagonistic to non-Muslims. The dominant concept implies that they should be treated with 'fairness', but excluded from political participation. The statements of the Islamists on this subject often sound quite insulting by implying that the non-Muslims do not actually belong to their native countries, but belong somewhere else. Zainab al-Ghazali, leader of the Muslim Sisters in Egypt, seems to suggest something like this when she lists the rights of *ahl al-dhimma* in Islamic lands, and then says:

I state that we [the Islamists] will never treat the Christians and Jews . . . in the same way as *their* governments treat the Muslim minorities in the homelands where they [Christians and Jews] are in the majority. Our faith commands us to be just with all people, and there is no need for the 'people of the book' to be apprehensive. (al-Ghazali al-Jubaili, 1988: 212 – emphasis added)

To this statement Fahd al-Fanik, a Christian Jordanian, gave the following pointed response:

So 'our' governments, of us Christian Arabs, are the governments of America, Britain and France – is this credible? I demand that the respected lady revises her statements, for we do not accept belonging to a foreigner since we are pure established Arabs (*aqhah*) who lived here before the Islamic conquest.

We should all agree that there is no *jizya* and no exemption from military service, and that there is equality in defending the fatherland, which I do not call Islamic lands, because it is mine as much as it is yours; otherwise it is upon you to tell me where my home is!

As for the rights mentioned by the respected lady, which include the protection of bodies and monies . . ., I was not particularly impressed – for the simple reason that these are basic rights that are secured by all states for foreigners, tourists, and even prisoners of war. (al-Fanik in Ibrahim 1988: 238–239; cf. also Salama in Ibrahim, 1988: 386–388)

One of the reasons for the untypically vicious religious strife that has taken place in Egypt since the seventies is the growing desecularisation that has occurred not only among Muslims but among the Copts themselves. For some years, the political leadership of the Copts has been shifting, from the *Wafd* mass party and from populist figures such as Makram 'Ubaid, until it ended up with the Coptic clergy, headed by the Patriarch himself (cf. Hanna, 1980: 94–98). While the strengthening of Coptic solidarity was certainly partly a reaction to vigorous Islamic resurgence, it was also, in some ways, a genuine revival on its own merits, especially under the leadership of the current patriarch Shenuda, who became Pope in 1971. Indeed, religious conflict probably became inevitable during this period: for if and when religion becomes the main concept of identity and the main focus of loyalty, then very little common ground can be established between citizens of different religions. From this point of view, the doctrines of Egyptian nationalism in the twenties and thirties, and of Arab nationalism in the fifties and sixties, were both markedly 'superior', as both were potentially conducive to reducing religious friction and to promoting socio-political integration.

The emergence of nationalism indicates, among other things, that secularism (*'ilmaniyya*) has not been entirely absent as a social and as an intellectual force in Muslim societies. In spite of its fragility, secularism has indeed established some roots in the Middle East. After Muhammad 'Ali abolished religious taxes, introduced general military conscription and established public recruitment and promotion largely on merit, secularism became a social force in Egypt, and later in other parts of the Middle East. Politically and intellectually, secularism manifested itself in the move towards Egyptian nationalism in the twenties and in the spread of Arab nationalist ideas from the beginning of this century, the two movements being very clearly 'secular' in the way they involved both Muslims and Christians.

Secularism has had its Muslims theorists, too, including some religious scholars. The most notable of these was Shaikh 'Ali 'Abd al-Raziq. Writing in the 1920s, 'Abd al-Raziq set out to prove that Islam (even in its Prophetic era) was purely a 'religion' and that it had no claim over politics. He maintained that:

> Muhammad . . . was no more than a messenger of a purely religious call, that is, not coloured by any inclination to govern or by any claim for a state. The Prophet had no rule or government, nor did he establish a kingdom in the political sense of this word or its synonyms. He was none but a messenger like those preceding him: not a king or a builder of a State or a proponent of monarchy. ('Abd al-Raziq, 1966: 135–136)

In an attempt to present a 'deconstructive history of Islamic thought', Mohammed Arkoun has also been able to 'discover a secular dimension of [Islamic] thought'. Some of the main lines he puts forward with regard to secularism (for which he prefers the French term *laïcité*) are the following: 'Secularism is included in the Qur'an and Madinan experience'. 'The Umayyad-'Abbasid State is secularist; the ideological theorizing by the jurists is a circumstantial product using conventional and credulous arguments to hide historical and political reality; this theorizing is built on an outdated theory of knowledge'. 'Military power played a pre-eminent role in the caliphate, the sultanate and all later forms of Islamic government'. 'Attempts to rationalize the *de facto* secularism and to develop a lay attitude have been made by the *falasifa*' [philosophers]. 'Orthodox expressions of Islam (sunni, shi'i, khariji, all of which claim the monopoly of orthodoxy) arbitrarily select and ideologically use beliefs and practices conceived to be authentically religious'. 'All political regimes which have emerged in Islamic societies after their liberation from colonialism are *de facto* secular, dominated by Western models, based on the Classical theory of authority and on intellectual modernity' (Arkoun, 1988: 71–72).[2]

Yet the *intellectual* – rather than the institutional or governmental – drive for secularism has never managed to entrench itself deeply in Muslim societies; it has always remained fragile and insecure, and its appeal seems, if anything, to be fading away rather than gaining strength. Some may argue that the concept of secularisation (as an 'imported' concept) was present only at a time when the Western-educated elites were dominant, and that with the rise to power of the more indigenously-educated elites, a corresponding decline in the influence of secularist ideals would therefore become inevitable. Part of the 'surprise' effect on Western politicians and scholars caused by events such as the Iranian revolution or the assassination of Sadat can be attributed to their mistaken presumption 'that secularization was occurring at both the institutional *and* the cultural-ideological levels' (Gilsenan, 1982A: 29).

'CONSERVATISM' VERSUS 'INNOVATION'

Like all others, Muslim communities have always alternated between the influences of conservatism and innovation. Islamic societies have not always been stagnant; on the contrary, until the end of the Middle Ages they possessed both the scientific practices and the commercial elites that later made Europe's industrial capitalist revolution possible. Why then did Europe develop into an industrial (and eventually into a post-industrial) society, while Muslim societies were unable to translate the scientific and mercantile achievements of the mediaeval period into a systematic process of capitalist (and cultural) accumulation? This is a difficult and a complex question, but the debate so far has revolved around two arguments. Max Weber and (in one way or another) the majority of 'Orientalists' have looked for factors within the Muslim societies themselves, and have considered these factors to be responsible for that stagnation. Weber, a puritan, thought that the 'warrior' tradition, the Sufi orders, the unincorporated guilds, and even the self-indulgence and sexual appetite attributed to Muslims, were all responsible for the arrested development towards capitalism (cf. Turner, 1974).

Other writers have challenged this thesis, which is based not only on a stereotypical and factually inaccurate understanding of Muslim societies coloured by contemporaneous popular legend, but also on Weber's own personal likes and dislikes. This approach overlooks the fact that both the Muslim world, as well as the rest of Asia and Africa, which were not dominated by Islamic influences, were stagnating, and that this was occurring in correspondence with the colonial expansion of Europe. As Maxime Rodinson has argued, there was nothing in the Muslim societies of the Middle Ages that would have prevented them from developing into capitalism, for they did indeed have many of the prerequisites for such a transformation. If development did not take place, then it must have been because of an 'external' factor – because of colonialism, which dominated politically and exploited economically, and which also led to cultural humiliation and the loss of self-confidence (Rodinson, 1978; and cf. Turner, 1978).

Intellectually, too, Muslim societies have had their own tools for cultural innovation and renewal; yet, as with most other societies, they tended in times of weakness and stagnation to take refuge in the certainty of conservative tradition. The conflict between *taqlid* (imitation; following; traditionalism) and *ijtihad* (independent interpretation and judgement), or between *'aql* (reasoning) and *naql* (copying), is an old one in Islamic jurisprudence. According to the taqlid stream, religion should be viewed as a revelation that can be clearly understood through the strict and literal reference to the original sources – the Quran, plus the *Hadith* (sayings of the Prophet Muhammad) and the *Sunna* (traditions of the Prophet Muhammad). In ijtihad these original sources are interpreted in an independent way and are also frequently supported by *qiyas* (reasoning by analogy) and *ijma'* (consensus of the learned).

Although these two streams have normally existed together, there was undoubtedly a tendency to emphasise ijtihad during times of advancement when innovation and creativity were required, and to stress taqlid in times of decay and stagnation, when the rulers did not tolerate difference and freedom, and when the populace looked for elements of certainty in the midst of confusion or for consolation in the face of oppression. Indeed, the shutting of the open gates of ijtihad in the 'household of Islam' by the religious jurists was a characteristic feature of much of the later Abbasid and of the Ottoman periods of Middle Eastern history, as we have already seen.

The gates remained more or less closed until the emergence of Jamal al-Din al-Afghani (1838–1897), a scholar (probably of Persian origin) who was active mainly in Egypt and Turkey. Afghani revived the ijtihad stream and in a way initiated 'a renaissance of Muslim philosophy, encouraging the direct study of the works themselves rather than the study, then customary, of the usually sterile commentaries or supercommentaries' (O. Amin, 1966: 92). He also advocated the Mu'tazilite doctrine of freedom as opposed to fatalism. His Egyptian disciple, Muhammad 'Abdu (1849–1905), was a 'rationalist' who influenced and inspired not only a whole school of thinkers and reformers, including many graduates of Al-Azhar mosque-university in Cairo (the oldest university in the world), but a number of non-Egyptians and even non-Muslims as well. This school of Islamic reformers tends to apply a freer approach in reading and interpreting the sources, stressing *qiyas* (argument by analogy) and also *istihsan* (the principle of 'desirability'), as well as the principle of *al-masalih al-mursala* (general interests of the community).

Revivals of the opposite stream have also occurred. The Wahhabi movement in Arabia in the eighteenth century, and the Sanusi movement in the Great Sahara and the Mahdiyya movement in Sudan, both in the nineteenth century, were strict, puritanical movements whose motivation was primarily a response to internal decay rather than to external threat (Esposito, 1987: 39), and who were strongly inclined towards fundamentalist simplicity.

The *salafiyya* tradition (veneration of the tradition of early Muslim leaders and jurists) has also been revived, intellectually by individuals such as Muhammad Rashid Rida in the twenties and thirties, and socially by the Muslim Brothers who started up in Egypt in 1928 and who now also have offshoots in Syria, Jordan, Sudan, Arabia, North Africa and elsewhere. This is a trend which often develops into a curious combination of negative and rejectionist attitudes towards Western values on the one hand, and a 'passive, uneasy, ineffectual acceptance of European institutions and social practices' on the other (Kerr, 1966: 221). In spite of their activities in social and economic spheres, the 'Islamic groupings' (such as the Muslim Brothers and the smaller but more 'extreme' Muhammad's Youth) 'did not produce a modern applied theory for economic and social organisations, or a comprehensive educational approach; which led the people in charge of such agencies to revert to borrowing, perhaps until now' (Bayyumi, 1979: 321).

Islam has undoubtedly had a 'renaissance' of sorts, initiated by the schools of Afghani and 'Abdu. Even so, this renaissance was never complete and to this day remains fragile in the extreme. Kamal 'Abd al-Latif would in fact argue that the 'Islamic reformers' had not really accepted modernism as an integrated philosophical outlook (related to concepts such as liberty, individualism, social contract, etc.), but that they borrowed eclectically as it suited them, always extracting the 'modern' concepts out of their (European) intellectual and social context, and trying to subsume them instead under familiar Islamic concepts believed to be analogous to them. Thus the Islamic reformers had read and interpreted the liberal philosophy and the phenomenon of the State only according to their own idiom, informed by the vocabulary of *al-siyasa al-shar'iyya* (religious politics). This act of intellectual compromise, 'Abd al-Latif would maintain, was understandable as a defence mechanism under the existing conditions of Western hegemony. Gradually, with Muslim societies no longer needing to act in such a defensive way, the later generations of salafis and of fundamentalists have resorted to removing the eclectic, compromising touch and to revealing again the essential Islamic concept of *hakimiyya* (God's absolute sovereignty) which cannot be reconciled with foreign concepts such as that of the 'social contract' (cf. K.'Abd al-Latif, 1987).

Whether we agree or not with 'Abd al-Latif's analysis in its entirety, there is little doubt that the attempts by people such as Afghani and 'Abdu to initiate reform were mainly prompted by external stimuli, by confrontation with a technologically superior and politically dominant Western presence. Their reforms tended, therefore, to carry the marks of a hurried attempt at intellectual compromise that quite often arrived at an abrupt and inconclusive dead end. Yet the seeds for an innovative cultural revival were certainly present in the writings of people such as Afghani and 'Abdu, to a degree that provoked some citizens to claim that the two pioneers were not true and sincere Muslims: in the case of Afghani, both his ethnic origin and his religious affiliation were called into question, while it was said of 'Abdu that he was an atheist, or at least an agnostic (cf. Kedourie, 1966; Keddie, 1968).

An important point to be made here is that if the Muslim reformers did not wholeheartedly embrace the full philosophical thrust of the (European) 'enlightenment', this was not really because of a certain 'essentialist' character in Islam as a belief system that would necessarily have constrained such an intellectual development. Rather, it was the distorted and incomplete nature of the capitalist transformation of Muslim societies that stood in the way of a full adoption of the values and thinking patterns of bourgeois liberalism. Thus, as Samir Amin has argued, a certain dualism has established itself within the Egyptian, and subsequently the Arab, culture (which has continued more or less to the present), whereby dogmatic or at least conservative hermeneutics of Islam are juxtaposed with pragmatic, piecemeal borrowings from the modern sciences (cf. S. Amin, 1985: 119–133). The constraint over the development of rational liberal thinking – which continues in some respects to this day – was caused not simply by the resistance of a stubborn religious tradition, but more importantly by the fact that the formation of a native industry and a native bourgeoisie has been belated and incomplete (compare also 'Isa, 1986: esp. 583–595).

The so-called 'Islamic resurgence' of the seventies and eighties is in some measure an indication that the earlier reforms were not able to answer all the nagging questions. More concretely, it represents a response to a variety of secular development experiments that appeared not to have 'worked': neither Ataturk-ism in Turkey and the 'White Revolution' in Iran, nor the Nasserist Egyptian and the Ba'thist Syrian varieties of 'Arab Socialism', seem to have delivered what was promised.

On the other side, however, Israel – which is perceived by most Middle Easterners as a 'religious formula' – has conquered and flourished. It is not altogether surprising, therefore, that most aspects of the current religious revival in the Arab world appear to have followed closely behind the 1967 defeat by Israel: not only was there a marked growth in general religiosity and an increase in the membership of the 'mystic' orders after this tragic event, but on a more militant level, the emergence of what I have termed the neo-fundamentalist Islamic groups also followed the traumatic experience of the Six Day War, and was to a large extent influenced by a 'religious interpretation' of Israel's victory and the defeat of the Arabs (Ayubi, 1980B).

Yet in spite of all the difficulties, and apart from the case of Iran (where the religious scholars managed to transform a middle-class revolution into a near-theology), 'secular' governments seem to be managing to hang on – though only just. Under pressure both from populations that show every sign of a growing religiosity as well as from a number of small militant Islamic groupings, these governments have had to make concessions, by re-incorporating religion into laws, schools and organisations. On the other hand, they cannot afford to concede too far, since the very foundations of their legitimacy – which are supposed to be political, not religious – would otherwise be undermined. Thus, for example, at the same time that Sadat (in 1980) conceded a fundamental change in the Egyptian constitution – stipulating for the first time that the shari'a was to be the *main* source of legislation – he repeatedly used the slogan: 'No religion in politics and no politics in religion'.[3]

Meanwhile, the Iranian revolution remains the sole political embodiment of an Islamic ideology in modern times. Yet the intellectual contribution of this revolution has remained quite limited. After a brief but promising glimpse which suggested that the turmoil might be about to produce a revitalising and dynamic 'cultural revolution', focuses altered and directions changed as a result of political and strategic developments, and there now seems to be very little coming out of Iran in the way of innovative solutions to its major human and societal problems.

On the intellectual level, Muslim thinkers continue their search for a new formula that can combine 'modernity' with 'authenticity'. As is often the case, many of these attempts at renewal are frequently caught up into the paradigm and idiom of a particular Western philosophy: Cartesian, Kantian, Positivist, Marxist, or whatever. Interesting examples can be found in some of the writings of Zaki Najib Mahmud, 'Abd-Allah al-'Arawi, Muhammad Aziz al-Ahbabi, Sadiq J. al-'Azm, Adonis, and others. On the other hand, there are indications of a trend among Islamic thinkers which seems to be trying to find its way, not through rejecting Western philosophy (liberal and radical) but by aspiring to surpass it. Islamic thinkers of the fifties and sixties, like the early Sayyid Qutb and the early Khalid Muhammad Khalid who were inclined to interpret Islam in a liberal-radical fashion, seem to have been followed since the seventies and into the eighties by a few thinkers who are attempting to create 'a new radical Islamic theology' (Bezirgan, 1979). Hasan Hanafi, who would probably consider himself the Arab equivalent of the Iranian 'Ali Shari'ati, is probably representative of this trend. Not only is he well-grounded in Islamic teaching, but he is also thoroughly familiar with the phenomenological and Marxist philosophies, and he tends to adopt a 'Third World-ist' orientation that renounces in particular all aspects of cultural dependency while calling for a genuine renewal of the national heritage (cf. Hanafi, 1980).

THE POLITICAL ROLES OF ISLAM

It should be clear from the previous analysis that despite what many 'Orientalists' and 'fundamentalists' would have us believe, Islam is different things to different people: it is both understood differently and utilised differently (cf. Hudson, 1980: 13–24). This applies to all areas of life; and in politics the various roles of Islam may range anywhere from being on the one hand a tool for legitimisation and for the preservation of the status quo, to being a vehicle for protest and a spearhead for revolution on the other.

Both trends are inherent in the Muslim political tradition. For instance, much of Islamic political jurisprudence (as we have seen in Chapter 1) had been related to a doctrine of civil obedience. The caliph performed some religious duties but he was basically a political figurehead. The *ulama* (religious scholars) often taught that anyone in effective possession of political power had to be obeyed, and that an unjust ruler was better than civil strife; this was particularly the case in the mainstream Sunni tradition.

Following this tradition, there are several contemporary examples for the use of religion as a vehicle for legitimisation. In Saudi Arabia, Islam is utilised to mask and to counterbalance the regime's excessive military and cultural dependency on the West, as well as the hedonistic and indulgent pursuits of some sectors of the elite. In Morocco, the monarchy bases its legitimacy on a claimed Sharifian (related to Muhammad) ancestry that places the king, in his capacity as 'commander of the faithful', above the ethnic (Arab/Berber) and the tribal divisions of the population. Islam was also used as a 'mask' by Sadat in Egypt to disguise the rather offensive manifestations of *infitah*, the 'open door' economic policy, and the ever-growing corruption that surrounded it.

But as rulers try to use religion for their own political purposes and against their own political enemies, they frequently end up by having to 'swallow the same poison' that they have forced upon others. For religion is not a monopoly of the rulers; it can also be invoked by the ruled. As Bruno Etienne has argued, both the rulers and the ruled are in some way competing for the same 'cultural and symbolic capital' represented by Islam (Etienne, 1987: 153–154). The Saudis, for example, have always used 'religious weapons' to justify their own policies and to resist the spread of radical influences, especially from Egypt, not only financing some Islamic organisations there but also providing refuge for Islamic militants fleeing from that country. This was particularly true during the time of Nasser, but the trend continued beyond that period. In 1977 certain members of the Egyptian neo-fundamentalist group *al-Takfir w'al-Hijra* (looked at in detail below) escaped to Saudi Arabia after killing an ex-Minister; the Saudis, in accordance with their previous norm, refused to return them to Egypt to stand trial. Two years later, some members of *Takfir* were reported to have been among those who participated, in the name of Islam, in the violent takeover of the Most Sacred Mosque at Mecca (cf. *Al-Siyasa*, 27 November 1979; *Al-Nahar*, 28 November 1979; *Al-Safir*, 28 November 1979).

In Egypt the story is more intricate. After Sadat came to power, he perceived Nasserists and leftists as being his real political enemies: to counterbalance them, he released all members of *Al-Ikhwan al-Muslimun* (the Muslim Brothers, a fundamentalist organisation first formed in 1928) who were still in detention, permitted their publications to circulate, and discreetly gave all manner of encouragement to what was then being called 'the Islamic trend'. Partly as a result of this, Islamic groups became enormously powerful and eventually got completely out of hand, turning finally against Sadat himself – it was members of one of these groups (*Al-Jihad* organisation) who assassinated him.

Just as religion can be utilised as a tool for preserving the status quo, so it can also work as a catalyst for change and a spearhead for revolution, and Islam has always had incorporated in it a certain tradition of revolt. As we have already seen, the socio-political unrest of the first century of Islam (especially following the death of the Prophet Muhammad in AD 632) had led among other things to the emergence of the Shi'a sect. This might have been prompted partly by the need among non-Arabic speaking groups, especially the Persians, for a measure of equality and self-realisation *vis-à-vis* the dominant Arabs; in any case, Shi'ism soon attracted the interest and support of the underprivileged classes. (The spread of 'non-conformist' Protestant sects among the non-English peoples of Great Britain offers a later historical analogy.) The Shi'ites eventually developed a rather elaborate clerical hierarchy, and their ulamas often collaborated with those in political power, especially after Shi'ism had become the state religion of Persia in the sixteenth century. Nevertheless, Shi'ism continued to host a rich literature on the justification of revolt and the glorification of martyrdom against unfair and corrupt rulers, a heritage that Ayatollah Khomeini and his colleagues were able to invoke and draw upon for the purposes of the 1978–79 Iranian revolution. This was a movement that began as a social revolution of the professional middle class, the Bazari merchants and the urban lumpenproletariat, which was then turned into a clergy-led religio-nationalistic revolution (see Akhavi, 1980; Keddie, 1981; Halliday, 1988: 31–63, and in MERIP, 113, 1983: 3–8).

Another source of the 'revolutionary' tradition within Islam is the Kharijite (seceding, 'deviant') movements which emerged during the reign of the fourth caliph, 'Ali, and which continued to flourish while the Umayyad dynasty (AD 661–750) and the Abbasid dynasty (AD 750–1258) were in power. There were around two dozen of these groups, which were composed of ultra-zealot puritans or militants who applied very strict moral criteria, and who often murdered those who did not measure up to their standards because they considered it necessary to rid the community of impious and tyrannical rulers and their followers. In modern times, in the case both of Saudi Arabia and of Egypt, the groups that revolted against the rulers were termed *kharijites* by the authorities, and indeed several similarities can be observed between some of the present-day movements of Islamic dissent and certain historic movements such as the *khawarij* (see Chapter 6).

Yet, as we shall see, such movements do not necessarily have to look back to the Kharijites or to the Shi'ite tradition in order to justify civil rebellion, for within the Sunni mainstream tradition itself there are several sources that can be called upon in this respect. Militant Muslims who are particularly concerned with the cause of equality have always been able to invoke the ideas of an individual like Abu Dharr al-Ghifari, a contemporary of the Prophet Muhammad particularly sympathetic to the poor, while those concerned with the issues of strict moral conduct and resistance to the outsider have been able to turn to the ideas of a person such as Ibn Taimiya, the uncompromising Syrian Hanbalite theologian (see Chapters 1 and 6).

Related to the fact that Islam can be used either to justify the status quo or to change it is the fact that, in doing this or that in the name of Islam, there is no single formula that is recommended by all scholars and believers. Here there are three main areas on which opinions vary:

1. In terms of the scope of political activity. A sizeable group believes in the complete and holistic nature of revealed Islam so that, according to them, it encompasses the three famous 'Ds' (*din*, religion; *dunya*, life and *dawla*, State). There are others, however, including some religious scholars, who believe that modern politics and economics are more of a civil domain for the ordinary citizen to ponder and to improvise upon, in which belief they come very close to what in Western terminology would be called separation between Church and State. Typical of the first trend is, for example, the distinguished Islamic writer Yusuf al-Qardawi. He maintains that Islam is an integrated totality that offers a solution to all problems of life. It has to be accepted in its entirety, and to be applied to the family, to the economy and to politics. To him, furthermore, the realisation of an

Islamic society is predicated on the establishment of an Islamic State, that is, an 'ideological State' based on the comprehensive precepts of Islam (al-Qardawi, 1983: 45-115). It should be emphasised, however, that in spite of the pervasiveness of the holistic view, the concept of the 'Islamic State' as such is very new, and can be regarded as an alternative to the concept of the defunct caliphate; it was developed by Muhammad Rashid Rida (1865-1935) and by the Muslim Brothers in response to the dissolution of the Turkish caliphate and in reaction to the pressures put on Muslim societies by the Western powers and by the Zionist movement (cf. Enayat, 1982: 69ff; Donohue and Esposito, 1982: 55-97; Piscatori, 1986: 76-100; Ayubi, 1988A: 17-52).

On the other hand, others have argued the case of separation of Church and State, including Shaikh 'A. 'Abd al-Raziq in the twenties (1925, new ed. 1966: 135ff), and Shaikh K. M. Khalid in the fifties (1950: 157-196; and 1981) (see Chapter 9). Writing in the seventies, the Islamic thinker Muhammad 'Imara articulated the argument in the following terms:

> Islam as a religion has not specified a particular system of government for Muslims, for the logic of this religion's suitability for all times and places requires that matters which will always be changing by the force of evolution should be left to the rational human mind, to be shaped according to the public interest and within the framework of the general precepts that this religion has dictated. ('Imara, 1979: 76-77)

2. In terms of the degree of political control and participation. There are some who believe that Islamic government is not about participation, and that the Muslim ruler is not obliged to take into consideration the advice and opinion given to him by others (al-Sha'rawi, 1982). There are those who believe, on the other hand, that the Islamic principle of *shura* is exactly equivalent to the term 'democracy' in its modern connotations. As the Egyptian thinker Khalid Muhammad Khalid puts it, '*Shura* in Islam is the democracy that gives people the right to choose their rulers and their deputies and representatives, as well as the right to practise freedom of thought, opinion and opposition' (K. M. Khalid, 1982).

3. In terms of the type of socio-economic system and the scope of State intervention in the economy. Here there are those who, in emphasising Islam's condoning of private ownership, end up by justifying the status quo, the class system (*ba'dukum fawq ba'din darajat*: [you were created in] levels that are one above the other), and a capitalist-type economy. They do not normally put it in so many

words, because they usually maintain that Islam has its own genuine economic system which is neither socialist nor capitalist. But their recurring emphasis on Islam's hostility to what they call 'materialism, atheism and communism' is often an indication of their capitalistic inclinations. This is typical, in Egypt for example, of the writings and pronouncements of 'Abd al-Halim Mahmud, Mustafa Mahmud and Mutawalli al-Sha'rawi (cf. Hammuda, 1987A: Ch. 11).

There are also those, such as the Mujahidin Khalq of Iran – representing from a leftist perspective the main opposition to the Khomeinist regime – who maintain that 'true Islam is . . . progressive and revolutionary, and has always fought against oppression' (Mujahidin Khalq Iran, 1979: 5). A similar revolutionary perception of Islam is expressed by Hasan Hanafi, the Egyptian leftist Islamic thinker, when he argues that the purpose of the Islamic sermon should not simply be to call for passive piety and devotion, but rather

> to call for struggle and for retrieving the rights of the poor from the rich; it is to strengthen the wretched and to confront Zionism and imperialism. For the mosque is a [political] party, the prayer [meeting] is a call, the *imam* [leader of prayers] is a guide of the people, and religion is politics. (Hanafi, 1979: 2)

'Religion is politics' – this is indeed the main feature that distinguishes a number of the contemporary Islamic movements from many of their predecessors. To a large extent the current Islamic resurgence is an indication of the existence of a disillusioned popular mass in many countries of the Middle East. As remarked above, the hopes of people in the Arab world in the fifties and sixties hinged upon socialism and pan-Arabism; when these failed (and Israel succeeded), there was a strong 'return to Islam', but this time with a fairly right-wing orientation. Nor did Kemalism in Turkey or the 'White Revolution' in Iran appear to have succeeded as developmental models. Thus, Islamic revival can be regarded at least partly as a function of the eclipse of the Arab radical nationalist movement and of other developmental experiments in the Middle East. In the uncertainty created by the demise of such experiments, it was natural to seek refuge and reassurance in the older and more familiar concepts: for example, for the Egyptians it was an identity based on Egyptian patriotism and religion (with revival among both Muslims and Christians), while for Saudi Arabians it was an identity based on Arab ethnicism and Islamic guardianship.

In theological terms, the main intellectual inspiration for most contemporary Islamic movements has come from the staunch Islamic thinker, Ibn Taimiya, who lived in Syria during the eclipse of the

Abbasid dynasty. Horrified by the atrocities of the nominally Muslim Tatars and disgusted by the compromises of contemporary politicians towards the Mongol invaders and the Crusader settlers, he incorporated into his tracts some strong justifications for disobeying the corrupt rulers. Ibn Taimiya's teachings have always had an impact on those puritanical, militant movements that expressed a kind of Islam more oriented towards the past. Among his disciples, in one way or another, were Muhammad ibn 'Abd al-Wahhab in Arabia and Muhammad al-Sanusi in North Africa, both in the nineteenth century, and to some extent Rashid Rida, the conservatively inclined Syrian thinker who lived in Egypt in the early part of this century (Kerr, 1966: Chs 5 and 6).

Certain contemporary Islamic thinkers have also strongly influenced many of the militant Islamic groups, including in particular the Pakistani Abu al-'Ala al-Mawdudi, and the Egyptian Sayyid Qutb. The main thrust of their ideas revolves around adherence to the principle of 'God's absolute rulership' (*al-hakimiyya l'illah*) and a belief in the total pagan ignorance (*jahiliyya*) of all contemporary governments caused by their failure to apply this principle and to enforce the application of religious law (shari'a). The way out of such a ghastly state of affairs, the neo-fundamentalists maintain, is to go back to the primary sources of shari'a, i.e, the Quran, and the Sunna (sayings and traditions of the Prophet), and to discard *fiqh* (jurisprudence) which has been 'polluted' with human and political vested interests over time.

As in Protestantism, the importance of discarding the Church's teachings and 'going back to the sources' is the resulting egalitarian and participatory ethos that makes everybody able to understand and interpret the word of God without the barriers raised by clerical rank or theological education. The idea, of course, is to exclude the ulama who, to all intents and purposes, have become part of the ruling Establishment and who are therefore – from the Islamists' point of view – unable to see things properly. Traditionally, the ulama were in charge of *ijma'* (consensus of the learned), which is an important complementary source of the shari'a. They practised this through *ijtihad* (independent interpretation), guided by the following: (a) traditions of the Prophet's Companions, Madina people and the imams and leading jurists, and (b) logical methods such as *qiyas* (reasoning by analogy). Understandably, this allowed for a fair amount of improvisation and innovation in interpreting religion. Neo-fundamentalists in particular reject all such philosophical and logical 'tricks' and 'ploys' (*hiyal*), and with them, the main source of the ulama's influence. In confronting the scholars of the ancient mosque-university of Al-Azhar, for example, they claim that nobody has a monopoly over interpretation, that all Muslims are *mujtahids* (those who apply independent reasoning), and that indeed they possess overwhelming arguments that are unknown to the ulama and to which the ulama would be unable to reply (cf. e.g. *Al-Liwa' al-Islami*, no. 19, 3 June 1982; no. 20, 10 June 1982).

A TAXONOMY OF ISLAMICITY

It should be clear from this introductory survey that modern Islam is quite varied in its intellectual expressions and political roles. Indeed some people prefer to speak of various Islams rather than of one essentialist Islam (cf. Eickelman, 1981: Ch. 9, and 1987: 13–30; Roff, 1987: 31–52). It may therefore be useful to conclude with a schematic outline of the various categories of 'Islamicity' which may help, among other things, in avoiding the confusion that can often arise when Islamic 'revival', 'resurgence' and other such concepts are discussed.

First, there is the simple category of being a *Muslim*; that is to say, a person born to Muslim parents, whose name is Muhammad or 'Ali, Fatima or 'A'isha, and the like. One step further along, there is a *mutadayyin* Muslim, that is an observant Muslim who upholds the 'credo' (*al-shahadatain*)[4] and fulfils the duties of prayer, fasting, pilgrimage and zakat (tithes or obligatory alms). Various levels of piety may, of course, be expressed through a variety of good works, and various levels of religiosity may manifest themselves in things such as religious learning or even belonging to a *sufi* (mystic) order.

The group of writers usually known as the 'Islamic reformers' or the 'Islamic modernists' (e.g. Afghani and 'Abdu and their various contemporary followers such as M. 'Imara and M. Khalafalla) can only be designated 'Islamic' because they deal in Islamic subjects. The intensity of their personal religiosity and the orientation of their social and political ideas often vary significantly – even Afghani and 'Abdu seem not to have been strictly practising Muslims (cf. Haidar, 1987: 9). But 'Islamic reformers' tend generally to hold that Islam as a belief system is broad and flexible enough to be able to accommodate itself effectively to the changing requirements of time and place.

Thus far we are still close enough to the concept of religiosity as it is known, for example, in the Christian West. Then we start to move from the area of belief and more into the area of orientation and intensity of doctrine; we also at the same time move from the 'general public' to much smaller intellectual or social groups. Here we may get a *salafi*, that is one who believes, often to the exclusion of other sources, in the good example of Prophet Muhammad and his companions and of the *early* caliphs and jurists: the earlier somehow the better (some stop after the first two caliphs). The term salafi is almost impossible to translate, but it is derived from the word *salaf* meaning ancestors or predecessors. The salafis are therefore inclined to be scripturalist and traditionalist. Many of the ulama could be regarded as salafis in their main orientation, although the term is more often used with reference to non-clerics. The eighteenth- and nineteenth-century puritanical desert-generated movements of Wahhabiyya, Sanusiyya and Mahdiyya may be regarded as a special branch of the Salafiyya orientation. But Salafiyya is better illustrated by the teachings of Rashid Rida and the early Muslim Brothers, such as Hasan al-Banna. The Salafis tend to be strict Sunnis, opposed to the veneration of saints and often to Sufism, and hostile to non-Sunni sects. Their doctrinal dogmatism, however, is often combined with political flexibility (Haidar, 1987: 120–134).

Fundamentalism, and its French kin *intégrisme*, are more complex terms to define, being originally Christian (Protestant and Catholic) notions that were subsequently superimposed on to the Muslim world. The term 'fundamentalists' even seems to have crept up on some Arab writers who call such people *al-'usuliyyun*. Like the salafis, fundamentalists prefer to go back to the early sources, but they are generally less sympathetic to fiqh (jurisprudence). This is a tendency to which fundamentalists of all religions incline, except that in its Islamic variety it also seems to adhere strongly to a holistic, comprehensive notion of Islam, better expressed by the term *intégrisme*. Hence the slogan of the three 'Ds', already mentioned above – Islam is meant to be *din* (a religion), *dunya* (a way of life), and *dawla* (a State). This holistic perspective seems also to imply the necessity of collective action, to bring the totality of Islam into play.

The neo-fundamentalists are often splinter groups from the larger fundamentalist gatherings, and are usually more radical or militant in orientation. They tend on the whole to be more eclectic in their selection and in their reading of the authoritative sources, and they are generally more inclined towards *immediate* action of one sort or another. Examples of such groups are the *Takfir* in Egypt, and the *Jihad* in Egypt and in several Arab countries.

The term Islamists (*al-Islamiyyun*) is usually applied to the last three categories (i.e. salafis, fundamentalists and neo-fundamentalists). It implies a conscious, determined choice of an Islamic doctrine, rather than the simple fact of being born a Muslim, or even of being a pious practising one. The term 'political Islam' (*al-Islam al-siyasi*) is more often confined to the last two categories (the fundamentalists and the neo-fundamentalists) as these are the ones that tend to emphasise the political nature of Islam, and to engage themselves in direct anti-State activities.

A variety of 'cultural Islam' (*Islam hadari*) is also emerging among certain intellectual circles, and seems to be aimed at integrating Islam into a nativist, nationalist or culturalist world view, the politics and economics of which are often of some 'corporatist' description. 'Adil Husain, Tariq al-Bishri and Galal Amin are representative of this trend, to which the occasional Christian, such as Anwar 'Abd al-Malik or even Victor Sahhab, may also loosely belong.[5]

The rest of this book will consist of a study of the ideologies and movements of political Islam (i.e. mainly of the fundamentalists and neo-fundamentalists), and of the debates and counter-debates that they have stimulated within and among various Arab societies.

4   The Islamic movements: some country studies – part 1

How does 'Islamism' manifest itself in various countries? It can be suggested, at the outset, that the various manifestations of Islamism in action are very much contingent on certain historical conjunctures and political conditions (cf. Halliday and Alavi, 'Introduction', 1988: 1-8). For instance, Islamic militancy is likely to be more vigorous against avowedly secularist regimes than it is against regimes that proclaim themselves to be Islamic – where opposition is more likely to take a nationalist or leftist form. Nikki Keddie is basically right in her observation that

> Islamism is not strong in states which are *really* largely traditional and have not experienced a major Western cultural impact, though such states are increasingly rare as Westernization impinges almost everywhere. The people in such states may still follow a number of Islamic laws, but militant mass movements calling for an Islamic state and the end of Western influence are relatively small. (Keddie, 1988B: 16)

This observation is by no means absolute, however, as shown by the Saudi Arabian case where Islamic opposition, both Shi'i and puritanical-Sunni, has taken place, and in Iran where the religious-leftist Mujahidin Khalq oppose the clergy-based Islamic government. But in general the political context would give the Islamic movement its specific character. Thus, for example, Islamic opposition in Afghanistan and Syria, where the governments proclaim 'progressive' policies, has come to be 'traditionalist' in orientation, whereas in opposition to the Westernising policies of the Shah of Iran, of Sadat in Egypt, and of Bourguiba in Tunisia, it has been of a more 'radical' inclination.

A more detailed study of the Islamic movements in various countries is needed before one can generalise about them or compare the social contexts in which they may flourish, and this will be attempted in the following pages. The six Arab countries selected for review in this and the next chapter have been chosen for a number of reasons. To start with, they are all Arab because, apart from the Iranian case which will be touched on from time to time, the phenomenon of political Islam, as defined in this work, manifests itself most clearly in the Arab world. On the whole they host significant Islamic movements, but there are very interesting differences among them. Egypt, of course, has the oldest and most influential Islamic movement, both domestically and regionally. Several Islamic movements in the Mashriq (Arab East), Sudan, North Africa and even the Gulf started as branches or offshoots of the Egyptian Muslim Brothers. Syria is interesting, among other things, because of the special character that the Sunni–'Alawi rift has given to its Islamic movement. Saudi Arabia and Jordan are given as cases of 'traditional' monarchical regimes that have tried to 'incorporate' and not simply to 'control' their religious establishment. This incorporation is, of course, much more in evidence in Saudi Arabia than it is in Jordan. Jordan is also interesting because it hosts, in addition to the Muslim Brothers, the Islamic Liberation Party which is also influential among the Palestinians and which has sympathisers in other countries such as Egypt and Tunisia. Tunisia's Islamic movement represents a distinctive and rather 'cultured' response to what has perhaps been the most 'Europeanised' experiment in the Arab world. Sudan is interesting not only because of the major role recently played by the Islamic movement in the actual government, but also because of the light it sheds on the implications of declaring an 'Islamic government' in a country with a substantial non-Muslim minority. Like Pakistan (and to some extent Libya), the Sudanese case is also illustrative of what an 'Islamic government' installed by the army officers may look like in reality.[1]

Islamic movements exist, of course, in other Arab countries not reviewed in these two chapters, and a glance in passing at some of these may be in order. In addition to the cases studied in this and in the following chapter, Sunni Islamic movements (similar to the Muslim Brothers) exist in Lebanon, Iraq, Kuwait, Dubai, Yemen, and among the Palestinians. The rising Islamic movement in Algeria and the smaller Islamic movements in Morocco have also been partly inspired by the Muslim Brothers, although a certain group in Algeria represents in some ways a continuation of the line of the Islamic nationalist Malik Bin Nabi. The Indian-inspired *Jama'at al-tabligh al-Islami* (Society for Propagating the Message) which is more missionary than political, seems recently to have gained some ground in

Egypt, the Gulf and even North Africa. A few Shi'i Islamic movements also exist in the Arab countries where Shi'is live, most notably Lebanon, Iraq and the Gulf (for details cf. Etienne, 1987: 249–252).

We now proceed to our case studies of the Islamic movement in six Arab countries.

THE ISLAMIC MOVEMENT IN EGYPT

The Islamic movement in Egypt is arguably the strongest in any Arab, or possibly Muslim, country at the present time (for a coverage of the period preceding the seventies see Chapter 6, pp. 130–42). In order to understand the situation properly, it is important to realise that the recent 'Islamic revival' in Egypt is 'multi-layered'. For political analysis it is useful to distinguish between the following four levels:

1. Growing religiosity among the populace at large, as manifested by things such as increasing participation in prayers and pilgrimages, modesty in dress, higher consumption of religious literature, and growth in the *Sufi* (mystic) orders and in charitable societies. This is basically a 'psychological' phenomenon that dates back to the 1967 defeat and that seeks to offer refuge in the spiritual and the 'authentic'. It is the same phenomenon that gives popular encouragement and 'custom' to the 'Islamic companies' (which are thought to have between two and three million depositors and an estimated capital of £E12 billion), and to the proliferation of a network of 'Islamic' hospitals, schools and welfare centres.

2. Growing social and political criticism by some mosque preachers. Although most preachers started their careers within the traditional 'Establishment Islam' of the al-Azhar and other official religious institutions, some of the best orators among them have become outspoken critics of government policies since the later Sadat years, when his abuse (and arrest) of a number of them served to add to their popularity. Perhaps the most famous among the preachers now is Shaikh Hafiz Salama, the leader of several demonstrations pressing for the immediate application of Islamic law, and who has recently called for a holy war against Israel. Other popular preachers, whose cassette-recorded speeches are now favourite items, include Shaikhs Khishk, Mahallawi and Matarawi. In a slightly different category is Shaikh Mutawalli al-Sha'rawi, a favourite television star; although he does not address political issues directly, his highly expressive 'populist' sermons have a distinct political message (being, for example, anti-socialist, supportive of Islamic finance, and so on).

3. Mainstream Islamic salafism/fundamentalism. This is best rep-

resented by the Muslim Brotherhood, which first appeared in 1928 and could now be regarded as the oldest and most established movement of 'political Islam'. Members who were persecuted and imprisoned under the monarchy and under Nasser were released under Sadat, and they were permitted to circulate their literature (most notably *Al-Da'wa*) in the hope that they would counter-balance the Nasserists and socialists. Under Mubarak they entered politics through coalitions with existing political parties – the Wafd in 1984 and Labour in 1987. They have thirty-six representatives in the parliament (elected in 1987) and they are involved in the formal political game without completely renouncing militant options. They have penetrated the boards of several professional syndicates (lawyers, physicians and engineers) as well as some university staff associations (Cairo and Asyut universities). Their main weakness is the advanced ages of their leaders – a new head, Hamid Abu al-Nasr, was nominated in 1986 on account of his seniority. Their main activity now is to increase pressure on, and to 'nibble away' at, the existing secular legislations. They are also active within the 'parallel economy' and the parallel welfare system.

4. The neo-fundamentalists. These consist largely of splinter groups from the Muslim Brothers which proliferated during the 1970s and 1980s, mainly in correspondence with the 'open door' economic policy (*infitah*). They may be regarded as the 'Youth Wing' of the movement for political Islam. Their membership consists mainly of university students or young graduates, from the new urban quarters of the large cities or from smaller provincial towns but with recent rural origins. They have a more militant ideological outlook, and believe in the necessity of challenging the whole existing order. They control most university student unions, but they have also made inroads among professionals, technicians and officers. The authorities estimate that there may be up to twenty such organisations, with fluid and interchangeable membership, including about half a dozen that are particularly significant:

a. Smaller militant organisations: these include the Islamic Liberation Party (involved in a failed attempt to take over the Technical Military Academy in 1974), and *Al-Takfir wa al-Hijra*, 'Excommunication and Emigration' (involved in killing a Minister for Religious Affairs in 1977). More recently, members of the *Samawiyya* Organisation were brought to trial in 1986 for setting fire to several video clubs and shops. The 'Saved from the Inferno', *Al-Najun min al-nar*, Organisation has been behind the attempted assassination of two ex-Ministers of the Interior and a critical magazine editor in 1987. Also known to exist as broadly defined gatherings are such groups as the one known as *Al-Qutbiyyun*, an offshoot of the Muslim Brothers that is particularly influenced by the teaching of Sayyid Qutb, the exclusive group of *Al-Firmawiyya*, followers of an elderly Shaikh who have withdrawn themselves from certain types of work and activities and who are said to adopt a rather ritualistic orientation, and the group called *Al-Tawaqquf wa al-tabayyun* (repose and meditation) whose name suggests a presumably more 'ethical' orientation.

   b. Al-Jihad: the most significant of the small organisations. It appeared in 1978, merging and absorbing various factions while it planned and then carried out the assassination of Sadat in October 1981 and battled with the police forces in Asyut province for several days afterwards. It is an extremely militant organisation which believes that Islam is not merely a belief for the heart but is a full social and political order that should be enforced by the sword against the wishes of an unwilling ruler. Although it may be a heterogeneous organisation both in terms of its ideology and its leadership, Jihad is the most active politically, leading demonstrations, organising exhibitions, holding seminars, and so forth. Its members often take the law into their own hands in the provincial towns (especially in Asyut and Minya), preventing the mixing of the sexes, prohibiting the sale of alcohol, and harassing Christian citizens. They are actively engaged in discussions with other trends with the aim of attracting the youth element among the Brotherhood, the Nasserists and other groups.

   The assassination of Sadat by a team of militant Islamists naturally brought to the fore the significance of such radical Islamic groups in present-day Egypt. Indeed there are many who believe that if these groups had not, to a certain extent, pre-empted themselves by killing Sadat, a more serious Islamic revolution, similar in some respects to that of Iran, might well have occurred in Egypt sooner or later. These secretive Islamic groups (*jama'at islamiyya*) had in fact become very influential, having managed, in addition to establishing strongholds on university campuses, to penetrate some of the legal Muslim societies (*jam'iyyat islamiyya*) and to secure the support of some older religious preachers and the use of several well-frequented mosques for the propagation of their views and the preparation of their activities.

   Sadat had to a large extent contributed to creating the problem; in his attempts to use the 'religious weapon' for his own political purposes, he went too far, failing to realise until much too late that the Islamic movement had acquired an independent life and logic of its own. Religious associations were initially encouraged by the government during the early seventies, in an attempt to counterbalance the Nasserist and socialist trends and indeed – according to the testimony of various academic officials – they were supported organisationally and financially by the authorities (cf. e.g. *Sabah al-Khair*, no. 1350, 19 November 1981). By 1977, however, the militant Islamic groups felt strong enough to go their own way, first by persecuting Christian students, then by harassing secularist faculty members, and then by confronting the government authorities with a direct challenge.

The social outcome of the economic policies of Sadat's regime, especially the infitah policy, helped only to fuel the frustration and anger of the religious youth (cf. Ayubi, 1982: A.'Abd al-Latif, 1978: 30–31). For the religiously-inclined, the notorious Pyramids Road came to symbolise, morally and socially, all the obscenities of infitah, as the 'oil shaikhs' and the 'nouveaux riches' scattered their money endlessly around the depraved fleshpots of this infamous highway on alcohol and immorality! In the 'food riots' of January 1977, bearded youths (i.e. members of the militant Islamic groups) were seen setting fire to the nightclubs and cabarets and smashing the wicked whiskey bottles. The belly-dancing and other sinful activities around these night spots were considered a particularly serious affront during Ramadan, the Muslims' holy fasting month. The government's solution to this conflict between 'touristic' considerations and religious sensibilities was typical of its 'masking' techniques; in 1979 it was decreed that the belly-dancing could continue during the holy month provided that each performance included some religious songs in between the usual items! (*Al-Jumhuriyya*, 15 July 1979; *Al-Akhbar*, 8 August 1979). It is easy to appreciate how people who took their religion seriously were outraged by this sort of humbug.

In the meantime, Sadat continued to put on his religious face, in which, however, the dedicated did not believe. As Hasan Hanafi wrote sarcastically

> President Sadat has been given the title 'the Believer-President'. He is always called by his first name, Muhammad. He is shown in the mass media in his white *jallabiya*, going to the mosque or coming out of it, with a rosary in one hand, Moses' stick in the other, and with a prayer mark on his forehead... He murmurs in prayer, closes his eyes and shows signs of humility and devotion. He begins his speeches with 'In the Name of God', and ends them with Qur'anic verses signifying modesty and asking for forgiveness. (Hanafi, 1982: 63)

Apparently believing that this cultivated image of piety and religiosity did actually impress people, Sadat gradually lost touch with his own folk, failing to realise that, to the Islamic youth, such affectations could not camouflage the economic crisis and the lack of jobs, the self-indulgent consumerism and unabashed corruption, and the uncritical subservience to the Israelis and the Americans. He seems to have woken up to the potential danger of the militant Islamic groups only in mid-1981. In September he reacted, in a pre-emptive move, by arresting over 1500 people (most of whom were neo-fundamentalists though many secularist opponents of all political shades were also detained), and by threatening that if the fundamentalists did not behave themselves, he would arrest 5000 more. Trying in their turn to pre-empt any further action by Sadat, some members of the militant Islamic groups, led by a young man whose brother had been arrested, proceeded to assassinate the president barely a month later. For a few days following the assassination there were sporadic and in some instances vicious armed encounters with members of other militant Islamic groups as the government set out to arrest thousands of suspected members and sympathisers, and there was a genuine atmosphere of apprehension all over the country as to what they might do next.

After President Husni Mubarak came to power, the situation calmed down to some extent, but since the mid-eighties, religious and sectarian unrest have both picked up again. Although the militant groups remain too small to represent a serious threat to the regime, nobody can be absolutely sure about future prospects (Ayubi, 1988B: 60-63).

It may be useful at this point to consider in some detail certain features of these secretive underground Islamic groups. Most of them have philosophical or organisational roots that at some point or other grew away from the older Islamic societies, especially the Muslim Brotherhood (*Al-Ikhwan al-muslimun*), and its more extreme contemporary, Muhammad's Youth (*Shabab Muhammad*). One of the most widely publicised of the neo-fundamentalist groups, and the one that was initially suspected of Sadat's murder, is the group known by the authorities as *Al-Takfir w'al-Hijra*. This title has normally been translated as 'repentance and flight', although it would be more faithful to the exact meaning to translate it as something like 'excommunication and emigration'. Another group, currently of more importance, is *Al-Jihad* (struggle or crusade), some of whose members were actually convicted of, and executed for, the assassination of Sadat in 1981 (cf. al-Aswani, 1985).

It is believed by some that the early beginnings of such newer offshoots from the older Islamic groups date back to around 1965, when young members of the Muslim Brothers, arrested that year in a conspiracy against President Nasser's government, were cruelly tortured; this provoked a mutiny in the detention camp in May 1967 which in turn led to the younger and more rebellious elements being isolated in special confined quarters. Presented thus with the opportunity for intensive discussion of religious and political matters, they started from the proposition that rulers who tortured people just because the latter believed sincerely in their own religion could not themselves be real Muslims even if they were nominally so. From this, there emerged the basic concept of *'takfir'* – meaning to judge somebody as being infidel (or as I have termed it for brevity, 'excommunication') – which was very much influenced by Qutb's book *Ma'alim 'fi al-tariq* (Signposts on the Road). Qutb was executed two years after its publication, with other leaders of the Muslim Brothers, in 1966 (see Chapter 6).

In 1967, the Arab states were crushingly defeated by the Israelis in the Six Day War. This was taken by the detainees as an indication of the total corruption of regimes that 'deserted God and so were let down by God'. A legal officer who had access to the files of the Takfir case has described their beliefs: they felt that the solution was to work for a real Islamic society and to fight anyone who might stand in the way. Deliberations as to how this was to be achieved led, however, to the emergence of at least two trends. One group believed that the situation was not yet ripe for radical change. They thought in terms of 'stages', and called their movement 'action through understanding' (*al-haraka bil mafhum*), in the sense that they would not yet declare their total rejection of the society although it was understood within themselves. They would thus separate themselves from the society only emotionally, while for the time being continuing to interact with it physically. During the intermediate stage they would work for the installing of the Meccan verses of the Quran (which, historically, had appeared before Islam was completely victorious in Arabia); then, as Islam became more powerful in Egypt, they would proceed gradually to enforce the more strict verses revealed in Madina (when Islam was triumphant in Arabia) (cf. Tawfiq, 1977: 163–187).

The other trend, calling itself the 'believers' community' (*jama'at al-mu'minin*), opted for immediate action and open confrontation, using a strategy of retreat in order to reconquer (emulating the practice of Prophet Muhammad in emigrating to Madina in AD 622). They had therefore to emigrate somewhere into the deserts or the mountains of Egypt or Arabia in preparation for the victorious comeback, under absolute and unquestioning allegiance to their *imam* (leader and guide), and following a very strict code of conduct covering all the details of life and behaviour (such as, for instance, the way of taking a drink or entering a bathroom). Failing physical emigration they were to boycott all aspects of the existing order within the society – employment, education, military service, etc. – as well as the prevailing political and representative organisations and institutions. In their religious belief and practice they would rely completely on the primary sources, the Quran and Sunna, since, in their view, 'wasting effort over something that has no textual support is Wrong itself', and because '*taqlid*' (scholarly or institutional religious tradition) 'is blasphemy against the Great Almighty' (members of Takfir in a religious debate published in *Al-Liwa' al-Islami*, no. 21, 17 June 1982). The group is therefore strictly fundamentalist and strongly anti-traditionalist.

Following some debates and disagreements, the leadership of this group ended up in the hands of Shukri Mustafa, a young man born in Asyut in Upper Egypt, who was a student at the Faculty of Agriculture. In one of his monographs, he wrote that the entire world was infidel and evil, and that it was in need of a special leader who would guide a special group of believers towards the establishment of a real Islamic society (Tawfiq, 1977: 170). His message, which echoes the ideas of Qutb, clearly shows the total rejection of the present order, but also stresses the role of an almost messianic leader (with a shadowy suggestion of the *mahdi*) who would come to save his people. Shukri was a handsome young man with long hair and penetrating eyes, charismatic, and probably autocratic. His movement was tightly organised in small, and to some extent specialised, cell-like units (*majmu'at*); there were missionary units (*da'wa*), survival and catering units (*i'sha*), as well as units for arms training, intelligence, and so on. The organisation was, however, based mainly on personal allegiance (*bay'a*), strong internal discipline, and severe punishment for deserters. It was also the only neo-fundamentalist organisation to have included a relatively large number of girls (with accompanying rumours of semi-communal social relations within the group).

Although it was discovered by the government in 1973, Takfir came into open conflict with the authorities only when its members abducted an ex-Minister of Religious Affairs as a hostage for the release of some of their jailed comrades, and eventually killed him. Following their trial, their imam and three other leaders were hanged, while thirty-six of the 204 who had been tried were imprisoned. The rest, however, as well as possibly hundreds of supporters and sympathisers, remained at large, many of them being re-arrested just before and just after Sadat's assassination.

The organisation to which Sadat's assassins belonged was reported by the government to be Al-Jihad, a group that was first uncovered in 1978 when some of its members were involved in anti-Christian sabotage. In March 1982, five people (led by Khalid al-Islambuli) who were held to have been directly responsible for the assassination were sentenced to death, and seventeen others to imprisonment. A considerable time passed before another 302 members of Al-Jihad were brought to trial and sentenced in March 1984. Of these, 192 were pronounced not guilty, ten leaders were given life sentences, and the rest received prison sentences of between two and fifteen years (cf. Hammuda, 1985).

As an organisation, Al-Jihad seems to lay less emphasis than Takfir on the cult of the leader, being more oriented towards organised action, and rather than withdrawing from contemporary society, it seems to be more interested in the infiltration of governmental and military institutions and in confrontation with the Egyptian State. Internally, Jihad is based on a kind of 'democratic centralism', and a system of commissars (*mas'uli tanzim*). On the central level the organisation is said to have had a governing 'scholars' council' and a 'consultation council', as well as three commissions, one for armament, one for finance, and one for preaching. At a lower level there are believed to have been revolutionary committees and mosque units, in addition to well-armed militias formed of student and skilled worker elements (reported in *Mayu*, 2 November 1981).

Although not as unorthodox as al-Takfir, members of Jihad seem also to believe that those who do not abide by the details of the shari'a should be considered infidels whose blood is defiled. The religious Establishment noted with some truth that, in equating *jihad* almost with the meaning of 'holy war' (though this is not actually its linguistic or its religious meaning), this group appears to have been greatly influenced by both the Kharijite and the Orientalist concept of *jihad*. Another distinction is that, whereas Takfir believes in stages of struggle, Jihad believes in *levels* of struggle which decide the worth of everybody in the eyes of God. They consider that the crusading spirit is a more important factor for Islam than, say, learning and education: for 'what did the Ulama of al-Azhar do when the troops of Napoleon were desecrating the Muslim soil of Egypt?' Such ideas were incorporated in *Al-Farida al-gha'iba* (The Absent Commandment), a monograph attributed to one of Jihad's leaders, 'Abd al-Salam Faraj, and heavily influenced by the teaching of Ibn Taimiya (cf. *Al-Ahram*, 8 December 1981, and quotes therein).

Both organisations reassert in their own way a limited repertoire of key elements that are mythologised and presented as a once-existing

ideal state. Yet, by displacing the nature of the existing social crisis
into the level of Utopia, they may have helped – as Michael Gilsenan
argues – to negate the energies that they had released, and to turn
Egyptians away from a grasp of the factors determining the conditions
of their society. Initially, these groups were tactically useful for the
Egyptian State as a force to counteract the leftist groups. But as the
Egyptian State was soon to discover, especially with the somewhat
aggressive Jihad organisation, such religious symbolism and idiom
could easily become the language through which the petite bourgeoisie
and lower classes expressed not only their resentment of corruption,
decadence and inequality, but also their hostility towards the very
state machine that embodied these evils (Gilsenan, 1982B: 225–226).

Although there seems not to have been a dominant personalised
leadership in the Jihad organisation, 'Abbud al-Zumur, a young army
officer, appears to have played an important organisational role. He
actually believed that the group should delay political action for a few
years until an Islamic revolution could count on the popular support
that would give it the same kind of success that the Iranian revolution
had enjoyed. Another important figure – because of his religious
education and because he was one of the very few middle-aged persons
among the leaders of the neo-fundamentalists – was a blind professor
at the Theological College in Asyut, 'Umar 'Abd al-Rahman, who is
said by the authorities to have issued religious *fatwas* for the group to
justify such actions as stealing money from Christians.

Ideologically, all these groups share two notions: belief in the non-
separation of religion from politics, and the necessity of immediate
application of the shari'a, by force if appropriate. Concerning foreign
affairs, they tend to share with the older fundamentalists the belief that
Muslims are confronted by a large-scale conspiracy whose partners are
the 'atheists' (i.e. Communists), the 'Crusaders' (i.e. Christians), and
the 'Zionists' (i.e. Jews) (cf. Rizq, 1981: 16–17).

It is interesting, however, with regard to the ideology of the militant
Islamic groups, to observe that in spite of the lavish verbosity of many
of their members, some appear to have at best a fairly sketchy
knowledge of the finer points of Islam; nor have they managed to
attract many members who are graduates or students of the religious
and theological colleges. Indeed, according to the fundamentalist
scholar 'Umar 'Abd al-Rahman, 'most members of *al-Takfir w'al-
Hijra* do not remember the Qur'an, do not know the rules of grammar,
and are often mistaken even in the names of the books on which they
base their arguments' (quoted in *Al-Musawwar*, no. 3013, 9 July
1982).

The deficiency in the religious knowledge and learning of many of the militants suggests that their doctrine – however important it might be – is perhaps not the most significant or telling of the various aspects of the militant Islamic movements. Available reports of trials (always assuming that they have not been distorted out of all proportion), have revealed that members of these groups are not always particularly knowledgeable about the technicalities of their religion. Therefore it is possible that comparatively few of them were inspired to join the various movements basically or simply for doctrinal reasons. If we add to this factor an analysis of the socio-economic background of the membership, it can be suggested that most of the members join for reasons that are social and psychological, rather than strictly ideological (religious). We will consider and compare here two communities of 'joiners' of the Islamic movements – those in the mid-fifties, and those in the late seventies and the eighties.

The Muslim Brothers who were brought to trials before the fifties were predominantly civil servants, teachers, white collar workers, small merchants, businessmen, a few artisans and, of course, students. In a list of 'wanted' Brothers published by the government in 1954, the typical occupations were civil servants, teachers, clerks, workers and craftsmen, professionals, a few police and army officers and, as the largest single group, students, as well as quite a few unemployed. The hundreds who were tried between 1954 and 1955 came from more or less the same types of occupations. The Brothers in general represented certain fractions of the lower middle class that included recently-urbanised employees and clerks on the one hand, and relatively well-to-do artisans and technicians on the other. The chief of the 'Revolutionary Tribunal' who tried members of the 'secret apparatus' of the Brothers commented sarcastically on their social background: 'Thank goodness the entire 'secret apparatus' is [formed of] haberdashers, welders and minor employees: I haven't come across a single engineer or department director'! (Ramadan, 1982: 53).

Very few of the important Brothers lived in rural areas. A listing of their Consultative Assembly in 1953 showed that out of 1950 members, all but twenty-two of them belonged to the *effendiyya* (urban, European-costumed) groups. The top leadership of twelve was of a higher educational, cultural, and possibly social level. But even among the followers and sympathisers in general who attended the evening meetings of the society in the early fifties, people wearing either the informal or the decorated *galabiyya* (the native dress) were certainly in the obvious minority (Mitchell, 1969: 328–329).

The personnel of the militant Islamic groups of the seventies and eighties show some even more telling aspects (Ayubi, 1980B; S. Ibrahim, 1980), reflected in the following characteristics. In terms of age, the leaders tended to be in their twenties or early thirties and their members in their late teens or early twenties. In terms of education, they were mostly university graduates or students, especially in scientific subjects. In terms of socio-economic background, they tended to come from a lower middle (or middle) class background, and those of them who were working tended to be teachers, civil servants, military and police officers, engineers and physicians, shopkeepers and technicians. In regional terms they tended to be urban but with recent rural or small town backgrounds, with a proportionately higher percentage appearing to originate from Upper Egypt (i.e. the *Sa'id*) rather than Lower Egypt (i.e. the Delta).

From within the leadership of the militant Islamic groups, the 14 *amirs* (or commanders) who were arrested in September 1981 reflect some interesting features. Their median age was 28 years; only one of them was 50. Most were born in the countryside but were active in the cities; 9 were born in Upper Egypt, 3 in the Delta, and only one in Cairo, while one was born in Cairo but brought up in Upper Egypt. Four of them were physicians, 4 were civil servants, 3 were teachers, and there was one private white-collar, one technician, and a science student (my figures, compiled from *Al-Ahram*, 7 September 1981).

The age factor shows that to an extent this is a typical youth revolt, reflecting a real generation gap and a profound mood of frustration and disillusionment. The rural–urban factor points to a developmental crisis and to the tensions and pressures of recent immigration into decaying cities that have serious and escalating problems (for further details see Chapter 7). Indeed, activities of the neo-fundamentalists are most obvious in Egypt's three major cities – Cairo, Alexandria and Asyut – where the concentration and the volume of business and commerce lead to many practices that such people would easily define as morally corrupt, and where the existence of sizeable Christian minorities increases the possibilities for embarking into sectarian competition, friction and agitation.[2]

The occupational composition of the leadership indicates clearly that these are not just peasant-type traditionalist movements but are basically militant (though quasi-fascist, not leftist) movements of the petite bourgeoisie. There is a high percentage of university students (particularly in the sciences) among the membership; their belonging to such groups may, therefore, reflect their anxiety over career prospects since, under the impact of the economic liberalisation policies followed in the seventies, unemployment of the educated has become an increasingly serious problem. The proportion of science students is also larger because scientific colleges tend to recruit from those with higher grades; hence their expectations will be higher and as a result more painfully shattered by unemployment or misemployment.

After Sadat's assassination, the government's policy of continuing to encircle and categorise members of the militant Islamic groups, and the growing number of studies made of their socio-economic background, increasingly clarified the link between the proliferation of membership of these groups on the one hand and aspects of what might be termed the 'urban crisis' on the other. (For further details see Chapter 7.)

Using the government's list of 302 persons accused of membership in the Jihad organisation and its affiliates (published in the Egyptian press on 9 May 1982), Hamied Ansari confirmed (1984A) that most of them did indeed come from neglected areas where living conditions were hard and where the presence of government was relatively weak (hence, for example, the proliferation of *ahli* – private – rather than government-sponsored mosques in such districts). Many of the active members came from the provincial capitals of the relatively more underdeveloped Upper Egyptian region. Among single provinces, Greater Cairo had the highest percentage of the membership (26.1 per cent), closely followed by the adjacent Giza province (23.9 per cent), and in both provinces, recruitment was unmistakably stronger within suburbs characterised by recent rural migration and shanty dwellings (e.g. Matariyya, Rod al-Farag, al-Sahil, Bulaq-al-Dakrur, etc.). By contrast, no evidence was found of significant militant membership in the older and more stable communities in popular suburbs such as Old Cairo or Sayyida Zainab. In the northern belt of Greater Cairo and its northwestern section, the most destabilising event was the influx of numerous families who were forcibly evacuated from the centre of Cairo to make way for the construction of luxury hotels and tourist centres. They were relocated in al-Zawiyya al-Hamra, the scene of ugly communal riots in June 1981, and in 'Ain Shams, near the housing complex in which Khalid al-Islambuli's sister lived and where some of the group leaders met to plot the assassination of Sadat (Ansari, 1984A: 130–136).

In terms of socio-economic background, active Jihadists belong mostly to a certain segment within the lower middle classes which is economically humble but which rates relatively high on the scale of literacy, mobility and political consciousness. Being still quite close to their recent rural and provincial origins, the educated militants who dominated the leadership of Jihad in the seventies had managed by the beginning of the eighties – and with the help of their kinship networks – to break into the ranks of the lower middle classes at large and to recruit important elements from among such sections of the population as artisans, bazaris and clerks (i.e. a grouping similar to the following of the Ikhwan). Thus, if the Takfir group could be described as eccentric and messianic, the Jihad appears to be more firmly rooted in the social and popular map of Egypt.

Analysing the same official list of 302 defendants (as well as smaller earlier samples), Gilles Kepel further amplifies the argument concerning the geographical as well as the social background of the militants. The Jihad movement seems to have two important axes, one in the Greater Metropolis (including Cairo, Giza and a few small Delta towns), the other in Upper Egypt, concentrated in particular in the three provinces of Minya, Asyut and Sohag. The notable exception of Alexandria is most probably accidental, for Islamicist dissidence has not spared that city; half the defendants in the Military Academy trial were from Alexandria, and the *Jama'at islamiyya* has a strong base there as well. Within Greater Cairo itself, 'the concentration of defendants in those areas of the poverty belt west of Giza where most housing units are sub-standard, is striking' (Kepel, 1985: 22, 217).

The most important observation by Kepel about the Jihad group, however, is social, and it concerns the higher percentage of non-students among its members. The group is about equally divided between students and non-students, with the students having a slight edge. This compares to the 81.5 per cent of student and graduate members in the Military Academy group (of 1974):

> In the absence of fresh information to the contrary, we can only assume that the Islamicist movement, or at least its *Jihad* component, did manage to break out of the campus ghettos, as 'Isam al-Din al-'Aryan had hoped. If true, this new characteristic could be a source of strength for the Egyptian Islamicist movement in the future. (ibid.: 216)

A similar trend is illustrated by the slightly higher age average among the Jihad defendants. Furthermore, slightly less than a third of the Jihad defendants were students in the elite faculties of medicine and engineering, a proportion which, though far higher than the national average, is definitely below the record levels of the Military Academy group. So not only is Jihad proportionately less student-based, but its students are also more representative of the student population at large. The other important group is that of artisans and merchants (nearly 41 per cent of the membership), which prompts one to wonder whether this means that 'these social layers, which in appearance have benefited from the economic opening, have a deeper reason for challenging the regime?' (ibid.: 217).

In terms of political action, there is little doubt that the Islamic movements in Egypt have registered some notable victories in recent years. They maintain their pressure – often augmented by mass demonstrations and sit-ins – for larger proportions of the shari'a to be incorporated into the legal system. A court ruling in 1985 that the fairly liberal family law, passed by Sadat in the absence of parliament, was unconstitutional, was taken as a victory for the Islamists' line, even though the ruling concerned the form and not the content of the legislation.

More impressive was the success of thirty-six Islamists (mainly Muslim Brothers) in gaining seats in the parliament in the elections of 1987 (cf. Ayubi, 1988B: 60–66). Since then the Islamists have been acting as the main parliamentary opposition group. There have been signs to support the expectation by some that as the more respectable Muslim Brothers become a parliamentary force, they may contain and constrain the more militant of the twenty or so Islamic groups, and particularly Jihad (whose ideological adviser, Dr 'Umar 'Abd al-Rahman, gave last-minute support for the Islamists to enter the elections, as part of an alliance with the populist-Islamist Labour Party and the right-wing Liberal Party). However, attempted political assassinations around the middle of 1987 (including one attempt against a former Minister of the Interior which was claimed by the Jihad organisation) suggested that such fringe militant groups might very well be acting on their own. Many, however, are apprehensive that the Islamic movement may be indivisible and that the Muslim Brothers may be no more than its parliamentary façade. By the subsequent arrests of several hundred members of such militant groups later in the year, the government was obviously attempting to draw a distinction between parliamentary religious opposition on the one hand and 'terrorist' underground movements on the other.

Leaders of the ruling National Democratic Party (NDP), as well as of the liberal/rightist Wafd Party (that had led the opposition in the previous parliament) were surprised by the performance of the Islamists in the April 1987 elections, which was better than anyone had expected. It is presumed that high financial resources are necessary to guarantee success in the current Egyptian electoral process – such support is provided through State resources in the case of NDP candidates. In the case of the Islamic candidates (mainly Muslim Brothers), there were reports that financial support was being supplied by the Islamic banks, and more specifically from the so-called Islamic 'Money Utilisation Companies' (MUCs). It is significant that shortly after the elections, President Husni Mubarak condemned these MUCs, and that following the Egypt–IMF negotiations which took place soon after, Dr 'Abd al-Shakur Sha'lan, an IMF executive (of Egyptian nationality) and a participant in the negotiations, openly criticised the companies (for details see Chapter 8).

How can one explain the growth and relative success of the Islamic movement in Egypt? It is our contention that the main cause behind the surge in political Islam is a 'developmental crisis', whereby many new social forces have been unleashed without their energies being politically absorbed and without their economic and social expectations being satisfied. With growing social inequality and cultural alienation, increasing numbers of the urban youth have been inclined to think that what is wrong are the secularist formulas that are being tried, whether socialist, capitalist or otherwise. A prevalent tradition in interpreting Islam as an all-encompassing set of principles for organising life in its totality has made it possible to express all kinds of grievances in religious terminology. From a political point of view, the fundamentalists have been tactically effective in not spelling out the economic and political details of their alternative project. Their call has more appeal (and avoids possible embarrassment) since it remains simple, pure and abstract. The fundamentalists may not be offering workable solutions to everyday problems but they are likely to be more successful in presenting people with an alternative domain of concerns over collective morals and family life. Because of this, some of their ideas have been gaining ground among wider segments of the population.

The government's strategy in confronting the fundamentalists has been two-fold: (a) to suppress them through the use of a technically narrow 'police and security' kind of approach; and (b) gradually to introduce increasing doses of religion into legislation, education, the media and elsewhere. Neither method has proved effective, for the first overlooks the socio-political dimensions of the problem and may inadvertently be adding to the popularity of the persecuted movements, while the second may well be encouraging the militants, as they interpret the government's actions as revealing its weakness, consequently to increase their pressure for yet more concessions. Furthermore, it is quite possible that the greatly increased coverage of religious affairs in the government-run radio, television and press is not deflecting people's attention from the attraction of the militants' message, but rather is preparing the ground, both educationally and intellectually, for a much readier acceptance of the fundamentalist call.

Although they repeatedly challenge the authority of the government, the neo-fundamentalists do not represent an immediate and serious threat to the existence of the regime, as long as they remain small and dispersed. However, a major crisis situation or a break in public order could well prompt certain elements within the armed forces that are sympathetic to these groups to take speedy action. The government admitted that some of the Islamist supporters who were arrested in 1987 were army officers. But even if no such crisis situation occurred there could, as already remarked, be another possible source of challenge to the regime – from the Muslim Brothers. Although it is more likely that the Brothers intend to act more or less like an ordinary political party for certain segments of the Egyptian bourgeoisie, and to influence (and change) politics mainly through the existing legal framework, one cannot rule out the possibility that, under presssure or through temptation, they might re-establish their links with the more militant wing of the Islamic movement (and with Jihad in particular) and thus escalate their campaign for power both on the political front and through the use of violence.

THE ISLAMIC MOVEMENT IN SYRIA

Like Egypt, Syria has witnessed a remarkable expansion of the activities and the apparatus of the State under quite a similar strategy of 'Arab socialism' or 'State capitalism', and like Egypt, Syria was also subjected to the humiliating defeat of 1967. However, the native commercial bourgeoisie in Syria has always been more socially and politically important than its Egyptian equivalent. The fact that the merchant community is overwhelmingly Sunni, whereas the leadership of the encroaching State apparatus has, since the late sixties, been disproportionately 'minoritarian', has made the Syrian Islamic movement in recent years appear to be more of an oppositional social and political force, than of a profound intellectual trend.

Various Islamic associations appeared in Syria in the thirties and forties, such as *Al-Gharra'*, *Al-Hidaya* and *Al-Tamaddun*, among others, but the Muslim Brothers Society – established in the late thirties as an offshoot of its Egyptian counterpart – was to take the lead over all such societies (and to unite several of them) by the second half of the forties. From the beginning, the Muslim Brothers were different from other Islamic societies in following party-style organisational methods and in involving themselves in a wide range of cultural, social and economic activities.

The Syrian Muslim Brothers branch became the main centre in the Arab world for the activities of all Ikhwan, following the clamp-down on the Brothers' activities in Egypt in the mid-fifties. However, the Syrian Brothers themselves were soon subjected to direct harassment from the Egyptian State machine during the period of union between Egypt and Syria from 1958 to 1961. The movement resumed its activities openly after the secession, registering significant electoral successes in 1962. But with the Ba'th resuming power in 1963, suppression of the movement escalated; the membership resisted fiercely in 1964 and 1965, then again in 1973 and 1976, and their resistance reached new heights in 1979, 1980 and particularly in 1981 when the Hamah massacres took place (as we shall see in detail later in this chapter). It seems that such confrontations with the State apparatus have led to a split in the leadership of the movement, leaving its leader 'Issam al-'Attar in a relatively moderate politically-inclined faction, whereas Sa'id Hawwa, 'Ali al-Bayanuni and 'Adnan Sa'd Al-Din had opted for a more militant action-oriented faction intent on *jihad* and continued confrontation.

The Islamic movement in Syria draws intellectually on some of the writings of the earlier Islamic reformers, and in particular on ideas of the Syrian neo-Hanbalite school (e.g. Jamal al-Din al-Qasimi), as well as on those of more recent Syrian Islamists such as Rashid Rida and Muhammad Kurd-'Ali. They are more inclined, however, towards an action-oriented approach, inspired by the tracts of the Egyptian Hasan al-Banna and the more contemporary Muslim Brothers (al-Janahani, 1987: 125–127).

Like their Egyptian counterparts, the more militant Islamic elements in Syria tend, by their own admission, to derive much inspiration from the mediaeval jurist Ibn Taimiya (Carré and Michaud, 1983: 151–153). In fact he has for them a more immediate relevance, since not only was he Syrian and Hanbalite, but because he also wrote some of the most biting attacks ever directed at the Nusairis (i.e. 'Alawites – the name given to them by the French). Ibn Taimiya considered that the 'Alawites were

> more infidel than Jews and Christians, indeed more infidel than many polytheists, and their harm to the community of Muhammad is greater than that of the fighting infidels such as the Tatars and Franks . . . They are always on the side of every enemy of the Muslims . . . the day the Christians would take the cities of the

Muslims (God forbid) would be their greatest festival . . . There is
no doubt that fighting these . . . is a great sign of obedience (to God)
and his duties; it is superior to fighting polytheists and 'people of the
book' who do not fight the Muslims.

Such was Ibn Taimiya's antagonism towards the 'Alawites that one
contemporary commentator contends that the Islamic radicals who
imparted a political character to his militancy were mistaken, because
'his intellectual struggle was not with kings and princes, but with those
whom he regarded as adherents to myths and fantasies' (such as the
'Alawites) (al-Aswani, and his quotations from Ibn Taimiya, 1985:
53–64).

In the early fifties, the Syrian Muslim Brothers were active in social
and political affairs, and some of their members and sympathisers
became interested in the formation of political parties. Like its
Egyptian equivalent, the movement also became interested in social
and economic affairs during the fifties, especially under the impact of
Mustafa al-Siba'i (cf. al-Siba'i, 1962). This was partly a response to the
growing popular concern with such matters following independence,
and partly perhaps a corollary to the intellectual struggle with the
Communist movement and other influential socialist trends during
that period. As usual, the Islamic movement tried to present an
Islamic alternative based on collaborative rather than on conflictual
concepts – and in this respect it might have been representative of the
perspectives of the petite bourgeoisie, although it would, of course, be
excessive to claim that its endeavours were simply 'a new formula for
class struggle' (compare al-Janahani, 1987: 137–140). A concept of the
Islamic State was also elaborated upon by Muhammad al-Mubarak,
an Ikhwan sympathiser. He agreed with the fundamentalist thesis that
Islam was both religion and State, and that the Islamic State was a
doctrinal or ideological one, guided by the shari'a, although he
conceded that the specific form of government might be open to some
improvisation (al-Mubarak, 1981).

In its earlier stages, the confrontation between the Muslim Brothers
and the Ba'thi state tended to revolve around defining the religious
character of the State, with the Brothers insisting that the Constitution
should openly describe Islam as the State's religion. Bloody clashes
occurred in 1973, with the State conceding only that Islam should be
the religion of the head of State, not of the State itself. In the
meantime, the movement concentrated internally on educational
affairs, and on organisational matters, by way of preparing the ground
for reviving the 'Islamic personality' (Hawwa, 1979).

The literature of the Syrian Brothers, like that of all Islamists, maintains that there is a specifically Islamic order that is suitable for all of humanity, based on the sovereignty of God, on the rule of the shari'a, and possessing a specific 'comprehensive Islamic economic system' [3]. In general broad terms, their literature has portrayed the Brothers as the guardians of the native popular culture against the distortions of foreign and secularist ideologies (Jad'an in 'Abdalla, 1987: 155–156). In spite of his being an elderly *'alim*, the ideas of Sa'id Hawwa are rather akin to those of the neo-fundamentalists. Like them he calls for absolute sovereignty and rulership (*hakimiyya*) to God, believes that all Muslim countries are not currently Islamic in the true sense but are deeply immersed in 'apostasy' (*ridda*), and calls for the establishment of the Kingdom of God (*dawlat Allah*) in all countries, since this is the only way to guarantee the enforcement of God's commandments in their totality and the fulfilment of the *jihad* duty (Hawwa, *c.*1980: 5–48).

What is the socio-economic background of the Islamic movement in Syria? Hanna Batatu has produced some very significant data on this subject (Batatu, 1988). The earliest generation of Syrian Muslim Brothers tended to be from families of ulama of middle income and status (e.g. M. al-Mubarak, S. al-Shash, Mustafa al-Siba'i, 'Isam al-'Attar, etc.). Traditionally, there has always been a substantial degree of coincidence between this religious shaikhly strata and the class of tradesmen. The shops of tradesmen-shaikhs were usually located in the neighbourhood of mosques, and several of the Ikhwan founders and devotees were descended from the class of merchants and artisans (Batatu, 1988: 115–117).

The financial independence of this strata relieved its members from reliance for their livelihood on the State, and afforded them closer links with the religiously-inclined urban community. Since the sixties, however, the State has been tightening its grip over the clerics and the religious institutions, and especially through the Ministry of Awqaf whose personnel grew from 298 in 1962 to 2759 in 1978, and whose budget expanded from SL 1288 thousand to SL 8859 thousand during the same period (B. Yasin, 1985: 118–131).

The geographical dimension is also significant. The Ikhwan movement first took shape in Aleppo, a large and substantial city. The division of the Near East into 'modern' territorial states, from the twenties and thirties, resulted in the severing of Aleppo's traditional social and trading links with both the north (now Turkey) and the east (now Iraq). The situation was made worse by the influx of thousands of Armenians and other Christians from Turkey in the 1920s, since this disturbed not only the denominational balance of the population in the city but also the position of its trading and artisan classes. Aleppo was cut off from its natural outlet to the sea and from its natural markets and hinterland, a development that harmed the Muslim trading community much more deeply than it did the Christian merchants, the latter having been connected more with European than with inter-Ottoman trade. If one also takes into account the climatic and environmental character of Aleppo with its barren landscape and its dry and relatively severe climate, it is possible, suggests Batatu, to understand why the Aleppan Muslim Brothers have been tougher and more inclined to violence than, say, their Damascene counterparts (the Islamists moved their headquarters to Damascus in 1944 and adopted the formal title of Muslim Brothers in the following year) (Batatu, 1988: 118–121). Several interesting parallels can be drawn in this connection between Aleppo in Syria and Asyut in Egypt.

The growing political radicalisation of the Muslim Brothers in Syria cannot be understood except in relation to their increasingly conflictual relationship with the Ba'thi State following the Ba'thists' rise to power in 1963. From the beginning, the ardently secularist tendencies of the Ba'th had alienated the traditional Islamic circles, especially the clerics. This had already led to a number of clashes that included outbreaks of strikes in the suq and demonstrations against the publication of an 'anti-religious' article in an army magazine in May 1967, the protests being led by Shaikh Hasan Habannaka who denounced the government as 'godless' (Hinnebusch, 1982: 159).

In spite of certain phases of relative prosperity for the merchants, the main development of the Syrian system has been towards the building up of a powerful and expanding State apparatus, with a strong economic arm that stretches into the domain of trade as well as agriculture and industry. The agricultural and trading cooperatives established by the State on a large scale adversely affected the interests of the members of the large trading and artisan community who – with their dependents – easily accounted for one-sixth of the population in the early seventies (Batatu, 1988: 120). Recent Syrian politics have been characterised by an acute conflict between, on the one hand, the Ba'th Establishment, firmly installed in the villages and dominating the three largest and best organised institutions in the society – the army, the party and the bureaucracy – and, on the other hand, the forces of politicised Islam, deeply rooted among the traditional clerics, and with strong sympathy and support from the urban suq and the old notables (Hinnebusch, 1982: 165–166). Social problems aggravated the situation further from the mid-seventies onwards. Accelerating peasant migration to the cities induced a mounting rate of inflation that was combined with growing corruption, while the 'economic liberalisation' policy adopted by President Hafiz al-Asad in the early seventies began to produce disorienting social and cultural effects similar to those of its counterpart infitah policy in Egypt.

A major difference from the Egyptian case, however, has been induced by the disproportionate representation of members of the 'Alawi minority in the control and security apparatus of the Ba'thi State. This gave the situation the character not only of a conflict between fundamentalism and secularism but also of a confrontation between a 'natural' majority and an upstart minority. In turn, both conflicts were to some extent 'masking' another conflict, between an encroaching state bourgeoisie and a beleaguered commercial bourgeoisie (Ayubi, 1984: 44). It is perhaps too simplistic to agree wholeheartedly with the claim of one observer that 'behind the mask of religion stands the Khumasiya, the wealthy former owners of Syria's largest industries, who suffered from Ba'th nationalisation measures in the sixties and now would like to regain their former position' (in Hudson, 1986: 86). Yet there is much to support the view that 'the Ikhwan may to some extent be the façade behind which a number of displaced secular, but nominally Sunni elitist groups have mobilized, using the power of Islamic ideology to legitimate their own specific interest in overthrowing this regime' (ibid.: 93).

Although the class dimension is present, the Islamic movement in Syria takes mainly the form of a struggle *against* the State, and, ultimately, *over* the State, intensified in that country by the sectarian and functional dichotomy between the Sunnis and the 'Alawites (compare: Carré and Michaud, 1983: 163–192). What the Ba'thists describe as the 'State of the masses' is interpreted by others as the 'state of a clique'. And given the prevalent sense of a blockage in the social system, not only on the political level but also to an extent in daily economic activities, the 'youth without a future' are bound to represent the mainstay of the forces of Islamic fundamentalism (Carré and Seurat, 1982: 22–23).

The Muslim Brothers escalated their offensive against the Ba'thi State's organisations and its 'Alawite personnel from the mid-seventies, apparently aiming at exposing the 'sectarian' character of the regime, and possibly at provoking State retaliation that would broaden the scope of popular-religious opposition to the regime. By the beginning of the eighties, they were successful also in provoking fairly extensive demonstrations and shutdowns of shops and schools in Hamah, Aleppo and elsewhere. During this process, the movement has obviously been developing a militant 'youth arm', which has not, however, broken loose from the mainstream Brothers (as happened in Egypt). Socially, while merchants and artisans form a major component of the older and mainstream membership of the Syrian Ikhwan, the most militant activists tend to be drawn from among their offspring or their educated elements – students and members of the intelligentsia. The militants who attacked the party institutions, the military academies and the government buildings are young men in their twenties and early thirties. Out of a total of 1384 arrested by the government between 1976 and 1981, some 27.7 per cent were students, 7.9 per cent schoolteachers, and 13.3 per cent were professionals including 79 engineers, 57 physicians, 25 lawyers and 10 pharmacologists. The profile of the leaders of the militant sections of the Muslim Brothers indicate a similar characterisation, the activists being members of the intelligentsia who are sons of merchants or clerics (Batatu, 1988: 118, 129).

The most dramatic episode in the confrontation between the Muslim Brothers and the Ba'thi State was the Hamah uprising of February 1982, which resulted in the brutal massacre of many thousands of people and the destruction of whole quarters of the city. It was obviously a blow from which the movement would not easily recover, especially since, legally, mere membership in the Ikhwan is now a crime, punishable by death. If anything, it probably reinforced the inner solidarity of the frightened 'Alawite community. The Islamic movement has had its own weaknesses too. Although membership of the Ikhwan was growing fast in the mid- to late seventies, it was becoming clear that the organisation was not succeeding in turning itself into a broadly based popular movement that could reach beyond the traditional urban concentrations of the Sunnis of Aleppo and Hamah.

Although the radical wing seemed to have had an exaggerated perception of its own strength, as expressed, for example, in the 'Manifesto of the Islamic Revolution in Syria' (IRC, 1980), the crushing defeat of 1982 has caused most members of the movement to lose heart and seems to have generated a wave of divisions and conflicts within its organisation (CPSS, 1988: 235–236, 241–243). The failure to make substantial inroads in the capital city has also been a serious shortcoming. The strong presence of the State apparatus there, combined with the relative prosperity of the commercial class (due to workers' remittances, the Lebanese 'transit' trade, and through partial coalition with the state bourgeoisie to exploit the limited degree of economic liberalisation available), and with the more noticeable influence of the leftist trends in the capital city (cf. Gran, 1987: 107–125), all seem to have put a check on the penetration of the Brothers into Damascus.

It is factors such as these which may by now have pushed the Syrian Muslim Brothers into a corner, forcing them to confine themselves to actions of assassination and sporadic violence. Indeed, there was an assassination attempt in 1987 on the President, the blame for which was placed on the Brothers; following this attack, further numbers of alleged members of the Ikhwan were arrested and detained by the authorities. It is obvious that the story of the confrontation between the Islamic movement and the Syrian State has by no means come to an end.

THE ISLAMIC MOVEMENT IN JORDAN

Although the Islamic movement in Jordan is less vocal than it is in some other countries, it is still of some intellectual and political significance. The Hashemite rulers of Jordan are, of course, descendants of the Sharif of Mecca, and although his 'Arab revolt' is usually interpreted as representing a blow to the last, Ottoman, caliphate, the Jordanians prefer to see in the rule of Husain ibn 'Ali and Faisal I the beginnings of a new and dynamic Arab-Islamic revival, which *followed* the practical end of the caliphate and which was in some ways a replacement for it (cf. al-Hasan ibn Talal in Ibrahim, 1988: 259–261). Whatever the case may be, the Jordanians have increasingly followed a policy of cooperation with, and coop-tation of, the ulama, and have striven to appear as the sponsors of an intellectual and cultural Islamic tradition that would be perpetuated by institutions such as the Ministry of Awqaf, the Higher Council for Islamic Affairs, and the Mu'assasat Al al-Bait.

The Jordanian State has also increasingly incorporated the local preachers into its administrative and financial web. The village preacher is no longer just a 'culture broker' in the sense of bridging the 'great tradition' of the Islamic literati with the 'little tradition' of folk Islam (Antoun, 1989: 42–43). He is also now, socially and politically speaking, 'caught between the expectations of the bureaucracy (in that he is the lowest figure on the bureaucratic totem pole), and the expectations of the community of which he is a member' (ibid.: 26ff). As happened previously in more established states, the expansion of State power from Amman now includes 'the education, training and confirmation of local preachers and their partial bureaucratization through emoluments from the Ministry of Religious Endowments' (ibid.: 189–190). The preachers become increasingly bureaucratised and financially dependent on the State, particularly as they take up ancillary duties (e.g. as marriage officials or pilgrim guides). Of course, many preachers are capable of 'conveying their own message and at the same time confounding the message of the State' (ibid.: 242), but there is no doubt that the overall process of incorporating them into the State machinery is on the increase.

The Muslim Brothers initiated their associations in the Levant in the second half of the thirties. The presence of voluntary Ikhwan combatants from Egypt and Palestine in the period between 1936 and 1939 must have left a distinct impact among the Palestinians. In 1945–46 the Society of the Muslim Brothers of Palestine was formed; its first group was established in Jerusalem and it subsequently expanded into various Palestinian and Jordanian towns. In the inter-Arab general congress of the Muslim Brothers movement that was held in Amman in 1953, a Jordanian Society for the Muslim Brothers was publicly declared. In the years that followed, the Jordanian (and for a period the Syrian) Muslim Brothers helped in providing support for the Egyptian Ikhwan who were persecuted by the Nasserist regime in the period between 1954 and 1967. The relative degree of tolerance accorded to the Muslim Brothers in Jordan during that period was partly a function of the 'Arab Cold War' which put Jordan in a camp that was ardently opposed to Nasserism, as well as to Ba'thism and Marxism. Gradually the Jordanian Muslim Brothers, under the leadership of 'Abd al-Rahman Khalifa, were to become in effect an essential component of the Hashemite regime (Carré and Michaud, 1983: 208–210).

The occasional friction that at times characterised the Ikhwan's relations with the Jordanian authorities was tempered by their consistent support for King Husain and their shared distaste for the nationalist group. The Muslim Brothers even participated in various Jordanian parliamentary elections. The movement thus operated legally from Amman, with official local offices in various towns (Shadid, 1988: 661–664). Following the 1967 Arab–Israeli war and the loss of the West Bank, the relations of the Palestinian Muslim Brothers with the Jordanian monarchy appeared to improve even further, for reasons of mutual interests and benefits.

The Jordanian Muslim Brothers prefer to be seen as legalist and reformist. As such, they are accorded a fair degree of influence within the government administration, notably in the Ministries of Justice and Education and in some universities. As we have mentioned, some

Ikhwan sympathisers also manage to be represented in parliament (for example, Ahmad Kufani and 'Abdallah al-'Akailah in the 1984 elections) (Etienne, 1987: 212). Thus it can be seen that the Jordanian monarchy, as a conservative if modernising regime, has been able to arrive at a fairly effective formula for the partial incorporation of the milder elements of the Muslim Brothers into its institutions.

More recently, such a policy has become of even greater importance for the regime, which now seeks to use the Muslim Brothers as a counterpart to the Palestine Liberation Organisation (PLO). Muhammad Shadid claims that 'the Jordanian government's current strategy is to forge an alliance with the Muslim Brotherhood in the West Bank in order to undermine PLO support, an objective that serves the interest of both parties' (Shadid, 1988: 675). This policy is not without its difficulties, however. As many of the Palestinian and Jordanian Ikhwan of the younger generation become more radicalised, their relatively conservative leadership has to walk a tightrope. As the head of the Executive Bureau of the General Islamic Congress for Jerusalem – based in Jordan – explains,

> The leadership is sometimes obliged to take contradictory positions: while it is committed to a 'reformist' approach of which it is in reality convinced, it has to surround that position with a 'revolutionary' language. This situation was used by the ruling authorities as a justification for taking a hostile stand towards the [Islamic] movement, because they held it accountable for the apparent pronouncements, not for the implicit intentions. (Al-Sharif, 1988: 254)

In Jordan proper, official toleration by the regime of the Muslim Brothers has on occasion been used as a foreign policy device *vis-à-vis* the Syrians, whose problems with the Ikhwan have been particularly acute. Leaders of the Syrian Muslim Brothers who have been given refuge in Amman have included their main contemporary leader, Sa'id Hawwa, who died there in March 1989.

No empirical study is available on the social background of the Ikhwan's membership in Jordan. I gather, however, that the main recruitment ground is among the youth in urban centres and refugee camps, especially students, teachers and officials. They are on the whole people from the middle classes, mainly from the towns (although some may have a rural background), and some of them have family connections in commerce.

The Jordanian and Palestinian Muslim Brothers have also faced increasing competition from more militant movements, the most important of which is the Islamic Liberation Party (ILP). The Islamic Liberation Party (*Hizb al-tahrir al-islami*) was established by the Palestinian lawyer Taqiy al-Din al-Nabhani (d. 1977) in Jerusalem in 1953, and from its inception it has competed with the Muslim Brothers. It is unique among Islamic movements in declaring itself openly as 'a political party whose principle is Islam and whose activity is politics' (ILP, 1985: 5). It aims at re-establishing the Islamic caliphate as a unitary, not a federated, State for all Muslims in the world. The basis of Islamic government, according to the Party's perspective, is that sovereignty should be for *shar'*, not for the umma – the umma enjoys only *sultan* or executive, immediate power (ibid.: 71–79). In economic matters, the Party is most 'conventional' in maintaining that 'the economic problem in the perspective of Islam . . . is the distribution of wealth, not the production of wealth' (ibid.: 83). In domestic and international affairs, the Party certainly ranks among the most radical movements. It adopts *jihad* as the overall strategy, and it believes that all countries of today's world do not implement Islam and are therefore 'a household of infidelity (*dar kufr*), even if their inhabitants are Muslims' (ibid.: 103).

The ideas of Nabhani are believed to have influenced the thinking of the Egyptian fundamentalist Sayyid Qutb and a number of the smaller and more militant groups that have splintered away from the Muslim Brothers in Egypt, as well as groups among the Palestinians, Jordanians and others in the Arab East (cf. Jadaane, 1987: 128–139). In fact the Islamist group that attempted a takeover of the Technical Military Academy in Egypt in 1974 was led by the Palestinian–Jordanian Salih Sirriyya, who had belonged to the ILP in his younger days. Furthermore the Jihad organisation that was eventually involved in the assassination of Sadat was formed in 1980 by an amalgamation of three groups, one of which was led by the Jordanian Salim al-Rahhal who also believed in the importance of military methods for the takeover of power (Sayyid-Ahmad, 1988A: 66–78).

The most distinctive feature of the ILP is its openly and avowedly political nature. According to a Jordanian critic who is himself a supporter of the Ikhwan and who admonishes the ILP for being too nationalistically inclined, the initiators of the Party seem to have believed that they could take over power and establish an Islamic state probably within thirteen years of its inception, and in any case within no more than three decades (Sadiq Amin, 1982: 76–78). From the mid-sixties, the Party started to show interest specifically in taking over power: thus a takeover was attempted in Jordan in 1968, and another attempt is said to have taken place a few years later (ibid.: 170–173).

ILP sympathisers seem to have been involved in a number of violent political acts in a number of Arab countries, including Iraq, Tunisia and, as we have seen, Egypt.

The Party seems to require a high level of intellectual juridic sophistication from its followers and to emphasise the crucial role of culture and education, an emphasis that has been seen by some other Islamists as excessive in its attention to minute juridic detail. To avoid possible disagreement based on the diversity of juridic sources, the ILP appears to resort to a practice that it terms the principle of the 'adoption of tenets' (*tabanni al-ahkam*). This is really an extension of a 'political party' practice, whereby not only policies but also even ideas become binding upon all members once they have been authoritatively adopted by the organisation.

From this it can be detected that the interest in intellectual formation, although important, is regarded as subservient to the requirements of political action, to which paramount priority is given; this often leads to immature, hurriedly prepared acts. The Palestinian issue, however, seems to be a curious exception – the ILP has been opposed to the Palestinian resistance on the grounds that Israel is a State and has therefore to be confronted by other *states* (Haidar, 1987: 137–166 and refs. cited).

Although there has been no open confrontation between the ILP and the authorities in Jordan in recent years, there is no doubt that the regime regards it, together with the more militant offshoots of the Ikhwan that function under the name of Jihad, as basically hostile. Such Islamists were blamed by the authorities for the disturbances on university campuses in 1986, and more explicitly for the 'price riots' that broke out in various Jordanian towns in 1989.

It can be argued that the controlled incorporation of some Islamic elements within the Hashemite Establishment, combined with the relative prosperity and dynamism of the Jordanian economy since the mid-seventies (due to substantial remittances and to generous foreign aid to a country with a small population), were together responsible for the restrained militancy against the State by the Islamic movement. However, with the economic and social problems that have begun to build up in recent years, the potential for a more radicalised Islamic movement cannot be ruled out of hand. In addition, it is possible that the growing politicisation of the activities of the Muslim Brothers (especially their Jihadist branches), as well as the rise of the Islamic Resistance Movement, *Hamas*, in the West Bank and Gaza, may also have some spill-over effects among the Palestinians who live in Jordan.

5 The Islamic movements: some country studies – part 2

THE ISLAMIC MOVEMENT IN SAUDI ARABIA

The armed takeover in November 1979 of the Most Sacred Mosque at Mecca by a militant Islamic group took many people by surprise, and proved beyond doubt that even the supposedly 'very Islamic' Saudi Arabia was not completely immune to the forces of 'Islamic resurgence'.

In Saudi Arabia, religion is used as a main tool for social control and political legitimisation, and achieves these through institutions such as the shar'i (religious) courts, the Organisation for the Enforcement of Good and Prevention of Evil (established in 1929) and the moral police (*mutawwi'*) system (cf. Piscatori, 1980: 123–138). Furthermore the Saudi Royal Family has historically allied itself with the Wahhabi movement (*al-Muwahhidun* is the term favoured within Arabia), a puritanical Sunni movement that, to a large extent, follows the strict Hanbali school of Sunni jurisprudence. The Royal Family has also relied significantly on the sanctioning and support of the prestigious body of ulama inside the country. In one of the several attempts to unify most of the Arabian territory under one command, the Sa'uds had relied on a movement known as the *Ikhwan* (not to be confused with the Egyptian *Al-Ikhwan al-Muslimun*). These were Wahhabi-inspired nomadic groups that organised themselves around the turn of the century in *hujar* (singular: *hujra*, from literary Arabic *hijra*), or agricultural/military colonies. They cooperated with the Sa'uds in unifying much of Arabia before the Sa'uds turned against them and suppressed their forces, especially in the major confrontation that occurred in 1929–1930 (cf. the excellent treatment in

Sharara, 1981A). Since that date, some of the defeated tribes seem to have continued to harbour antagonistic feelings towards the Saudi Royal Family.

But in the same way in which the rulers have used Islam to legitimise their rule, several opposition movements in Saudi Arabia also utilise Islam to express their antagonism in religious terms. The 'Islamic Revolution Organisation' emerged after the riots in the Eastern region in 1979, and is probably still centred there. Its adherents believe in creating an Islamic republic in Arabia based on popular participation internally and full independence in foreign policy. It also appears that there is a radical branch of the Egyptian Muslim Brothers, whose Saudi members believe that *salafi* Islam (i.e. that based on precedent of the early pioneers) is being utilised in Arabia today to mask corruption and oppression, which the Brothers have set themselves to resist.

The existence of such Islamic groupings indicates that Saudi Arabia also seems to witness certain aspects of the general phenomenon of the political revival of religion that now spreads through most of the Middle East region. Many observers have wondered why there should be an 'Islamic revival' in a country that is already supposed to be such a strict follower of the path of Islam. But what is not given proper attention is the fact that such movements are more often movements of socio-political protest, in spite of their being clad in religious garb, and that as such they are often related to socio-economic contradictions, to cultural dislocation, and to generational differences. The people who launched the Mecca takeover were a neo-puritanical movement who, in invoking strict 'fundamentalist' teachings, were actually expressing social criticism of, and political protest against, what they regarded as the false and opportunistic utilisation of Islam to hide corruption, decadence and oppression as well as subservience to 'the foreigner'.

The Mecca uprising proved that the process of 'routinisation' of fundamentalism that was taking place in Saudi Arabia was not without problems. Admittedly, the majority of the ulama were won over to the side of the regime, and tried to walk a tightrope between tolerating 'modernisation' while opposing 'Westernisation' (cf. Abir, 1988: 24–31). Yet modernisation could not easily be divorced from Westernisation and the headlong rush into capitalist economic relations that was accompanied by the spread of consumerism, permissiveness and 'corruption'. Neither was the process of modernisation or the distribution of the 'petroleum spoils' achieved evenly and equitably all over the Kingdom. The desert-inspired, inward-looking Wahhabi puritanical ethos was still basically at odds with the consumerism, indulgence and 'materialism' that resulted from the incorporation of the Saudi

Arabian 'rentier' economy into the world system of capitalist relations of exchange.

The Mecca rebels, clustered around a revived *Ikhwan* nucleus (see the passage above on the *Ikhwan*), were thus retrieving a type of neo-Wahhabism in order to strike back at the Saudi society and the Saudi State. Several of the leaders of the takeover were from Najdi nomadic tribes which were traditionally opposed to the Al-Sa'uds, and which continued to live in less-privileged regions where the benefits of the oil bonanza were fewer and where there was relatively less penetration by the Saudi State. The leader of the movement was Juhaiman al-'Utaibi (born 1936), who was brought up according to beduin traditions by a father who was deeply learned in tribal customs; his grandfather had been killed in the Sabla battle with the Saudis in 1929. He hailed from al-'Arja, one of the Ikhwan *hujars* on the Riyadh–Mecca route. He was married to the daughter of the Amir of Sajir, who was the sister of Muhammad 'Abdalla al-Qahtani; both men were among the Mecca conspirators, with the latter presented as the long-awaited *mahdi* (a kind of messiah). There was thus a distinct familial and tribal nucleus to the movement, with several of the leaders being grandchildren of individuals from the 'Utaiba, Matir and Yam tribes who had fought with al-Dawish against 'Abd al-'Aziz ibn Sa'ud in previous generations (IRO, 1981A: 25–26).

Juhaiman worked for the tribally-based National Guard for about eighteen years, then joined the Islamic University of Madina for a period. He subsequently resigned from the Guards, some six years before the events at Mecca, in order to propagate the Ikhwan's message through writing and distributing various tracts – *rasa'il* – until his death, at the age of 43, in the uprising. Several of his followers were also students of the Islamic University; indeed, according to some sources, students represented about 80 per cent of the nucleus of the neo-Ikhwan organisation (IRO, 1981A: 100).

The ideological position of Juhaiman represents a neo-Wahhabi orientation, whereby (i) the puritanism of the original Wahhabism is now being unleashed against the corruption of Al-Sa'ud and the self-indulgence of Saudi society under the oil bonanza; (ii) the xenophobia of the original Wahhabis is now directed against the 'Christian ambassadors, experts and educators' who are now 'our teachers' and whose Christian flag 'flies next to the [Islamic] unitarian (*tawhid*) flag'; and (iii) the militancy (*jihad*) of the original Wahhabis is now directed at the attempt to 'routinise' Wahhabism, through government organisations such as *Al-'Amr b'il-ma'ruf*, *Al-Ifta'*, *Al-Da'wa*, and others, and with cooperation from the official clerics that Juhaiman calls the

Shaikhs with 'degrees, ranks and social pursuits' (cf. Juhaiman in Sayyid-Ahmad, 1988B).

The actual seizing of the mosque is said to have involved some 2000 rebels who were well-armed and provided with food supplies, presumably in preparation for and anticipation of a long siege or struggle, and was obviously well-planned and carefully prepared (for example in the smuggling of weapons into the sacred sanctuary). The intention was clearly to present an alternative leadership for Arabia, presumably counting on the support of the praying masses, and the siege lasted for twenty-two long days, being crushed only at considerable political cost with the deaths of some 450 rebels and around 2700 government troops.

The choice of the Most Sacred Mosque of Mecca, rather than the capital city of Riyadh, was interesting: was it an indication of the movement's emphasis on the religious rather than the political nature of the act, or was it more 'tactical', through relying on the difficulty and sensitivity for the government of attempting to reconquer the sacred sanctuary? Significant too was the fact that the *fatwa* (juridico-religious verdict) by the ulama sanctioning the government's actions in storming the mosque took several days to be secured and was not signed by all the leading ulama, indicating that some of them were either sympathetic to the objectives of the takeover or reluctant to agree to the use of force in a zone absolutely prohibited for fighting or struggle. It is possible that although several clerics were in 'ideological' agreement with many of the ideas of the rebels, they did not favour the specifying of Qahtani as the awaited *mahdi* and/or the use of force to attack the State (cf. Sayyid-Ahmad, 1988A: 34ff). The main detailed source for the Mecca events is the clandestine book by Abu Dharr [pseud.], 1980).

The sociological profile of the movement is also significant here. Most of Juhaiman's followers were students or graduates in their twenties or thirties, the majority coming largely from the Islamic University of Madina (established in 1960), and from other universities. They would meet him in mosques and houses in Mecca, Madina and other cities to study and to discuss, among other things, the *rasa'il* that he published of his own writings or of his interpretations of Ibn Taimiya. The movement also had a certain 'pan-Islamic' dimension to it, as it had included members from other Muslim countries, some of them students at the same Islamic University. Among the sixty-three individuals who were eventually executed for their part in the takeover plot were one Iraqi, one Sudanese, three Kuwaitis, seven Yemenis, and, most remarkably, ten Egyptians.

In short, therefore, participants in the Mecca takeover can be described as young, urban and educated. In addition, there is a tribal and regional dimension that points to the uneven distribution of the rewards of the oil boom among the various tribes and regions. Because of the sensitivity of the tribal issue, the Saudi authorities denied that the dissident group had had any tribal or even familial dimension to it (cf. *Al-Riyad*, 9 December 1979). However, over two thirds of the forty-one Saudi citizens who were executed in January 1980 came from the relatively underpriviledged Najd region, and 25 per cent were from the less-than-friendly 'Utaiba tribe alone (Abu Dharr, 1980: 248ff *et passim*). Others were from the tribes of Qahtan, Harb, 'Unaiza, Subai', Shamar and other tribes that are not entirely reconciled to the political hegemony of the Al-Sa'ud family.

As was to be expected, the Mecca takeover was put down in the name of Islam, although with the sharp edge of the sword. The rebels were classified as kharijite deviants, and a *fatwa* was obtained from the ulama to justify the storming of the Mecca sanctuary in their pursuit. But the Mecca events had a wider significance beyond their immediate alarming impact. They revived the controversy about the Islamic legitimacy of the monarchical form of government (since most fundamentalists believe that Islam does not sanction the rule of kings). Also, and not unusually, they highlighted the problems of 'corruption on earth' that in the Saudi case were exacerbated by the impact of the oil bonanza. The official strict Islamic posture of the ruling elite does not blend smoothly with the stories of huge 'commissions' and bribes, pornography parties, overseas gambling adventures and 'love' affairs, not to mention the less secretive but equally profligate expenditures on royal palaces, private aircraft, wedding ceremonies, camel races and falcon hunting expeditions!

The impact of the oil bonanza combined with the nature of the existing socio-political system has, indeed, led to widening disparities, not only among the various social classes and among the religiously educated, the secularly educated and the illiterates, but also between the urban centres on the one hand, and the beduin and the rural centres on the other. In recent years the inhabitants of the latter areas have experienced increasing discomfort as drought has crept into most of the desert, and as the government's policies have become ever more biased towards the urban centres to the detriment of the desert- and country-dwellers. If religion is to be used again in Saudi Arabia as a vehicle for protest and as a catalyst for revolt, such 'relatively deprived' groups are quite likely to be among its users.

The expectation of the rebels that they would succeed appears to have been quite unrealistic, given that the Islamic movement does not seem to have penetrated the various segments of Saudi society, and that it remained isolated from other secular and Islamic protest movements, including those of the Shi'a who were rising in the Eastern provinces against the regime at about the same time (cf. IRO, 1981B). The Hanbali–Wahhabi emphasis of the movement would obviously reduce to a minimum any possible cooperation with the Shi'i radicals, and might not necessarily appeal to the large educated-technocratic elites who are perhaps more attracted to ideas of 'Islamic reform' like those propagated in Arabia and the Gulf by 'Abdalla al-Nafisi and his sympathisers (cf. e.g. al-Nafisi, *c*.1980).

The main outcome of the Mecca events was, in the final analysis, a reinforcement of the moral and social authority of the ulama in preserving the main Wahhabi characteristics of the Saudi regime (and increasingly the 'conservative' outlook in the Gulf at large), as long as they – the ulama – refrained from interfering with the manner in which the Al-Sa'ud wielded power.[1] That conduct of power has become much stricter since the beginning of the eighties and, from the mid-eighties, has increasingly been couched in religious terms. The king has recently dropped the title of 'his royal majesty', replacing it with the new one of 'servant of the two sanctuaries' (*khadim al-haramain*) of Mecca and Madina. Although most of the lists of alleged 'political prisoners' that are currently circulated by the opposition appear to include mostly Shi'ites from the Eastern provinces, one would not be surprised if the repercussions resulting from the decline in oil revenues were, in the not too distant future, to spark off new types of religious and/or political opposition among the young, educated elements of the mainstream Sunni community.

THE ISLAMIC MOVEMENT IN SUDAN

Sudan presents some interesting insights into the relationship between religion and State. Not only does the country have a significant Islamic movement, but it also has to deal with a sizeable non-Muslim minority in the South. Together with Zia's Pakistan, Numairi's Sudan also represents a fascinating case study of what a so-called Islamic government, launched by a military regime, may look like.

From quite early on, Sudanese Islam acquired a distinct Sufi character. The reasons for this are many, including the fact that in Sudan, Islam came to prominence relatively 'late', nor was it imposed by a military conquest, or through an organised *da'wa* by the ulama; rather, it was spread by merchants and by tribal leaders. Interest in theoretical and juristic matters therefore tended to develop rather later, while the role of ritual, ceremony and example had become predominant. The Sufi groups were quite successful in spreading Islam in this manner, retaining at the same time several characteristics of the local, pre-Islamic culture. Furthermore, the Sufi leaders came to represent the embryonic origins of the traditional Sudanese intelligentsia, especially as their role was not confined to purely religious matters but also extended into various aspects of social and political life ('Ali, 1987: 79ff)

The nineteenth-century Mahdist movement combined an attack on colonialism with a puritanical quest to restore simplicity and 'orthodoxy' to Sudanese Islam. Although the Mahdi was defeated by the Anglo-Egyptian forces at the end of the nineteenth century, Mahdism was revived in the twentieth century by Sayyid 'Abd al-Rahman al-Mahdi, and its supporters, the *Ansar*, were organised under his 'conservative-style leadership' (Woodward, 1983: 99–101).

During the nineteenth century, the *Khatmiyya* order was established on a countryside basis, and it acted as a major opponent of Mahdism; this order was further strengthened at the beginning of the twentieth century. Given the limited role of the formal ulama elite, the Khatmiyya and the Ansar were the most influential and certainly the better organised of all the groups in modern Sudan, functioning at the grass roots level through their specific local *fakis* (Arabic: *faqih*-s) (Voll, 1983: 117ff).

In the post-war period, this sectarian (*ta'ifī*) division characterised the emerging political parties, the main ones of which were the *Umma*, which was pro-Mahdist and sympathetic to the British, and the *Ashiqqa'*, which was pro-Khatmiyya and sympathetic to Egypt. The differences in sectarian organisation and ideology were reflected in the structures of the respective parties. Thus the reluctance of the Sufi leaders to assume political roles gave primacy to the secular 'modernising' nationalists within the Nationalist Union Party (which developed around the Khatmiyya), whereas the activism of the Mahdist movement ensured the primacy of the sectarian, Ansar, leadership within the Umma party (Cudsi, 1986: 36–38).

The Islamic Movement for Liberation, which was a more obviously fundamentalist group, emerged in 1949 from within student circles, and eventually formed an association with the Egyptian Muslim Brothers in 1954. Hasan al-Turabi subsequently established an Islamic Charter Front, in 1964, and became a leader for the Sudanese Muslim Brotherhood which, however, remained rather small in size (Voll, 1983: 128–129).

For the first twenty-five years of the country's independence, political life in Sudan was dominated by the influence of personalities and organisations, both political and military, with the background division between the Khatmiyya and the Ansar always looming on the horizon. A *coup d'état* in May 1969 brough Numairi to power, and established a new regime with socialist and Arabist leanings. Such an orientation was responsible for, among other things, the bloody armed confrontation between Numairi and the Ansar that occurred on the Aba Island in March 1970. However, an attempted leftist-oriented coup in July 1971 turned Numairi against the left, causing him to purge most socialists from his government and to replace them with men of Sufi backgroud or connections, and, eventually, to establish a system that was based on the 'politics of collaboration' (Cudsi, 1986: 41–46).

While wanting to enforce a separation between sects and the State, Numairi also wanted to preserve a close relationship between religion and society. Thus the Constitution of 1973 stipulated that Islam was the main source of legislation, and a committee was formed in 1977 to review laws and to bring them in line with the principles of Islam. The Muslim Brothers were naturally the first to cash in on the benefits of such an orientation. Although strongly anti-leftist, the Muslim Brothers, as a group that had benefited from modern education, appeared to be proponents of economic development and political modernisation (ibid.: 47–48).

In his crackdown on the powerful Communist Party of Sudan, Numairi was obviously interested in reaching a reconciliation (*musalaha*) with all anti-leftist forces, and the Muslim Brothers were neither sectarian-based nor strong enough to represent an immediate threat to him. Hasan al-Turabi's group thus dissolved its Brotherhood organisation, and joined ranks with Numairi in the Sudan Socialist Union (SSU), whereas a less conciliatory group that was opposed to this collaboration continued to function under the banner of the Muslim Brothers and under the leadership of Sadiq 'Abd al-Majid. Sadiq al-Mahdi, the leader of the Ansar, also benefited from the 'national reconciliation' of 1977–1978, and joined the SSU for a brief period, though he resigned a few months later.

Hasan al-Turabi represents in many ways the distinct type of following that characterises the Sudanese Muslim Brotherhood. The son of a judge, he was born in 1932, lived in various parts of the Sudan, studied law in Khartoum and London, and obtained his doctorate in law from the Sorbonne. He worked as a lawyer until Numairi summoned him to join a cabinet that had been set up to neutralise the entire opposition; here he was a Minister of Justice and

Chief Public Prosecutor, along with another Muslim Brother, Ahmad 'Abd al-Rahman, who functioned as Minister of the Interior. In addition, Turabi gained further influence through his appointment to the politburo of the SSU, and was later designated Foreign Policy Adviser to Numairi. However, the Brothers continued to be a somewhat isolated movement of the intellectuals that lacked any particularly close links to the ordinary Muslim masses who frequented the humble mosques. In answer to a question about the connection that the Brotherhood might have had with the country's mosques, Turabi remarked that there was 'not very much at all. We work in mosques, but also in schools, universities and factories. We are present in clubs, football associations, artists' organisations.' (Dietl, 1984: 201).

In their alliance with Numairi, the Muslim Brothers had to accept a 'supplementary' role to Numairi's policies and thus, to some extent, needed to adjust their own vision of the features of an Islamic state. Yet there is no doubt that the Brothers' interest in political power had led them, on more than one occasion, to give religious legitimisation to Numairi's growing authoritarian inclinations. Hasan al-Turabi's ideas on the Islamic state are in tune with mainstream fundamentalist thinking. An Islamic State, he believes, is part of Islam's comprehensive, integrated way of life, where there is no division between the private and the public, between the State and the society (al-Turabi, 1983: 241ff). Its ideological foundations lie in the doctrine of *tawhid*, whose function is to serve God through the pursuit of shari'a. The Islamic state is neither secular nor nationalist, nor is it a sovereign entity – because it is represented by an umma that is ultimately subject to the will of God. Turabi maintains that politically an Islamic State 'rules out all forms of absolution', since Islamic government is essentially a form of 'representative democracy'. Islamic government, he confirms, is a limited, not a totalitarian government. Under Islamic rule, non-Muslims have a guaranteed right to hold their own religious convictions and to regulate their private lives, education and family affairs. If there is any rule in the shari'a which they think is religiously incompatible, they can be absolved from it (al-Turabi, 1983: 242–250).

As he became increasingly involved in real politics, however, Turabi had to admit that, in comparison with its achievements in personal or economic affairs, Islamic jurisprudence in political matters was less profound and less current and up-to-date. Indeed, he spoke about a 'crisis in political jurisprudence' which he attributed to the fact that such an 'energy of belief' was being released by the Islamic revival that it far exceeded the expressive capacity of the Islamic political jurisprudence that was currently available (in Haidar, 1987: 39–40).

The 'Islamic order' enforced by Numairi on Sudan, with support from Turabi and the Islamists (i.e. The Islamic Charter Front, later to become the National Islamic Front – NIF), did not live up to the ideal image postulated by Turabi. Numairi claimed that he was fighting the religious sectarianism that expressed itself through the conventional party system, and that he was setting out to establish a more integrated, cooperative society based on true Islam (cf. Numairi, 1980). In September 1983, the application of shari'a laws was announced, followed some months later, in June 1984, by amendments for certain clauses of the Constitution that were submitted by 'Imam' Numairi (cf. AOHR, 1984). These included: an open presidential term from the date of *bay'a* (selection oath) for life; the right of the president to specify a successor; the absolving of the president from any questioning or trial; the Speaker of parliament to be appointed by the president; the judiciary, headed by Numairi, to be responsible before God, and the president to be in charge of the higher judiciary council; and finally, and most important, any reneging on *bay'a* to be regarded as high treason.

Such amendments enraged quite a number of people in Sudan, and Numairi was unable to get his own way in the People's Assembly (whereupon he turned the proposals over to specialised committees for further study). However, it is undeniable that Numairi had identified the application of shari'a in his own mind with absolute rule for himself, and indeed he moved swifty to imprison Sadiq al-Mahdi when the latter dared to criticise the pace and the methods by which the shari'a reforms were being introduced. In addition, in January 1985, and in spite of pleas from many quarters, he executed the 80-year-old Mahmud Muhammad Taha, leader of the small Islamic group of The Republican Brothers, for daring to criticise his application of the shari'a laws. This application was indeed both sweeping and severe, and was imposed quite summarily, arbitrarily and cruelly (often involving the devastating chopping off of hands and feet) against both Muslims and Christians, by special emergency courts. According to the emergency law of 1984 the president or his delegates formed these courts, which consisted of three individuals, one or two of whom were military or police officers. They often passed judgment (frequently in a televised performance) on the same day, with the accused deprived of any professional legal services and with no right of appeal. The new penal law of 1983 that they applied, together with the law on *usul al-Ahkam* (legal sources of rulings) that supported it, were themselves also excessive in their severity.

Other 'Islamic' laws, on civil and commercial affairs, on judiciary procedures, and even on traffic matters, were passed in a great hurry and within a period of less than a year during 1983–1984. The Islamists were proud that they had contributed to 'the first applied effort to codify Islamic jurisprudence, in which respect the Sudanese have preceded all others'. They tended to play down the fact that this was done under a basically dictatorial regime, claiming that their participation had enlarged the scope for expanding justice while at the same time revealing the corrupt aspects of the regime (al-Kabbashi, 1986: 13–14; 62–67). To complement the general atmosphere of authoritarianism, individuals belonging to thirteen different professions were deprived of the right to form, or to belong to, trade unions, including lawyers, physicians, engineers and others (Fawda, 1985: 121–141).

Needless to say, Numairi's new Islamic order did not help to solve any of the escalating economic and social problems that were besetting the country. On the contrary, combined as it was with the arbitrary redivision of the Southern regions (in violation of the 1972 Addis Ababa Agreement), it further inflamed the rebellion of the non-Muslim South. Socio-economic problems had been piling up since the mid-seventies with the opening up of the Sudanese economy to external forces and influences (both Arab, foreign and international) over which the State had little control (given especially the meagre resources of the Sudanese administrative apparatus and the country's limited planning and managerial capabilities). Popular protest escalated in the North too, and expressed itself in demonstrations and strikes, the most notable of which was by the doctors early in 1984.

The emergency laws announced by Numairi in the same year were supported by Turabi who claimed that they had precedent in the Islamic tradition. But the new legislative and organisational changes that were introduced caused such serious dislocations in the State machinery that whatever little effectiveness it still possessed was quite removed. The social and political situation was getting out of hand, and the Islamic movement realised fairly swiftly that its support for Numairi's arbitrary power had gone too far; it was at this juncture that the Islamists apparently decided to attempt a sort of internal coup in order to take matters firmly into their own hands. However, their intentions were unravelled by the State authorities, and the Islamist leaders, including Turabi, were arrested and detained in January 1985 (CPSS, 1988: 243–245).

The escalating socio-economic crisis, combined with Numairi's eccentric arbitrariness, resulted finally in the big popular explosion of March 1985. It all started in the Omdurman Islamic University, and then spilled out into the streets, where the lumpenproletariat or *shammasa* (those who live and work perpetually under the sun) of the Omdurman and Khartoum markets joined in. Next came the professional syndicates and the railway unions, who were subsequently joined by a substantial proportion of all popular forces (including women), and eventually this widespread marshalling of popular resentment led to the removal of Numairi (Mus'ad, 1985: 201–210).

There is little doubt, however, that the Islamic movement had utilised its period in government with Numairi to consolidate its organisation and to spread its influence within the country's educational and administrative institutions. The Islamists' falling out with Numairi shortly before his removal and their participation in the civil rebellion against him in March 1985 saved the movement from the fate of total popular disgrace, and it now emerged indisputably as the third active political force in Sudan, although various political groupings, especially the left, still regarded it with suspicion and abhorrence. This is perhaps the reason why the Islamic Front did not participate in the National Gathering, which included most political and syndicate forces in Sudan, during the period of transitional government from April 1985 to April 1986 (when a military council assisted by a non-party civilian cabinet was in government). Yet the Front continued to flex its muscles during this year, winning in most student elections, and organising some large demonstrations that were hostile to the mainly southern Sudan People's Liberation Movement (SPLM); in 1986, these manoeuvrings brought a coalition government to power, with Sadiq al-Mahdi as prime minister.

The elections of April 1986 proved how much power the Islamic Front had gained in Sudanese politics. By managing to take 51 out of 227 elected seats (including some in wards traditionally dominated by Sufi groups with whom the Islamists had no intimate relations), they thus represented the third largest parlimentary party, and the main opposition force. Furthermore, the Front then mounted a strong campaign that prevented the new coalition government from being able to consider any reversal of the shari'a laws passed under Numairi, or to adopt a more conciliatory stand towards the resistance in the South. Of course, Sadiq al-Mahdi himself is an Islamist of sorts, except that his influence is mainly derived from, and tempered by, his symbolic communal leadership of the Ansar. His Islamic concepts are not as fundamentalist as those of Turabi. He maintains, for example, that there is no particular system of Islamic government, nor any particular Islamic economic system. All those who theorise about such systems have, in his view, simply expressed historically relevant means of applying Islamic injunctions. Even the most specific injunctions, such as those pertaining to canonical punishments or *hudud*, permit, according to him, a high degree of flexibility in their application (al-Mahdi, 1983: 230–240). Yet Sadiq al-Mahdi could not afford to be seen as less zealous than Turabi or Numairi about enforcing the shari'a or resisting the 'intransigence' of the non-Muslim South.

There is no special profile available of membership in Sudan's Islamic Front. However, its main constituents are among members of the 'new' middle class, with modern education (although possibly with some Sufi family background), and studying or working in the cities, especially Khartoum. As well as being strongly represented in the students' unions, they won twenty-four out of the twenty-eight seats allocated for university graduates in the 1986 general elections (CPSS, 1988: 245–246). Furthermore, the election commissioners' results, reported in the press at the time, indicate that the National Islamic Front gained 42 per cent of the seats available in the Khartoum area in the same elections, which is illustrative of their strength in the urban centres. There are indications too that the politicised form of Islam represented by the NIF is attracting growing numbers of people who are young, educated and recently urbanised, but who nevertheless hail from families with Sufi or traditional backgrounds. The socio-economic blockage that such elements face because of the accumulation of problems resulting from the failure of State policies, in some ways brings them closer to the 'newer' Islamic forces and erodes some of the conventional divisions between the two camps.

Ironically, therefore, the Islamists appear to be a rather 'modernist' group, small but non-sectarian and well organised, whereas the government itself had gone back to an uncomfortable coalition between the conventional forces of the Ansar and the Khatmiyya, including those members of the intelligentsia who had been unable to break loose from their traditional, conservative leaderships ('Ali, 1987: 93–94). The large demonstrations and counter-demonstrations of 1987 brought such a contradiction into focus: thus, whereas the Islamists were capable of launching well-organised demonstrations by students and the urban forces numbered in their tens of thousands, the governing coalition was capable of launching counter-demonstrations in the order of hundreds of thousands that mainly included supporters of the Ansar and the Khatmiyya from the countryside (CPSS, 1988: 250). Although both sets of demonstrations were flexing their muscles at each other, there is much to suggest that both were also trying to hint to the army that they were the more reliable and trustworthy force in the country.

Riots and demonstrations escalated throughout Sudan during the last few months of 1987, with the country's economic and political problems seemingly deadlocked. In an attempt to broaden the coalition government and to dislodge the Islamists from their critical position towards the regime, the National Islamic Front was attracted to a new coalition government formed in May 1988 (with the Umma and the Unionists). In it the NIF was represented by five ministers, including Turabi as Minister of Justice and Prosecutor General. During the period from December 1988 to March 1989, the five became seven with the appointment of another two ministers after the withdrawal of the Democratic Unionist Party (DUP) from the coalition, and Turabi was made Minister of Foreign Affairs. In addition, members of the NIF held a number of other important posts which included that of governor of the capital city, deputy ruler for the Northern region and the Darfur region, regional ministers in all northern regions, as well as the post of Speaker of the Constituent Assembly or parliament (*Al-Rayah*, 16 March 1989).

Social and economic matters did not improve; if anything, they became increasingly worse with the escalation of the uprising in the South. Attempts to strike a deal with the Southern forces were strongly resisted by the NIF, and the possibility of the military intervening openly in politics became very close. In March 1989, the National Islamic Front decided to opt out of a newly formed coalition government that was intent on reconciliation with the Southern rebels and their Sudan People's Liberation Movement. To appease the Southerners, the government had decided to delay the issuing of a new Islamic penalties law which had been prepared in 1988 to replace the one passed under Numairi (with the aim of freeing the Islamic legislation from the tarnish of Numairi's dictatorial rule). The NIF was, of course, strongly opposed to this. Although the armed forces appeared to be in favour of the reconciliation plan, negotiated initially by the DUP, the NIF continued to court the army and to express unequivocal support for it. The Front also tried to give the impression that it was a modernist and integrationist movement opposed to what it called 'parties of the jungle' (i.e. the SPLM) and 'parties of the desert' (i.e. the sectarian-based Umma and Unionist parties) (*Al-Rayah*, 30 March 1989). At the same time it encouraged the formation of 'people's defence forces' to confront the 'rebellion' in the South (*Al-Rayah*, 26 May 1989), while escalating Islamic demonstrations in protest against demonstrations launched in Khartoum in support of the national reconciliation by the Southerners, the Unionists and other sympathisers (such as the Marxists and the Ba'thists).

It can thus be seen that the strong Islamist ideas and feelings of the

NIF leadership have turned the Front into an ardent opponent of any measure that can be remotely interpreted as a concession by Muslims to non-Muslims. The broader issue of Southern autonomy, as well as the more specific issue of the comprehensive application of shari'a, are both regarded in this light. Although the NIF was no longer part of the ruling coalition, the Sudanese government was made too fragile to be able to press ahead with the reconciliation process in the face of escalating opposition from the Front, which thus revealed its continuing ability to influence events, however negative and obstructive that influence was. Once again, too, the Front proved to be tactically astute. When the instigators of a new *coup d'état* took power on 30 June 1989, the National Islamic Front, being no longer part of the coalition government, could therefore escape many of the purges that inevitably followed this latest change.

THE ISLAMIC MOVEMENT IN TUNISIA

The sudden emergence and speedy expansion, from the late seventies, of a significant Islamic movement in Tunisia has caught some people unawares, given that this country appeared to many to be thoroughly 'modernised', and even secularised. Yet it was that 'Occidental saturation' itself, through which a large segment of the population was marginalised both economically and culturally, which explains the growing appeal of the Islamic tendency In Tunisia, and which, ironically, imparts to it its distinctive features (Grandguillaume, 1982: 55–57).

Since the independence of Tunisia in 1956, Bourguibism has been one of the most avowedly secularist political strategies in the Arab world. Among its main policies have been the secularisation of personal statute laws, the liquidation of shari'a courts and of religious endowments (*habus*), and the restriction of the influence of the religious Zaituna university and other Quranic schools. Religious practices such as pilgrimages, the fast of Ramadan and traditional ceremonies of a religious nature were also played down (Vatin, 1982: 238–239; Anawati and Borrmans, 1982: 216–217). Such changes were bordering on implicit Europeanisation, creating among the less well-to-do, less educated and traditionally overlooked sectors of the population a distinct sense of alienation.

The beginnings of the Islamic movement came about in 1970, centred round a review called *Al-Ma'rifa* in which opinions were exchanged on the alienation of Islam in its own land. This was followed during the early seventies with a revival of religious teachings in the Zaituna university particularly by Shaikh Bin Milad, his disciple Shaikh 'Abd al-Fattah Muru, and others. Another influence came from the Arab Levant, when Rashid al-Ghanushi and Hamid al-Naifar returned from their studies in Syria (where they had become familiar with the ideas of the Syrian and the Egyptian Muslim Brothers), and joined the Tunisian Quranic Preservation Society. The Quranic study circles, which enjoyed government support, were soon to spread within the university, where they indulged in typically idealistic discourse, contemptuous of the corrupting outcomes of the 'open door' economic policies of the seventies.

In the Tunisia of the seventies, as with other post-populist regimes making the suden transformation from state capitalism to an open door policy, incomes in the 'business' sector rose very fast while those of the salaried sectors moved very slowly. While the State was mainly obsessed with confronting the leftist tendencies and the labour movement (culminating in the bloody conflict with the General Workers' Federation in January 1978), growing segments of the youth were mulling over the Arab weakness against Israel, excessive cultural Westernisation and the success of the Islamic revolution in Iran. Readership of Islamic literature grew and distinct Islamic circles started to take shape.

By the late seventies the Mouvement de la Tendance Islamique (MTI) had emerged as the main Islamist organisation in Tunisia, one of its main leaders being Rashid al-Ghanushi. Other smaller organisations were also believed to exist in the eighties, such as the Islamic Shura Party, the Islamic Progressive Tendency, the Islamic Vanguard Movement and the Islamic Liberation Party (Boulby, 1988: 590, 602). Having emerged much more recently in Tunisia than, for instance, in Egypt or in Syria, the Tunisian Islamic movement is at the stage of declaring itself to be more concerned with the moral and social Islamic matters than with the establishment of an Islamic State. It also now calls for the extension of public liberties, has joined ranks with the nationalist movement, and is even integrating itself gradually with the labour movement. As al-Ghanushi has remarked, his movement, the MTI, does not reject modernity, but seeks only to 'Islamise' it (Jones, 1988: 21).

The main problem, according to the Islamists, lies in the incongruency between the style of social organisation based on European institutions and the collective consciousness based on an Islamic culture and spirit, which results in a disorienting kind of 'cultural dualism' (al-Hirmasi, 1987: 276–279). But cultural emphasis notwithstanding, the political action of the trade unions in 1978 took the

Islamic movement by surprise and made it look rather marginal to popular concerns. After this, the movement developed a greater interest in social and economic affairs and as a consequence became more politicised, though it had not yet put itself in the position of the exclusive actor with rights of moral tutelage over the society at large.

This tutelage over society, characteristic of the Ikhwan and other Islamist trends, is pointedly criticised by Rashid al-Ghanushi, who claims that his movement draws on various intellectual sources: the Tunisian religious tradition; the *Salafiyya* school as represented by the Muslim Brothers and other intellectual and political Islamic approaches in the Mashriq; and the 'Islamic Rationality' trend, that is influenced by the *Mu'tazila* (Mu'tazilites) and is sympathetic to the pluralist and oppositional groups of Islamic history (such as the Khawarij, the Shi'a, the Qarmatians, etc. (al-Ghanushi, 1987: 300–302). Such intellectual 'openness' has enabled the MTI to interact more dynamically with the Iranian Revolution and the Sudanese Islamists, as well as with the older Islamic trends in the Arab world. The same 'openness', it is claimed, also enables the MTI to accept a pluralist formula for Tunisian politics that includes even secularists and Communists, and to adopt a 'sociological' perspective based on social analysis as well as on active cooperation with the dispossessed groups in Tunisia, and particularly with the country's labour movement (ibid.: 305–308). Such an open intellectual perspective certainly distinguishes the MTI from other Islamic movements in the Arab world, but one cannot help wondering whether that is simply a tactical approach in view of the movement's recent existence and relative weakness, or whether it will become one of the more lasting features of the Islamic movement in Tunisia.

When Bourguiba initiated a limited political liberalisation in 1980 and a number of parties were allowed to form, the MTI was not permitted to do this, and indeed several of its leaders were dismissed from their posts, harassed and arrested. This policy of suppression seems to have increased the movement's popularity within the universities in the period from 1981 to 1984 and thus it came to dominate the student movement. During the same period other Islamic movements, most particularly the Islamic Liberation Party, involved themselves in violent action against the State, including, reportedly, within the armed forces, members of which were sent to trial and prosecuted in 1983 (CPSS, 1988: 247–248).

The socio-economic background of the Islamists reveals a typical pattern. Based on a study by 'Abd al-Baqi al-Hirmasi, in which he polled fifty members of the MTI and a national representative sample of 800 Tunisians, it can be seen that the average age is around 25 years and that 50 per cent of all personnel are below 30 years (the age perhaps being even younger among followers and sympathisers), although there are some older ulama and mentors from Zaituna University. The fact that the leaders are not so young (Ghanushi is in his fifties and Muru in his forties) indicates that the Islamic movement has apparently not been split along generational lines as happened, for example, in Egypt. Some 80 per cent of members are students and, among those detained, no fewer than seventy-five were teachers and students (especially in the sciences – as in Egypt), the remaining 25 per cent being minor functionaries and technicians (al-Hirmasi, 1987: 252).

It seems from Hirmasi's study, and given the relatively high level of secularisation in Tunisia, that one should distinguish between general Islamic adherence and commitment on the one hand (what we term 'religiosity'), and more determined, action-oriented Islamism on the other. Thus, whereas general Islamic adherence is concentrated on the coast, and in the capital Tunis (but to a lesser extent in the middle and the south of the country), there is a general impression both among the Islamic leaders and the State security apparatus that determined, action-oriented Islamism is more typical of the rural middle and south (ibid.: 252–254). Obviously more accurate studies will be needed before one can decide whether this view is based purely on impression and speculation, or whether the Tunisian interior is the equivalent – with regard to the Islamic movement – of, say, Aleppo in Syria and Asyut in Egypt. In the Sahel, Islamists face strong resistance in places where groups of earlier settlers, dispersed from the countryside by colonialism, have settled in governmental and modern sectors and possess a distinct nationalist–secularist outlook. Only after the mid-seventies and as a result of the tourism and other industries brought to the coast by infitah policies, could the Islamists encroach on this region (ibid.: 291, 297).

Hirmasi's study also indicates that most Islamists belong to the middle and lower-middle classes. Among the parents, 48 per cent were illiterate, 27 per cent were secularly educated (to modest levels only), and 19 per cent were religiously educated. Professionally, 21 per cent of the parents were middle functionaires, 46 per cent were urban or agricultural workers, and 29 per cent were of very impoverished family backgrounds (ibid.: 254–255).

Although the Islamic movement has become increasingly politicised, the activities of its militant wing have contrived to emphasise a sort of culturalist and moralist symbolism. Unlike the Islamic militants in Egypt and Syria who concentrate their attacks on government buildings and personnel and on other symbols of State power, the Tunisian militants (though active in the 'food riots' of 1984 and in university strikes during 1986–1987) have acted only indirectly against State institutions, focusing their attention more directly against such symbols of moral laxity and cultural decadence as cafes and patisseries that serve food and drink during times of fasting, or hotels that cater to the tourist hordes of 'semi-naked' Europeans and Americans. Such actions were bound, however, to exacerbate the tensions that already existed between the regime and the Islamists, given the regime's growing reliance on tourism and foreign trade. The confrontation reached its peak in September 1987 when, following the arrest of al-Ghanushi in March 1987, the subsequent and spectacular trials of the Islamists were to result shortly afterwards in Bourguiba's demise. Apparently displeased with the 'leniency' of the sentences that had been passed, Bourguiba asked for a retrial and for a specific number of convictions (Boulby, 1988: 608–614). At this point, in November 1987, an insider military man 'Zain al-'Abidin Bin 'Ali, who was then Prime Minister, felt obliged to step in and take over power in order to avoid more serious and uncontrollable repercussions.

The parlimentary elections held in April 1989 under President Bin 'Ali did not result in any formal opposition candidates winning any seats in the Assembly. Yet the Islamist 'independents' managed to win around 17 per cent of the vote, thus displacing the secular left, with around 3 per cent, as the main opposition (Halliday and Molyneux, 1989). The Islamists were encouraged too by the release of hundreds of political prisoners, among whom were many of their fellow members. A few symbolic gestures, such as the broadcasting of the *adhan* (call to prayer) on radio and television (which had not been allowed under Bourguiba), also had the desired effect of appeasing broader sectors of the religious public at large. There were other reports, however, in the summer of 1989, concerning the arrest of some Islamists who were accused of belonging to the illegal Islamic Liberation Party (*Al-Islah*, 7 July 1989).

Although seven political parties were recognised by the Bin 'Ali regime, parties holding 'exclusive' claims to Islam have not been permitted, which is why the MTI was, in 1989, seeking recognition as a political party under the new name of *Hizb al-nahda al-Tunisi* (The Renaissance Party of Tunisia). It is obvious, therefore, that, for the time being, the MTI is prepared to act in a legal and reconciliatory fashion. It remains to be seen, however, how long the party's strategy, not to mention the reaction of the authorities to it, will permit this state of affairs to continue.

CONCLUSION

It should be clear from this brief survey of the Islamic movements in a number of Arab countries that an important element of variation exists, depending on the historical conjunctures and political conditions in each country. The intellectual sources and the socio-economic bases will be given further consideration in the next two chapters. A brief comparative note, however, may be in order at this point. It is perhaps possible to generalise by saying that movements of political Islam appear to be more vigorous in countries that have openly discarded some of the symbols of 'traditionalism' and have clearly declared a schema for 'modernisation'. In monarchical regimes that still claim religion and/or Sharifian (related to Prophet Muhammad) descent as one of the bases for their legitimacy, the Islamic movement remains relatively muted. This is true, as we have seen, of Jordan and Saudi Arabia, but it is also true of Morocco and to some extent of the smaller Gulf countries. It should not be forgotten, however, that practically all these countries also have access to means that bring financial resources in sizeable or at least significant magnitude directly to the State (oil, phosphates and foreign aid). Thus these countries are able to support the sources of their religious (or 'traditional') legitimisation with substantial amounts of financial resources. Several of these regimes have 'incorporated' (rather than simply 'controlled') the religious establishments within the State machine and allowed the ulama to play an important role in educational, judiciary and social affairs. In the case of Saudi Arabia and of Morocco, the religious movement was on the whole a partner in the process of State-building.[2] The monarchical regimes seem to strike a more genuine alliance with the religious elite, because they conceive of the nationalists and leftists as their major antagonists.

Saudi Arabia is in a way an exception that proves the rule. Apart from the Mecca incident, the anti-State religious movement does not seem to have a serious presence. The grievances of the Shi'is are grievances of a sectarian minority and therefore have a somewhat different character. The Mecca incident itself, though revealing some of the familiar youth frustrations, might have been more tribal in its driving force than it was religious. In any case, Saudi Arabia has a strong tradition of Wahhabism which is bound to cause occasional friction between the puritanical ethos of the desert, and the consumerist drive of modern urban life.

It is therefore justifiable to argue that political Islam appears to be basically a response movement to regimes that are avowedly more 'modernist' and secularising. In such cases the State appears to be exercising a more 'alientating' impact, in cultural terms. The State is also dominant economically, but what distinguishes this variety of State from the previous one is that it derives its economic power from the surplus it extracts directly from the population, and not from a 'natural' or external source of finance. What this State does may not only appear to be culturally alien, but it may also 'hurt' financially and socially.

This variety of State has encroached more seriously on the civil society, utilising against that society resources that are derived directly from its individuals and social classes. The State does this in the name of development. But when development falters and the promised rewards are not achieved, segments of the civil society rebel against the State using 'religion' as a catalyst for mobilisation and resistance. This 'religion' that the militant Islamists use, however, is not simply a 'traditional' set of beliefs that is being retrieved, but is largely a novel religio-political body that they improvise. In the following chapter we will set out to illlustrate that 'political Islam' is not an old doctrine that is currently being resurrected, but rather a new doctrine that is in the process now of being invented.

6 Political Islam: intellectual sources

We have argued repeatedly in this work that although Islam is a religion of collective morals, it is not particularly a political religion. The main Quranic concept of the *body politic* (*umma*), as noted earlier, is not necessarily a religious one; nor did the Quran or the Hadith specify how governments should be formed or what they should look like. If there ever was an imagined ideological Islamic State based entirely on 'pure' shari'a, such a state was in dissonance with the 'historical Islamic State' which relied in most stages of its existence on extra-canonical sources of law, such as custom, convention and the ruler's will (*qanun, nizam, iradeh*) (cf. Vatikiotis, 1987: Chs 1, 2 and 3). There was indeed a connection between religion and politics throughout much of the history of the Islamic State, but this was the outcome of the State (already strong owing to the nature of the mode of production) taking over religion as a legitimising shield for its activity. Islam did not give the historical Muslim State its character; on the contrary, the historical Muslim State had, over the centuries, imparted its features on the Islamic tradition. This process, incidentally, was the reverse of the process in Europe, where it was the Church that interfered in politics and not the other way round.

It is important to note, however, that the ruler, in taking on Islam as a legitimiser, could not avoid paying attention to some of its precepts, nor could he avoid, from time to time, being taken to task by his opponents on the basis of Islamic tenets. In other words, the State historically appropriated Islam to legitimise itself, but the State could not *monopolise* the use of Islam for itself – by its very nature, religion is a *shared* belief and experience.

It could, in my view, be argued that in the area of political economy the Islamic State enjoyed a high level of relative autonomy from society. The assuming or the alternating of political authority did not rely to any critical degree on the support of any distinct social classes, being mainly an act of power – military, political and organisational. As the modes of production were mainly control-based, the ruler who controlled them was thereby given a significant degree of autonomy *vis-à-vis* the producers and their groupings and organisations.

In the area of political culture, however, the State was far less autonomous from society. Although the ruler had usually assumed power by force or intrigue, he tried to legitimise his continuation in power on the basis of his overseeing of and guardianship over the realisation of a good Islamic society. Because his rule had very little popular base (since, as we saw, the principles of *shura*, *'aqd* and *bay'a* were in reality not practised), he had to trace it back to some 'divine' source; he had to derive his legitimacy from claims to be the implementer of the Word of God on earth. Of course, he had also to make sure, by sponsoring various jurists and clerics, that the Word of God would always be interpreted in ways that enhanced his position or at least minimised any threat to his rule. Such an ideological posture in some ways legitimised, and in some ways masked, the ruler's control over the polity and the economy.

But this ideological posture also rendered the ruler somewhat vulnerable, for he was not the only Muslim: the ulama, who were presumably more knowledgeable about Islam than he was, wielded in consequence a tremendous amount of intellectual power, and although the majority of them supported the ruler at most times, there were those who criticised, corrected or protested. Various social movements could also articulate their demands in terms of religion – that is, in the way they saw and interpreted the texts. However, the task of such movements was very difficult because although, in a manner of speaking, the Quran was theirs too, the various patterns of reading and interpreting it had long been monopolised and slanted in the direction of the ruler and the State.

In contemporary Middle Eastern countries the State also enjoys, in most cases, a high degree of relative autonomy in the economic sphere, resting as it does on an extensive infrastructure of nationalised industries, large-scale hydraulic projects, large public services, petroleum sectors, transit trade (e.g. the Suez Canal, trans-statal oil pipelines, etc.), and foreign (i.e. 'external' to society) aid.

Yet unlike their traditional counterparts, the contemporary states have on the whole tried to rid themselves of the ideological shield of religion by claiming to be secular. Their new slogans have encompassed things such as national independence, economic development and Arab unity. When these did not materialise, nobody could blame God, but they could blame the State, and now it was the opposition, not the rulers, who had first call on religion, since it was one of the very few things that the government could not confiscate completely for itself. What is more, religion seemed to belong to the people alone, since in the heyday of nationalism, modernism, socialism and other such secular 'isms', the government did not even appear to be interested in it. It was only when the opposition began to beat the State with the whip of religion that the State started to put on a religious face – but it was too little and too late by the reckoning of the Islamists: it is they who have now taken the initiative in the game, forcing the State to play the defensive role, to react and to counteract, and to try to manipulate the Islamic movements.

The contemporary territorial state in the Arab/Muslim world (for all its 'artificiality' in terms of borders and in terms of cultural/social delineation), has not only accepted the existing juridic and political 'world-of-nations' system, but has also, on the whole, accepted the existing international economic order. While the first system does not give Muslim States any advantages over non-Muslim ones (indeed there are no Muslim States, for example, among the permanent members of the Security Council of the United Nations), the existing economic order places most Muslim countries – the rich Gulf ones included – in a position of dependency *vis-à-vis* the capitalist 'core'.

In their relationship with the rest of the world, no special treatment is given by Muslim States to fellow Muslim States: ambassadors are exchanged in the normal way, and the principle of State sovereignty is adopted in any multi-national organisation that brings Muslim States together (e.g. the League of Arab States and the Islamic Organisation Conference) (cf. Piscatori, 1986). In terms of political behaviour there is no automatic support of a Muslim against a non-Muslim country (e.g. Cyprus, India, Pakistan). In economic relations no preferential treatment is given to other Muslim countries in terms of trade, investment or importation of manpower, etc. In economic aid given by Arab development funds there is no preference given to Muslim countries as such. Although some priority in direct State aid is given to Muslim States by Saudi Arabia, in absolute terms the main bulk of Arab aid, Saudi aid included, is to Arab – rather than Muslim – countries, some of which (such as Syria and Jordan) are not particularly known for their pro-Islamic policies (cf. Ayubi, 1984).

Opposition Islamic movements are now using religion to challenge such a 'religiously-neutral' State: their call is for a society where God's word is the only source of ethics and legislation, and they want a specifically Islamic – not a patriotic or a nationalist – concept of the community, and a revival of the concept of *jihad* as a basis for restructuring the world order. Thus we can see that, contrary to the familiar historical pattern of Islamising political practice (i.e. the imparting of religious legitimisation upon real, power-based politics), contemporary Islamic opposition movements aim at politicising Islam (i.e. at turning Islam into an action-oriented force not only in the traditional areas of morals but also in the areas of collective ethics, domestic politics and international relations). This is what several commentators have come to call 'political Islam'. By political Islam here, I mean a process that goes in the opposite direction from the historical one of Islamised politics. It is an attempt to link religion and politics not by way of legitimising government, but rather by way of resisting it – political Islam is thus still on the whole a protest movement (with the partial exception of Iran).

Although it may sound unorthodox, political Islam (though drawing on older sources such as the ideas of the Khawarij and Ibn Taimiya) is just as modern a concept as, say, Arab nationalism. Its two main components are much more recent than many Orientalists and fundamentalists have led us to believe. Domestically, the concept of an Islamic *State* (i.e. that Islam is both religion and politics: *din wa dawla*) is fairly recent, dating broadly to the end of the Ottoman Empire and more specifically to the teachings of Mawdudi and some Muslim Brothers. Internationally, its deliberately and specifically religious rendering of the term *umma* is also fairly recent (although it does, of course, have historical precedents). When the Arab Nationalists began to use the term *umma* to describe all Arabs (*al-umma al-'arabiyya*), they were not mistakenly or figuratively imparting a new meaning to an old (religious) concept, for indeed the term had always been used in the classical literature to mean either people/nation or a community of believers (see Chapter 1).

For the civilian, Western-educated fundamentalists, the Islamist doctrine was not a ready-made body of knowledge that was simply neglected in the past and was now being re-adopted. The Islamists have had to 'dig' for the sources and to struggle over re-interpreting and re-constructing them. For the last hundred years or so, Islamic jurisprudence has not formed part of the standard learning or reading of the average educated person in the Arab countries most affected by radical Islamism.[1] Thus the Islamists were not peeling away a thin veneer of 'Westernisation' that was concealing an intact treasury of 'traditional' Islamic learning; rather, they were going through a process of rediscovery and reassembly of pieces long since scattered and dispersed.

The counter-ideology of the Islamic movement confronts the

language of rationality and development espoused by the territorial bureaucratic State with a language of piety and authenticity. Within the bounds of Islamic sources it is highly eclectic; however, the eclecticism of the Islamists is not as transparent as that of the ruling elites – it is glossed over with the devout repetition of 'divine words' about an eternal promise, and with the nostalgic dream of retrieving a Golden Age (that never really existed). The eclecticism is not transparent because there is nothing to 'measure it with': the language is so abstract that it is removed from both time and place – inconsistencies therefore become irrelevant.

From a historical perspective, whenever 'extremist' Islamic movements (*ghulat* in traditional language, *mutatarrifun* in current language) emerged and involved themselves in opposition and protest, we knew that we were in a time of socio-political crisis. I think that this much can be established with good evidence. But why do social and economic grievances have to appear in the form of a religious discourse and address themselves in Islamic terms? Often, of course, there is no other channel for expressing grievances. But apart from this, I think that the reason is partly related to the nature of Islam itself as a belief system, and partly to the nature of the contingent social and political circumstances. The first factor imparts to most militant Islamic movements a certain similarity; the second makes them manifest themselves in different forms.

To start with the nature of Islam as a belief system: it is both a system of worship and a system of social morals and dealings (see Chapter 2) – it is thus well endowed with a wide ethical and social vocabulary that is capable of a broad range of applications. Secondly, Islam calls for total submission to God (that is, after all, what the word 'Islam' means), and for an almost total epistemological break with anything that preceded it – this is normally referred to as pagan ignorance (*jahiliyya*). And although Judaism and Christianity are recognised, it is believed that their available texts have been distorted over time. Therefore those who take their Islam (too) seriously tend to want to apply purely Quranic analysis to, and to seek (if possible) purely Quranic sanctioning for, whatever they may be trying to do. There is no doubt that textual literalness (scripturalism) is a dominant trend in the Islamic tradition (see Chapter 1), but the text is comprehensive and general enough to render itself, in various areas, open to many interpretations. These are thus the two most characteristic features of Islam as an 'idea system': a certain inclination towards 'collective morals' and a certain inclination towards 'sanctification of the text'. Practically everything else is contingent on the social and political conditions prevailing.

The point to be emphasised, however, is that although Islamic movements may emerge out of social conditions (that have to be carefully studied and understood), they do not represent doctrinally a mere mechanical reflection of social and economic concerns. Their discourse does often acquire an intellectual autonomy of its own, and the arguments and counter-arguments are capable of being debated as though they had little relationship to the stimuli that gave rise to them. To their members they do appear as though they seek nothing but the enforcement of God's Word, which is, after all, the duty of every true Muslim. As such we would be making a serious mistake if we applied a vulgar type of reductionism to the discourse of the Islamic movements and assumed that they did not really mean what they were talking about, or if we tried to impart a purely socio-economic significance to their discourse. Economic, social and political factors may *give rise* to specific movements at specific times, but such movements soon have a logic and a life of their own and their discourse certainly appears to their members to be self-sufficient and self-contained. It would also be naive to assume that man has no spiritual and moral needs, or that all such normative beliefs have to be subsumed under some easily tracked 'materialist' banner.

The way that the doctrine of political Islam has been developed is most interesting: it is based on a very selective choice and a rather unorthodox interpretation of older texts. The contingent nature of the ideology of political Islam can sometimes be understood through the detection of some similarity between the social conjunctures that produced the original, older idea on the one hand, and the conditions that surround the contemporary 'edition' produced by the modern Islamists on the other.

OLDER SOURCES

The first and oldest source of inspiration for the doctrine of political Islam is the *khawarij* (see Chapter 3). Like the khawarij, the militant Islamists tend to come from a relatively harsher ecological-social background. Like them, they were lured to, but then not effectively absorbed by, the city. Failing to win the game they turned against the city to condemn its rules altogether. From the khawarij, the political Islamists seem mainly to have borrowed three concepts: (a) God's absolute sovereignty and rulership (*al-hakimiyya li Allah*); (b) the judging as infidel and the 'excommunication' (*takfir*) and even assassination not just of those who blaspheme but also of those who simply sin (*murtakib al-kabira*); and (c) the refusal to establish leadership on any ethnic, class or even educational (theological) basis (compare, e.g. al-Sayyid, 1984A: 45–76; Huwaidi, 1987: 247–252).

The second old intellectual source for political Islam is the stern Syrian jurist Ibn Taimiya (see Chapter 3). In his most renowned book *Al-Siyasa al-Shar'iyya* he does not sound particularly militant. He follows the orthodox consensus on the necessity of government and leadership (*al-imara*) to all societies and especially to Muslims by way of the need to avoid strife and to enforce religious commandments (Ibn Taimiya, 1983: 138–144). On *jihad* (holy struggle or war) he is also fairly conventional, explaining that it is mainly required against infidels. However, there are some nuances here: any person who constrains or prevents (*mana'a*) the total piety to God should be fought (ibid.: 106); anyone who opts out of, or deviates from (*kharaja 'an*) the Islamic shari'a should be fought even if he utters the 'credo' (ibid.: 109).[2] Following the most strict jurist Ahmad ibn Hanbal, he recommends the punishment, even perhaps the execution, of those who do not pray (ibid.: 111).

For the more relevant, contingent and action-oriented rulings, however, the contemporary militants have had to dig into Ibn Taimiya's multi-volume *Fatawa* (religio-juridic rulings/opinions). Here Ibn Taimiya has gone one step further, by specifying situations where a Muslim, and more specifically a Muslim *ruler*, is to be 'excommunicated' and fought. Pertaining to specific questions that are presumably related to real problems, and being prescriptive in nature, the *Fatawa* are more reflective of Ibn Taimiya's life and times: a disheartened and persecuted man in a time when the Islamic empire was fragmenting into smaller statelets, governed by Mamluks or other ethnic/military cliques, and exposed to the threat of the Crusaders from the West and to the advancing march of the Mongols (Tatars) from the East. It was also a time of growing religious and philosophical controversy and uncertainty, and of escalating numbers of non-Orthodox sects, such as the Nusairis (or 'Alawis), and of Sufi orders (cf. al-Sharqawi, 1982). Suffering persecution, Ibn Taimiya had to travel several times within Syria, and between Syria and Egypt; his ideas were refuted and opposed, and in both countries he was on occasions incarcerated, eventually to die in prison 'without his pens and papers' (See Preface in: Ibn Taimiya, 1983).

Ibn Taimiya was asked to advise on the case of the invading Mongols, who were formally Muslim, and about Muslim local rulers, such as the prince of Mardin, who gave allegiance to these Mongols.

Ibn Taimiya replied that such people were infidels who should religiously be fought by the believers because, though they were nominally Muslims, they actually adhered among themselves to a Turkic 'common law' of nomadic origin called the *yasa* (Ibn Taimiya, 1965, Vol. 4, no. 515: 332–358).

The *yasa* is similar to the *'urf* (customary law) of the Arabs, and although it is not codified, it is believed that its 'secular' precepts governed the internal relations of many ruling Turkic-influenced elites: the Mongols, the Mamluks, and also the Turks themselves. Al-Maqrizi (AD 1365–441) maintained that it was of Mongol origin, and that it was used by the Turks and the Mamluks. He even claims that it is the origin of the term *siyasa*, which he defines as the 'law posited for guarding manners and interests and for regulating affairs'; as distinct from *shar'* which is God's religious orders ('Imara, 1983: 87–90).[3]

Ibn Taimiya's writings had a strong impact on the formulation of the Wahhabi call in Arabia from the eighteenth century on. However, it is mainly the Jihad organisation in contemporary Egypt, and similar militant organisations in the Arab world and the Indian subcontinent, that have given Ibn Taimiya's thoughts a fresh relevance and significance: it is sometimes argued that the 'dependent' rulers of the contemporary Arab countries are the equivalent of the mediaeval prince of Mardin – Muslim in name but ruling by another non-religious law and owing allegiance to foreign infidel powers (see below).

The modern rediscovery of Ibn Taimiya in Egypt and Muslim India is – as Sivan maintains – probably not a mere accident (though his equal popularity in Saudi Arabia rather clouds the argument):

> For these two lands were among the first to come under the impact of the West. Western influence thus had time to penetrate the local culture. Many were alarmed by what they considered the undermining of Islam from within and despaired of coming to terms with that alien culture without forfeiting their ancient identity – and they found in the Ibn Taimiyya doctrine a kind of inspired solution. The analogy of the Mongols and the concept of the pre-Islamic jahiliyya would be reinterpreted to suit the new state of affairs. (Sivan, 1985: 101)

ABU AL-A'LA MAWDUDI

One of the most important contemporary sources for the doctrine of political Islam is the writings of the Pakistani journalist/author Abu al-A'la Mawdudi (AD 1903–1979). Most of Mawdudi's political ideas were developed in India in the period between 1937 and 1941 when any strict orthodox Muslim must have felt beleaguered on all fronts: current rule and sovereignty were for the 'infidel' British, and prospective rule appeared to be destined for the 'pagan' Hindus (cf. 'Imara, 1987: 221–222, 234–244). In such circumstances a siege mentality seems to have led Mawdudi to adopt an extremist, ultra-conservative position about practically everything: science and technology, the position of women, the status of non-Muslims, relations with other cultures, and, of course, politics and the State. Traditional Islamic jurisprudence had never indulged to any great extent in theorising about the situation of Muslims in countries with non-Muslim majorities. Mawdudi's writing was in some ways a plea not to be left out or left behind. His 'fundamentalist' call might have been partly the outcome of idealism, partly a reflection of anxiety: 'anxiety seems to decrease when one decides to act vigorously in a certain direction', and an unequivocal fundamentalist interpretation of the scripture often makes people 'emotionally strengthened' (McDonough, 1984: 95–96).

Yet Mawdudi was just as opposed to the Muslim League as he was to the Congress Party – for him both were equally secular. What he wanted was not a *Muslim* State but an Islamic State: an Islamic State, he says, is 'an "ideological State", that should be run only by those who believe in the ideology on which it is based [the Quran and the Sunna] and in the Divine Law which it is assigned to administer' (Mawdudi, 1982: 256–257). Consequently Mawdudi directed much of what he wrote between 1937 and 1941 against nationalism and against democracy – in his view, both would lead to the predominance of Indian and/or non-Islamic forces and influences (cf. Metcalf, 1987: 135ff). Mawdudi's solution to the problem of Muslims in India was that they should become better Muslims, and cast off any Indian, Western or secularist ('non-religious', *la dini*, as he called it) influence that might have adhered to them (Adams, 1983: 102–106).

Up to that point, Mawdudi's ideas had been shared by only a very small number of dedicated followers with no clearly identifiable class base. This situation changed as the 'Pakistan movement' (mainly expressing the interests of the multi-ethnic Muslim salariat throughout India), appeared to be succeeding in its aim of establishing a Muslim State in the Indian subcontinent. Mawdudi formed the *Jamaat-e-Islami* in 1941, and subsequently migrated to the new state of Pakistan which was established in 1947.

What concerns the political scientist most about ideas is not so much their logical consistency or intellectual elegance as their popular appeal and social backing. Mawdudi's ideas were to find their main 'social sponsors' only after the Partition, and this – as is often the case in Islamic history – was once more among recent migrants. The partition of the subcontinent and the large-scale repatriation that followed must have been one of the most traumatic events of recent history. 'The *Jamaat* attracted a new following among Urdu-speaking refugees from India, the *muhajirs*, who felt insecure and bitter about India, because of their suffering in the course of their enforced migration.' As Hamza Alavi explains, 'they responded readily to the chauvinistic rhetoric of the *Jamaat*' (Alavi, 1988: 92ff). Soon afterwards, big businessmen and landlords in Pakistan and conservative powers from the Middle East started to support the Jamaat with generous donations because of its value in combating radical and left-wing groups. This function was made physically easier with the incorporation of 'armed thugs, an element that was re-inforced by the repatriation from East Pakistan of members of Al-Badr and As-Shams, its fascist paramilitary organisations, after the liberation of Bangladesh' (ibid.: 95).

Mawdudi further elaborated his ideas within a Pakistan in which the concept of 'Muslim nationalism' was obviously not working. These ideas were to have a marked impact on several fundamentalist groupings all over the Muslim world, and were to become a major source of the doctrine of political Islam. A particular idea that would be widely echoed was his khawarij-inspired concept that total and absolute sovereignty was with God (*al-hakimiyya*), humans only being delegated to implement the holy law, which is far superior to, and far more just than, any political or economic system improvised by man (cf. Mawdudi, 1984: 119ff, 169ff, 217ff, 353ff). Also influential was his emphasis on the Khawarij-Ibn Taimiya concept that what makes a Muslim is not simply acceptance of the 'credo' (*al-shahadatain*) but rather active involvement of oneself in a collective endeavour for 'commanding good and prohibiting evil' (*al-amr bi al-ma'ruf wa al-nahiy 'an al-munkar*), that is to enforce the Islamic moral order on the legislative, political and economic affairs of society (cf. Mawdudi, 1987: 47ff, 111ff, 143ff, 189ff). This is what needs to be done to escape from the current state of *jahiliyya* (total pagan ignorance) in which the contemporary Muslims live.

Mawdudi was indeed quite unorthodox in applying the jahiliyya description (meant originally to characterise the pre-Islamic condition) to contemporary Muslim society. In his view, modern jahiliyya had two sources: a 'traditional' source derived from the practices of all political leaders following Muhammad and the first two caliphs, and a

'Western' source brought into the Muslim world with colonialism and imperialism. This was indeed the main 'theoretical contribution' of Mawdudi, or at least of the 'Indian School',[4] that was subsequently to arouse much controversy, and which specifically influenced the thinking of Sayyid Qutb and several radical Islamic activists ('Imara, 1987: 75ff).

HASAN AL-BANNA AND THE MUSLIM BROTHERS

The Muslim Brotherhood (*Al-Ikhwan al-Muslimun*), established by Hasan al-Banna in 1928, is the parent organisation and/or the main source of inspiration for many fundamentalist organisations in several other countries in addition to Egypt (e.g. Syria, Sudan, Jordan, Kuwait, North Africa, etc.). The movement's leaders may be considered the main initiators of the early formulations of a concept of political Islam in the Arab world.

Born in 1906 in a small Delta town to a family of clerics and artisans, Hasan al-Banna established his first religious society in the Canal zone town of Isma'iliyya, which at the time functioned under the heavy yoke of the British presence. Initially, the organisation was announced as a purely religious and philanthropic society that aimed to spread Islamic morals and good works.

However, the emergence of the Muslim Brothers was part of a general reaction to a number of alarming developments that were engulfing the Muslim world. Not only were the Arabs divided into spheres of influence by the European powers, but the caliphate was abolished in Turkey in 1924 and a conference attempting to restore it failed in 1926. Western influence also appeared to make serious inroads into and encroachments upon the Islamic culture of the region. Not only were openly secularist ideas being propagated by writers such as Salama Musa and Taha Husain, but even some of the Al-Azhar scholars were adopting apparently Western approaches to the analysis of 'Islamic' issues, a trend that reached its most disconcerting point with the publication in 1925 of 'Ali 'Abd al-Raziq's book on Islam and government in which he denied that Islam was in any way concerned with politics (cf. Shamuq, 1981: 29ff).

As a school teacher and gifted orator, al-Banna was able to attract to his movement various members of the local intelligentsia, as well as some artisans, and a few workers from the British camp workshops. Moving to new, humble headquarters in Cairo in 1932, he continued his activity of spreading the message, in regular evening sessions which attracted a majority of artisans and minor merchants, described by one of the Ikhwan leaders (Labib al-Buhi) as people 'with no education and no interest in learning' (Al-Sa'id, 1977: 64).

The society became increasingly interested in public affairs, developing a distinctive conception of the 'comprehensiveness' of Islam which placed it in a contrasting position to both the established clergy and the existing conventional philanthropic charities. As Muhammad al-Ghazali, one of the Ikhwan leaders, remarked, there were in Egypt two Islamic blocks, an official one formed of Al-Azhar personnel, and one formed of the 'Islamic societies' – and the two would never meet. He added that 'Al-Azhar scholars have gone to sleep, and the Muslim society has followed them' (Al-Sa'id, 1977: 57).

There is no doubt that al-Banna, influenced as he was by the ideas of Rashid Rida, had called for a comprehensive and activist Islam. Less clear, however, is the extent to which this activist Islam was to be a specifically 'political' Islam. Richard Mitchell has argued that the ultimate goal of the Muslim Brothers was the creation of an 'Islamic order' (*nizam Islami*) rather than an Islamic State. He takes at face value the view attributed to al-Banna and expressed by his successor in the leadership of the Ikhwan, Hasan al-Hudaibi, and in some writings by leading members of the society (such as 'Abd al-Qadir 'Awda), that the existing constitutional and legal framework of Egypt at the time would, if reformed, satisfy the political requirements of Islam for a 'Muslim State'. From this he infers that 'the precise nature of a Muslim State was not a burning question' for the Muslim Brothers (Mitchell, 1969: 234ff).

It seems to me, however, that in al-Banna's perception, the Islamic State was a significant ingredient of the Islamic order that was aspired to. The fact that there was, as Mitchell puts it, 'a paucity of "official" organization literature about it' can be attributed to a number of reasons. First is the simple fact that conventional Islamic jurisprudence was not particularly rich with regard to matters pertaining to politics and the State. The Ikhwan movement was still fairly young and had not developed its own detailed vision on politics. The Ikhwan leaders probably did not consider the assumption of political power as an imminent possibility; there were more immediate concerns such as the continued British occupation and the rising nationalist movement that required more direct attention. At such an early stage in the Society's formation and development, the tasks of moral reform (*islah al-nufus*) and of agreeing on an Islamic approach and 'methodology' (*minhaj Islami*) must have appeared more appropriate for the requirements of that phase. Too much emphasis on government might also have subjected the Society to even more suspicion on the part of the authorities.

Thus, although the Ikhwan's message was concerned mainly with establishing an 'Islamic order', there is little doubt that an 'Islamic State' was a main ingredient in that order. This was clear in the dictum that eventually was to develop and to become, to this day, the Brothers' slogan: 'God is our objective; the Quran is our constitution; the Prophet is our leader; Struggle is our way; and death for the sake of God is the highest of our aspirations'. Al-Banna was clear in describing his message as an 'Islamic' one, and for him the word 'Islamic' 'had a broad meaning, different from the narrow meaning understood by people – for we believe that Islam is a comprehensive connotation and involves all affairs of life' (al-Banna, 1954: 13). This is Islam in al-Banna's understanding: 'if this is of politics – then it is our politics. If the one who calls for such principles is a politician, then we are – thanks to God – the most established people in politics' (ibid., 45–46). He maintained that the Brothers were prepared to engage in the highest level of struggle (*jihad*) to achieve their ideal. The starting point, however, was unambiguously in the moral sphere, for 'the formation of nations, the education of people, and the realisation of hopes and principles, requires of the nation that strives for them or at least of the group that calls for them, a tremendous *psychological power*' (ibid.: 59 – emphasis added). This is to be supplemented with a clear Islamic methodology (*minhaj*) which, if applied properly, is capable of presenting solutions to all social concerns such as those pertaining to the family, to nationalism, internationalism, socialism, capitalism, Bolshevism, war, the distribution of wealth, relations between the producer and the consumer, and all that relates to such social and political concerns (ibid.: 62–63).

The Ikhwan did not identify themselves as a political party, although they set up their organisation and ran their affairs very much like one: 'we are not a political party, although politics on a foundation of Islam is in the heart of our concept' (ibid.: 26). But politics was only one of the concerns of al-Banna and his society, and – at that stage – possibly not the major concern. Al-Banna defined the Ikhwan as 'a *salafi* call, and Sunnite order, a *Sufi* reality; a political institution, a sports team, a cultural association, an economic company and a social concept' (ibid.: 14–16). In achieving their goals, the Brothers would not necessarily require the government for themselves and would support whoever ruled by a 'Quranic method'. If they could not find such a ruler, then government is one of their [i.e. the Ikhwan's] means, and they will strive to take it away from any government that does not comply with the commands of God. Yet the Ikhwan are more wise and strict than to proceed to the task of government while the souls of the nation are in the condition they are in. A period is required wherein the principles of the Ikhwan will spread and dominate, and the people will learn how to put public interest before private interest. (ibid.: 38–39).

It is thus not the lack of interest in politics that explains the paucity of detailed discussion of matters of government and the State in the pronouncements of Hasan al-Banna and the early Ikhwan, but rather the fact that in their thinking 'personal piety and the good community [were] the conditions' for a good Islamic State (cf. Zubaida, 1989: 33–34). Their more immediate task was to reform souls and to enlighten minds. Government would follow in due course, and even at the early stage of al-Banna, they had a few of its features in mind. This would involve a one-party system that, after completing the process of the nation's independence 'would set the fundamentals for general internal reform. Events would then suggest patterns of organisation, [which should be] inspired by the unity commanded by Islam' (al-Banna, 1954: 49). Further details elaborated on by al-Banna suggest a 'corporatist' type of system inspired by Islamic ethics and grounded in a just 'moral economy' (cf. ibid.: 50–80; Mitchell, 1969: 232–294).

It could be argued that the activities of the Ikhwan acquired more of a political character from around 1938. From that date, they started their weekly *Al-Nadhir*, which on occasions threatened to 'fight any politician or organisation that did not work for the support of Islam and the restoration of its glory'. By now the Ikhwan had more than 300 branches that espoused their ideas (Ramadan, 1982: 27–31). Up till then, however, they had been careful not to antagonise the Palace, which, in fact, appeared to be quite supportive of them as a force capable of checking the popular Wafd party. A conflict with the Egyptian and the British authorities at the beginning of the forties led the Ikhwan to avoid confrontation with the British at any price, while building up their own organisational and para-military capacity. A special 'secretive organ' was established within the movement, and special 'phalanges' were formed, sometimes under the guise of scout organisations. The Ikhwan also built their own companies, factories, schools and hospitals, and infiltrated various organisations, including the trade unions and the armed forces, to such a degree that by the end of the forties they had almost come to represent 'a state within the State' (ibid.: 42–77).

By this time, al-Banna had also escalated the 'terrorist' attacks on Jewish and British interests in Egypt, which inevitably killed or injured many Egyptians. The government was forced to respond by dissolving the Brothers, and the confrontation between the two reached its peak late in 1948 and early in 1949, with the assassination by the Ikhwan of the prime minister, Nuqrashi, and the assassination by the government of the leader of the Ikhwan, al-Banna himself.

Whether one decides to play up or to play down the significance of political violence in defining the general outlook of the Ikhwan, there is no doubt that their activist conception of Islam has had a lasting effect. Hasan al-Banna had, above all, asserted a thesis on Islam's comprehensive and totalitarian character. The 'political' was a significant but, tactically, not an immediate concern. Al-Banna's personal charisma, combined with his 'practical' (survivalist) inclinations, meant that his theoretical contribution would remain rather limited (cf. al-Tilmisani, 1984: 123ff). He was basically a 'teacher' who believed in the efficacy of tutoring his following. It was the disappearance of the charismatic leadership of al-Banna in 1949 and, more specifically, the confrontation between the Ikhwan and the new revolutionary regime in Egypt in the 1950s, which caused the Ikhwan to raise the 'political' to a much higher rank within their order of concerns.

SAYYID QUTB AND HIS DISCIPLES

Whether it was the establishment of an Islamic order or an Islamic State that had initially concerned the Muslim Brothers, the catalyst that turned many of the Ikhwan into a determined movement of political Islam was their confrontation with the Nasserist State, after it had come to power in 1952.

The Muslim Brothers were no strangers to the Free Officers who launched the 1952 coup. Their various contacts with the Officers enabled them to escape the fate of dissolution after the coup, since they were classified as a 'movement' or a 'society' and not as a political party. Many Brothers, including their new 'general guide' (*murshid*) Hasan al-Hudaibi, seem to have hoped that, given the affinity between the two movements, the Free Officers would be prepared to allow the Ikhwan direct participation in government after the Revolution ('Abd al-Halim, 1985: 115–140). When this hope was frustrated, relations between the two forces deteriorated, resulting in a bloody confrontation, repeated imprisonment and severe torture, and it was this confrontational atmosphere that eventually effected a shift in the thinking of the Ikhwan sympathiser Sayyid Qutb, a shift that subsequently was to colour the ideas of most of the regiments of radical political Islam in Egypt, which had set themselves the task of challenging the contemporary Egyptian State as formulated by Nasser and his successors.

Members of the Muslim Brothers existed in most of the political cells that were secretly active within the Egyptian armed forces in the late forties and early fifties. They included Mahmud Labib, A. 'Abd al-Ra'uf, A. 'Ab al-Hayy and Ma'ruf al-Hadari. Anwar al-Sadat belonged to the Ikhwan at some stage, and even Nasser is said to have joined them for a while and to have hidden some of the arms and documents belonging to the Free Officers with members of the Ikhwan. This link led 'Umar al-Tilmisani, leader of the Ikhwan in the seventies and eighties (d. 1986) to claim that it was Hasan al-Banna, the initiator of the Muslim Brothers, who had established the Free Officers movement, and that the Ikhwan had played a leading role in the successful outcome of the Free Officers' assumption of power in July 1952 (al-Mahdawi, 1986: 110; Sayyid-Ahmad, 1985: 31–34; Muru, 1985: 55–59).

Whatever the case might have been, there is no doubt that the Ikhwan had issued a declaration of support for the Free Officers movement, and a number of them had assumed positions in the revolutionary government. Muslim Brothers detainees were released in October 1952, unlike members from other political, popular and trade union organisations. It seems that some Ikhwan leaders had hoped that through their cooperation with the new regime, leftist, secularist and democratic forces would be liquidated, thus paving the way for a greater influence for, and possibly a total takeover of power by, the Ikhwan. The Free Officers might have had a similar objective of relying on the popularity and support of the Ikhwan until they had managed to consolidate themselves in power.

However, confrontation between the two forces was soon to follow. It began with the revolutionary government intervening in a conference held by the Brothers at Cairo University in January 1954. The Brothers retaliated by participating in the mass demonstrations that forced the military regime and its Nasserist leadership to return Muhammad Nagib (the figurehead leader of the revolution) to the presidency a few weeks later. Alarmed by the organisational capability of the Ikhwan in moving the masses, Nasser resorted to proposing a 'deal' with Hasan al-Hudaibi (the Brothers' leader) whereby the

Ikhwan could continue their activities and receive governmental support in return for giving their support to the Nasserist wing against the Nagib wing. This indeed took place during the events of March 1954 with the result that Nasser was confirmed in power.

The Brothers promptly sought a reward for their support, asking for distinct political gains for their movement within the new regime, but without accepting any changes in the nature of their organisation or in the composition of its leadership. This was apparently the point at which each of the two sides realised that the other was using it tactically for its own purposes. The rift was already widening, and culminated in a bloody confrontation between the two forces in October 1954. An attempt made on Nasser's life on this date in the Manshiyya square in Alexandria was blamed by the regime on the Ikhwan. The latter maintained all along that this was an act staged by the regime to provide an excuse to liquidate the Brothers and, from then on, this perception of the 'treason' of the revolution towards its previous allies was to represent an important element in forming the intellectual and psychological attitude of the Ikhwan towards the Nasserist experiment and the Nasserist State. The attempted assassination was followed by extensive arrests and the imprisonment of tens of thousands of Brothers (including Sayyid Qutb), who were ridiculed in the military 'People's Courts' and tortured in detention, while fifty of their leaders were executed and hundreds detained for years without court judgements.

In spite of the persecution to which the detained Ikhwan were subjected, a number of their remaining leaders gathered and formed study groups to analyse the nature of the Nasserist State and to consider ways of confronting it. Their ideas at that time 'were a mixture of Hasan al-Banna, Sayyid Qutb, al-Mawdudi and Malik bin Nabi' (Ra'if, 1985: 235). In 1959–1960, the organisation resumed its activity with a new committee of five in the leadership. They met regularly in the house of the Muslim sister Zainab al-Ghazali, discussing the corruption of the government and the evil of its president. The committee agreed to delegate the influential 'Abd al-Fattah Isma'il to select a suitable man to lead the movement, and he chose Sayyid Qutb, whose writings 'had found their way to the Organisation by being smuggled from the prison . . . until they eventually came to form the main feature of the Muslim Brothers' thought' (ibid. 243).

Sayyid Qutb was born in 1906 in the village of Musha in the austere province of Asyut. Like many others he emigrated to the capital to seek further education and employment. He was not particularly amused by Cairo and thought that below the surface trappings a sick, ugly and miserable face was revealed (Diyab, 1988: 36). He worked as a teacher and on occasions became culturally and morally confused, as for instance when he started to advocate the concept of nudism (ibid.: 94). He also became increasingly sensitive to issues of poverty and injustice, publishing in 1949 a book on social justice in Islam, and in 1951 another on capitalism and the Islamic struggle (S. Qutb, new ed., 1958; 1951). He visited the United States for training in 1948 and was not at all impressed by what he saw; indeed, his American visit seems to have sparked in him the desire to seek sources of cultural and moral authenticity.

Until a few months before the 1952 revolution Qutb was describing himself merely as 'a friend of the Islamic call', and was sometimes critical of the positions adopted by certain Muslim Brothers. He joined the Muslim Brothers movement only in 1953; arrested with the leaders of the Ikhwan in 1954, he was sentenced to fifteen years of hard labour. Because of his poor health most of this sentence was spent in hospital, where he was able to concentrate on what became his increasingly radicalised writing; this was systematically smuggled to other Muslim Brothers still outside prison.

During this time, 'Abd al-Fattah Isma'il frequently travelled abroad to mobilise the forces of Brothers who had escaped arrest. 'Money and arms' were considered essential for achieving the Brothers' objectives of 'defending themselves'. Ikhwan meetings occurred in which the importance of military training was reiterated and the possibility of assassinating political leaders was discussed. In the meantime, in 1964, Qutb was freed from prison, ostensibly for health reasons, though his release may have served as a trap to enable the regime to recognise certain Ikhwan leaders. Certainly there was a further wave of arrests in August 1965 that resulted in the detention of most of the members of the new Ikhwan organisation on charges of conspiracy to overthrow the regime. A number of the leaders were executed, including the ailing Sayyid Qutb.

This second tragedy of the Ikhwan irrevocably confirmed Qutbian thought as the predominant influence over the movement, especially as its author had died as a 'martyr' at the hands of the regime. This influential thinking, consisting mainly of Qutb's new ideas, emerged from a suffocating prison atmosphere that was conducive both to feelings of anger and to an inclination to be abstract and simple. Transformed by the painful experience of his imprisonment, his thinking had become markedly different in orientation and in tone from his earlier literary and social writings. Assembling elements from the sub-continental Islamic thought of Mawdudi and Nadwi (governed as it was by a desperate 'siege mentality'),[5] Sayyid Qutb then reproduced such ideas in a more extreme, single-minded and action-oriented fashion that was deeply imbued with his feelings of frustration and anger towards the revolution. The 'politics of despair' had now acquired a 'religious' theory.

For it should not be forgotten that Sayyid Qutb was no outsider to the revolution. He had met Nasser before the coup, and pinned great hopes on his movement. Indeed he had cooperated directly with the revolution from the beginning and had an office at the headquarters of the Revolutionary Command Council, where he was in charge of restructuring school curricula for the new regime. He was also later appointed as secretary-general to the Liberation Rally which had been announced in 1953 as the regime's first experiment with the single political organisation formula. Qutb also knew Kamal al-Din Husain, the Free Officer with Ikhwan sympathies who proposed him as a Minister of Education and who required the teaching of his nationalist hymns in government schools. Indeed Qutb's support for the revolution was so strong that he sent an open letter to Muhammad Nagib asking the latter to establish a 'just dictatorship' in the land through the revolution (Hammuda, 1987B: 107–115; Diyab, 1988: 98–102).

Thus, when the Free Officers and the Muslim Brothers fell out with each other, Qutb's frustration at the mutual accusations of treason and despair over the regime's execution, torture and imprisonment of the Ikhwan must have been shattering. The confrontation between the two forces developed not as a religious disagreement, for example over interpretations, but as a political struggle over power. The defeat of the Ikhwan at a point where they had at last felt themselves close to participation in government, must have been psychologically devastating, especially to those like Sayyid Qutb who were so closely associated with the Free Officers.

In the painful confines of detention, Qutb's bitterness was to intensify and his hatred and detestation of the Nasserist state was to grow. He saw in it everything that was bad: it was both a disguised 'American regime' that nevertheless applied an ideology 'originating in the socialism of Karl Marx', and it held youth camps dominated by 'Communist directives and by moral degeneration' (text of the court trial in Hammuda, 1987B: 172). On a general ideological level, the detention of Qutb and his colleagues was to lead to an overall revision of the movement's thought: 'the nucleus had been there, but with the ferment of events, its major part had now grown into a hatred for the State and for the regime' (Diyab, 1988: 103–104).

The Qutbian ideas that have come to influence most of the contemporary movements of political Islam are mainly the ones to be found in the writings he produced between his two imprisonments (Haddad, 1982: 226). These include in particular: *Hadha al-din* (This Religion), *Al-Mustaqbal li hadha al-din* (The Future is for this Religion), and most specifically *Ma'alim fi al-tariq* (Signposts along the Way; first published in 1964). The key concept in this later Qutbian discourse (especially that of the *Signposts*) is undoubtedly that of *jahiliyya* (total pagan ignorance). Inspired partly by Ibn Taimiya but most specifically by Mawdudi, Sayyid Qutb extracted this concept from any historical or geographical context, giving it a universal validity that covers all contemporary societies, Muslim ones included:

> We are today in a jahiliyya similar to that contemporaneous to Islam or worse. Every thing around us is a jahiliyya: people's perceptions and beliefs, habits and customs, the sources of their culture, arts and literature, and their laws and legislations. Even much of what we think of as being Islamic culture, Islamic sources or Islamic philosophy and thought is in fact the making of this jahiliyya. (S. Qutb, 1985: 21–22)

Around the same time that the *Signposts* was published, Sayyid Qutb's brother Muhammad Qutb published another book with the specific aim of elaborating this concept of the 'twentieth century jahiliyya' (cf. M. Qutb, new edn 1981). According to the thesis of the two Qutb brothers, which is echoed by all subsequent neo-fundamentalists, a complete epistemological break has to be effected with modern civilisation if Muslims are to be real Muslims. In order to arrive at this conclusion, modern civilisation has been divorced in their analysis from its intellectual sources, and a simplistic reading of its shortcomings and drawbacks is offered, taken mainly from Abu al-Hasan al-Nadwi's critique of Western civilisation (which in turn is based on the reading of a few basically conservative and pessimistic European critics of this civilisation) (cf. al-Nadwi, 1977; 1984). Modern culture (capitalist and socialist alike) is abridged into a few simplistic categories that can be easily understood by people with modest education and that show it as being basically materialist and anti-human (especially anti-Muslim). Furthermore, the critique of modern civilisation is not presented as a thesis that may be discussed and debated, to raise consciousness of the self and of the other, but rather as a militant ideology that does not lend itself to discussion because it is premised on a sincere devotion to a divine method and design (al-Sayyid, 1988: 345–354).

The way out of such jahiliyya, as prescribed by Sayyid Qutb, is also simple: it is a declaration of the total sovereignty and rulership of God, otherwise known as the concept of *al-hakimiyya*:

> To declare divinity for God alone . . . means a full revolt against human rulership in all its shapes and forms, systems and arrangements . . . It means the destroying of the kingdom of man to establish the kingdom of God on earth . . . the wresting of power from the hands of its human usurpers to return it to God alone; the supremacy of divine law alone and the cancellation of human laws. (S. Qutb, 1985: 81–83)

This is, of course, originally a kharijite concept, although again it is more directly derived from Mawdudi and given a more extreme applicability by Qutb. To achieve this goal, the *jama'a* (an organic, dynamic community inspired by the early Companions of the Prophet) should be re-formed in isolation from all polluting influences and according to a purely Islamic method (*minhaj*) and culture, that is purged of any non-Islamic influences such as those of patriotism, nationalism and suchlike (cf. Diyab, 1988: 110–152; Haddad, 1983: 81–93).

Strongly affected by such ideas, the imprisoned Ikhwan, in their pain and isolation and with the ever-present memory of their martyrs, were to weave an alternative project to Nasserism – indeed, as Hafiz Diyab explains, a 'counter project' which reflects the maturation of the contradictions between the Brotherhood and Nasserism. The Qutbian discourse had achieved its full ideological structure in its capacity as a counter-discourse to the Nasserist project. Thus, whereas the Nasserist project was historically required to reconstruct authority and to build the State, the Qutbian counter-discourse was premised on the solidarity of belonging to the divine design, and on challenging the human rule that aims at reproducing the world system. In other words, as Diyab succinctly puts it, if the Nasserist project had sanctified the political, the counter-discourse of Sayyid Qutb was to politicise the divine (Diyab, 1988: 155–178). The Qutbian discourse is therefore essentially political, pertaining to thoughts and actions that deal with the State and society. As Qutb expressed it, the establishment of the kingdom of God on earth will be achieved only through struggle (*jihad*).[6]

> It will not be achieved merely by teaching and preaching, for those who inflict the yoke on the necks of the people and who usurp the authority of God on earth will not concede their position through such explanation and sermonising. (S. Qutb, 1985: 82–83)

Yet the Qutbian discourse is political only in a rather unusual sense. It tends to influence people's thoughts and actions in a psychologically tense way that creates in the individual not the ability to reconstruct reality, but rather the dream of breaking with that reality. It is a position of utter refusal to enter into any dialectical relationship with objective realities or to prepare any societal alternatives to the status quo. Rather, the task is to obliterate the existing order completely, and it is only then that the opportunity for applying options and solutions may emerge. Yet, at least in theory, this obliteration of the existing social order cannot be achieved except by confronting the State and fighting it (Diyab, 1988: 172–178). The later Qutb was particularly careful to emphasise that the priority was to remove the non-Islamic order and to establish the Islamic society, after which one could worry about the detailed laws and systems of such a society:

> This is the correct order for the steps of the Islamic method . . . It may seem to some that the presentation of the fundamentals of the Islamic order – even of Islamic legislation – to the people would make the task of the call more easy and would fondly attract people towards this religion; [but] this is an illusion generated by misguided haste. (S. Qutb, 1985: 46–47)

But why did the political-ness of the Qutbian discourse express itself in the form of a total epistemological break with, and psychological emigration from, the existing social order, rather than in an attempt to outline the features of an alternative project? Obviously the 'psychology' of the Muslim Brothers at that stage was crucially important. As we have noted, to come so close to power and then to be suddenly deprived of the fruits of a project to which they believed they had generously contributed – must have generated in the Ikhwan a deep sense of betrayal, frustration and anger, feelings that the imprisonment, torture and execution of their members could only have nurtured and intensified. Yet the frustration of Qutb and other Ikhwan leaders must also have been at least partly a disillusionment with themselves, because, the religious terminology apart, the Nasserist project had many features to which Qutb and the Ikhwan had previously subscribed – the concept of social justice, the corporatist alliance of social classes, the one-party formula, and several other aspects. Nasser had in some ways appropriated their project for himself – and a few years into the sixties it did not seem to be working very well, either. The Islamists had no 'social' project apart from the corporatist one; now it was being applied by their enemy, and it no longer appeared as attractive. The immediate task had therefore to be to break completely with that project and with all its possible intellectual and political sources, and to transmit the whole situation to the Almighty in the hope that, with His grace, something better might eventually emerge.

The construction of the Nasserist State and the reformulation of the Qutbian discourse undoubtedly coincided closely in terms of time. Yet can one claim with any confidence that the two were causally linked? This is a difficult question to answer, for it would be an exaggeration to suggest that the Nasserist State alone was responsible for the swelling current of political Islam. The Muslim Brothers had indeed emerged and demonstrated their interest in politics well before the revolution, while the moment for the dynamic flourishing of political Islam actually occurred under the Infitah policy of Sadat. Yet it seems fairly reasonable to suggest that the emergence of the Qutbian trend was at least in part a reflection of the Nasserist State's failure to deal with ideological and political movements. Indeed the appeal of the Qutbian thesis must be viewed as a symptom of an ideological and political vacuum which had particularly affected the younger generations under the Nasserist State. Qutb's formulations were thus an attempt at providing an ideological response to the Nasserist project, a project that emphasised State building but lacked intellectual and political fulfilment. Yet the Qutbian trend was in turn a mirror image of the Nasserist project, revolving similarly around the State and regarding the act of government as the main approach to changing society. Unlike Nasserism, however, Qutbism derived its legitimacy not from any claim to 'revolutionary achievements', but rather from allegiance to supreme divine values that were considered far superior to any attempt at human improvisation.

Last but not least was the defeat of the Nasserist State in the Arab–Israeli war of 1967, which was to enable the Qutbian trend to gain greater influence and to claim an indirect victory against the 'enemies of God'. From then on, Qutb's ideas were to represent the main intellectual influence on the younger, militant Muslim Brothers, and indeed to shape the entire thinking of a whole regiment of political Islamists who have come to be known as the Qutbists, *Al-Qutbiyyun*[7] (Mardini, 1984: 139).

THE JIHADISTS AND OTHER NEO-FUNDAMENTALISTS

The ideas of Sayyid Qutb have exercised the strongest influence on the ideology and the discourse of the radical Islamists of the seventies and the eighties. Almost all these Islamists agree on total sovereignty being to God (not to the 'people', to 'law'. . . . or whatever), and all of them share a strong rejection of existing social and political realities because these do not live up to that principle either in theory or in practice.

There are various differences, of course, but they should not obscure the ideological affinity and the mutual exchange of members among the various neo-fundamentalist groups. Thus, for example, whereas Al-Jihad reserves the act of *takfir* (i.e. to judge someone as being infidel) for deviant rulers only, not for the society at large, Al-Takfir wa al-Hijra believes that the entire contemporary Muslim society is infidel. In a monograph by Shukri Mustafa, the executed leader of Takfir, entitled *The Caliphate*, he diagnoses the problem and pre-scribes the solution in the following words:

> All that is seen before you now on earth of men and women, of money, soldiers, arms and ploys, of constitutions and laws, wars and conciliations . . . represents a front for God's enemies, led by evil on earth [*al-taghut*] . . . Within this reality a man will come who, together with the believers who would follow him, will erase this reality, fight the infidel entity and establish the Islamic body. (in Tawfiq, 1977: 170)

Operational differences consequently emerge as well, so that Al-Takfir is more inclined to engage in long-term ideological training and socio-organisational preparation, whereas Al-Jihad is more inclined to engage in direct and immediate activism, with the intention of infiltrating political and military institutions. However, the ideas and the recruitment population (of the disaffected educated youth) are so similar that it is believed, for example, that many ex-Takfir members had joined the Jihad organisation when the former was being harassed by the Egyptian authorities during the late seventies.

A reading of the monograph *Al-Farida al-gha'iba* (The Absent Commandment), attributed to Muhammad 'Abd al-Salam Faraj, would make it clear that the objective of the Jihad organisation is more centred around the immediate 'establishment of an Islamic State', since this is conceived of as the only method possible for 'returning Islam to this community' (Faraj, 1982: 8–9). This objective should be achieved via *jihad* (militant struggle by all methods, especially military fighting), *jihad* being in the view of Faraj (one of the leading militants who was executed for the assassination of Sadat) a commandment that Muslims everywhere have ignored or overlooked (see also Youssef, 1985; and Jansen, 1986).

The fighting should be launched in particular against rulers who stand in the way of creating that state by their failure to apply God's laws. Such rulers are apostates who are just as infidel as the Tatars were in Ibn Taimiya's day, and it is the duty of all Muslims to fight them (Faraj, 1982: 9–14). Faraj speaks with disdain about the idea of working through religious and philanthropic societies to persuade people to live up to Islam: 'Is the Islamic State going to be established by such works and pieties? The immediate answer is without doubt: No' (ibid.: 14). The Islamic State can only be established through struggle, *jihad*, against oneself, against the devil, against the infidels and against the hypocrites. And this struggle to build the Islamic State should start immediately and not be delayed for fear of failure, nor should it be divided into distinct escalating stages but must be launched in one big strike, provided that the leadership can be entrusted to those who are up to it and that good planning for the struggle is achieved (ibid.: 21–28). Despots should be removed 'by the sword', while 'confrontation and blood' is the way for establishing the Islamic State: without delay, without compromise.

As is often the case, Faraj has achieved his extremely militant formulation through a process of selective interpretation of the original texts. Only the militant verses of the Quran are quoted, only the 'combatitive' definitions of *jihad* are adopted and only the most stern jurists are referred to. Ibn Taimiya is obviously the Jihadists' main inspiration but even here they often extract passages out of their proper context, misunderstand the terms and overlook what they do not like. For example, and contrary to established opinion, they almost equate sin or deviance (*ma'siya*) with infidelity (*kufr*) and apostasy (*ridda*). They also overlook Ibn Taimiya's praise of the role of the Mamluk rulers in defending the 'abode of Islam', even though – like the Tatar – they also applied the secular *yasa* law among themselves ('Imara, 1983: 55–95).

It is obviously the angry state of mind of the Jihad leaders, inflamed by a whole range of moral and social grievances that were only aggravated by the implementation of the infitah policy, which pushed the author of *The Absent Commandment* into such a very selective assembly of ideas in such an unorthodox way, but with the unmistakable emphasis on the importance of *the political factor* for re-creating any truly Islamic society.[8] This is made all the more clear, as one relates such theoretical debates to the more concrete critique of the Egyptian order incorporated in the Jihad's clandestine monograph entitled *Muhakamat al-nizam al-siyasi al-misri* (A Trial of the Egyptian Political System) (cf. Huwaidi, 1987: 230ff).

Some of these themes are reiterated by one of the neo-fundamentalists in a recent book on the so-called 'contemporary jahiliyya' ('A. Yasin, 1986: 163–165). The contemporary society in general and the Egyptian system more specifically are defined as pagan because in them 'servitude to God' is not absolute. Egypt is Muslim in name, but she is still rather attached to her previous Christianity, and she has become, since 1875, too faithful to her secular laws, which are of French or Roman origin (ibid.: 41–44).

'Abd al-Jawwad Yasin corroborates the Mawdudi–Qutb thesis that the Muslim's belonging and allegiance should be to his religion alone. Any patriotic or nationalist loyalty is therefore regarded as pagan (ibid.: 53–64; 173–183). He consequently condemns the Egyptian Constitution for proclaiming equality between Muslims and non-Muslims, and he follows Mawdudi and Qutb in adopting an exceptionally harsh position towards Christian citizens:

> Under an Islamic State, there is no escape [for the Christians] from the *jizya*, no participation in government, no relying on them in defence or war. Rather, they should always be in a state that makes them feel the strength of Islam, its grandeur and supremacy, [as well as] its goodness, generosity and tolerance; that is a state that would push them – on the whole – to enter Islam. (ibid.: 59)

What is the way towards achieving such a purely Islamic society where absolute sovereignty is for God alone? The answer is unequivocal. Internationally, it is '*jihad*', and just in case somebody may think this to be only 'ideological', he adds 'and conquest' (ibid.: 34). Domestically, the real Islamic society cannot be achieved without a 'State' of its own:

> Islam is a State. . . . It is a religion of a State, or of a community ruled by a certain authority . . . that spares no effort to enforce the stipulated rulings. . . . The Islamic call today should not turn its back on this basic pillar of Islam, it may not postpone it or circumvent it . . . For it cannot be said that Islam is established unless it takes the form of a State. (ibid.: 163–165)

The fundamentalists have thus completed the circle. From calling for an Islamic order, they proceeded to condemn the existing society and its rulers for not being purely Islamic, and then concluded that the only way out is to establish an Islamic State through military struggle. The politicisation of religion has now been made complete.

AYATULLAH KHOMEINI AND THE IRANIAN REVOLUTION

Iran has witnessed the only contemporary experiment in putting the ideas of political Islam into practice – hence its extreme intellectual and political significance. Since this book is concerned mainly with the Arab world, no attempt will be made here either to locate Khomeini's ideas within the intricate debates on the nature of government in Shi'i thought, or to give a systematic analysis of the causes and developments of the Iranian revolution. Rather we are mainly interested (a) in finding out the extent to which Khomeini's theory of government might, like all other theories of political Islam, be a novel rather than a traditional theory; and (b) in discovering what kind of general appeal Khomeini's formulations may find among political Islamists in the Arab world.

Hamid Algar suggests that the Islamic revolution of Iran

> differs from other events of the present century that have been given that designation by being firmly rooted in history. Far from being a radical break with the essential and profound developments of the Iranian nation, it is, on the contrary, a continuation and fruition of long years of political, spiritual and intellectual development. (Algar, 1983: 39)

While this may be true in a very general sense, it would be quite mistaken to argue that the form of 'Islamic government' pertaining in Iran today and greatly influenced by Khomeini's ideas, is in any major sense traditional or conventional.

While the idea that the *faqih* (jurisconsult) has a right to act as a political ruler is not entirely new to Shi'i political theory, Khomeini's theory of the 'guardianship of the jurisconsult' (*wilayat-i faqih*) does, at the very least, 'represent an unexpected revival of an old, dormant theme' (Enayat, 1986: 163). Khomeini's doctrine is obviously predicated on a belief in the existence of an Islamic form of the State, a belief which has been advocated by other fundamentalists such as Rashid Rida and A. Mawdudi. There is nothing specifically Shi'ite or Khomeinist about this belief that an Islamic state is necessary and possible.

> [Khomeini's] most daring contribution to the modern debate on the Islamic State is his insistence that the essence of such a State is not so much its constitution, or the commitment of its rulers to comply with the *Shari'a*, but the special quality of its leadership. He thinks

that this special quality can be provided only by the faqihs. (ibid.: 164–167)

Khomeini in fact suggests that, with the obvious exception of the privilege of receiving the divine revelation, all the other responsibilities and powers of the Prophet have been devolved on the ulama after the disappearance of the Twelfth Imam. Put so categorically, Khomeini's theory constitutes a radical departure from the classical Shi'i view of government. He did not simply retrieve an old belief system but rather he brought about 'a re-interpreted, ideologized conception of the old system' (Bayat, 1983: 50).

Khomeini did not 'make' the Iranian revolution, nor was he its initial ideologue ('Ali Shari'ati holds this latter position) (Abrahamian, 1988: 289–297). Yet the transformation of Khomeini's political theory from a conventional 'advisory' one to an innovative action-oriented one did not take place in isolation from the developments that paved the way for the revolution in Iran. Indeed, his most renowned lectures on 'Islamic government' were delivered after his (and the ulamas') confrontation with the Shah and while he was languishing in forced exile in Iraq. This is not to suggest that Khomeini's theory was produced as a direct blueprint for a revolution against the Shah, for even as late as the summer of 1978, neither he nor his followers predicted an early removal of the Shah or a government of Iran by the religious leaders (Bill, 1982B: 31; Keddie, 1988B: 307). Yet, as we know, Khomeini's ideas acquired their importance from his eventual undisputed leadership over the revolution and the incorporation of his theory into the Constitution of the Islamic Republic of Iran.

Khomeini was born in provincial Khumain in 1902, and received his religious education in Arak and Qum; his first tract of a political nature, entitled *Kashf al-asrar* (Revealing the Secrets), was produced in 1943. He recommended a traditional advisory stance towards government: 'Bad government is better than no government. We have never attacked the Sultanate; if we criticized, it was a particular king, and not kingship that we criticized' (Fischer, 1983: 166–167]. By 1960, Khomeini was claiming the legacy of the Iranian Constitution (of 1906) for the ulama, and by the seventies he was arguing that monarchy was altogether incompatible with Islam (ibid.). Such changes in his position developed in large measure as a response to events that were taking place in Pahlavi Iran. M. Reza Shah's attempts to further centralise and modernise the monarchy and to speed up the industrialisation of the country encroached upon the financial, educational and social prerogatives of the clergy. Conflict occurred over local elections in 1962 and over land policies in 1963, and the ulama, especially Khomeini, responded vigorously with denunciations of the ruling family, social corruption and American patronage. Khomeini was arrested and subsequently exiled for a period of nearly fifteen years (during which time his elder son was assassinated), returning eventually to Iran in 1979 as the triumphant leader of the revolution.

The revolution was the outcome of a complex and painful process of rapid and uneven economic development. The main reason why it occurred was that 'conflicts generated in capitalist development intersected with resilient institutions and popular attitudes which resisted the transformation process' (Halliday, 1988: 39). Although the opposition forces were formed of a broad coalition of 'modern' as well as of pre-capitalist or pre-industrial sectors, Islam had come to play a major and growing mobilisational role in the process. Islam was the only force within the civil society that the Shah had not managed to crush, and it was thus able to provide the organisation and ideology that all revolutions need (ibid.: 39–49). Furthermore, the combination of modern and traditional, and indeed of 'leftist' and 'rightist', that was uniquely provided by the Khomeini discourse, was particularly suited to the articulated formation of the Iranian society, and therefore accounted for the initial success of the revolution (compare ibid.: 54–57).[9]

What are the features of this unique combination of 'modern' and 'traditional' that Khomeini provided? It should be remembered, to start with, that Khomeini's theory of *wilayat-i faqih*, which he developed in a series of lectures delivered at Najaf in Iraq in 1970, could not – by his own admission – be conclusively established by textual demonstration from the Hadith. Rather, he argued that it was logically self-evident from the nature of Islam. It could be supported by the examples of the Prophet and the imams, and through the joint consideration of a series of Hadith, none of which individually is unambiguous, but taken together would, in his view, constitute a clear position (Fischer, 1983: 157). For example, he considers the various financial levies required by Islam and particularly the large *khums* (one-fifth) levy required by the Shi'i jurists 'from the largest ship owner and the smallest vegetable peddler' alike. He then surmises that such a large income could not be meant simply for feeding the poor or supporting people with blessed ancestry (*sadah*). Rather it is meant 'to secure the expenditures of a great sovereign State', a function requiring a complex process of coordination that should be performed by the Imam and his government (Khumaini, 1979: 29–31; 1986: 27–29). Thus, both the 'obligatoriness' of Islamic government and the requirement that the jurisconsult should become the guardian of such a government are mainly predicated on the 'logic of Islam' as understood by Khomeini. One method he used was for the argument over *ulu al-'amr* (the Quranic formula in Surat al-Nisa' pertaining to 'those who are in charge'), to be merged with the discussion over the formula of *wilayat-i faqih*, thus extending the political jurisdiction of the guardian jurisconsult (cf. Fischer, 1983: 167). The important point to observe is that by shifting the emphasis from the shari'a to the jurisconsult, any act of rulership that the latter might deem appropriate could then be defined as being 'Islamic'.

With the instalment of Khomeini as leader of the revolution, this improvisation of his was to transcend the world of theory and to be incorporated into the Islamic Constitution of Iran passed in 1979. It is referred to in article II and more specifically in article V:

> In the absence of the mahdi imam (may God hasten his arrival) the guardianship over the affairs of the community shall be charged to the just faqih, who is pious, knowledgeable about the times and courageous; an administrator and a manager; known by the majority of the masses, who will accept his leadership. If no faqih can achieve this majority, a leader, or a leadership council composed of faqihs meeting all the requirements, will shoulder this responsibility. (Islamic Republic of Iran, 1979: 22)

It seems however that the Constitution did not entitle the faqih to as many powers as Khomeini would have liked. As he expressed in an interview:

> The Constitution makes some provision for the principle of the governance of the *faqih*. In my opinion, it is deficient in this regard. The religious scholars have more prerogatives in Islam than are specified in the Constitution, and the gentlemen in the Assembly of Experts stopped short of the ideal in their desire not to antagonize the intellectuals. (Khomeini, 1985: 342)

The end result of such a shifting of emphasis from the shari'a to the jurisconsult has been, in practice, to give precedence to the political, blending both religious and secular concepts and practices in a way that can still claim an Islamic legitimacy. Islamic concepts such as *mustazafin* (those made weak) and *mustakbirin* (those making themselves haughty) are imbued with modern social meanings such as those of the 'oppressed' and the 'oppressor'. A traditional term such as *maktabi*, originally meaning 'textual' or 'bookish', is now used to mean 'according to the book' and is used as a device to exclude anyone who does not adhere to Khomeini's interpretation. Likewise concepts such as 'Westoxification' (originally used by Jalal al-Ahmad) or 'alienation' (more typical of 'Ali Shari'ati) become part of the repertoire of the Islamic republic's vocabulary once they are used by Khomeini in his speeches (cf. Fischer, 1983: 168–169).

On the other hand, 'secular' institutions such as the 'republic', the 'constitution', the 'cabinet' and the 'parliament' *(majlis)* are incorporated in what is taken to be Islamic. Sami Zubaida has argued convincingly that

> Khomeini's 'fundamentalism' is problematic in that while it draws on traditional sources and forms of reasoning, it reaches very novel conclusions, and that these conclusions are only possible and plausible if we add the assumption (implicit in Khomeini's work) of a modern nation-state and its peculiar form of politics. (Zubaida, 1989: 3ff)

The 'Islamic' forms used in Iran today 'are not revivals or continuities with historical instances but quite novel creations'. These in turn are intermingled with forms more typical of modern nation-states. Thus, for example, there is a duality in the Constitution between the popular will (article VI) and the principle of the guardianship of the jurisconsult which gives 'sweeping, almost arbitrary powers to the ruling faqih'.[10] Popular sovereignty is embodied in parliament, but its legislative powers are subject to the approval of the faqih and the 'Council of Guardians' (half its members appointed by Khomeini and half by the *majlis*) in line with Islamic principles. Additionally, although the Constitution states that the Islamic shari'a is the basis for all legislation, in practice many of the civil law codes survive from the previous regime and are administered by civil *(madani)* courts. The element of the Republic that has been most 'Islamicised' is the political field and its personnel: 'after defeating, banishing or subordinating their opponents and rivals, the Islamic Republic became basically a government by clergy'. Zubaida concludes that the Iranian case indicates that the Islamic elements of the Republic fit in very well with the nation-state model, both in terms of state organisation and of the structure of the political arena and its discourses (ibid.: 3–7).

A further testament to the 'novelty' of Khomeini's ideologised Islam is the fact that there is no *marji' al-taqlid* (the highest traditional juristic authority) who is prepared to associate himself with the regime, and that several of such high jurists have actually criticised the regime's practices (Katouzian, 1989: 10–11). Khomeini described such critics as 'fossilised clerics', 'promoters of American Islam' and 'enemies of the Prophet'. As Homa Katouzian suggests, the tone of these descriptions is strangely reminiscent of the Shah's description of the scholars as 'bearded idiots' (ibid.: 12). Significant disagreements among the jurists and the Islamic ideologues continue over the extent to which the religious leadership should be involved in the running of the State and also over specific public policies espoused by the Khomeinists, especially with regard to the power of the State over the rights of private property.

It was in the context of such disagreements and the endless wranglings between the Cabinet and the Council of Experts over them, that the primacy of the 'political' in Khomeini's concept of Islamic government was to become crystal clear, with his issuing of the controversial proclamations of December 1987–January 1988 concerning the powers of the Islamic State. These culminated in a letter from Khomeini to the president of the Republic, Khamini'i, in which he wrote:

> Your interpretation of what I have said, to mean that it [simply] signifies that the government has power [only] within the Commandments of God, is entirely contrary to what I had intended.
>
> I should point out that government (which is a branch of the Absolute Guardianship of the Prophet . . .) is one of the primary rules of Islam, and that it has priority over all subsidiary rules, even including [those governing] prayers, fasting and Hajj.
>
> The [Islamic] government can unilaterally break [even] those contracts which it has made with the people on the basis of shari'a rules, whenever the contract may be contrary to the expedience or interest (*maslaha*) of the country and Islam. It can also stop any activity – be it spiritual or temporal – whose continuation would be contrary to the expedience or interest of Islam, for as long as this is the case. (in Katouzian, 1989: 15–16)

Thus Khomeini has carried his theory of the guardianship of the jurisconsult to its logical conclusion, emphasising that his guardianship (now analogous to that of the Prophet) is absolute, even if it contradicts the stipulations of the shari'a. It is now the government that is supreme, not the shari'a; the State, not the ideology. As tends to follow with all revolutions, this was probably part of a process of trying to expand the 'autonomy of the State' (compare Halliday, 1988: 62, n.36). Once the Communist party, for example, takes precedence over the Marxist ideology, it is the 'State' that consolidates itself, not the revolution. In its initial stages, Khomeini's theory might have fulfilled a certain function of 'expressing the exasperations' of certain social classes while at the same time seeking a number of 'universalistic values' (Fischer, 1983: 170–171). With the 'revolution' firmly in power, Khomeini's more clearly articulated theory and the criticism it has generated reflect not so much a class conflict as 'a disagreement about the nature and extent of the power of a state which does not depend for its legitimacy – and much of its income – on the social classes' (Katouzian, 1989: 22; 1981).

What is the likelihood of a wider impact for Khomeini's ideas on other parts of the Muslim world, and especially the Arab countries? There are, of course, various assessments of the extent of Iran's influence over Islamic movements in various Arab countries. Although Iran's Islamic revolutionaries do undoubtedly exert an influence among the Shi'i communities of Lebanon, Iraq, Bahrain and Kuwait, the dominant opinion, especially in the West and among conservative Arab and Muslim governments, has tended to exaggerate the extent of Iran's ideological and political influence in the Muslim world at large (Hunter, 1988: 730–749; Bill, 1982A: 29–45). Whatever the case may be, it is the likely intellectual influence of Khomeini's ideas and of the Iranian revolution that concerns us most in this context.

To start with, it should be emphasised that the success of the Iranian revolution was received most favourably in the Arab world, since it represented for many people both a defeat of the unpopular Shah and a victory over Western hegemony. It was through the revolution that intellectuals in the Arab world came to learn of Khomeini's ideas on political Islam. For the Islamists in particular, the success of the revolution meant that an Islamic revolution was a real possibility, not just a far-fetched dream. Although the general popularity of the revolution waned following accounts of a reign of terror in Iran and with the eruption and continuation of the Iran–Iraq war, some of the Iranian religio-political terminology continues to leave its imprint on the writings and parlance of the Islamists in the Arab world; e.g. words such as *mustad'afun*, *mustakbirun*, *ifsad*, *taghut*, etc.

On a more specifically intellectual level it can be argued that Khomeini's theory has generally reinforced the case for political Islam. Yet the theory's Shi'i aspects, as well as its specifically Khomeinist touches, obstruct the way in which the theory is able to exert a detailed influence on the discourse of political Islam in Sunni societies. Doctrinally, there are significant differences between the Shi'i and the Sunni traditions with regard to the subject of leadership and rule (*imama*). Whereas for the Shi'is it is one of the fundamentals (*usul*) of the belief, for the Sunnis it is merely one of the branches (*furu'*) of jurisprudence. Thus, although Sunni and Shi'i scholars may agree on rejecting all political theories that would trace the origin of the (Islamic) State to the family, to power, or to social contract, the Sunnis would try to deduce the Islamic State from the shari'a, whereas the Shi'is would lay emphasis on regarding 'the State [as] a Prophetical phenomenon; a continuation and escalation of the work that the Prophet had started at a certain stage of the life of humanity' (cf. al-Sadr, 1986: 51–53). This is obviously what Khomeini meant when he increasingly spoke of the 'pure Muhammadan Islam' (*Islam-e nabi Muhammadi*) and when he stated that government was 'a branch of the Absolute Guardianship of the Prophet'.

Given such doctrinal differences, it is unlikely that Khomeini's theory would influence, except on a very general level, the ideas of Islamist thinkers in Sunni societies. To illustrate this statement, a few examples are given here; all are taken from Egyptian writers since Egypt has the largest Islamic movement in the Arab world and also enjoys a degree of freedom of expression that allows for a relatively open discussion of such Islamic topics.

In his introduction to an Arabic version of Khomeini's book on *Wilayat-i faqih* (significantly published under the title of 'Islamic Government'), Hasan Hanafi, the Egyptian Islamic philosopher, views Khomeini's contribution as a welcome addition to the literature on political Islam and regards it as part of the 'revolutionary approach' subscribed to by A. Mawdudi and S. Qutb (Hanafi, 1979: 4ff). To him 'the great Islamic revolution of Iran is not a revolution of the Shi'i sect but of Islam', and 'Khumaini, like Afghani, is leading an Islamic revolution that transcends the boundaries of sectarian differences, by going back to the initial revolutionary [spirit] of early Islam that is inherent in its sources of the Qur'an and the Hadith'. He does not detect in Khomeini's book any prominent elements of the conventional Shi'i concepts that are contested by the Sunnis, such as the sanctity and infallibility of the imam – although in this Hanafi is not altogether accurate.[11] He regards it as a non-sectarian Islamic tract on the necessity of Islamic government in the contemporary age, that would provide a methodology for confronting imperialism and Zionism and for resisting the exploitation and oppression suffered by Muslims (ibid.: 24–25).

However, Hanafi has a few reservations on Khomeini's work, including in particular its main innovation, the theory of the guardianship of the jurisconsult. Although this guardianship is – according to Khomeini – of the 'relative' administrative/political (*i'tibari*) type and not of the absolute existential/supernatural (*takwini*) type (cf.

Khumaini, 1979: 49–52), his elaborations in this regard are not entirely void of a certain metaphysical connotation to that guardianship derived, in Hanafi's view, from the old philosophical sources of the Shi'i sect (Hanafi, 1979: 26).[12] Nor does Hanafi condone the explicit emphasis on the role of the good leader and the authority of the pious imam, rather than on the importance of a broader cultural enlightenment and social change (ibid.: 26–29).

Another Egyptian Islamic writer, Muhammad 'Imara, equally regards the political thought associated with the Iranian revolution as 'pioneering'. Yet he finds Khomeini uncritically faithful to the traditional Shi'i theorisation about the imamate, considered 'excessive' by the Sunnis in its attaching of a divine rather than a human character to political authority. To him, Khomeini 'puts revolutionary values and progressive objectives into an old and conservative, even a reactionary, container' ('Imara, 1982: 11–34). Again, he is particularly critical of the concept of rule by the jurists and considers it a non-Islamic innovation, with strong anti-democratic implications. He also implies that Khomeini's theory has little relevance, except for the Iranian Shi'is, and wonders rhetorically: 'Is it an Islamic revolution in Iran, or a Shi'ite – Persian – Islamic revolution in Iran?' (ibid.: 43).

Fahmi Huwaidi, another Islamic Egyptian writer who has actually visited revolutionary Iran, is more sympathetic. He is aware of the fact that the imamite Shi'is have had to live for twelve centuries without a state of their own because the existing rulers were regarded, doctrinally, as usurpers of the legitimate power of the imam. While this stand had given the Shi'i religious establishment a greater social role to play (as an 'alternative' to the State) it has tended to postpone any practical concern with Islamic government among their jurists. Although the concept of the 'guardianship of the faqih' is not entirely new in Shi'i jurisprudence, Khomeini's main achievement, in Huwaidi's view, is that he brought it to the fore as the form of Islamic government that should be applied without delay. What is particularly important is Khomeini's call to the Shi'is to end their traditional wait for the hidden imam to appear and to involve themselves directly and immediately in an Islamic government. The further details and elaborations may be open to criticism, but this is less important in Huwaidi's view (Huwaidi, 1988B: 95–108).

Huwaidi examined about a dozen educational books taught in schools in revolutionary Iran and concluded that they were void of the traditional Shi'i themes that cause conflict with the Sunnis (ibid.: 339–351). This would suggest a general Islamic, rather than a strictly Shi'i, significance and appeal to the Iranian revolution. He observed that in reality, however, Sunnis are inadequately represented in the political bodies of revolutionary Iran, and this, to an extent, reinforces the revolution's sectarian colouring.

In short, therefore, Huwaidi is very appreciative of the general religious and political significance of the Iranian revolution, but he is equally aware of the doctrinal (and societal) specificity of the Shi'ite, and more particularly the Khomeinist, position on Islamic government. Thus, for example, in his estimation it is highly unlikely that Egypt will experience a replication of what happened in Iran (Huwaidi, 1988A: 293–302).

It is possible to conclude this section by arguing that Khomeini's main theoretical contribution has been to offer an innovative, if not completely novel, formula that has legitimised for the Shi'is the act of bringing to an end their doctrinal boycott of government. Rather than waiting endlessly for the hidden imam to reappear, this formula sanctions the immediate establishment of an Islamic government, here and now, and requires that this government is overseen by the jurists. As such, Khomeini's theory, especially because it has also, uniquely, been seen through to implementation in Iran, has given a boost to the thesis of political Islam. However, his concept of the guardianship of the jurisconsult, which is the main substantive component of this theory, continues to be very controversial, to some extent inside Iran itself, but particularly among Sunni Muslims all over the world. Indeed, if anything, Islamic movements in Sunni societies – where the clerics have historically played a completely different social and political role – show signs of becoming increasingly anti-clerical.[13] Thus it seems that 'the great Sunni-Shi'i division still holds sway over Islamic radicalism. It still looks as if the Shi'i and Sunni radical movements will each have to pursue its own revolutionary path' (Sivan, 1989: 1–28).

CONCLUSION

A few concluding remarks on the intellectual sources of political Islam would be in order here. While each author has his own style and flavour, the writers briefly reviewed in this chapter all share a similar philosophical outlook. They are all, to one degree or another, 'fundamentalists' in the specific sense of believing that a man is incapable of understanding the world and of shaping it according to his own wishes. Rather, the human existence can only have meaning inasmuch as it shows devotion to the Divine Will. Further, it is believed that this Divine Will is entirely clear and unambiguous to any person who reads the original sources.

Without denying their 'philosophical' implications or belittling their real, abstract meaning to those who hold them, we have tried in this chapter to relate the ideas of the neo-fundamentalists to their socio-political context. From this analysis of the ideas in their context, two themes emerge.

First we observe that, far from representing a return to something original or essential, the fundamentalist ideas, Sunni and Shi'i alike, are in reality new improvised formulations. Even when the original 'scripture' is invoked and when the old jurists are quoted, the methodology applied is highly selective, and the concepts assembled are then radically reconstructed. This point is perhaps partly related to the fact that, with the only exception of the Shi'ite Khomeini, none of the important proponents of political Islam has been a member of the traditional ulama. If anything, the political Islamists are often quite antagonistic towards the religious Establishment and rather unmoved by its traditional concerns. Even Khomeini, the cleric, seems to have expressed in his last years (d. 1989) a certain element of disdain for the conventional inclinations of the clergy.

Secondly we observe that the intellectual process of reconstruction has taken place in relation to a particular socio-political context. More specifically, the emergence of doctrines of political Islam has represented a response to the actions of the modern, secular State. Thus fundamentalism, which might have emerged first as a religio-philosophical inclination, has become increasingly concerned with the 'social order', and has ultimately developed into a highly politicised type of discourse. This outcome is also new, in that it reverses the familiar historical pattern. If the link between Islam and politics was mainly effected, historically, by the State appropriating religion, contemporary political Islam is mainly an attempt by religious groupings to appropriate politics (and is therefore, in the immediate instance, an anti-State phenomenon). Historically, the State Islamised politics; currently, the fundamentalists want to politicise Islam.

Islamic jurists and preachers had always sought to reform people. The innovation of the fundamentalists was to link this reformation to the State by making personal piety and the moral community the conditions of a good Islamic State (cf. Zubaida, 1989: 33–34). The neo-fundamentalists have developed the linkage between religion and State even further, and in some way have reversed the conditional relationship. Rather than personal piety and the moral community being the conditions of a good Islamic State, they seem to suggest that it is the Islamic State which is the condition of personal piety and the moral community. Thus with the neo-fundamentalists 'the "political" has become the master of all precepts and rulings (*ahkam*), and Islamic action has come to mean, in the first and last resort, a quest for the establishment of an Islamic State' (Jad'an, 1989: 286).

7 Political Islam: socio-economic bases

Our country studies as well as our survey of the intellectual sources of political Islam and their social context must have made it clear that the so-called Islamic revival is a multi-layered phenomenon. Part of the confusion that constrains our understanding of the phenomenon is due to the fact that many observers simply lump together all such manifestations without any analysis of their social bases. While one of the 'functions' of ideology is quite often to gloss over differences and to mediate contradictions, it is up to the social scientist to trace the various ideological/cultural manifestations back to their social roots.

It should be emphasised that while signs of general religiosity and of sympathy to the Islamic cause can be seen within a broad trans-class social base, militant Islamists represent a much more specifically defined social group. Naturally, usage of the same moralist terminology allows the radical political Islamists to converge with a more broadly based Islamic resurgence, which can be regarded as a kind of rising 'cultural nationalism' whose main drive is the quest for 'authenticity'. The anti-State thrust of the Islamic militants may also strike a sympathetic chord with various social groups who, for a variety of reasons, fear and/or despise the State. Yet in many respects the very distinctive social background of the militant political Islamists sets this group apart. The Islamist discourse of the latter group is better seen as the moralist/culturalist expression of a developmental crisis, that has resulted in the frustration of the rising expectations of the lower middle class in general and of the intelligentsia and the students in particular.

That militant political Islam is a movement of the intelligentsia should have become clear, albeit with few local reservations, from our country studies. With the partial exception of Syria (where the sectarian split skews the phenomenon in a certain distinct way), political Islam – as our case studies illustrate – is a movement of the students and of the 'new middle class' of officials (including army officers), professionals and technocrats. Members of the 'traditional' class of merchants and artisans have been active in Islamic movements in Iran and in Syria, and even on a limited scale in Egypt. Yet apart from Iran and from the special Syrian case, bazaris do not form a major component of the contemporary militant Islamic movements in any Arab country. This is also true of the traditional clerical elite. Again, apart from Iran where the Shi'i clergy have played a histori- cally and socially different role, the militant Islamic movements have sometimes benefited from the support of some individual Sunni ulamas (e.g. 'Umar 'Abd al-Rahman and Hafiz Salama in Egypt; Sa'id Hawwa and Hasan Habannaka in Syria), but these movements have not been movements of the clergy; in fact they are very often quite hostile to Establishment Islam.

Nor have the contemporary Islamic movements succeeded in attracting the industrial proletariat. In fact, as we illustrate below in the present chapter, the Muslim Brothers were more successful in mobilising workers in Egypt during the forties than any of the contemporary Islamists have been anywhere in the Arab world. The so-called 'workers' who appear on some official lists of Islamic militants are often technical artisans (e.g. mechanics, electricians, metal forgers, etc.) who do not work in large, modern factories. Iran seems again to represent a partial exception to the rule; yet even here 'it was only in the decisive oil-field and factory strikes of 1978 that workers played an important role in the revolution. And these strikes were in fact often initiated and led by middle-class employees in management' (Munson, 1988: 98–100, and refs cited).

Henry Munson is basically correct in his observation that

> generally speaking, the least educated and most traditional social strata were not active in the fundamentalist Islamic movements of the late twentieth century. Peasants have been conspicuously absent from such movements, as have the urban poor and blue-collar workers with regular jobs – although the latter two groups did eventually participate in Iran's revolution . . . In sharp contrast with the Iranian situation, most Sunni fundamentalist movements have been incapable of mobilising support outside the ranks of university students and recent graduates or dropouts. This is especially true of the more radical and militant movements. (ibid. 103–104)

If it is indeed the case that political Islam is a movement of the middle strata and particularly of the intelligentsia, then this surely is in need of some explanation. In a nutshell it can be argued that while the middle strata have been expanding in size and in proportion in most Arab societies, their rising expectations (stimulated in particular by the acquisition of higher education and by the move to urban centres), are being severely frustrated because of the constrained nature of economic development in these societies. Let us now consider this proposition in a little more detail.

To start with, it should be stated that there is now sufficient documented evidence pertaining to most Arab societies in the last three decades to show that their class structure is skewed in a rather unusual way. Whereas the petite bourgeoisie involved in commerce and the services (and more recently in increasingly capitalised agricultural activities) has continued to be quite sizeable, the ranks of the 'new' middle strata (*couches moyennes*) as well as of the sub-proletariat and the lumpenproletariat have swollen most remarkably, possibly dwarfing by comparison the working class proper (the proletariat). This process has been documented for Egypt, Morocco, Iraq and Sudan, and there are indications that it is also true of countries such as Syria, Tunisia, Algeria and others (cf. 'Abd al-Fadil, 1988: 111–131).

Given the available data, it is difficult to regard such 'in-between' or 'intermediary' classes as being of only secondary or insignificant importance within the social structure of contemporary Arab societies. However, several of these classes, strata and fractions are transitional, liquid and/or heterogeneous in character, and several of them represent 'intermediary' groups that are 'caught in between classes'. For example, it is not always easy to delineate the boundaries between the petite bourgeoisie and the *couches moyennes*, or between artisans and workers. Many members of the proletariat and the peasantry have also become 'capitalised' in recent years (via employment in the oil-exporting countries) and their class identity and consciousness must be rather ambivalent. The general rise in Islamic ideological formulations is in some measure a reflection of this fluid class map, as such formulations tend to be more successful in stressing cultural 'identity' and in seeking independence from the State, than in spelling out class-specific social and economic objectives. Leonard Binder has expressed the process most concisely in these passages:

> The Muslim bourgeoisie has, to a considerable extent, abandoned nationalism in its earlier form. The bureaucratic–authoritarian state, identified with the Ba'th, Nasser, Ataturk, Reza Shah and Boumedienne, transformed liberal nationalism and used it to strengthen the state. But the inadequacy of the capacity and the

resources of the national state, its cultural alterity, and its over-extension in international affairs, all led to a limited achievement and growing opposition. In time, this opposition was sustained by a coalition of traditional regimes (led by Saudi Arabia) and some Western powers (led by the United States).

In a sense, the rise of Islam is an ideological dimension of the movement to restrict the power of the State – a movement constituted of a loose coalition of bourgeois fractions, some rural agrarian capitalists, notables and estate owners, and the virtually proletarianized members of the state-employed petite bourgeoisie, the under-employed intelligentsia, and the larger student population. The interests that these segments appear to have in weakening the state apparatus, or in gaining a larger share of influence within it, are not compatible, so one of the purposes of the contemporary ideological process is to mask the divergence of these interests. This may be one of the functions of new Islamic ideological formulations. (Binder, 1988: 16–17)

Within this 'loose coalition' there is little doubt that the 'virtually proletarianized members of the state-employed petite bourgeoisie, the under-employed intelligentsia, and the larger student population' are the main sponsors of the most militant of the Islamic tendencies that have now as their sole objective the defeating of the State and the dismantling of the current social order on which it is premised. The enlightened Islamic writer Fahmi Huwaidi has wondered why the Kharijite thought finds popularity in current times. He says that his Islamic writings bring him a great deal of mail from young, educated people who condemn the entire contemporary society, especially its economic and moral corruption, and who adhere to the 'contemporary jahiliyya' thesis. He writes:

I have received many letters that agree with the idea of condemning the society with jahiliyya and which concentrate on two issues: moral corruption and economic corruption. I have noticed that these letters launch a severe attack on society, and my attention was drawn to the fact that a high percentage of the letter writers were from the youth generation: *some are university students and some recent graduates in law, medicine, accountancy, etc.* . . . One of them sent a letter of five long pages . . . [that was] all accusation against the entire present order . . . In the last three lines of the letter, its writer mentions that *he had graduated in commerce four years earlier and had not found work until now*, and was thus devoting himself to self-education and to compiling a list of all aspects of corruption that are published in the newspapers, of which he had already collected 4632 published cases! (Huwaidi, 1987: 247–248 – emphasis added)

Thus we can see that a major source of frustration is over the unfulfilled promise of education. Individuals and families go through tremendous sacrifices to enable the young to acquire higher education in one of the vastly expanding universities (for details on Egypt see Ayubi, 1978; Abdalla, 1985), in the expectation that the qualification will improve their lot – but it does not because they end up being unemployed, or poorly employed (and poorly paid).

A second major source of frustration is over the unfulfilled promise of urbanisation. Individuals and families move to the city in search of better opportunities and better facilities. What they often get is not only the moral vulnerability brought about by the indiscriminate mixing together and the anonymity, but also the degradation brought about by the excessive crowding and the appalling state of utilities. This is made all the more painful for the financially-constrained but status-conscious lower middle class as it is often obliged to live in close proximity to and to rub shoulders with the urban sub-proletariat or even the lumpenproletariat.

To illustrate our argument, let us consider in some more detail the case of Egypt (see also Chapter 4). If one considers the geographical and the social background of Egypt's radical Islamic movements, two 'spaces' become immediately apparent as breeding grounds for the militants: Upper Egypt and peripheral Cairo – the two being actually and symbolically linked together by a certain process, that of migration.

It should be observed, first, that we do not have a full picture because although nearly 5000 Islamists were arrested in September and October 1981 (after Sadat's assassination), only 302 of them were on the Public Prosecutor's list of the accused; of these, 271 were actually tried (the remaining 31 being fugitives or dead). But the available data, however limited, should still be of some significance. Geographically, the provinces of Cairo and Giza together (i.e. Greater Cairo) accounted for 135 (49.82 per cent) of the prosecuted individuals, Upper Egypt (the *Sa'id*) for 117 (43.17 per cent), and Lower Egypt for only 19 (7.0 per cent) (see Sayyid-Ahmad, 1988A: 96–97, and cf. Junaina, 1988: 116–117; and Ansari, 1984A: 130–131). Given that Lower Egypt has about double the population of Upper Egypt, the percentage of militants from the Sa'id is *proportionately* even higher.

Table 1 Distribution of the accused Jihad members by occupation and age

Occupation	No.	% (100)
Students	123	43.9
Workers	41	14.6
Professionals	35	12.5
Unemployed	30	10.7
Shopkeepers	16	5.7
Government officials	15	5.4
Police and military	14	5.0
Farmers	6	2.2
Total	280	100.00

Age	No.	% (100)
below 20	49	17.5
21–30	196	70.0
31–40	30	10.7
above 40	5	1.8
Total	280	100.00

Source: Ansari, 1984A: 133

In terms of social profile, available figures – whether of the accused or of the sentenced Jihad members – confirm (a) the preponderance of militants from among the intelligentsia/lower middle class, and (b) the predominance of young militants from the 20–30 year-old age group. Tables 1 and 2 should make this quite clear.

It is obvious that students represent the major category (around 44 per cent in both lists), followed by professionals/officials and then by workers (including modern-type artisans/technicians). Shopkeepers (or the traditional bazaris) account for less than 6 per cent of the total, and farmers/peasants for a mere 2 per cent of the total. Militant Islamism is therefore basically a movement of the students and the intelligentsia.

It is also obvious that the youth (age group 20–30 years) form the most significant category among the militants. In fact further scrutiny illustrates that there are proportionately more members in the 20–25 age group than there are in the 25–30 group. The movement of political Islam therefore carries many of the features of a youth movement. This should not come as a great surprise, since the problems of identity and authority tend to be seen most sharply

Table 2 Distribution of the sentenced Jihad members by occupation and age

Occupation	No.	% (100)
Students	45	44.55
Professionals	25	24.75
Workers	15	14.85
Shopkeepers	6	5.9
Police and military	4	3.96
Farmers	2	1.98
Unemployed	4	3.96
Total	101*	99.99

Age	No.	% (100)
below 20	9	8.91
20–25	42	42.57
25–30	35	34.65
above 30	15	12.87
Total	101*	99.00

*This table includes only the 101 individuals sentenced by the Supreme State Security Court. There is no information about nine other individuals listed as fugitives in the records.

Source: Junaina, 1988: 142–143

among a nation's youth. As David Apter explains, identity problems among the youth are often exaggerated in 'modernizing' societies, because identity choices often lead to discontinuous sequences and usually coincide with a process of 'role search' that is replete with anxiety. This anxiety can in turn lead to temporary alienation from society.[1] All these socio-psychological strains are often then 'expressed' in symbolic, ideological forms which may include 'the use of historical myths, the re-writing of history, the search for a golden age' (cf. Apter, 1964: 20ff, 60ff). This is precisely what has happened with the Muslim youth.

It would be interesting at this point to consider the linkage, if any, between the *Sa'idi* background and the Cairene circumstances of Islamic militancy in Egypt.

ISLAMIC RESURGENCE OR URBAN CRISIS? A TALE OF TWO CITIES

There is, it seems, some linkage between Upper Egypt and peripheral Cairo, in that a proportionately higher percentage of new immigrants into the latter city tend to come from the former region. They presumably bring with them their grievances and frustrations, their prejudices and feuds, including a more heightened sense of Muslim–Christian competition and friction, that are made even worse in the metropolis because of the new conditions of excessive overcrowding and poor housing conditions.

The fact that the majority of the Islamic militants in Egypt hail from the *Sa'id* (Upper Egypt) may warrant some explanation, especially as it has not received adequate coverage before. The Sa'id is the narrow strip of land tucked between the hills on both sides of the Nile from the bottom of the Delta to the cataracts of Aswan. It is arid, hot, and – until the Aswan High Dam – only partly 'hydraulic', and is naturally an inhospitable part of the country. It is economically and socially less advanced than the Delta, with distinctly lower standards of living. When the Arabs settled in Egypt, the Northern, more nomadic, tribes preferred the similar environment of Upper Egypt, whereas the Southern, Yemeni, more 'agricultural' tribes preferred the rich stretches of the Delta. The Arabian nomads took with them to the Sa'id their accent and their social norms, and they were more resistant to mingling into the original Egyptian population than were their relatives in the Northern part of the country. Until relatively recently the distinction in the Sa'id between Arab (i.e. Arabian of nomadic origin) and Fallah (i.e. farmer of 'purely' Egyptian origin) was still valid and significant. Within the fallahin, another stratification existed between Muslims and, at a lower level, Copts. Social stratification and status rituals were fairly rigid, with members of the lower groups having, for example, to dismount from their animals, give way and walk on the left in the presence of members of a higher-status community. The 'Arabs' kept aloof from agriculture and normally engaged in carrying arms and some trade; they 'protected' the peasants (Muslim and Christian) and on their behalf carried on vendettas with other villages/tribes who might have attacked them.

Sometimes as the nomads eventually became sedentarised and inter-married with the peasants, a fresh wave of vigorous nomads, in a typical Khaldunian cycle, would arrive and assume supremacy (in power and thus in status) over the rest. This was most obvious, for example, in the Qina province where the most recently arrived North African Hawwarah nomads (possibly of Berber origin) stood at the top of the social hierarchy, below them the so-called 'Arabs', then Muslim 'peasants', and then Coptic 'peasants'. It was also probably the nomads' disinclination to intermarry with the local peasants that kept the percentage of Copts higher in Upper Egypt than it had become in the Delta.

The nomads spread within the Sa'idi society at large their values of extreme generosity, obsession with honour and the related practice of vendetta. They also carried with them their fiercely independent and ardently anti-State attitude. Carrying arms has been a normal pattern and violent crime has been rampant, with the 'mountain' providing a convenient hide-out for those wanted by the government for murder, the cultivation of drug-producing plants or desertion from the army. The fact that various governments have neglected or overlooked the Sa'id in their developmental programmes has meant that the old social structure was able to retain its hold for much longer than it did elsewhere in the country – if the government *would not* reach out with schools, clinics and factories, it *could not* reach out with its police forces either.

This situation started to change drastically in the middle of the nineteenth century, especially in the towns and most particularly in the city of Asyut. This old Pharaonic town (Siut) was now actively engaged in extensive trade between Egypt and the Sudan, made easier by Britain's subsequent rule over the two countries. The main camel trade route from Sudan passed by Asyut and a prosperous class developed in the city that traded in the camels themselves as well as in grains, dates and spices from the Sudan. Thriving artisan industries also developed on the side: ivory carving, woodworking, cane furniture-making and the weaving of woollen carpets.

A significant percentage of the merchants were Copts (the percentage of Copts in Asyut province being the highest in the country), who now, under the new laws of the mid-nineteenth century, could also buy land, and who sent their children enthusiastically into the many new schools that were being built both by their community and also by the missionaries. At this period, there was an influx of American Protestant missionaries into Asyut city and of Catholics into the town of Tahta, to an extent that seriously alarmed the Coptic Orthodox patriarch. Such Copts also extended their commercial activities throughout the country, using the network of permanent and temporary Coptic emigrants to other Egyptian cities – especially Cairo, Alexandria and Suez – where they were involved in the trading of gold, grains, carpets, groceries and fruits, as well as in some money-lending.

As a result of such developments, the old network of social relationships was changing fast and coming under tremendous pressures. Foreign trading communities (especially Greeks) also increased in the Upper Egyptian cities, involved mainly in wholesale cotton trade and export, and bringing with them their own way of life including restaurants, cafes and bars. European consulates were established in Asyut and the European businessmen as well as the Greek traders tended to prefer dealing with the Copts, who were more mobile and better at foreign languages. Some of the leading Coptic merchants acted as consular agents or representatives of European commercial interests in Upper Egypt, of which Asyut was regarded as the regional capital (Walz, 1978: 113–123). The dusty, drab city of Asyut now started to possess magnificent baroque palaces and comfortable residential areas that housed the emerging classes of semi-feudal landlords and prosperous cosmopolitan merchants. The city was obviously changing radically and fast, and the old status ranking was being shattered: being 'Arab' (i.e. beduin) was no longer prestigious; even the feeling of superiority at being Muslim was no longer of much account.

The economic situation did not change significantly after the 1952 revolution, for there was very little industrialisation introduced into Asyut, but a university was built in 1957/58 to which admission, as for others around the country, was by grades. The presence of the State became more obvious as, for example, the old 'feudal' palaces were taken over and turned into government departments and quarters for the Arab Socialist Union. But because no industrial expansion was taking place, and since even Asyut's long-established trading role was diminishing (following the decline in traditional Egyptian–Sudanese trade), the newly-mobile Muslim youth must have felt their aspirations for social promotion were severely blocked, while many Copts must have seen their privileges gradually eroding. By the late sixties, there must therefore have been quite a number of angry people in the province of Asyut, who, given their 'semi-nomadic' cultural outlook, were also habitually inclined to act impulsively and violently over perceived grievances. And it is understandable that much of the anger would be directed at the State – the State which the Sa'idi sub-culture traditionally despised, and the State which, revolutionary and modernising slogans notwithstanding, had failed signally to do anything to develop the region.

The appointment by Sadat of a governor for Asyut, Muhammad 'Uthman Isma'il, who was known for his fundamentalist sympathies and anti-Christian biases, did not make things any better. The man remained in this sensitive post for an unusually long term – from 1973 to 1982, at which point he was removed by President Mubarak.

According to the account of an Islamic sympathiser, he played during this time

> an undisguised role in pushing the Islamic groupings and the secretive movements towards expansion and hegemony, until they appeared at a certain moment to be larger than the regime itself. He also played the most evil role that a Muslim in Egypt may play, which was to manipulate the sectarian strife until it reached the brink of a civil war. (Mahfuz, 1988: 169–170)

Is it therefore simply a coincidence that Sayyid Qutb and Shukri Mustafa, as well as a very high percentage of the membership of the militant Islamic groupings, came originally from the province of Asyut?[2]

Although the significance of the Sa'idi background of many militant Islamists is important by itself, its national impact is made all the more noticeable because the Sa'idis tend to form a proportionately high percentage of new immigrants into Cairo, where the appalling housing and social conditions add further fuel to their old grievances and prejudices. A brief look at the problematic 'urban' conditions in Cairo would therefore be in order.

Recent urban studies confirm that the Cairo periphery in general and the northern and north-western quarters in particular have witnessed the most intense levels of immigration since the sixties. These quarters include Bulaq al-Dakrur, Matariyya, Shubra al-Khaima, Newer Heliopolis, Hilwan and Newer Ma'adi, Sharabiyya and Imbaba. The annual rate of increase in some of these areas has ranged between 10 and 20 per cent per annum in recent years (Musailihi, 1988: 385–387, 396). Most have witnessed religiously-coloured disturbances, and a proportionately higher percentage of Islamic militants reside there. Not only would recent immigrants in such quarters feel 'morally vulnerable' with regard to their families' 'honour' (see Chapter 2), but the dreadful housing, sanitation and transportation conditions would simply add insult to injury.

Most of the 'urban' growth affecting these quarters has been sporadic and haphazard, supported mainly by informal housing and unplanned utilities and facilities (Hanna, 1978: Chs 3 and 4). As much as 84 per cent of all new houses built in Cairo between 1970 and 1981 was 'informal, unplanned housing' (Musailihi, 1988: 404–405). Some of that housing is almost 'illegal': 56 per cent is on non-registered land, 38 per cent consists of non-registered buildings, and 73 per cent of the houses were constructed without building permits. In terms of facilities, 35–43 per cent of the buildings had no running water, 29–44 per cent were unconnected to sewage networks, 10–12 per cent were not connected to electricity grids, and most did not adhere to regulations regarding space, ventilation, lighting, etc. (ibid.: 305–306). This is the type of housing that expands fastest, rather than the shanties (*'ishash*) which proliferated particularly in the period between Egypt's two major wars with Israel, when housing resources were extremely constrained both for the public and the private sectors; as much as 30.8 per cent of all Cairo shanties were built between 1968 and 1973 (ibid.: 407).

Around the same time, and extending into the seventies (although the trend has now declined markedly), residence in cemeteries began. In spite of being symbolically ominous – and prohibited by Islamic tradition – the practice was widespread, though confined mainly to other Cairenes and to people from neighbouring provinces. Socially, cemetery life was not such a bad move, since most of the occupied tombs were spacious and solidly built around courtyards, and usually contained an entrance hall, two or four rooms, a kitchen and a w.c., as well as a small garden plot (ibid.: 420–434).

Two-thirds of the inhabitants of the sporadic urban quarters (67.2 per cent) are immigrants, and the rates of room crowding in these areas is markedly higher among immigrants than among Cairenes moving into these areas from other Cairo quarters (e.g. 5.6 person/room for immigrants as compared to 4.4 person/room for Cairenes in Bulaq al-Dakrur) (ibid.: 408–409). In the northern shanties, the one province that provides the highest percentage of immigrants is al-Minufiyya, the most densely populated rural province of Egypt. But most other immigrants come from Upper Egypt, especially from the provinces of Asyut, Minya, Qina, Suhag and Bani Suaif (ibid.: 414). Predictably, the main source of immigrants for the southern shanties is the Upper Egyptian provinces, especially Asyut, Suhag, Qina and Minya (ibid.: 417).

No extensive surveys are available, and they are certainly badly needed, of the occupational profile of the inhabitants of the shanties or of the sporadic quarters. Scattered sample studies and personal observation would suggest that typical occupations in the shanties would be: peddlers and itinerant vendors, horse cart drivers, construction and decoration casual workers, minor artisans in leather, plumbing and metals, car body repairs, janitors, servants and guards in government offices, factories and houses. Their wives might work as servants, washerwomen, vegetable or offal vendors. These are basically occupations of the urban sub-proletariat, a class that is represented on a small scale among the Islamic militants.

Although their very limited income may oblige members of the sub-proletariat to survive spatially very close to elements of the lumpen-proletariat (cf. Hanna, 1988: 50–51), these two social categories should be carefully distinguished from each other. Such 'co-habitation' was the case, for example, in the Qulali/Turguman area. In the 'Ishash al-Turguman shanties over 80 per cent of all families lived in shared houses, and some of them were reputed to be involved in activities such as drug pushing, monkey juggling, theft and pickpocketing, professional begging, and male and female prostitution. Significantly, most inhabitants of this shanty town were evacuated by the government in 1979 and rehabilitated into the already crowded and rapidly growing immigrant quarter of al-Zawiya al-Hamra, where they harboured bitter feelings about their uprooting and also became involved in conflicts with the existing inhabitants that eventually led to the flare-up of ugly sectarian Muslim–Christian strife in summer 1981 (cf. Ansari, 1984B: 408–409).

The lumpenproletariat come from the segments in society which, economically speaking, are deeply deprived. Because of the collapse of their family support system and because they lack any productive role in society, they have little self-respect or social/class identity and are pushed into a life of ignorance, corruption and degradation. These are the types that generate the rough gangs and the urban bandits, provoke riots and skirmishes, indulge in drugs, alcohol and deviant sexual behaviour and use a 'vulgar' argot of insult and base sexuality. Although they may join in mass uprisings, such as the Egyptian food riots of 1977, they are lacking in consciousness and are inclined to resort to destructive violence and looting, and can be rather easily manipulated by governmental and/or Fascist type forces (compare with Iran in Jazani, 1980: 141–143). Thus, although the lumpen-proletariat have not joined in Islamic movements, they are likely to participate in any large-scale Islamic uprising once it is in motion.

By contrast, typical occupations among inhabitants of the new sporadic quarters would be: minor functionaries and civil servants, clerks, typists and minor accountants, policemen and soldiers, tea-chers and clerics, mechanics, electricians and metal technicians, taxi and lorry drivers, grocers and skilled workers. They will usually have non-working wives and several children who are school or university students, or unemployed recent (or not so recent) graduates. This is a typically conservative middle class population, struggling desperately for upward mobility or scared stiff of downward mobility (as in the case of minor officials, clerks and some merchants). Milad Hanna observed that such new sporadic quarters house a strange mixture of people from various professions and classes (many of them recent immigrants), including minor officials, artisans/technicians, newly-married recent graduates, as well as a few itinerant vendors. He saw in them a strange heterogeneous blend of rural and urban influences, a natural environment for breeding intellectual and religious extremism, and the source of potential threat to 'social peace' in the country (Hanna, 1988: 59–62). Indeed, as we have already seen, this is precisely the environment in which the militant Islamists have emerged in their largest numbers (cf. Ch. 4; also Kepel, 1985: 216–217; Ansari, 1984A: 130–136), adopting in the process the concepts assembled from the repertoire of the Kharijites and Ibn Taimiya.

One of the characteristics of late, uneven and dependent capitalist 'development' is that the rates of growth in urbanisation, education and bureaucratisation are never matched by similar rates of growth in industrialisation. Capitalist relations of exchange and the capitalist culture of consumerism and fetishism envelopes the peripheral economies more easily and at a much faster pace than the rate at which capitalist accumulation can take place. A relatively small consumerist class is created in the cities, whose counterpart is usually a noticeably large sub-proletariat involved in the services and a fairly large lumpenproletariat scavenging for the leftovers of the consumerist segment. Such potential opportunities in the services sectors and the informal sectors do, however, pull increasing numbers from the rural communities towards the cities, especially as the growing monetarism and commercialisation in the agricultural sector push increasing numbers of people out of their villages.

The earlier phase of this process of distorted transformation towards capitalism did produce its variety of immigrants to the city in the twenties, thirties and forties. But at that stage the rate of migration was still comparatively slow, and the services and artisan sectors were still capable of expansion, since, although the initial capitalist penetration of the non-capitalist social formation restricts the artisan industries and commercial activities in certain areas, it does, however, extend them in other areas – this is true both in general terms and in specifically Middle Eastern terms (cf. Taylor, 1979: 225–226; Owen, 1982: 289 *et passim.*). Other factors also ameliorated the situation: the miseries of the newly urbanised might have been lessened through membership in Sufi orders and through partial association with the traditionally-oriented bazaars and crafts guilds (which were weakening and transforming but which had by no means completely disappeared). The anti-colonialist nationalist struggle of that period also provided the various classes and fractions with a common and obvious target for their main struggle.

Such a situation of complex, transitional articulation of modes of production had generated its recommended formulas for political action, represented by various 'populist' and 'corporatist' tendencies. The Islamic movements of the forties in the larger Muslim countries – e.g. Egypt, Iran, Morocco and Syria – subscribed to the emerging trends that were moving towards a variety of economic modernisation premised on solidarity rather than on conflict among the classes. Indeed, the interest shown by the Muslim Brothers in economic and social problems during the forties culminated intellectually in the fifties in works such as Sayyid Qutb's *Social Justice in Islam* (in Egypt) and Mustafa al-Siba'i's *The Socialism of Islam* (in Syria).

It is significant that, following Hasan al-Banna's arrest in 1943 and his final rupture with the Wafd, the largest secular party in Egypt, the Muslim Brothers were to adopt a more populist and activist stance that eventually included a more assertive position in the workers' movement (Beinin and Lockman, 1987: 365ff). Characteristically, however, the Brothers became increasingly opposed to the encouragement by the Communists of trade union independence from non-workers patrons (which was typical of that period) and of greater labour militancy, which they saw as sowing conflict and social discord among Muslims. They engaged in a fullscale organised campaign that was aimed at supplanting the left as the leading force, especially among the private sector workers of Shubra al-Khaima: here, in 1946, they even established a textile mill of their own called the Muslim Brothers' Spinning and Weaving Company with the intention to 'protect its members from unemployment'. More generally it was intended as a working demonstration of the viability of Islamic principles in the management of an industrial enterprise. All workers were required to buy at least one share, so that conflict between labour and management would be eliminated – this was a concrete expression of the Brothers' view that there was no class conflict in a justly ordered Islamic society. A form of unemployment insurance was also established by the Brothers in Shubra al-Khaima through which full wages were paid to members who lost their jobs, and whereby solidarity was shown through the personal charity and other types of support that were offered (ibid.: 371–375, 378–379).

But although the Brothers upheld an individual's right to private property, they opposed the materialist values and attitudes which they felt were promoted by capitalism. Foreign-owned enterprises in particular bore the brunt of their attack on capitalism, being also seen as the economic wing of occupation in Egypt (ibid.: 377; Goldberg, 1988: 228–241). Such a nationalist dimension was particularly sharply felt at the Suez Canal Company and at the Shell Oil Company and its subsidiary, Anglo–Egyptian Oil Fields, and it is therefore no accident that the unions in these enterprises and throughout the Suez Canal Zone generally were significant centres of the Muslim Brothers' strength within the Egyptian workers' movement (Beinin and Lockman, 1987: 378).

The Brothers' vision of a just Islamic society based on a solid 'moral economy' held a strong attraction for workers who, having recently arrived in Cairo, the Canal Zone and other urban centres, had been

> wrenched from their rural and preindustrial social networks and confronted with the harsh regime of industrial discipline, dominated by what appeared to be specifically European rather than simply capitalist values and norms. This vision also appealed to small independent artisans and craftsmen whose markets and very livelihoods were under attack from commodities produced by large scale capitalist methods. (ibid.: 378)

Indicative of the Brothers' corporatist inclinations is the fact that although they expressed their sympathy towards the demands of the workers, on the whole they never openly supported strikes by workers except, and only in a veiled and implicit manner, against foreign-owned enterprises (ibid.: 379–380). Indeed from 1948 the Brothers became more radicalised, and were involved in terrorist attacks against Jewish and foreign interests. The death of the Society's General Guide, Hasan al-Banna, had led to the loss of its organis-ational coherence and this eventually resulted in the ascendancy of the radical trend as expressed by Sayyid Qutb, Muhammad al-Ghazali and al-Bahyi al-Khuli, as well as some writers in *Al-Da'wa* magazine, who, although they were not official spokesmen for the Society, appealed to the general membership through their anti-capitalist writings and open support for workers' strikes in the late forties and early fifties (ibid.: 388–393).

In general, however, the Islamists' sympathy towards the workers remained of a moralist nature. The workers were not really viewed as a distinct social class, but rather as individual Muslims who were subject to cultural and 'national' as much as to economic oppression. Such an understanding of employer–employee relations made sense in the framework of Islamic populist moralising as long as the men in charge of discipline were foreign. 'Once that changed, moral suasion ceased to be a viable tactic to better the lot of workers', and 'one mode of continuing to improve the conditions of workers was to move the trade unions directly into the state under the auspices of a corporatist nationalism' (Goldberg, 1988: 240–241). And that is precisely what was done after the 1952 revolution.

Now it can be argued that Nasserism (and Ba'thism, Bourguibism, etc.) could be regarded as being in some ways the secular, State-led version of the same populist/corporatist recipe that the Islamists call *takaful*.[3] It should be remembered that it took many years for the Free Officers and the Muslim Brothers to be disentangled from each other in Egypt (see Chapter 6 above), and that Nasser was fairly friendly to the Brothers in Syria and had indeed publicised Siba'i's book on Islamic socialism (cf. Jad'an, in 'Abadalla, 1987: 157–158). Of course, Nasserism and Ba'thism subsequently expanded nationalisation beyond what the Brothers would have liked, and increasingly even used pseudo-Marxist terminology to describe their economic and social programmes, but semantics and terminology apart, the two approaches were premised on similar 'collaborative' rather than conflictual class lines.

When Nasserism, Ba'thism and Bourguibism all failed to sustain a process of comprehensive independent development, and to live up to their promises to bring about decent life for all citizens, the Islamic populist theory was to make a spectacular reappearance.[4] As Michael Gilsenan most aptly expresses it:

> Societies continue to be marked by skewed and dislocated social and economic relations, in which a sense of being blocked becomes predominant. [And] no strata feel such distortions so acutely as do the urban masses and the petite bourgeoisie . . . Religion became closely entwined with the lives of displaced rural migrants . . . when the state was explicitly separating it from political and economic power . . . What we might call a kind of populist opposition to a ruling 'them', to big business, to foreign capital, and to the power of the banks easily takes on a religious form. (Gilsenan, 1982B: 255–261)

CONCLUSION

One of the most curious things about Islamic revival is that it appears to be bringing together groups with different social outlooks and political aims: e.g. radical students as well as conservative merchants. It should be emphasised, however, that the point where they all meet is a cultural one (a sense of alienation, a quest for authenticity, a demand for the enforcement of public morals), and possibly a philosophical one (a belief in the divine, not the human, ordering of man's affairs). In socio-political action, however, the various groups cannot go hand in hand – as the Iranian case has proved – except in transitional situations, because the social 'function' of Islamism is different for each group.

It is of course conceivable that a rapid process of 'modernisation' involving large-scale industries, European-style education and extensive rural–urban migration, would bring with it some seriously disruptive effects that dislocate the lives of traditional groups such as the artisans and the bazaris, not to speak of the clerics (cf. Munson, 1988: 107–116). Such groups may consequently find in the bond of religion not only a sense of psychological consolation but also a new focus of identity and an alternative network of relationships. If the 'development' process is of an 'imitative', dependent type, the social and cultural dislocations that it is likely to cause would render various groups susceptible to feelings of resentment about foreign domination and to calls for religio-cultural authenticity. Such an atmosphere may create a situation where potential *sympathy* to an Islamic call may exist. This is really the broader environment in which an 'Islamic revival' may emerge. A wide variety of groups are attracted to the Islamist thesis because this is expressed in a familiar devotional and moralist language that imparts a certain sense of intimacy and assurance, and because they may also share with the militants a certain degree of antagonism towards the existing social order and the State that keeps it in place. The Islamic language therefore represents a broad alternative system of meaning and power, to the hegemonic system represented by the existing socio-political order, which inevitably marginalises and/or alienates certain individuals and certain social groups. To an extent, the details of the Islamic thesis become less important than the fact that it is a very *different* thesis from that advocated by the State. The 'difference' itself seems to fulfil a certain function *vis-à-vis* an order that is deemed to be at most evil and corrupt, and at least a failure or a non-fulfilled promise.

As distinct from this general sympathy, however, the conditions that prompt certain people to become active political Islamists are much more specifically defined, in social terms. These are precisely the conditions of raised, but then frustrated, expectations. Nikki Keddie and Henry Munson have both utilised the theory of revolution of James Davies to explain the Iranian events of 1978–79. It is argued that revolutions are likely to occur when a period of rapid economic growth is followed by a worsening economic situation that frustrates the expectations heightened by the previous boom. This was indeed the case in Iran with the oil boom and its aftermath. But then there were some specifically Iranian factors which transformed the widespread grievances of various social groups into an Islamic revolution in Iran – and only in Iran (Keddie, 1988B: 306–311; Munson, 1988: 116–136). These include, among others, the ideological and organisational role played by the Shi'a clergy, who are much more involved with the 'popular base' (rural and urban) than any of their equivalents in the Arab world, and of course the role played by Khomeini as a charismatic leader with outstanding credentials in resisting the Shah.

No such 'Islamic' revolution has taken place in any Arab country, and none is likely to take place in the immediate future (with somewhat of a question mark over the case of Egypt). Yet the same paradigm of 'frustrated expectations' that explains the Iranian revolution would also explain, albeit on a smaller scale, the recruitment into militant organisations of political Islam. Although most of the Arab countries witnessing a serious Islamic revival have not enjoyed an oil boom, they have in general experienced important developments in the areas of education, urbanisation and industrialisation. These developments were also accompanied, and this is very important, by great hopes and aspirations among many sectors of the population, especially of the middle strata. By the seventies, however, it had become clear that the 'modernising' states could not deliver their promises. Defeated militarily and/or exhausted financially these states have become too poor and inefficient to offer the youth jobs and houses and too frightened and lacking in confidence to allow them political participation.[5] It is precisely such youth with heightened, then shattered, expectations that form the mainstay of the militant Islamic movements in Arab countries (cf. Khoury, 1988: 213–234).

Regardless of the country-specific peculiarities, there are similar socio-economic conditions under which all radical Islamic movements function; in a way, they are all a manifestation of, and a reaction to, a developmental crisis in the Muslim part of the Third World. They have all appeared in an environment of rising expectations, poor achievements and frustrated hopes. They are almost all movements of the upwardly mobile, formally educated and recently urbanised youth, who were 'released', often mobilised, but not completely assimilated and rewarded by the national State, because of incomplete industrialisation and unfulfilled modernisation. Their sense of 'relative deprivation' (cf. Runciman, 1989: 36) may therefore explain much about their general anxiety and about the adoption of religion as a goal-replacement mechanism.

As such, these movements have emerged not really as an expression of moral outrage against a modernisation that was going 'too fast', but rather as a reaction to a developmental process that was not going fast enough. The Islamic militants are not rebellious because they are opposed to development (or even, to an extent, to modernisation), but rather because they desired it so strongly and yet could not get it. Theirs is the proverbial case of 'sour grapes': they hate modernity because they cannot get it! The Islamists are not angry because the aeroplane has replaced the camel; they are angry because they could not get on to the aeroplane. There is little doubt in my mind that had Nasserism (and other similar developmental projects) 'delivered' in the sixties, we would not be witnessing the same political revival of Islam that we see today.

8   Islamic banks, companies and services, or the rise of a native commercial bourgeoisie

By the late seventies and early eighties, it could be observed that the so-called Islamic banking had 'taken off' in various parts of the Muslim world (cf. Wilson, 1983: 80–98). Although it is too simplistic to argue that 'the boom in oil exports has, more than anything else, caused the recent Islamic resurgence' (Pipes, 1982: 45), there is little doubt that the financial and political self-confidence brought about by the oil boom has enabled people in the Gulf countries in particular and in the Muslim world in general to begin to think about trying to do things their own way, and to seek a distinctive place for Muslim countries within the emerging 'new international economic order' (cf. ICO: 1982). Indeed, under the leadership of Saudi Arabia, the conservative Arab regimes have, during the third quarter of this century, invested a great deal in developing an 'Islamic' policy that they used as a means for gaining influence and power within the Third World through institutions such as the Islamic Conference Organisation (ICO) and its affiliates. The efficacy of this policy was made easier by the relative state of stagnation that had overtaken the non-aligned movement in the Third World around the same time (cf. 'Abd al-Malik 'Awda, 1988: Chapter VI, Section 6). Such a policy was also able to acquire an important 'financial' dimension following the oil boom of 1973–1974. As is already well known, Arab OPEC countries had in 1980 an aggregate surplus of US $120 billion, and considerable reserves were available to individual natives of these countries and to millions of expatriate personnel working in them. New outlets were obviously needed for investing these funds.

ISLAMIC BANKS

In economic affairs, part of this new thinking has been related to the perceived Islamic prohibition of *riba* (usury). Although some Muslim modernists have maintained that this Arabic term applies only to usurious interest rates on consumptive credits and not to payments resulting from productive investment, the more widely accepted juridic interpretation is that any interest, irrespective of the level of the interest rate and the purpose of the credit, is prohibited because it is a positive, predetermined return on capital (cf. e.g. 'Uwais, 1986: 41-74; also the debate in *Al-Iqtisad al-Islami*, July 1989: 2-18). The availability of surplus funds, to Muslim states and to individuals alike, in the aftermath of the 1974 oil boom, combined with the general atmosphere of Islamic revival in the seventies and eighties, has given the religiously-inclined an opportunity to experiment with so-called usury-free investment *(la rabawi)* ('Uwais, 1986: 137-167). Such a drive would also have appealed to a number of 'nationalistically' inclined people, as a way of limiting the growing financial dependency of the Gulf economies *vis-à-vis* the Western capitalist world. It should be observed, however, that the highest estimate of funds deposited with the Islamic banks put them at some $10 to $13 billion in 1984. In the meantime, the main bulk of Arab surplus funds continued to be 'placed' at Western interest-paying financial institutions, which in turn extended interest-taking credits to Third World countries – with Arab countries alone suffering an external indebtedness of $136 billion in 1984 (Taha, 1988: 177-179).

But to what extent are the proliferating Islamic banks really 'Islamic'? It is our contention that, although a certain element of Islamic symbolism is involved, the expansion of Islamic banks has initially represented part of the general phenomenon of an ascendant *pax Saudiana* within the Middle East. Increasingly, however, the expansion is becoming more specifically representative of the rise of a native commercial bourgeoisie in the Arab world. In the following pages we set about explaining this contention.

The origins of the Islamic banking formula were not 'Islamic' at all. All accounts trace the original idea to the local development of cooperative/savings banks that were established in the Egyptian countryside (with equivalents, it seems, in India and Pakistan) in the sixties. Mutual savings arrangements were already a known practice in Egypt among families, neighbours and friends. The new banking experiment started in 1963, during the Nasserist era, when a provincial local savings bank was established in Zifta and Mit Ghamr, in the rural Nile Delta region. The scheme was initiated by Ahmad al-Najjar, 'an academic with practical experience in local savings banks in West Germany, who later became secretary-general of the International Association of Islamic Banks, and a member of the board of directors of the Faisal Islamic Bank of Egypt' (el-Ashker, 1987: 155). The initiators of the first experiment thus drew their inspiration not from Islamic economics, but from the theory and experience of German cooperative and mutual savings banks (Nienhaus, 1986: 5). Since then, however, al-Najjar has been hailed as 'the spiritus rector of the Islamic banking movement' (Klower, 1982: 44).

The Mit Ghamr bank was a no-interest local savings centre, helping small farmers and entrepreneurs to run small projects, providing them with immediate access and saving them from any undue financial exploitation. A borrower had to have a deposit account with regular savings for at least six months before he could be considered for credit facilities. The formula was ideologically acceptable to the political leadership, and the bank was regarded as a public sector institution enjoying 'a degree of operational autonomy but ultimately accountable to the State' (el-Ashker, 1987: 155–159). A special fund was set up by the bank for pooling local *zakat* revenues paid voluntarily by individuals, to be used for the purpose of supporting social services. Within five years of its inception, the bank had become fairly prosperous and several provincial branches had been opened. However, the uncertain financial and political atmosphere following the defeat of 1967 had subjected the bank to competing influences and in the end it was placed under direct state control, eventually to be absorbed into the mainstream banking system.

The Nasser Social Bank, established under Sadat in 1971 (before the 'socialistic' orientation of the regime was reversed), was a revival of the Mit Ghamr Bank, with Najjar still the driving force behind the new endeavour. This time, the new Nasser Social Bank (being affiliated to the Ministry of the Treasury) was to receive financial support from the State, which enabled it to fulfil functions that were similar to, but wider than, those of its predecessor. Again it was a non-interest organisation, but it benefited from government donations, pension and insurance contributions, from exemption from all taxes and fees, and from a number of investments in public and in private projects, in addition to *zakat* contributions from individuals. It accepted savings (for investment purposes) and extended credits to small entrepreneurs. The *raison d'être* for the bank was expressed in pseudo-socialistic terms:

> In a society of 'sufficiency and justice', believing that work is the main foundation of society . . . capital has, above all, a social function, and – unlike in a capitalist society – it should be subjected to the requirements of serving its individuals, and should be freed

from any suspicion of exploitation or injustice. Thus it has been decided to replace the principle of fixed interest with a principle of 'partnership'. For a society of 'sufficiency and justice' is required to put capital in the service of every citizen who wants to work but is unable to pay for the cost of obtaining the means of work. (in 'Atiyya, 1987: 33–34)

This was the organisational model for all the 'Islamic banks' that emerged in the Arab world following the oil boom. Egypt had encouraged the idea of Islamic banking on an international level as part of her efforts in the seventies to attract petro-dollars. In 1973 the Islamic Conference Organisation decided, on the basis of an Egyptian study, to establish an international development bank, and this was duly inaugurated in 1975 as an inter-governmental Islamic Development Bank.

The first private commercial bank carrying the Islamic label was the Dubai Islamic Bank, established in 1975 by Shaikh Sa'id Lutah. It was followed, on a larger scale, by an initiative from Prince Muhammad al-Faisal of Saudi Arabia in 1977 to establish the Faisal Islamic Banks, with important contributions from leading Saudi businessmen such as Prince Sa'ud bin 'Abd al-'Aziz, Shaikh Salih Kamil, Shaikh Fahd al-Shubukshi, Shaikh Husain al-Harithi, Shaikh Ahmad Jamjum, and others. Thus emerged the Faisal Islamic Bank of Egypt, and the Faisal Islamic Bank of Sudan, to be followed by the Islamic Bank of Jordan, the Bait al-Tamwil of Kuwait, and the Islamic Bank of Bahrain. Salih Kamil also initiated the Al-Baraka financial group in 1982, which was soon to cover a wide geographical range in and outside the Muslim world (including Al-Baraka Ltd. in London). And Prince Muhammad al-Faisal Al-Sa'ud initiated the Geneva-based Dar al-Mal al-Islami in 1981, which also spread its branches to several countries.

Other Islamic financial institutions subsequently followed in other Arab and Muslim countries (e.g. Malaysia, Turkey, the United Arab Emirates, Tunisia, Senegal, Bangladesh, Mauritania), with some even being established in non-Muslim countries (such as the International Islamic Bank in Denmark and Al-Baraka International Bank in Britain). In addition, other banks were established which were directed jointly by a number of governments of Muslim countries, such as the Islamic Development Bank based in Saudi Arabia, which was established, as already noted, by the Organisation of Islamic Conference, and the International Islamic Bank of Investment and Development, which is based in Egypt. Some ordinary banks also started to take advantage of the rising tide by opening special 'Islamic' departments.

In the eighties, two 'Islamic' governments obliged all their banks to follow non-interest practices: Pakistan through a series of laws culminating in 1985, and Iran in 1984. Many of the Islamic banks have joined the International Association of Islamic Banks, whose articles of association were signed in 1977.

Sudan represents a case in between, as the entire banking system there was 'Islamised' for a while under Numairi, when all banks were instructed in December 1984 to follow Islamic banking practices and not to charge interest. Seven banks in Sudan were based specifically on the principle of Islamic banking: the Faisal Islamic Bank of Sudan, established in 1978, was the first and was followed by the Islamic Cooperative Development Bank, Tadamun Islamic Bank of Sudan, Al-Baraka Bank, Islamic Bank of Western Sudan, and the Bank of Northern Sudan (EIU, 1987–1988: 37). Until February 1984, Islamic banks were exempt from business and 'development' taxes, and this contributed to their success in offering higher returns than conventional banks. Some of the banks also established their own 'Islamic' companies (e.g. the Islamic Company for Trade and Services, the Islamic Insurance Company Ltd., etc.).[1]

Islamic banks, as we have seen, possess respectable funds (around $12 billion in 1984), but their share of total banking in the region is not in any way particularly remarkable. Only two of the largest Islamic banks are to be found in the annual list published by *The Banker* of the top 100 banks in the Arab world. The Kuwait Finance House entered the list on rank 94 in 1979 and climbed to rank 32 in 1984 as the sixth of seven Kuwaiti banks in that list, and the Faisal Islamic Bank of Egypt entered on rank 77 in 1981 and climbed to rank 51 as the seventh of thirteen Egyptian banks in 1984 (Nienhaus, 1986: 6). Most Islamic banks presented impressive growth rates in their earlier years, in terms of capital, deposits and total assets. This was partly due to the exemption given them from normal banking, financial and taxation regulations in several countries, and to their initial success in mobilising funds. They were able to offer competitive rates both to shareholders and to depositors at most times. However, the banks tended to suffer from over-liquidity as it became increasingly difficult for them to find adequate and legitimate profitable utilisations for their funds. Furthermore, the profitability of the banks is probably not as impressive as it appears, due to their practice of lumping together as profits in their balance sheets both the profit shares to shareholders and the profit (interest) shares due to depositors (ibid.: 8).

In some cases, bringing the Islamic banks under the controls enforced by the national central banks on all credit institutions resulted in constraining their profitability. For example, the attempt by the Bank of Sudan to subject the Islamic Banks in Sudan to normal banking regulations and controls has resulted in their development being hampered (Ahmed, 1988: 227–228). The Faisal Islamic Bank of Egypt enjoyed exemption from all normal banking and financial regulation, and was exempt from all taxes for its initial fifteen years, which ended in 1981. Apparently, however, the bank resorted to a number of 'malpractices' to keep its profits high, including foreign currency speculation, which is not allowed by the Egyptian authorities (*Al-Ahram al-Iqtisadi*, 9 March 1987). In order to evade regulation by the central banks, the Islamic banks resorted, in some cases, to registering themselves overseas, such as with the Islamic Banking System incorporated, which was initially registered in Luxembourg (and which is now the Islamic Finance House Universal Holding, owning the equity of the International Islamic Bank of Denmark, the fully licensed Islamic bank in Europe), and Dar Al-Mal al-Islami incorporated, which is registered in the Bahamas (and managed from Switzerland).

The practices of these banks can be described as 'Islamic' only in a very broad and generalised sense. As one involved practitioner admitted, some Islamic banks delegate the job of investing in international markets to conventional banks that act on their behalf. The non-Islamic bank then performs the transactions on behalf of the Islamic bank according to its own systems, organisation and personnel, thus engaging the latter in usury and other prohibited dealings at one remove ('Atiyya, 1987: 71).

Islamic banks have also found it extremely impractical to apply the conventional juridic concepts of *mudaraba* and *musharaka* to banking operations.[2] They tried to improvise various profit–loss sharing formulas, but this was not always easy, especially within countries where the total *economic* system was not fully 'Islamised', which is the more prevalent case. The Islamic banks have had to resort to a great deal of innovation (which they tend to describe as *ijtihad*) in order to arrive at profitable, but ostensibly Islamically legitimate, patterns of dealings. Apart from government-sponsored 'Islamic' banks, most have taken the form of commercial banks, acting as public limited companies. The earlier inclination towards the idea of cooperative banks was not expanded, nor were local development banks or specialised investment banks initiated. A very small percentage was spent by the Islamic banks on medium- and long-term investment financing (5 per cent of the total in the case of the Faisal Islamic Bank of Egypt and 2.5 per cent in the case of the Kuwait Finance House in 1983) (ibid.: 166–179).

Although Islamic banks have criticised conventional banks for having separated money from its owner who, it is claimed, should be directly involved in its utilisation, especially in *socially* rewarding activities, 'the reality of most Islamic banks has gone in a completely different direction' (ibid.: 180ff). Thus, for example, in 1983 the Kuwait Finance House placed and / or invested 18 per cent of its assets, the Faisal Islamic Bank of Sudan 19 per cent of its assets, and the Faisal Islamic Bank in Egypt 34 per cent of its utilisations, all into foreign banks (ibid.: 181–183). Even deposits by an Islamic bank into the central bank of its country of domicile (which is a government requirement in several countries) is quite a tricky business. Some Islamic banks do indeed accept interest payments from their central banks, though they deny that such payments represent usury by claiming that the rates are usually *administratively* fixed (that is, they are not determined through market fluctuations).

In addition, the Islamic banks have expanded too much into the lucrative *murabaha* field at the expense of the more Islamically-legitimate, if rather risky, instruments of *mudaraba* and *musharaka*. This represents a departure from the original Islamic ideal, since *murabaha* is an indirect form of financial involvement whereby the return of finance is represented by a pre-determined margin of profit that is not directly related to the activity of the client who bought the commodity. Further, the main area for *murabaha* sales is in the commercial sector and is very limited in industry and in agriculture. In fact the main field is in financing foreign rather than local trade, particularly in the area of importation, which is not a very attractive activity from a developmental point of view. It can thus be concluded that whereas the Islamic banks appeared initially to favour financing small artisans and entrepreneurs in order to emphasise the role of work and diligence, they have ended up financing the already well-to-do. And although they have claimed to work for a comprehensive Islamic economic order, they have ended up being 'servant institutions to the capitalist world system, acting within the same framework of economic and financial relations of dependency, even though they have hung an Islamic label on each of the existing systems, instruments and contracts' (ibid.: 184–192).

The ascendance of Islamic banking cannot be explained simply in terms of growing religious piety. It is true that such institutions resort outwardly to a great deal of Islamic symbolism: the appointment of *shar'i* controllers or consultants, the appearance of Quranic verses everywhere, the modest dress of Islamic bank officials, and the strict observing of prayers during working hours. More instrumental to the whole process, however, has been the growth of financial reserves resulting from the oil boom, which has affected the rich and the not-so-rich in the region.

The Islamic banks represent an endeavour by the rising Arab commercial bourgeoisie to employ petro-dollars in the highest paying types of mercantile activities (Ghunaim, 1986: 298–307). For this reason, the banks have been criticised by many for their excessive emphasis on commercial activities and particularly for speculation in foreign currencies and precious metals. This last is another point of friction between them and their respective governments, since state laws often prohibit such speculation while the religious advisors of the banks permit it, with evidence to show that in any case the ban was not complete (Huwaidi, 1987: 173).

To enable the Islamic banks and companies to impart religious legitimacy to their activities, they employ well-paid and high-ranking religious scholars (*ulama*) to offer religio-legal consultation about their activities. In Egypt, six members of the highest Islamic authority (the Islamic Research Combine) are advisors to Islamic banks, and these individuals have been accused by some (reportedly including the President) of refusing – because of their vested interests with the Islamic banks – to issue a religio-legal counsel authorising the State's investment bonds (ibid.: 153–158).

The emergence of Islamic banking has been part of the rise, both financially and politically, of the regional *pax Saudiana* which followed the 1973 oil boom. This is a conservative, pro-Western, but *culturally* Islamist variety of Islamic influence that some local critics call 'petro-Islam' and others call 'American Islam' (since the United States and the Gulf ruling families are presumed to be strategic allies within an American-led world capitalism) (cf. Zakariyya, 1986: 21–26). The sudden availability of an abundance of funds in societies not previously familiar with managing credit on a large scale according to Western methods was a very important factor in the growth of Islamic banking. Whatever surpluses had been available to the princely circles before the oil boom were customarily invested in Western and in Lebanese banks. The sudden flow of money into the hands of larger groups of people, both Gulfian and expatriate, encouraged the experimentation with financial practices that would have more of a 'native' feel to them. This, of course, would include perceived Islamic principles as a major part of the native culture.

The Al-Rajhi Company for Currency Exchange and Commerce is a good case in point. Starting as a money exchange house in Saudi Arabia before the big boom, it found itself after the oil bonanza with huge deposits that were a temptation to invest. In 1983 it obtained a royal decree that allowed it to engage in a full range of banking activity, based on Islamic principles. The company expanded with more than 275 branches throughout Saudi Arabia and now invests on behalf of its depositors in foreign company bonds and in commodity trading. Two-thirds of the Al-Rajhi Company's total assets of about $5 billion are held in cash as bank balances, and the remaining amount is utilised in mainly short-term 'Islamic investment' activities (Nienhaus, 1986: 6–7). A set-up such as that of Al-Rajhi is more accessible and has a more familiar look and feel about it, especially for first-time dealers, customers and depositors, than a branch of a Western-style bank. Banks carrying an Islamic appellation are more likely to attract people who have not traditionally used banking services. Thus, for example, the Bahrain-based Al-Baraka Islamic Investment Bank, which started operations in 1984 with the specific aim of creating a secondary market in Islamic financial instruments, was, according to its general manager, to encounter 'an initial rush of deposits from Saudi Arabia and the Gulf States, 60 percent of which . . . came from people who did not use the banking system at all before' (Khouri, 1987: 23).

ISLAMIC COMPANIES

The expansion of Al-Rajhi from a money-changing house into a credit-taking and credit-giving commercial bank-cum-investment company has very little about it that can be considered specifically Islamic. Similar practices could be observed on a smaller scale in countries such as Lebanon, Jordan and Egypt, involving Christian as well as Muslim dealers.[3] The credit formula in such set-ups is not always interest-based, in the modern banking fashion (the financing of commodity or equipment purchases is a familiar practice). This is more of a 'native' type of practice in being – at this stage of development – a more mercantile form of using and circulating merchant capital. It is in this light that one can understand the so-called Islamic 'money utilisation companies' (MUCs) or *sharikat tawzif al-amwal* that have emerged in recent years. Al-Rajhi's is an important example of this genre, but the largest number of such companies exists in Egypt and to a lesser extent in the Sudan (Hamdi, 1989: 3).

To some extent, these companies try to emulate the practices of the larger and 'legal' Islamic banks. However, being subject to few legal requirements regarding their 'shares', budgets, investments and so on, they have had far more freedom of action than have the Islamic banks. In terms of their functions, the Islamic banks and the MUCs are technically quite similar, in that, albeit in different proportions, they are both deposit-takers as well as direct investors.

As with the Islamic banks, it is also our contention that the so-called Islamic companies are not really 'Islamic' except in the most tenuous of meanings. These are in some ways the most 'native' in style of Egyptian enterprises. They are personal (rather than 'anonymous' or 'limited') companies, usually run by a successful self-made entrepreneur assisted by family members, kin and acquaintances. The original capital would most probably have been obtained through working in, or doing business with, Saudi Arabia or other Gulf countries. As some of these businesses became successful (mainly in mercantile activities), holders of relatively small foreign currency reserves (usually again acquired from working in a conservative oil country) would ask the successful entrepreneur to 'employ their money for them'. Eventually, the 'Islamic' label is given to such companies (a) to impart a sense of respectability to what, according to Egyptian law, did not count as a proper company, and (b) to appeal to the conservative inclination of the holders of relatively small sums of foreign currency who are especially influenced by the growing Islamic religiosity, and who would therefore like to avoid investing in banks that offer 'interest' on deposits (interest being taken as another term for usury, which – they are being told – is Islamically prohibited).

It may be useful at this point to trace some of the origins of how, quite early on, the process of collecting financial capital acquired a certain 'Islamic' flavour. When the Nasserist regime nationalised all financial institutions and most business concerns in Egypt in the period from 1958 to 1963, the remarkable degree to which non-Muslims were represented within the financial and business elite was glaringly obvious. In the case of banks, the majority of employed personnel was also non-Muslim, and banks, for example, observed Sundays and Christian holidays. The sixties was a period when such businesses, with their partly foreign, partly 'minoritarian' cultural outlook, were gradually submerged into a growing state capitalism (cf. Ayubi, 1980A). In the process, a few Muslim entrepreneurs managed partly to escape the heavy hand of the nationalising authority. The most famous and the most important of these entrepreneurs was 'Uthman Ahmad 'Uthman, a contractor-engineer whose vast company played a large role in the construction of the Aswan High Dam, among other projects. Nasser's policies put the regime in confrontation with the Muslim Brothers (as we have seen in Chapter 6), many of whom fled to neighbouring conservative states, notably Arabia, the Gulf and Libya. There, while condemning Nasser's socialist policies as being atheist and ungodly, they received the protection of the rulers, and many of them managed to accumulate some respectable funds. Many of those Brothers who remained in Egypt were able to find a relatively safe haven in one of 'Uthman's companies.

'Uthman was born and raised in Isma'iliyya, where, according to his account, he was a pupil of Hasan al-Banna, the man who initiated the Muslim Brothers' movement. 'Uthman also admits to subsequent membership in the Brotherhood ('Uthman, 1981: 354–359). His companies employed many Brothers, to such a degree that Nasser was reported to have asked: 'Is this a contractors' company or a hideout for the Muslim Brothers?'. 'Uthman himself had a network of companies in various Arab countries, and using his extensive influence he managed to get round the travel restrictions imposed by the security authorities and to send Brothers 'in danger' to work in his companies abroad (ibid.: 373). He admitted (382–384) that he was 'so vulnerable when it came to granting any wish expressed by a member of the Muslim Brothers' that on occasion he was duped into recruiting engineers who claimed falsely to be members of the Society in order to gain access to his successful companies.

'Uthman was to exert tremendous influence on Sadat during the seventies, presumably because his example of capitalist success struck a responsive chord with the president. He used his influence to persuade the president to allow a political and economic rehabilitation of the Muslim Brothers, a process which included the return home of several by now wealthy Ikhwan from their hiding places in the Gulf, to participate in the infitah carnival. One of these was the Ikhwani millionaire 'Abd al-'Azim Abu Luqma, who bought the nationalised (ex-Swiss) and formerly chic Groppi tea halls, and declared them 'Islamic' by prohibiting them from serving alcoholic drinks. A nativist-cum-Islamic commercial bourgeoisie was now using infitah to establish its social and economic hegemony. 'Uthman was also instrumental in resolving the various crises that erupted between the Islamic groups and Sadat whenever the groups appeared to depart from the political line that the president had drawn up for them.

From the late seventies, and with the Islamic resurgence, several businessmen and entrepreneurs started to apply the appellation 'Islamic' to their enterprises. To live up to their Islamic description, their owners soon took to wearing white gowns, growing thick beards and holding long rosaries! Five such commercial and industrial enterprises are surveyed by el-Ashker (1987: 196–208). A good, if somewhat untypical, case in point is that of Al-Sharif Plastic Company. The founders of this company had been in business since the early fifties; their company was nationalised in 1961, but the ex-owners started another small enterprise for making the same products, which grew slowly and cautiously and mostly manufactured spare parts that were difficult to import. In 1973 the company raised funds from relatives and friends in Egypt, Lebanon and the Gulf and subsequently made use of the infitah policies to expand its activities. It is currently a parent company of a group consisting of about twenty associated companies that are owned by families and friends (estimated capital value of £E450 million), and by Egyptian standards it is considered large. It expanded into various fields in addition to plastics, such as netting, rope, cement bricks, tiles, glassware, building materials, electric equipment and ballpoint pens and stationery, and it was even considering investment in the motor industry. The Company is able to raise required equity finance on its own by seeking public subscription. Short-term financing comes from two main sources: trade credit and joint-venture investment with fund suppliers (ibid.: 195–196). The 'Islamic' character of the company is derived from practices such as 'no-interest' transactions and the holding of prayers at work.

Some sole proprietor enterprises also started to describe their businesses as being Islamic. Of these, Ashker has surveyed eighteen trading cases in the fields of grocery, haberdashery, clothing, housewares including electrical goods, tiles and sanitary fixtures (ibid.: 196–197). Their 'Islamic-ness' is again derived from no-interest dealings and symbolic manifestations of piety. A growing number of 'Islamic' grocery shops (e.g. those of Al-Salam company) play up their strict *shar'i* scrutinisation of foods and drinks, especially those prepared under 'modern techniques' (including imports in particular) with which the average consumer has traditionally been unfamiliar (cf. *Al-Da'wa*, 14 August 1981: 44). Indeed, some recent religio-juridic debates in the Egyptian press have been little more than an Islamic masking of capitalist competition. An interesting case in point has involved the producers and distributors of grain-fed and pellet-fed poultry, with the religious advisers of each group engaging in endless debates over whether poultry that had consumed feed containing a certain percentage of blood was Islamically prohibited or not (*halal/haram*) (Huwaidi, 1988A: 50–51).

Funds for such projects may be obtained from relatives and friends on the basis of *musharaka*. Sales may be conducted on a credit basis, whereby the selling price is increased by about 4 per cent per annum (is not this really 'interest'?). Most Islamic enterprises engage with Islamic banks in various types of transactions, especially *murabaha*, and although the 'Islamic' entrepreneur is involved in a fairly diversified range of activities, he is 'still regarded as risk averse' (el-Ashker, 1987: 207), in which respect he remains faithful to his 'native' business culture.

The so-called Islamic money utilisation companies have blossomed as part of this general wave. MUCs do not recruit their depositors publicly through general advertising, nor are their subscribers allowed to be shareholders or to participate in any decision-making. There are no issues of shares or bonds, but only of simple indebtedness receipts. Investors have no right to review or to inspect the company's activities, its budget or its projects, nor is there any legal control or financial auditing of its dealings, and technically they have no rights if or when the company or any of its projects go into liquidation. Many have argued that the high net profits distributed by these companies (2–3 per cent monthly or 24–36 per cent annually) could not be the result of any normal type of industrial or commercial investment, and there have been accusations of currency and metals speculation and even suspicions of trading in drugs. Indeed, it is now confirmed that many of the owners of such companies started their careers as black market currency dealers (Shuhaib, 1989: 27–47). Such a level of distribution must, at the very least, be based on the utilisation of the deposits of new customers to pay dividends to existing clients (i.e. the traditional 'pyramid scam' is in operation), and the practice certainly involves extremely high risks.

Capital accumulated by these companies was estimated in 1987 at £E12 billion, including at least $2 billion in foreign currency. One company alone had 300,000 depositors and £E3 billion in capital (which was double that of the Faisal Islamic Bank) (*Al-Ahram al-Iqtisadi*, 2, 9 and 23 February 1987). Although none of the 'financial' activities and practices of the companies is revealed, the image that the MUCs promote for themselves is rather that of involvement in productive investment projects. This is certainly true of the larger ones among them. Al-Rayyan group described itself as 'The citadel of Industry and the cornerstone of Construction' in Egypt, and advertised projects for such things as building, animal husbandry, textile and metallic industries and book publishing. Al-Sharif group described itself as 'the largest Egyptian integrated group working with an open mind, along proper scientific lines' and advertised projects in the fields of basic processing and manufacturing industries, and domestic and international trade as well as finance and investments. Al-Huda group described itself as 'the fastest growing investment company in Egypt', advertising manufacturing, trading and publishing activities, while Al-Hilal group trumpeted its involvement in paper mills, engineering, leather and plastics, cardboard, foodstuffs, agriculture, husbandry, oils, and so on. (cf. advertisements in the local press).

These companies are more a part of the parallel economy than they are a part of the Islamic revival: they are part of a native mercantile capitalism which, because of its origins and experience, is likely to be culturally conservative and therefore, incidentally, inclined to be sympathetic to the Islamic tradition. As such, these MUCs are not particularly 'Islamic', in spite of their appellation. Indeed, some of the money utilisation companies are run by Christians, and those which are not have Christian, or even Jewish, depositors: 'We are a money utilisation company, not a mosque,' said one of the major owners (cf. Shuhaib, 1989: 95, 103). With other members of the rising financial/ commercial bourgeoisie they have on occasion (most notably in 1985) sabotaged government policies that were aimed at the reform of the exchange, banking and imports systems (cf. Ayubi, 1988B: 58–60).

In terms of their social profile, the owners of such companies are on the whole young (in their thirties, late twenties or early forties). They are on the whole newcomers to the league of the wealthy, having usually emerged in the eighties or late seventies (Al-Sharif is a notable exception because he started his career decades earlier, and – untypically – had concentrated on industry). They come mainly from a lower middle class background, with a limited level of higher education and with little previous experience in financial or economic matters. Practically all of them, however, have worked or lived abroad, usually in the Gulf but sometimes also in Europe, where they started building up contacts with expatriate Egyptians working there and offering them services such as changing currency or helping with various purchases and investments in Egypt. Although several of the owners seem to have rather daring, adventurous personalities, they have on the whole had no previous political inclinations or activities until they started their flirtation with the Islamic movements in the mid-eighties. The only two exceptions are 'Abd al-Latif al-Sharif (who was a member of the Muslim Brothers) and Ahmad al-Rayyan (who was a member of Al-Jama'a al-Islamiyya) (Shuhaib, 1989: 53–64).

Among the members of such a class are those who finance the building of 'private' *Ahli* mosques, which have more than doubled in number since 1970, and which have become the meeting and recruiting arena for Islamic militants and religious opponents to the regime. It is also believed that some of the bigger Money Utilisation Companies had contributed financially in support of the Islamist candidates in the April 1987 elections. The Muslim Brothers gained thirty-six seats in this election, bringing into parliament some of their prominent leaders as well as the son of the founder al-Banna and the son of the second leader al-Hudaibi. Generous funding is needed if one is to compete successfully with candidates of the ruling National Democratic Party, who are supported by the powerful organisational, financial and informational network at the disposal of the State.

* * *

What are the political implications of the growth in the Islamic economic sector? To start with, it is not unreasonable to imagine that some rich Islamic personalities and financial institutions might be behind the political promotion of Islamist elements in certain countries. Such allegations were raised, for example, in Kuwait with regard to successful candidates from *Jam'iyyat al-Islah* who joined the Kuwaiti parliament after the 1975 elections (PDK, 1978); in Sudan with regard to successful Muslim Brothers' candidates in the 1985 elections (cf. *Al-Rayah*, 1 March 1989) and in Egypt with regard to successful candidates from the Muslim Brotherhood and other Islamic groupings in the 1987 elections (Ebeid, 1989: 43).

The case of Egypt is, again, particularly significant. Some observers suspect that the setting up of Islamic economic and financial institutions represents a conscious strategy by the Islamic movements for subsidising and financing their political, social and organisational activities, or at least for linking the supporters, the sympathisers and the religiously-inclined to the Islamic movement not only by spiritual ties but also by interest-based institutionalised bonds ('Abd al-Fattah in Ibrahim, 1988: 182).

If it is true that the Islamic movements have indeed secured for themselves such regular and reliable sources of finance, then this must represent a great qualitative improvement on earlier methods used by the Islamic organisations to mobilise capital. These had included the setting up of cottage industries and of kiosks for the sale of vegetables by the Takfir group, and rotated employment in Gulf countries and sporadic raids on Christian jewellers by the Jihad group. It seems that some doctrinaire Islamists who are opposed in principle to dealing with the institutions of an 'infidel' State have resorted to currency speculation as both a lucrative as well as a desirably anti-State activity (ibid.). And indeed some Muslim clerics, such as Shaikh Hafiz Salama and

Shaikh Salah Abu Isma'il, even issued *fatwas* maintaining that currency speculation was Islamically legitimate (Shuhaib, 1989: 126–30).

It does not seem to me, however, that the radical Islamic organisations have gone in for setting up Islamic enterprises in any big and organised way. Rather, it is the rising native mercantile bourgeoisie that has stretched its hand to the Islamic movement in order to impart to itself a certain element of religious legitimacy. In doing this, the mercantile bourgeoisie seems more often to have sought help from the more traditional and conservative segments of the Islamic movement. It is quite possible, of course, that the two forces will coalesce at some stage, but I think that the moving force behind such a process is more likely to be the mercantile bourgeoisie than the Islamic movement. If the 'Islamic' enterprises are now to be found organically linked to any other social forces, it is not really to the Islamic movement that they are tied but rather to the broader class of the 'lumpen' commercial bourgeoisie. If the Islamic movement and the commercial bourgeoisie seem to overlap at certain points, this is basically because of their shared hostility to the State Establishment. But unlike many radical Islamists, the owners of the so-called Islamic companies are prepared, for their own materialist purposes, to ally themselves with elements in the State apparatus and the official and non-official press (cf. ibid.: 113–126; al-Qa'id, 1988). Indeed the Islamic companies have coopted a number of influential political figures (including ex-ministers and governors) and outspoken editors and journalists (including some in the opposition press), and some of these coopted figures are far from being sympathetic to the radical Islamic movements.

The confrontation between the Islamic companies and the State reached its peak in mid-1987, at which time draft laws were being prepared by the government to regulate and to bring under control the activities of the companies (numbering 138 at that point). Zaki Badr, Minister of the Interior, condemned the companies and called for Egyptians to withdraw their savings from them. Remarking that some of the company owners were 'crooks' who were subverting the national economy, while some were financing 'extremist (religious) tendencies' and maintaining 'suspect' foreign contacts, he said that his ministry would play an important role in any vigorous confrontation with these MUCs. The Public Prosecutor also stated that recent investigations had revealed the involvement of some of these firms in cases that were 'detrimental to Egyptian national security', while the head of the military police confirmed that there was evidence linking the companies to 'antagonistic foreign interests' which were attempting 'to penetrate Egypt's national security system, subvert its stability and achieve internal economic control'. A statement issued by the Union of Egyptian Banks warned the public against putting their savings with these companies (cf. *Mid-East Mirror*, vol. 1, no. 134, 19 August 1987).

The Islamic companies responded vociferously and threatened to hold a mass protest rally in June 1988, thus obliging the government to pass a new law concerning the organisation of these companies' activities, which represented a considerably watered down version of the intended earlier drafts. Depositors continued to have no direct say in the management of the companies, government regulation remained only of a marginal supervisory nature, and plans to appoint official auditors to the boards of these companies were dropped. The new law on 'deposit-taking companies', as they are now called, has thus confined itself to converting the Islamic companies into 'standard' joint shareholding companies with regard to the method of their formation (*MEES*, 13 June 1988; *Oxford Analytica*, 22 June 1988).

Why did the State act so belatedly and so minimally with regard to the activities of the MUCs? Although the State authorities had been aware of the illegal practices of these companies since the early eighties, it was only the spectacular bankruptcy of some of them, their failure to pay out to their panicky depositors and the theatrical attempts by some of the owners to camouflage their crisis by resorting to mergers, that prompted the State to interfere. According to one interpretation, the State could not but interfere when the companies exceeded the 'permitted line of tolerance'. They did this, it is suggested, when they tried to involve members of the armed forces in an insurance project of theirs, and when they contributed to the finance of a number of militant Islamic organisations. The State must have been particularly alarmed to see these companies infiltrating and/or manipulating some of the State organs (the company owners boasted in 1987, for example, that they were behind the removal of the Governor of the Central Bank). However, that very infiltration of the State organs must also explain why the political action against the companies was slow and, in the final analysis, rather limited in its scope. Indeed, the political leadership was quite reluctant to interfere too soon with what was popularly regarded as successful business, and was obliged to do this only when the financial crisis of these companies became too acute to ignore without damaging the credibility of the State altogether (compare Shuhaib, 1989: 226-232).

There is no doubt that the MUCs have set about carving out for themselves – at the expense of the State – as large an economic and political space as possible.[4] In doing so, however, they have represented an ascending local capitalism with an Islamic face, rather than the economic wing of a growing Islamic fundamentalist movement. The Islamic banks and companies should be regarded more as part of a powerful parallel economy than as part of the 'Islamic revival' that is currently taking place. They represent an important component of a growing native bourgeoisie that, because of its origins and experience, is inclined to opt for mercantile activities in the economic sphere, and to manifest conservative attitudes in the cultural and political sphere. Although they appear to share with the Islamic movement a similar kind of vocabulary, and though they may on occasion ally themselves temporarily with some Islamists, the two groups are quite different. To use a familiar Arabic play on words, if the banks and companies are more representative of the action of *Al-Islam al-tharwi* (an Islam of wealth), the militant Islamic organisations are more representative of the action of *Al-Islam al-thawri* (a revolutionary Islam).

Within the phenomenon of *tharwi* (wealth) Islam itself one could possibly distinguish between a higher level and a lower level: at the higher level there are the Islamic banks which are part of the mainstream phenomenon of 'petro-Islam' and, as such, are closely linked to the world capitalist order. At a lower level there are the MUCs which are mainly an outcome of the spillovers (outside the Gulf) of the petroleum phenomenon. Even within the MUCs themselves, one should probably distinguish between the company owner-managers, who represent a rising native commercial bourgeoisie, and the depositors who are often people of lower- and middle-class backgrounds, trying to invest their relatively limited funds in a rewarding way. These latter are motivated to invest in such companies because of a mixture of religious piety, combined with the easier access to managers of such companies that is provided by family, friendship and neighbourhood networks.

ISLAMIC SOCIAL SERVICES

Another area that has witnessed a growing process of 'Islamisation' is that of social services. Here again, the most elaborate case, and the one on which we have the most information, is that of Egypt, but there is also evidence that Islamic charitable societies are expanding their social and medical services in other countries, most notably in the Sudan (cf. e.g. *Al-Rayah*, 2 February 1989: 2).

Voluntary social welfare societies, of which some may be religiously inspired or sponsored, date back to the late nineteenth and early twentieth centuries. The Islamic Philanthropic Societies (*Al-Jam'iyyat al-khairiyya al-Islamiyya*) have traditionally been among the most renowned of such societies, usually involving themselves in founding religious schools, orphanages, homes for the elderly, and other such charitable activities. Non-governmental societies of all descriptions have to be registered with the Ministry of Social Affairs: there were some 13,000 of these societies in Egypt by the end of 1986 (Amer, 1988). As we have just mentioned, only some of such voluntary societies are formed on a 'religious' basis. Up to the early seventies, there were *proportionately* more Christian than Muslim societies. Given that Islam is the State religion and given the large role played by the State in social affairs, it was understandable that non-Muslims would have required more voluntary societies to attend to their specific social and cultural needs. A parliamentary commission formed to investigate the sectarian clashes of 1972 reported that there were then 679 Muslim societies and 438 Christian societies registered with the Ministry of Social Affairs (Badawi, 1980: 71; *Al-Ahram*, 29 November 1972).

The relative retrenchment in the State's social and economic role in the seventies and eighties has, however, led to a decline in the level and quality of services offered by the State in various fields such as health care, schooling and vocational training. The government's job has been further constrained by various foreign and international donors who insist that the government should opt more and more out of such services and leave them to private and grass-roots bodies. The private mosques and the philanthropic societies have increasingly had to step in to fill the gaps that have resulted from recent governmental actions such as budget cuts, the removal of subsidies on food, clothing material and medicine, and the slowing down of the public employment of graduates. This, and the general atmosphere of Islamic revival, has led to a growth in the number of Muslim voluntary societies from about 600 in the early seventies to about 2000 in the mid-eighties (Amer, 1988). Some of these Muslim societies have grown in tandem with the so-called 'private' (*ahli*) mosques built by members of the community.

Ahli mosques have proliferated in the seventies and eighties. Since the forties, the Ministry of Awqaf has customarily been committed to providing each mosque in the country with an adequately qualified 'official' preacher, whose salary was government-paid. However, with the passage of time, public budgetary cuts combined with the availability of funds in private hands has meant that the Ministry of Awqaf could not cope with the demand for new preachers. In 1962 there were about 3000 government-controlled mosques and about 14,000 privately-owned ones. Twenty years later, the number of government-controlled mosques had doubled to about 6000, whereas the number of private mosques had nearly trebled, to over 40,000. (The number of private mosques was 20,000 in 1970 and had doubled by 1981) (Hammuda, 1987A: 214; *Rose al-Yusuf*, 1 March 1982).

In the mid-eighties, the Ministry of Awqaf could provide only about 5300 officially sponsored preachers. Other mosques rely on voluntary preachers who are often members of, or sympathisers with, the Muslim Brothers and other politicised Islamic groups. Whereas official preachers are either provided with formal sermon texts or apply a kind of self-censorship to their own sermons, voluntary preachers have often been more critical of the regime, and their mosques have often witnessed demonstrations and clashes between the worshippers and the police in Cairo, Alexandria, Minya, Asyut, Suez, Fayyum and elsewhere.

Many of the larger private mosques in the cities were sponsored by Islamic societies that were not particularly friendly to the regime, such as the Khulafa' al-Rashidun in Cairo, the Da'wa al-Islamiyya in Bani Suaif, the Ansar al-Sunna al-Muhammadiyya in Port-Said and Suhag, Fajr al-Islam in Suez, al-Jam'iyya al-Islamiyya li al-da'wa in Asyut, and al-Ihya' al-Islami in Fayyum (*Al-Ahram*, 6 September 1981). Some of their colourful preachers have become outspoken opponents of the regime, including the persistent Shaikh Ahmad al-Mahallawi of Alexandria, who drove Sadat into a temper in 1981, the blind Shaikh 'Abd al-Hamid Kishk of Cairo, whose ringing fiery voice is to be heard on cassette tapes everywhere, and Shaikh Hafiz Salama of Suez who, with his European suit, Turkish fez and long beard, seems to inspire a strange nostalgic mixture of Islamic fundamentalism and Egyptian patriotism.

Islamic societies have always had their conventional religious pursuits such as Quranic memorisation, religious publication, and burial of the dead. In the last decade, however, a growing number of Islamic philanthropic societies have begun to delve into new areas of social service for the community at large. As with 'Islamic' business, 'Islamic' social services also cover a broad spectrum of types and categories. At one extreme there is the lucrative commercially-run business, of which the Mustafa Mahmud Mosque/Society is the most representative. Mustafa Mahmud was trained as a physician but left his medical practice after a few years to become a 'progressive' journalist and story writer. A book by him on *God and Man* was censored in the Nasserist era for being too 'materialistic' in orientation. In the seventies, Mahmud changed his colours, took to presenting televised interpretations of the Quran in which he claimed that religion contained within it all the bases of modern science, and published a number of books that condemned Marxism (cf. e.g. Mahmud, 1982: 155–159). His formula fitted neatly with Sadat's slogan of 'Science and Faith' and appealed to the conservatively inclined in Egypt and in the Gulf. In the eighties, Mustafa Mahmud combined his medical and his mass-media credentials and directed them to the area of private enterprise. The Mustafa Mahmud Mosque, built in the flashy, upper–middle class/*nouveaux riches* suburb of Muhandisin, has a health centre that will soon contain a large ultra-modern hospital. The set-up attracts the well-to-do and appears to be profitable. As with Islamic banks, this is really capitalism with an Islamic face.

The more typical set-up would be a compound of services clustering around a 'private' mosque and a Quranic study circle, providing a small clinic, a kindergarten and possibly a primary school, and a vocational training centre. The Islamic society in charge of such a compound might also collect *zakat* (alms) donations to spend on social services for the needy. Such compounds, varying in size and diversity, are to be found in middle class suburbs, poor quarters and countryside villages. In the latter two categories, vocational training in such things as carpentry, sewing, and household building and repair would be particularly important. An 'Islamic' clinic would normally charge £E1–2 per consultation (about a tenth of what a normal clinic would charge). Another service extended by some of the societies is the provision of cheaper reproductions or photocopies of textbooks for university students. With their humble resources but good targeting of special needs, and in their proud recourse to self-help, such societies are a far cry from, and a stark contrast to the charitable societies that were sponsored on a large and showy scale by the ex-president's wife Jihan Sadat and which received huge donations from Egyptian and Arab dignitaries and from foreign and international agencies (cf. Imam, 1985: 60–69).

There is little doubt that the Islamic societies are increasingly providing an alternative social and organisational network to that sponsored by the State. They fill in the gaps created by the retreat of the State from some of its previous areas of activity, and build closer and more intimate links with the people at the grass-roots level, thus constraining the penetration of the State into society and eroding a great deal of the State's 'achievement-based' claim to legitimacy.

As with the Islamic banks and companies, however, no definite, immediate and automatic political role can be attributed to the Islamic societies as part of an imagined design for seizing political power. Like 'Islamic' enterprise – although admittedly to a lesser extent – Islamic social services involve people who belong to very different social classes, who may use the same religious vocabulary but who speak different political languages. The 'culture' of the users of these services may bring them together at some level, and many of them may share feelings towards the State that would range between hostility and frustration. Only in times of acute crisis, however, might they really act collectively (and most probably only tentatively), to use their growing 'alternative' networks.

* * *

To conclude this chapter we should perhaps reiterate its main theme. An alternative 'Islamic' network of banks, companies and social services is emerging in various parts of the Arab world. This network can be described as 'Islamic' only in a very tenuous sense. As Samir Amin has most persuasively argued, there is no essentialist 'Islamic political economy' that one can speak of regardless of historical contingencies or social forces (Samir Amin, 1985: Ch. 6). The class interests that lie behind the emerging alternative network are varied, and in many cases contradictory. The larger Islamic banks, although perhaps representing an attempt at cultural self-assertion, belong more closely to the 'corporate international bourgeoisie'.[5] The larger Islamic 'money utilisation companies' and some of the large commercially-run hospitals and schools represent the movement of a rising native commercial bourgeoisie. Small depositors in Islamic financial and investment institutions and most clientele of the Islamic social services belong more often than not to the middle and lower-middle classes (or even to lower classes). The owners and the clientele alike are joined together by a common Islamic symbolism that is perhaps more cultural in the general sense than it is religious in a specific sense. Many among them may also share, albeit for different reasons, a generally antagonistic attitude towards the State.

The emerging networks of Islamic banks, companies and social services do not – in my view – represent part of a concerted strategy by the Islamists to take over power. Although parts of the rising native bourgeoisie may at some stage ally itself or even coalesce with some of the Islamic movements, the two forces are not one and the same thing. It is difficult for me to believe that Faisal Al-Sa'ud, the Arabian prince and international financier, and 'Umar al-Tayyib, the humble

Sudanese grocer, are really 'in the same boat'; or that the luxurious Mustafa Mahmud health centre in the prosperous Muhandisin suburb and the drab Fath Islamic clinic in the shabby suburb of Matariyya are really concerned about the same Muslim public.

9 The Islamic liberals answer back

Throughout the seventies and up to the early eighties, the fundamentalists seem to have had the discursive arena practically to themselves. Their discourse had been the most widely heard, to such an extent that some rulers were obliged to 'put on a religious face' by way of pre-empting the Islamists, and to the extent that several previously nationalist and/or socialist writers found themselves increasingly having to use the vocabulary and sometimes the concepts of the Islamists in their debate. There were, of course, some who were answering the fundamentalists in the seventies, but these were either official clerics ('the Sultan's preachers' as the fundamentalists call them) whose discourse was brushed aside as being mere apologia, or else more avowedly secularist writers, most notably Fu'ad Zakariyya, whose 'intellectual alterity' often shed doubt on what they said in the view not only of the fundamentalists but also of some of the religious public.

By the early eighties, however, those whom we call the Islamic liberals had already begun to take the fundamentalists to task, especially with regard to their concepts of *jahiliyya* and *hakimiyya* and their emphasis on the 'politicality' of Islam.[1] Writers who are representative of this liberal Islamic trend are so far mainly, though not exclusively, Egyptian; but whatever is written in Egypt is, of course, read all over the Arab world. This is understandable as Egypt not only hosts the largest and most varied Islamic movement in the Arab world, but is also one of the countries with the longest secular 'tradition' in the region. It should perhaps also be mentioned in passing that the 'Christian liberals' have also started to answer back, both to the proponents of 'political Islam' and, sometimes, to the proponents of 'political Christianity'.[2]

The debate was revived in several explicit and implicit ways over a reconsideration of Shaikh 'Ali 'Abd al-Raziq's thesis of the mid-twenties ('Abd al-Raziq, 1966) that Islam was a religion (*din*) and not a State (*dawla*). Interestingly enough, another al-Azhar shaikh, Khalid Muhammad Khalid, had in the late forties arrived at a similar conclusion without having read 'Abd al-Raziq's book (K. Khalid, 1950). Both writers had argued that there is very little of a purely political nature stipulated in the Quran, that the political formulas adopted by the Muslims later on, such as the *khilafa*, were human improvisations, and that the insistence on merging religion with politics would threaten to harm both.

Apparently the vigorous fundamentalist discourse of the seventies had managed to persuade Khalid M. Khalid away from his previous analysis, and at the beginning of the eighties he published another book (K. Khalid, 1981) in which he restates the salafi argument of the totality of Islam, including the concept of a specifically Islamic umma and a specifically Islamic State. This new book, however, is smaller in size and less rigorous in method, and if one examines carefully Khalid's subsequent pronouncements, it becomes apparent that although he has reverted to the conventional Islamist terminology, his concepts are still close enough to his previous analysis. Khalid still argues in favour of *tajdid* (renewal, improvisation, innovation), and contrary to most fundamentalists he believes that *shura* (consultation) is mandatory in Islam and is exactly equivalent to the concept of 'democracy' in its current usage (cf. e.g. *Al-Dawha*, July 1981; *Mayu*, 8 March 1982).

Muhammad Ahmad Khalafalla is an Islamic liberal who has not changed his orientation over the years. The theme of his book on the Quran and the State that was first published in 1973, is still echoed in his current writings. According to Khalafalla all matters of government – political and administrative as well as economic and social – are not proscribed by the Quran but are delegated by God to the people (Khalafalla, 1981). He is clear that if any government is to be described as Islamic, it should be in the sense of 'Islam-the-culture' (*Al-Islam al-hadara*) and not of 'Islam-the-religion' (*Al-Islam al-Din*). The caliphate, in his conception, was a civil, not a religious system, improvised by people and in no way derived from God's authority or Muhammad's prophethood (Khalafalla, 1987: 88–90). Nor should the contemporary Muslims rely too heavily on the elaborations of the early jurists on matters of political and social organisation, because the current 'interests' of Muslims (*masalih*) are very different from the interests of those who lived nearly a thousand years earlier and who thus required different rulings and regulations (Khalafalla, 1985: 6–15).

Muhammad 'Imara is the most prolific of the Islamic liberals and reference has already been made to his ideas in various parts of this work. He also argues that Islam is against imparting a religious character to politics and the State, or uniting the two authorities in one.[3] This should be left for the endeavour of the people. *Imama* (leadership, rule), he reiterates, is not — except for the Shi'is – part of the 'fundamentals of religion' (*usul al-din*), but is a branch of jurisprudence (*furu' al-fiqh*) ('Imara, 1980). Religion and the State were distinguished from the beginning; thus the Quran could be regarded as the 'constitution' of the umma in its religious sense, whereas the *sahifa* (the 'Constitution' of Madina) was meant to regulate the affairs of the umma in its broader, political sense ('Imara, 1979; cf. also 'Imara, 1983, 1984, 1985).

Similar ideas are put forward by several contemporary writers on Islam and politics. Thus, for example, although 'Ismat Saif al-Dawla agrees that *'ibadat* (matters of worship) are *collective* rather than individual in Islam, he rejects the concept of the Islamic state either in the sense of a state including *only* Muslims, or in the sense of a state including *all* Muslims: either of these, he maintains, is 'a mythical state, not an Islamic state' (*dawlat awham la dawlat Islam*) (Saif al-Dawla, 1986: 107ff, 288). In his view, even the caliphate was not an Islamic State because it was based on a decision by the Muslims of the time, and not on a commandment from God or a recommendation from the prophet.

Husain Fawzi al-Najjar (1985) also maintains that although the shari'a has spoken of the community (*umma*), it never spoke of the State (*dawla*). 'The establishment of a State was not one of the objectives of Islam', although the phenomenon of the centralised State was known in the ancient world surrounding Arabia, and even on a limited scale – in its city-state form – in Mecca itself. Nor has Islam projected a form and system of government, although the Islamic principles adhered to by Muslims have tended to colour their governmental systems in certain ways (al-Najjar, 1985: 106ff, 167ff).

One of the most vigorous attacks on the doctrine of political Islam is that launched by Muhammad Sa'id al-'Ashmawi. He holds in no uncertain terms that 'God has wanted Islam a religion; but [some] people wanted it to be politics' (al-'Ashmawi, 1987: 7). No Godly government has existed after that of Muhammad. The neo-fundamentalist concept of God's *hakimiyya* is, in his view, a kharijite deviation, while, in his opinion, the excessive emphasis on shari'a is heavily influenced by Jewish tradition. Unlike Judaism, which is mainly a legislation, Islam is basically a message of compassion and morals, with legislation occupying a secondary place (ibid.: 34ff). Thus among the Quran's 6000 verses, fewer than 700 are of a legislative nature, and of these only about 200 verses deal with *mu'amalat* (regulations of *social* matters) rather than *'ibadat* (regulations of matters of *worship*). He argues that the legislative category has been the main one in Judaism, to the extent that Moses is called the giver of legislation and that the *torah* in Judaism is understood as an act of legislation. The Arabic term *shari'a*, on the other hand, originally meant path or method. Islamic thought has thus, in his view, followed Judaism without realising the difference in nature between the two religions (al-'Ashmawi, 1983B: 22ff).

He further argues that the term *hukm* in the Quran does not mean government as in contemporary usage, but rather adjudication (ibid.: 37ff). This point has also been argued by others such as Muhammad 'Imara, Husain Amin and Mahmud Mutawalli.[4] *Hukm* pertains to settling conflicts among people and to 'judiciary' judgement, whereas *'amr* is the nearest Quranic term to government and politics in the modern concept. 'Ashmawi also maintains that, in addition to legislative requirements being relatively limited in the Quran, some of them were contingent to their time or environment and others could be suspended when their context no longer justified them (ibid.: 45ff). He gives examples from 'Umar, the 'Just Caliph', and from the early jurists: 'Umar, for instance, suspended the penalty for theft during famine and prohibited temporary 'pleasure' (*mut'a*) marriage, even though both were religiously prescribed. On the other hand, there is no penalty for drinking in the Quran although it is considered sinful — the well-known and so-called 'Islamic' penalty of flogging was legislated subsequently by Muslims and can by the same token be removed. He elaborates further by remarking that the shari'a was very much contingent on the conditions of the time and place of its inception, it was greatly influenced by other traditions, and it was always premised on the fulfilment of a certain public interest. It follows that for shari'a to be complete, it should always correspond to social needs and revive itself in relation to developing public interests (ibid.: 51–86).

As for the so-called Islamic penalties (*hudud*), he holds that their application is not mandatory, either by the tradition of the Prophet or by the practice of the early 'guided' caliphs (al-'Ashmawi, 1987: 183ff), and that even in a purely Islamic society their application is contingent upon the establishment of the virtuous and just society where crime would definitely be a deviance. Otherwise civil or authoritative

penalties (*ta'zir*) similar to the ones improvised by the jurists throughout Islamic history should in most cases be sufficient.

'Ashmawi argues that Islamic political concepts, such as the key
concept of 'justice', had always been derived, under all Muslim States
from the Umayyads on, from juridic opinion backed by the State's
'sword'. He reiterates the familiar theme that it was very rare for jurists
to contradict the Sultan, and quotes the well-known statement by the
influential modern jurist 'Abd al-Razzaq al-Sanhuri, to the effect that:

> Public law in Islamic jurisprudence is less advanced than private
> law. It is still in its early stages, with insufficient progress. Appar-
> ently the arrested development of public law may be due to the
> succession of several despotic governments in Islam whose task was
> to suppress any juridic movement that would establish the principles
> of government on bases of political liberty and democratic public
> rights. As for private law in Islamic jurisprudence, it has advanced
> considerably, as despotic government was not harmed by its
> advance.[5] (Quoted in al-'Ashmawi, 1983A)

On political matters, 'Ashmawi concurs with the view that, historically, the Muslim public had either to acquiesce to sultanic interests
that were defended by the collaborationist jurists, or else to resort to
hypocrisy. The pursuit for 'Justice' had thus turned into an overwhelmingly formalistic act of legislation, and contained very little of
an individual consciousness (ibid.: 112–123).

'Ashmawi's characterisation of the contemporary neo-
fundamentalists is quite interesting. To him they are part of a general
world phenomenon of fundamentalism resulting from a widespread
disenchantment with current political and spiritual institutions. What
gives them their distinctive Muslim character is their obsession with
the values of 'nomadic Islam' – that of Madina (*Islam al-badawa*) –
rather than 'civilised Islam' – that of Baghdad (*Islam al-hadara*). He
detects a contemporary 'Arabian' influence, stimulated by migration
to the oil countries and by the influence of the Gulf states, which
imparts a certain inclination towards roughness, violence and vulgar-
ity that in his view is more nomadic than Islamic. He further detects
that people with such an outlook are opponents in a type of class
conflict, within an expanding middle class, between its higher echelons
with their more universal outlook and its lower echelons which are
more culturally introverted (al-'Ashmawi, 1987: 58–62).

'Ashmawi also contributes to the theory that the emergence of
political Islam has been a reaction to the dissolution of the last
caliphate and an expression of cultural and social alarm. He traces the

origins of this theory on political Islam to an article published in 1929 by the jurist 'Abd al-Razzaq al-Sanhuri at the height of the caliphate controversy, the opening sentence of which read: 'Islam is State and Religion' (ibid.: 157). Given the emotional state of affairs in Muslim countries at that time, the slogan found sympathetic circulation and was eventually adopted by many as a position, even as an article of faith. This trend continued, in spite of the fact that the shari'a (Quran and Sunna) is void of a single instruction on 'government' in the political sense, because many Muslims have been inclined to confuse shari'a with *fiqh* (which is an accumulation of *human* opinions on a number of affairs, including government). Thus the call grew for an Islamic government, strengthened by the claim that current regimes in Muslim countries were not Islamic, even though the majority of them were guided in most of their laws by Islamic principles and ethics and borrowed only the techniques of formulation from European positive law (ibid.: 157-163).

Husain Ahmad Amin, like 'Ashmawi, has acquired his reputation mainly through his replies to the theses of the religious fundamentalists and the political Islamists. Basically Husain Amin calls for a revival of *ijtihad* (independent reasoning in religion), which is to be achieved by, among other things, scrutinising the Hadith. The jurists attributed many sayings to the Prophet over the years, by way of filling a social gap and fulfilling a social need. This should teach the contemporary generation that social and political interests had played an important role in the development of the Islamic State, and should also reduce the excessive current inclination to rely too heavily on the Hadith (Amin, 1985: 60-61).

His prescription for reform is a kind of cultural Islam based on 'self confidence' and constructed around the values that the Islamic religion, the 'Eastern traditions' and the 'Arab intellectual heritage' can offer (ibid.: 128). Within this endeavour, an open mind has to be applied with regard to the Islamic text: consider, for example, the amputation of the hand, which was a suitable penalty for the nomadic society (where, given the transient state of most wealth, theft was almost tantamount to murder). This may not now be suitable, he maintains, at a time when ownership covers real estate and many other items. He offers similar interpretations with regard to the veil, which he attributes to pre-Islamic Persian traditions, and to several other issues (ibid.: 131-132). His recommended approach is to be inspired by what he calls 'the Spirit of Islam' and then by an open-minded interpretation of the text, rather than by what he calls 'the belief in the magic significance of the word' (ibid.: 132–138).

With regard to the popular call for the immediate application of shari'a, Husain Amin does not see this as a simple straightforward task, since the Quran and the Sunna have only limited legislative stipulations, while the fiqh tracts are replete with contradictory rulings (Amin, 1987: 186ff). Muslim rulers, including the early 'guided' caliphs, had also relied extensively on the local traditions, and had on occasion suspended or amended 'religious' rulings (ibid.: 190ff). At least, that is, until Shafi'i decided more or less to raise the status of Sunna to that of the Quran – and even higher – which resulted in a serious restriction of the scope for legislative freedom (ibid.: 193–194). One way round this inflexibility, he maintains, was for the jurists to 'invent hadiths, that would incorporate their opinions and could cope with current developments, and then attribute them to the prophet' (ibid.: 194). Other rulings were also attributed by the jurists to 'consensus' (*ijma'*) which is also raised by some to a very high level, to the extent that certain parts of shari'a (for instance those on the caliphate), are based almost entirely on *ijma'* (ibid.: 197). Having made the shari'a so inflexible, the Shafi'i and Hanafi jurists then proceeded to write dozens of books on 'tricks and ploys' (*hiyal*) to circumvent it, thus paving the way towards an unhealthy atmosphere of 'hypocrisy' (*nifaq*) which has come to 'characterise Islamic society in a manner that is hardly paralleled in any other society' (ibid.: 207). To be honest, however, jurists and interpreters should acknowledge explicitly that certain rulings of the Quran and Sunna were meant to deal with evils that were closely tied to their time (of the Jahili and of the Prophetic eras), and that subsequent generations have every right to modify these rulings, guided by the 'Spirit of Islam' and its broader perspectives (ibid.: 215–217).

One of Amin's interesting ideas in this respect pertains to the debate between the supporters of shari'a laws and the supporters of positive laws in Egypt. Tariq al-Bishri (referred to in various parts of this work) and others have recently argued that current Egyptian laws were alien (French) in origin and should, for the sake of 'authenticity', be replaced by Islamic laws derived from shari'a and fiqh. Husain Amin's reply to such a call is as follows:

> How can the views of jurists from Iraq, Afghanistan, Andalusia, Syria and Hijaz, dating from a thousand years or more be allowed to restrict the freedom of people in Egypt, for example? . . . I ask them [proponents of the Shari'a], how would they qualify the

systems that came to Egypt [from Arabia], in the seventh century AD, including the legal systems that they ask us today to go back to? Were these in accord with the traditions, values and historical evolution of the Coptic people? What would have been the position of such legalists if they had lived at the time of the Arab conquest of Egypt? And how many years would they consider as necessary before the 'intruding' or 'imported' systems (*wafida*) became a cultural heritage (*turath*) that we are attached to? Is it not possible by the same token that French laws in this land will become, with the passage of time, part of the cultural heritage?[6] (Amin, 1988: 231–235)

Husain Amin's analysis of the contemporary Islamic movements is particularly interesting. First he observes that, from the Muslim Brothers on, the Islamists are no longer individuals writing about reform or revival, but are *organisations* reacting to the social, economic and political problems surrounding them. The new Islamists also go further than the earlier generation of Islamic reformers in assuming that Islam alone, and on its own, can offer the solution to all problems. However, in spite of their insistence on the holistic nature of Islam, they emphasise and reiterate only a few themes, to the point of boredom: usury and interest; veiling and family control; Islamic penalties, and hostility to secularism and to equality between citizens regardless of religious belief (ibid.: 130–136).

What are the causes of this transformation? Amin seems to think that the roots in Egypt can be traced to the Nasserist and Sadatist eras, when traditional ties were dissolved resulting in an excessively individualistic attitude based on personal gain, mutual suspicion and social insecurity (notice the influence of community-based corporatist ideas on his thinking here) (Amin, 1987: 181–182). This rampant individualism, however, could not in Egypt's circumstances enable everybody to become upwardly mobile in reality – indeed several members of the old and new bourgeoisie are currently scared stiff of the likelihood of demotion into semi-proletarian ranks. Many reasoned that they could not avoid such a fate without resorting to deviance and corruption. Most of those who did not want to follow the path of corruption resorted to religion by way of self-defence, through a kind of moral challenge and symbolic resistance (ibid.: 234–236). Thus, under Sadat, a deep-rooted fear of social demotion produced among those unwilling or unable to ameliorate their situation through corruption, a type of religious solidarity that imparted a sense of collective purpose and action (Amin, 1988: 164–166).

At the same time, Husain Amin seems to imply, those who are benefiting from the existing distorted conditions and who are climbing up the socio-economic ladder, are also using religion to pave the way for their own kind of rule. He portrays a likely kind of scenario, similar to that which contributed to the emergence of Fascism. The 'Islamic companies' would encourage the religious movements to take over power, possibly via a *coup d'état*, to contain class conflict and to pre-empt any socialist prospects that this conflict might generate. The application of shari'a as a goal would distract people from their real exploiters, and non-Muslims towards whom their animosity was directed would provide them with a convenient 'scapegoat'. The secularists' wrangling with each other over trivia would give the theocratic/capitalist alliance an easier chance to take over power, and to establish their own 'Fascist' State of clerics and millionaires (ibid.: 309–326).

This observation by Amin is very important in that, although it does not express it in so many words, it confirms the thesis that there is no specifically 'Islamic' political economy: that both the downwardly mobile and the upwardly mobile classes and strata may be exposing their concerns in religious terms. We are suggesting elsewhere in this work that whereas segments of the lower middle classes, with a sense of blocked social mobility, have adopted radical Islamic tendencies, ascending segments of the petite bourgeoisie that have accumulated reasonable funds through the oil boom are more inclined to go for a kind of Islamic symbolism that serves as a spearhead for a rising native commercial bourgeoisie.

Perhaps the fiercest and most courageous criticism of the Islamists is that directed at them by Faraj 'Ali Fawda. Like many others, he is simply a liberal Muslim, and cannot be ranked among the *Islamic* liberals in the strict sense, for – unlike the writers we have already reviewed — he is openly and avowedly a secularist. Yet his significance to the Islamic debate derives from the fact that, unlike, say, Fu'ad Zakariyya, he does not shy away from confronting the Islamists openly with details derived from the traditional tracts on Islamic history and doctrine.

One of Fawda's main tasks is to de-mystify the Islamists' attachment to the Rashidun era as the epitome of the just and pious Islamic State. He reminds his fellow Muslims that of the four early 'guided' caliphs, three were definitely assassinated and the fourth possibly so, all within only three decades of the blessed Hijra and the prophetic rule (Fawda 1985: 15ff). He deduces from this that the Islamic utopia was never achieved by the Islamic caliphate even in its best 'golden age', for there has always been a divergence, and a gap, between Islam the religion and Islam the State. And from this he proceeds to call openly for separating religion from politics, as this will be better for both (ibid.: 23). He argues that the application of shari'a will inevitably lead to a 'religious state' – a concept alien to Islam — and will definitely ruin national integration (ibid.: 52–53). It will also lead to an authoritarian type of government under the banner of fighting the 'corruptors on earth' (*Al-mufsidun fi al-ard*) (ibid.: 63). He quotes extensive examples from the history of despotic and indulgent caliphal rule, where persecution was the fate of those who revealed the slightest degree of disagreement with the ruler (Fawda, 1988: 75–133).

Fawda's alternative is simply 'Egyptian nationalism' (Fawda, 1985: 99–114), the only way, in his view, to avoid the type of strife that erupted in Sudan when Numairi applied shari'a there (ibid.: 115ff). Indeed, Fawda thinks that the decline in the vigour of the nationalist movement is a main cause of the rise of political Islam, reinforced in recent years by the crushing economic crisis:

> If you wondered where the Islamic groupings are concentrated within Cairo, the answer will be: in the peripheral quarters of the extreme East and extreme West of Cairo, not as much in the industrial areas of Shubra al-Khaima or Hilwan, and certainly not in the well-to-do suburbs of Zamalek and Heliopolis. (ibid.: 170–174)

Fawda is unequivocal in stating his belief that the call for establishing a religious government represents 'a total cultural regression' (Fawda *et al.*, 1987: 11ff), whose main casualty would be national unity. The sources of sectarian strife are not foreign, as is often claimed, but are due precisely to calls for the revival of an Islamic State, which cannot, by definition, be tolerant (ibid.: 18). Thus the older competition in Egypt between the two communities of Muslims and Copts over governmental appointments and other opportunities (such as the right to build mosques and churches) is now reinforced by an escalating media campaign critical of the Christians and their beliefs, launched over the television by people such as Shaikh Sha'rawi and on cassettes by people such as Shaikh Kishk, and responded to via sermons and cassettes by people such as Father Bulus Basili (ibid.: 29ff).

Fawda argues that justice is achieved not via a religiously pious rule (because the application of shari'a by the Islamic rulers has not guaranteed it historically), but by a *system* of government based on checks and controls concerning which there are known rules and regulations. This is all the more so as contemporary societies have a whole range of social, economic and organisational problems for which the shari'a has nothing to offer by way of a solution (Fawda, 1988: 22-30ff). Fawda even dares to say that a reading of Islamic history would reveal that we now live 'in a society that by all counts is more superior in its ethical standards, a society that is more advanced and humane regarding relationships between ruler and ruled' and that we owe all this to 'the human culture (that does contradict the essence of religion) and to human rights (which do not contradict those stipulated by Islam)' (ibid.: 134). Only a distorted and selective reading of Islamic history would suggest otherwise. In any case eras long past will never return and it would be more productive for the youth to concentrate their energies on the strengthening of national unity, and on the solving of social and economic problems that are more typical of today's world (ibid.: 140-143).

In winding up this chapter, it is perhaps useful to present briefly the evaluation by a non-Egyptian, publishing outside Egypt, of the current 'Islamic revival'. Khalil 'Ali Haidar is sympathetic to the 'solidaristic' and anti-Imperialist potential of the Islamists' thesis, and appreciative of the fact that the Islamist movements are often an outcome of, and a reaction to, a deteriorating Arab situation with mounting political, economic and 'developmental' crises (Haidar, 1987: 201-205). However, he has serious misgivings with regard to the current Islamist revival. He is opposed to the fusion of religion with politics, economics and social affairs, believing that this would constrain progress and give rise to a number of social miseries. He regards the belief that a 'return to Islam' will solve all problems as a 'great myth' (ibid.: 205). He is particularly disconcerted that it is the graduates of science colleges who spend most of their energies arguing over ancient religious and juridic disputes, and he is also alarmed that, in their desperation, many conservative intellectuals, pious people, and simple folk are nurturing the myth that an assumption of power by religious parties will solve all political, economic and social problems. What he expects, if this was ever to happen, is a completely different picture:

> The religious parties will dominate the consultative council (*majlis al-shura*) preventing anyone whose loyalty appears suspect to them from entering it. The same will apply to the head of the state and to all incumbents of public positions. An iron hegemony will be enforced on all studies and personnel in schools and universities. Severe controls would be imposed on the press and publishing. All those in major positions in ministries, companies, trade unions and associations will be pawns in [the Islamists'] hands. *The religious*

Party will be at the mercy of the merchants, and the merchants will be at the mercy of the Party. There will be continuous conflict, and endless political, social and psychological strife. (ibid.: 206–207 – with some editing; emphasis added)

What makes him inclined to predict this dark image is the fact that although the features of the 'State' stipulated by the Islamists are far from clear, we know definitely that it is going to be an 'ideological State', a fact that is bound to generate divisions in the society, and we can also detect that its aim would be the establishment of a dictatorial, Fascist-type of State that persecutes all opposition and rejects all difference. He is concerned about the implications of the excessive 'superficiality' of the thoughts which the Islamists present, ripe as they are with conspiratorial interpretations that blame every difficulty on a hidden Christian, Jewish or Masonic hand![7] And he does not believe that creeds can replace nations or homelands (*awtan*) as a permanent refuge for peoples; for him 'the [Islamic] revival is temporary and the homelands are lasting' (ibid.: 207–214).

CONCLUSION

It should be clear from the foregoing review that the fundamentalists no longer have the discursive arena entirely to themselves. The Islamic liberals, and the liberal Muslims, have started to answer the challenge of the fundamentalists, and many of them are conducting this debate *in Islamic terms*, which must add substantially to the credibility of their argument. Those whom we call Islamic liberals vary considerably in their ideas and style, but they are generally less 'scriptural' and more historical and social in their understanding of Islam. They are also less hostile to the existing social order, and to its humanist, even to some extent its 'modernist', inclinations. They seek to blend certain elements of a 'modernised Islam' with certain elements of an 'Islamised modernisation'.

It is difficult at this stage to delineate any distinct 'class' character-istics of this group that we call the Islamic liberals. The debate appears to address basically doctrinal and cultural issues. However, it is possible to glean a few general features. The relative emphasis on things such as rationality, development, industrialisation and national independence may suggest that the Islamic liberals speak basically on behalf of a professional, technocratic and entrepreneurial class that is partly associated with the State and partly striving for autonomy from State control. This group can therefore be broadly distinguished both from the ascending mercantile bourgeoisie (of the 'parallel economy' and the 'Islamic' banks and companies), and from the 'proletarianised' intelligentsia (of the frustrated and socially 'blocked' recent graduates or near-graduates).[8]

We should perhaps also refer at this point to a small but distinct post-modernist trend that is emerging among some Arab writers who deal with Islamic topics. Although critical of the reductionism, divisionism and euro-centrism of the 'modernisation' thesis in its common version,[9] such writers are nonetheless concerned about the specific details of the current social and economic crisis, and interested in finding solutions that are both 'developmentalist' but also culturally 'meaningful', and nationally independent. Neo-Islamist writers with nationalist and/or leftist sympathies, such as Hasan Hanafi, Tariq al-Bishri, 'Adil Husain and even to some extent Galal Amin, may be loosely counted among this trend.

Although such neo-Islamists or, to be more accurate, *turathiyyun judud* (new partisans of the cultural heritage) as they are sometimes called, are often taken to be sympathetic to the fundamentalists' cause, they do in reality have more intellectual affinity with the Islamic liberals (compare Flores, 1988: 27–30). It would not be too far-fetched to imagine an eventual convergence between elements of the two groups into a common trend that one might broadly term 'culturalist Islam'.

10 Political Islam: why, and where to?

Eric Wolf (1982) has argued that each mode of production gives rise to a characteristic conjunction of social groups and segments, a conjunction that embodies its dynamic and reproduces the conditions for its proliferation, and that each mode also creates its own characteristic fissures and oppositions. He has furthermore suggested that the encounter of different modes spells contradictions and conflicts for the populations they encompass (Wolf, 1982: 386–387). Once we locate the reality of society in 'historically changing, imperfectly bounded, multiple and branching social alignments' we can also grasp the sense of the fluidity and permeability of cultural sets. Culture is therefore understood as a series of processes that 'construct, reconstruct and dismantle' cognitive and emotional material in response to identifiable determinants. Ideology, as part of culture, 'occurs within the determinate compass of a mode of production, deployed to render nature amenable to human use'. Ideologies 'codify social distinctions not merely as instrumental aspects of social relations, but as grounded in the essence of the universe – in the nature of nature, the nature of human nature, and the nature of society' (ibid.: 388–389).

Wolf further suggests that alternative systems of ideas take various forms, expressing both the relatedness of groups and classes within a given mode, and their opposition. They may appear as different accents or connotations imputed to the same communicative code by social actors occupying distinct points of vantage. These may sound a systematic counterpoint to the mainstream of communication, or may even develop heterodox visions of reality, carrying with them a threat of rebellion against the prevailing order. 'Such connotations, counterpoints, and heterodoxies, moreover, remain but rarely confined within a single social constellation or society. Religion and cults in particular tend to overleap boundaries and to convey ideological alternatives to audiences beyond the frontiers' (ibid.: 390–391).

Thus, if a mode of production gives rise to idea-systems, these are often multiple, and sometimes contradictory. Idea-systems in turn become weapons in the clash of social interests. If there is an 'articulation' of various modes of production in the society, the picture is likely to be even more complex and overlapping, and the definition of ideas is relieved from mechanical correlation with material realities. In fact the delineation of ideological positions may assume a quasi-autonomous character. This process of delineation may reflect not simply socio-economic interest or even the exercise or resistance of power, but also a whole set of cognitive and psychological components. In this process, the cultural repertoire is always being deconstructed and reconstructed in a perpetual process. To achieve hegemony or to counter hegemony, contending groups are forever trying to reach audiences beyond their immediate 'natural' following.

WHY POLITICAL ISLAM

The 'fluidity' of the class conformation in many Arab societies is bound to make cultural and ideological factors not only complex and multi-dimensional, but also exceptionally important both in mediating contradictions and in reconstructing social alliances. The current fluidity of the class conformation is attributable not only to the articulation of various modes of production, but also to the important reversal in many economic policies in several Arab countries in recent years (e.g. from 'socialism' to infitah) and to the important impact of 'other-than-production' criteria in the determination of people's income and status (e.g. 'rentier' types of revenue; temporary migration to the Gulf or to Europe, etc.). Upward as well as downward social mobility can be abrupt, fast and unexpected in such circumstances.

Such fluidity in class conformation, combined with the proportionately large size of the 'middle strata', is bound to blur the perspectives of class consciousness and class identity. Changes in people's social fortunes are likely to be attributed to metaphysical forces such as luck (*hazz*) or fate (*qadar*), or even blessing (*baraka*). Furthermore, many politico-economic facts may be transposed in people's minds in moral terms. Thus capitalist relations of production and of exchange are more likely to be perceived in terms of moral injustice and hedonistic self-indulgence; economic and technological dependency are more likely to be perceived in terms of cultural alienation; and despotic rule is more likely to be perceived in terms of moral corruption (*fasad*) and a desire to oppress (*istid'af*).

The penetration of capitalism into Muslim countries, as part of the 'periphery', has in the current phase brought to prominence a 'managerial bourgeoisie'[1] whose fortunes are affiliated in more ways than one with the State. The 'bureaucratic' fraction of this class spoke the language of 'rationalism', its 'intellectual' fraction spoke the language of 'secularism', and its 'corporate' fraction spoke the language of 'technicism'. The name of the entire game was 'modernisation'. When modernisation stumbled, failing to achieve the promised economic development and instead deepening the alienation and dependency of society, groups that were previously excluded or were promised what was never given, came forward with their alternative ideational system: 'Islam'. Having failed to reap any of the benefits of capitalism and modernisation, they have turned against them and embraced Islamism as 'a community-building movement, seeking to keep the noxious effects of the market, which is identified with secularist immorality, out of the community of believers' (Keyder, 1986: 13).

In suggesting such an explanation, one should of course be wary of the trappings of reductionism. The Islamic movements do indeed have their own Islamist worldview, premised on the concept that the major portion of human energy should be directed towards the act of devotion to God and submission to His will. The philosophical implications of such a belief are not the subject of this present exercise in political analysis. Without in any way belittling the true meaning and essential significance that such beliefs represent to their holders, our main concern here is over the political and socio-economic issues that may lie behind the religious terminology and the theocratic controversies.

Even then, one needs to be aware of the limited explanatory power of socio-economic factors with regard to certain cultural/ideological formulations. For example, socio-economic factors can tell us a great deal about why (and when) militant Islamic movements may appear. At the back of it all there is not only 'dedication to God' but also disappointment with what the various man-made 'isms and 'ocracies have been able to offer to individuals and to the collective membership of a society. However, these factors can tell us very little, and that only indirectly, about the content (the 'what') of their ideologies. Here, the tone, the pitch and the mood (the insistence, the impatience, etc.) are probably more important for political analysis than the 'theological' debate itself, though there are still a few trends that can be detected from the content.

Consider, for example, the inclination of the Islamists to pick up selectively from shari'a and fiqh, and to reconstruct according to their own often 'unorthodox' perspective. Behind this inclination is an attitude of deep distrust of established authority, both clerical and political, especially as these two are linked in the Islamists' thinking (hence the term *fuqaha' al-salatin* – the 'rulers' jurists' – for describing clerics who cooperate with the State). Consider, for another example, the Islamists' position with regard to non-Muslims. In conditions of hardship combined with desperation it is sometimes convenient to look for an easy scapegoat. The excessively anti-Christian positions of some of these groups may represent an attempt to exclude non-Muslims (or non-Sunnis) collectively from the hard competition over economic and organisational opportunities. This is also an easy area and a weak point (Achilles heel) at which to engage the State whose declared secularism obliges it to protect all citizens – attacking the minorities is therefore a convenient arena for challenging the State: if the State comes to the rescue of the Christians it can be condemned as caring about *al-mushrikun* (polytheists) more than about Muslims; if the State fails, it will appear as if it is getting weaker under the challenge of the Islamists.[2]

Trying to avoid reductionism and keeping in mind the limited (but still useful) explanatory power of socio-economic factors with regard to cultural/ideological matters, what can one suggest as the major concerns of the Islamic resurgence?

More than anything else the general Islamic resurgence represents a reaction to alienation and a quest for authenticity (compare Ajami, 1982: esp. 50–75 and Ch. 3). It is not really surprising that the Islamic revolution of Iran turned, more than anything else, into a movement for indigenous self-assertion. Islam had played a similar role in the Algerian war of independence against the French. For those resisting foreign dominance (political and/or cultural), Islam can provide a medium of cultural nationalism that is both defiant and self-assuring. This explains, for example, why Khomeini was joined by many secular (but nationalistically-oriented) people such as Abul-Hasan Bani-Sadr and Sadiq Qutbzadah. It also explains why Islam was so revered by many non-Muslim nationalists in the Arab world, such as Michel 'Aflaq, a leader of the Ba'th Party in Syria, and Makram 'Ubaid, a leader of the Wafd Party in Egypt. Indeed, it explains why several Christian Arabs, such as the Egyptian Anwar Abdel-Malek and the Palestinian Edward Said, have been foremost among those affronted by the frequent distortion of the image of 'Islam' in the West (for a somewhat contentious view of their position see Lewis, 1982: 50ff)

Islam can therefore serve as an effective weapon against the 'cultural dependency' that often results from the Westernisation policies passed off by various Middle Eastern rulers as developmental policies. Thus it should come as no surprise that, in reaction to the alienating policies of the Pahlavis, the Islamic revolution in Iran should have acquired somewhat of an anti-Western flavour. Nor should one find it strange that, after decades of Kemalist cultural disfiguration in Turkey, the country's main *Islamic* organisation should be called the *National* Salvation Party. The rather anti-Western colouring of many of the slogans of the neo-fundamentalists in Saudi Arabia and in Egypt should also be understood, in the same way, as being a reaction to various alienating policies that were enforced by the ruling elite in the name of modernisation but from which the majority of the people never really benefited.

What the Islamists are after is really a kind of 'cultural revolution', except that the 'neo-old' culture they want to impose is not ideologically informed by the aspirations of national struggle, class struggle or the like, but by what they perceive as the Divine Word: they are thus after a kind of 'nomocracy' (the reign of the Word and the Rule), not the reign of any group in particular (democracy, aristocracy or, for that matter, theocracy).

Resentment towards a perceived 'alienation' and a counter-quest for authenticity represent therefore a common concern that explains the *general* trend of Islamic resurgence. If, however, one considers the more specifically defined level of active involvement in movements of political Islam, another major concern is added. This may be described as resentment for a perceived sense of exclusion and a quest for a higher degree of participation. In different ways, and to different degrees, the Iranian regime under the Pahlavis, the Egyptian regime under Nasser and Sadat, and several others, were closed systems that did not allow genuine political participation, especially from the youth. A generation gap has often developed, and young people have found it impossible to be heard unless they oblige the listener by claiming more knowledge of and dedication to, the word of the Almighty. In Egypt, for example, where Sadat managed to silence most people by resorting to the prohibitionary concept of *'aib* (extremely shameful and 'not done'), it was only the young members of the militant Islamic groups who dared to challenge him in public, doing so in the name of religious righteousness. These youths also challenged religious scholars of the Establishment, confidently asserting that they knew their religion better than the scholars. There was also a rather perverse sense of glee in being able to stop a respectable university professor in mid-lecture when a member of an Islamic group would leap up and loudly announce 'the call to prayers'!

The invention of, and adherence to, a so-called Islamic costume by many neo-fundamentalist groups also emphasises the sense of participation and sharing, enhancing this with a feeling of simple equality with the insiders on one hand, and with an element of defiant distinction from the outsiders on the other. In fact, this participatory aspect distinguishes the neo-fundamentalists even from the slightly older fundamentalists (such as the Muslim Brothers) who had more respect for attributes like learning and age, and is reminiscent of the participatory brotherhood of some of the protestant movements in Christianity.

The quest for participation was not only confined to Muslims. The Christians of Egypt (the Copts) also resorted to religion to counteract the lack of political participation (which might have been even more severe in their case), but they did this, ironically, in quite the opposite direction. While militant Muslims to a large extent revolted against their own religious Establishment and formed their own neo-fundamentalist groups, militant Copts turned to their own clergy, not only for religious but also for political leadership (Hanna, 1980: 94–98). This development partly explains the deterioration in relations between Sadat and the Coptic Patriarch (whom Sadat accused of 'interfering in politics').[3] Like many of his Muslim counterparts, Pope Shenuda did indeed come to believe in the non-separation of religion from politics (cf. Heikal, 1983: 139–165; Yusuf, 1987: 161–182). Indeed he was the spiritual leader of a growing sector within the Church of educated, reformist clerics, of a lower–middle class background, who were increasingly attracted to a certain variety of what one may call 'political Christianity'; a development that cannot be completely isolated from the parallel emergence of a movement for political Islam (compare Farah, 1986: 47–51).

The official suspension of the Patriarch by the president in September 1981 was one of several decrees designed to confront what Sadat called the 'spectre of sectarian strife' in the land. It is interesting to note that among the religious agitators whom he subsequently arrested, most Muslims were young, anti-Establishment militants while most Christians were middle-aged and rather sedate Church clerics. A month after these extensive arrests, Sadat was assassinated. 'I killed the Pharaoh', shouted one of the assassins, indicating the sense of exclusion and lack of participation that had become a major grievance among such young people.[4]

It should also be emphasised that the Islamic militants' sense of 'exclusion' is not only political but also socio-economic. In the consumerist version of the capitalist mode of production that has dominated the Muslim world, as part of the 'periphery', 'success is demonstrated by the ability to acquire valued commodities: hence, inability to consume signals social defeat' (cf. Wolf, 1982: 389–390). In some ways at least, the radical Islamists, frustrated over the lack of jobs, houses and commodities, are seeking to turn social defeat into moral victory.

These two major grievances, over 'alienation' and over 'exclusion', and the two major concerns related to them, i.e. the quest for authenticity and the quest for participation, have in reality expressed themselves in the form of a confrontation between the Islamists and the State. For it is precisely the modern secular bureaucratic State which – in their view – has caused the alienation, while failing to provide the political and economic opportunities. Given this perspective, it is not easy to mistake the distinctively anti-statist colouring of the Islamists' discourse.

The transition from umma to State has not been easy in the Arab world. The 'modern' states have emerged piecemeal, partly under foreign pressure and partly under imitative borrowing. They were not the 'natural' outcome of developments of the market, of communication, and of individualism, etc., as was the case in Europe. They did not correspond to socio-economic realities, nor were they explained by a general political theory (Umlil, 1985: Chs 3, 6 and 7).

Burhan Ghalyun, a Syrian intellectual sympathetic to the 'Islamic revival', argues that, historically, the secular Arab state has emerged through a process whereby the State had voluntarily conceded its religious identity, while not succeeding in developing instead a modern, national identity that transcends religion. He maintains that not only was this process welcomed by the religious minorities, but it has also coincided with the interest of the State elite in excluding the masses from the sphere of power and politics (Ghalyun, 1979: 8–13). Popular resentment which was occasionally expressed against the religious minorities and the Westernised groups that dominated economic affairs, was increasingly being expressed in religious terms (ibid.: 38–39).

Separation of religion from the State came to the Muslim countries at the hands of the State herself, before the modern native elites were to adopt the [secularist] concept and promote its philosophical dimensions. It thus appeared as a continuation and promotion of a policy for increasingly separating the people from power, by liberating the state from the authority of religion – this latter being the last popular resort, and the only means of applying pressure that was available to those who lacked power and knowledge. (Ghalyun, 1979: 66)

The popular reaction to the State's encroachment had, by the nature of things, to be couched in religious symbolism:

> As long as secularism was tied to Authority (which was in turn tied to the Foreigner), the religious inclination was handed down to the opposition. And inasmuch as the social circles adopting secularism were to rise, religion (which in the past had protected Authority against vernacular heresies) was now to fall to the level of the man in the street. (ibid.: 55)

In a somewhat similar analysis, Munir Shafiq, a Palestinian intellectual who has recently embraced the Islamist perspective, views the Islamic revival as a 'return' by the broad popular forces to their original, real culture, from which they had been temporarily separated by the Westernised secular elites. Although the State was nominally independent from the imperialist powers, its 'small local sectors that were tinted by the European colours' had 'dominated the school and the court, the market and the word' (Shafiq, 1985: 8). When the problems of imperialism and of the dependent (*tabi'a*) but authoritarian (*tasallutiyya*) State were to accumulate, it was 'natural' for the popular forces to opt for the 'original' and to weed out the artificial. The popular forces are striving to achieve this by accepting Islam not simply as a component of their history and civilisation, but also as a 'comprehensive and self-sufficient theory for revolution' (ibid.: 5–11; cf. also Shafiq, 1983).

Owing to the special historical conditions under which 'modernisation' was 'introduced' in Muslim societies, culture and class have become intertwined in a certain way (i.e. the upper classes were relatively more 'Westernised' and the lower classes relatively more 'native' in their respective cultural outlook). Islamic symbolism may thus be invoked by the popular classes to express their antagonism towards the well-to-do, relatively more 'Westernised' classes. As Maxime Rodinson put it:

> [T]he conversion of these people (of the richer and more powerful groups) to such westernizing trends has reinforced the attachment to Islam, in its most rigidly traditional form, among the larger masses. The poor, driven to the limit of famine or wretched subsistence, direct their anger and recrimination against the privileges of the rich and powerful — their ties with foreigners, their loose morality, and their scorn for Muslim injunctions, the most obvious of which are

the consumption of alcohol, familiarity between the sexes, and gambling. For them, as Robespierre put it so well, atheism is aristocratic: and so is that 'sub-atheism' which is (supposedly) betrayed by the slightest ungodliness or departure from orthodox morality. These are not, as once was the case here [in Europe], old-fashioned priests or pious old maids railing against short skirts and kisses on the cinema screen; but angry crowds who indiscriminately attack shops selling luxury goods, hotels where the rich and the foreigners get their drink and debauchery, and (sometimes) the places of worship of 'heretics' or non-Muslim. (Rodinson, 1979: 4)

The fact that the modernising secular State has also partly disman-tled and partly dominated the economic sector has meant, by way of reaction, that 'culture' is turned *par excellence* into the arena in which the civil society may express itself and preserve its cohesiveness (Ghalyun, 1987A: 112–113). As the State has turned out to be an instrument for particularistic self-interest combined with total despotic power, and as the State involves itself in the 'dependent' process of opening up the society for new patterns of incorporation into the world capitalist system, 'it is not surprising for the structurally exhausted civil society, in such conditions, to try to reproduce itself, in isolation from the State, through ideology, myth and culture' (al-'Azmah, 1987: 24).

The reaction to the State's encroachment was not immediate, however, for the national State appeared in the fifties and sixties to be managing its socio-economic project and to be gaining ground against foreign hegemony. It is not a mere accident that this period witnessed a relative development of the 'modern' values of nationalism, develop-ment, socialism and suchlike. When the national State appeared to be retreating from its developmental path and weakening in its resistance to external encroachment, traditionalist, salafi and fundamentalist trends started to take their turn on the ascent. The middle classes that from the forties to the sixties championed the causes of liberation, nationalism and modernisation are the very classes that today with-draw into their traditional and primordial (including sectarian) retreats. And the process is mutually reinforcing, for the return to sectarian allegiances is bound to strengthen a religionist ideology. Thus, for example, the Muslim/Coptic rift in Egypt, or the Sunni/'Alawi rift in Syria reinforce, and are reinforced by, the rise in militant Islamism. For the greater the State's ability to realise and consolidate its national sovereignty and independence and to achieve its developmental objectives, the more the conflict will assume a social dimension, whereas when the State falters in the achievement of its economic and international objectives, the more likely it is that the conflict will both assume primordial (pre-nationalist, non-class) dimensions, and stress cultural, identity-bound struggles against the 'other' and the foreign.

The trouble with the modern, but dependent, State, is that it promised 'national honour' and promised 'goods and services' but (after a short, misleading spurt of success) ultimately failed to deliver either. When the secular regimes failed to deliver and when their 'developmental experiments' faltered, especially given that the Islamists were usually excluded from participating in carrying them out, it was in some ways natural that the Islamists would blame that failure on the experiments being un-Godly (secularist), and ignore or overlook the fact that their own so-called Islamic socio-economic premises might have been very similar. This may partly explain the fact that, unlike in the forties and fifties, the manifestos and action programmes of the Islamic movements are currently almost completely void of any socio-economic visions or prescriptions. The *secularist* colouring of the economic modernisation experiments of Nasserism, Ba'thism, Bourguibism and the like are singled out as the main cause of their failure, and gradually the condemnation of their secularism is practically turned into a condemnation of modernisation in general: its humanism (anthropocentrism), rationality and progressivism as well as its secularism. Modernisation is thus rejected, whether via private capitalism, State capitalism or State socialism. Modernity now appears to be the polite name for an authority that protects an alien project on the native soil, whereas the call for 'authenticity' appears to be a means to negate such an authority and to deprive it of legitimacy, and a prelude to attempts by the marginalised and the excluded groups to gain power (cf. Ghalyun, 1979: 97–100).

Above all, however, whereas the evil was perceived in the forties and early fifties to come from capitalism, which was closely associated in people's minds with colonialism and the 'foreigner', in the sixties and seventies the evil was perceived to come from socialism, which was closely associated in people's minds with the State. Now that the colonialists were no longer there, it is somewhat understandable that the Islamists would direct their hostility at the State, even though the State was now run by natives and, indeed, according to a 'corporatist' formula quite similar to what the Islamists had had in mind in the late forties and early fifties.

'This time', as Gilsenan rightly remarks, 'the enemy is within, the problems arise within and must be answered within; yet the solutions are the same and are cast in the same terms as they were forty years before' (Gilsenan, 1982B: 225). With one difference, I may add, which is that the doctrine is now expressed in more utopian terms, avoiding even more deliberately any mention of socio-economic problems or solutions – however minimal – that might have characterised the Islamist discourse of the forties and fifties. As such it can be argued that the Islamist discourse is becoming more and more utopian, relieving itself even further from the need to analyse in historical concrete terms and to prescribe in any specific social or economic terms. It places the perceived crisis

> within what is taken as a more real, truer and deeper scheme of meaning and purpose, underlying the unbelief of perversion or deviations of the present. It is the refounding of the original community . . . that is the issue and not specifically analysis of economic and political elements and relations, save in the most general and moral terms . . . The language of religion becomes used in a more and more repetitive and magical way, as though it could act on circumstances merely through the power of the Word and its reiteration (ibid.: 225–227)

Some writers, most notably Fu'ad Zakariyya (cf. Zakariyya, 1986; 1987), have been trying to argue with the Islamic movement at large and to illustrate that their propositions are illogical, inconsistent, or do not stand up to reasoned argument. This type of writing may convince the already converted or may influence a few hesitant or confused readers, but it is going to pass by the Islamic militants virtually unnoticed, precisely because of its rationality. Indeed rationality is the 'language' of the State with its (supposedly) legal–rational modern-type bureaucracy, and of the intellectuals with their (basically Western) scientific tenets and outlook. The target of hostility for the Islamic militants is often precisely that very rationality, which the State, usually with the connivance and justification of the intellectuals, has claimed exclusively for itself (compare Etienne, 1987: 86ff, 257ff). As Burhan Ghalyun rather acidly puts it, it is precisely the 'irrationality' of a trend such as 'Islamic fundamentalism' that is 'the source of its growth and the reason for its existence' (Ghalyun, 1987B: 321–323).

The Islamic militants are not about to play that game – theirs is the sword of absolute morality and the Divine Word: with this they lunge relentlessly at the State that betrayed them (which is the way *we* may see it), or that betrayed God (in *their* own view). In some ways, the Islamists are setting out to outplay the State and to surpass the political and socio-economic crisis by changing the 'arena' altogether: if Palestine cannot be liberated and people cannot be more prosperous, why not play the game that one *can* play more easily and strive to be more pious! This piety may also bring some micro-scale solutions to some of the hardships: a unified Islamic costume obliterates the need to compete socially through dressing up. Some collective Islamic solutions have also been tried by arranging marriages and by providing housing facilities as well as health and education services for members of the Islamic groups.

In Egypt, the State often organises indoctrination sessions, using the official religious scholars, to convince the Islamic militants of the wrongness of their ways; such attempts may shake the convictions of the occasional hesitant Islamist here and there, but more often it is the clergy (and sometimes, in trials, even the presumably secular judges) who are impressed by the militants' language of high morality and devotion. Many of the court trials and rulings against the militants sound quite sympathetic to their grievances and to their discourse in general (cf. e.g. Khalid, 1986; Hammuda, 1985). There is evidence available that in Egypt and in Tunisia, for example, the State machine (particularly the security apparatus) is far more hostile than the presumably 'secular' judiciary to the discourse of the Islamists.

The strength of the militant Islamic movements is derived from the fact that they are engaging the State on a battleground of their, and not the State's, own choosing, and that they are fighting with their own weapons and following their own rules. For the State to play the militants' game would be to accept a radical change in its basic character; for the State to ignore the militants' manoeuvres completely is to be seen to admit to incompetence, if not to straightforward defeat.

Thus it can be seen that the emergence of Islamism is an expression of a power struggle against the State, a State that is omnipotent on the one hand but incompetent and dependent on the other. But why should resistance and the struggle for power take a religious form? We have argued earlier that the historical pattern had been for the State to appropriate Islam in the generic sense, thus leaving for the opposition the more difficult task of formulating 'other' Islams – the 'true' Islam, the 'right' Islam, etc. – by way of resistance. We have also seen that the modern territorial State had adopted secularism and taken on the language of rationality and modernisation, with the intended, or unintended, result that certain popular sectors were excluded. It was natural then for the excluded and the disappointed to adopt a counter-ideology that is stark in its opposition to the official ideology. The opposition thus embraced 'generic' Islam, putting the State in the defensive position of having to argue for a qualified ('true', 'real', etc.) Islam. For disaffected or aspiring social forces to have adopted a religious expression of their movement is by no means a purely Islamic phenomenon. The early Protestants did so historically in Europe, and the 'liberation theology' movement does so now, in contemporary Latin America (Dagnino, 1980: 311–317).

It has been argued so far that Islamism has emerged, on a general level, as a reaction to perceived alienation and as a quest for a higher degree of authenticity, and that militant political Islam has in addition been motivated by a perceived sense of exclusion, developing therefore, at least in part, as a quest for participation. We have also argued that these two major grievances (alienation and exclusion) and the two pursuits developed as a response to them (cultural authenticity and politico-economic participation) have put the radical political Islamists, who are mainly of recently urbanised, middle-strata background, on a collision course with the State, whose cultural alterity, political authoritarianism and economic failure are taken by the Islamists to be symptoms of a deeper sin, which is betrayal of God. We have also illustrated that political Islam is an 'urban' phenomenon that takes place in the city. For not only is the city the space where the signs of 'alienation' are manifested most, but it is also the space where the presence of the State is most to be felt. Thus the city, which a few decades previously was the pride and joy of the nationalist, secularist elites, has now become the arena for a power contest between the government and the (mainly Islamic) opposition.

Now it should be observed that neither the search for authenticity nor the search for participation are a very specifically and exclusively Islamic pursuit. One cannot therefore help but wonder why these rather universal concerns have been given a specifically Islamic diagnosis (and a specifically Islamic prescription) in the Middle East? It is true that the quest for participation was paramount among the concerns of the youth revolution in the sixties in Western Europe and North America, while in the Third World at large, the quest for authenticity represents one of the major concerns now prevailing among many intellectuals and politicians of these predominantly non-Western countries. But while we agree that the militant Islamic groupings have much in common with the youth revolution of the sixties and with other popular movements in the Third World, we maintain that the Islamic movement still keeps a distinctive character and a particular vigour of its own which, we believe, is due to the specific historical experience of the Muslim world.

First is the fact that its own institutional and intellectual development has caused Islam to lend itself more comfortably than some other religions to a holistic, all-encompassing view of life that does not easily separate the religious from the social. Islam is therefore richly equipped with a quasi-political vocabulary and literature that can be of great assistance in arguing about political issues such as government and participation.

Secondly there is the history of rivalry and conflict between Christendom and *Dar al-Islam* (the Household of Islam). Of all the world's existing civilisations, only the Islamic civilisation was a direct source of learning for the West, and of all the Eastern civilisations, only the Islamic Empire ruled parts of Europe. The West's recent domination of Muslim societies, which until relatively recently had themselves been superior to Europe, has therefore been particularly painful and hurtful to Muslims. (Nor has the rivalry been completely forgotten in the West.) Many Muslims would therefore agree with Munir Shafiq's assertion that the 'European conflict against Muslim peoples has had a certain specificity' to it over and above what was necessitated by the general imperialist quest for 'plunder and domination' (Shafiq, 1986: 20–26). This gives particular depth and vigour to the call for authenticity in the Muslim world.

A third element which distinguishes the Muslim experience is the creation of Israel, whose impact on Muslims has been twofold. On the one hand it was agonising to watch the determined implantation of this 'foreign' body into the heart of the Arab world, to the detriment of the majority of the people who inhabited the land, the Muslim and the Christian Palestinians. To dedicated Muslims, the affront was compounded when Jerusalem, the second Most Sacred place in Islam, was occupied in 1967.[5] On the other hand, here was a polity based entirely on a religiously-defined concept of national identity which always succeeds and conquers. It is not just a coincidence that most neo-fundamentalist Islamic movements in the Arab world flourished particularly after the Six Day War of 1967. The idea was that if the Israelis could succeed because of their ardent adherence to their faith, Muslims would be all the more victorious if they were to adhere to their own good religion. As one Islamic writer in Egypt noted,

> The Pioneers of Zionism say that 'Jewish religious life is more than anything the secret behind the eternity of Israel' . . . So if only we would wake and realise that the only path for salvation, victory and

supremacy starts by making Islam a full lifestyle for all Muslims. (al-Khatib, 1978: 19)

The contemporary Muslim world is now experimenting with its own blend of 'religion-cum-politics'. In its own way, the Iranian revolution has increasingly emphasised religion as the primary basis for political identity and allegiance, and to a large extent the future of all Islamic movements aspiring for government in the Middle East will depend on the outcome of the Iranian experiment. In the meantime, however, this new 'religionisation' of politics has created difficulties for non-Shi'ites within Iran and has caused trouble for Middle Eastern countries with significant Shi'ite communities (such as Iraq, Bahrain, Lebanon and Saudi Arabia).

With two varieties of religious nationalism now reigning in Israel and in Iran, the temptations and/or pressures to move in a similar direction are escalating throughout the Arab world. Even within the ardently secularist Palestinian movement, the 'religious trend' seems to be gaining ground, while in most Arab countries, as we have seen, Islamic movements have increasingly become a reality of political life that has to be reckoned with.

Last but not least is the nature of the class structure in the countries of the Arab world. The articulated nature of their modes of production, combined with the rapid and enormous changes caused by the 'oil factor' and which have affected the oil-rich and the oil-poor alike, have created a class conformation that is both liquid and uncertain (for socio-economic status can be transformed practically 'overnight', for example by way of political action or through a 'lucky' contract from an oil-exporting country). It is also a class conformation that is characterised by the exceptionally large and fast-expanding dimensions of what may be vaguely described as the 'middle strata'. The resorting to a commonly understood Islamic idiom may represent an attempt at reconciling the differences between the various segments of such a gigantic 'middle class'. Yet given the rapid social mobility experienced by many Arab countries, maintains Galal Amin, this attempt may become increasingly dominated by the values and mannerisms of the relatively humble social groups, of recent rural origins, that are currently most highly mobile. In other words, the Islamic revival could be seen as a process of 'generalisation' of the cultural outlook of the newly urbanised and humble classes (with its important religious component). As Galal Amin suggests

it may not be at all far fetched to see a connection between this tendency to adopt rural and lower-class values, and the so-called resurgence of religious movements, and 'Islamic revival'. For what is involved here is not a strengthening of religious belief as much as the increasing observance of rituals and ceremonies, and the stricter adherence to an outward pattern of behaviour associated with Islam . . . What we are now facing is a mass movement of which both the members and the leaders belong to social classes that are more humble in origin, far less well-educated and with much stronger roots in the rural sector. (Amin, 1989: 118–119)

Amin's interesting idea may contribute to an explanation of the *general* and *broad* appeal of an Islamic idiom that now characterises much of the Arab world. It is certainly true that such an Islamic idiom is now used not only by the Islamists but increasingly by people belonging to various classes and to different intellectual and political persuasions. Even so, one has to be aware that 'the vocabulary may appear to be the same, but the language is not' (Keyder, 1986: 14). Many of the politicians, technocrats and intellectuals who currently use an Islamic vocabulary are still attached to the notions of nationalism, rationality, or even to an extent secularism, and hence their emphasis on referring to a 'qualified' type of Islam or of Muslims: e.g. 'true' Islam, 'real' Islam or else 'enlightened' Muslims, 'contemporary' Muslims . . . and so on. On the other hand, the newer class of prosperous traders, financiers and contractors who made a fast buck via the 'petroleum connection' or through speculative activities, may also resort to distinctly religious symbolism, partly by way of 'masking' their newly acquired wealth under the guise of Godly blessing (*baraka*). Other groups, mainly the lower, disaffected echelons of the salariat together with some members of the 'Third Estate' of minor merchants and artisans, may yet opt for a religiously-coloured language to express their socio-political protest.

Islamism, like all types of ideology, 'may mediate contradictions, but it cannot resolve them' (Wolf, 1982: 390). While an Islamic idiom may provide all such groups with a moralist/culturalist symbolism that is familiar to them all, and which many of them may cherish as part of a general quest for authenticity, that idiom can only mask, not solve, the social contradictions between these different social groups. As the Iranian experience has illustrated, the forms of conflict which are likely to be enforced by protest Islam may be too 'savage' to allow many intellectuals to feel any long-lasting enthusiasm for the 'Islamic alternative' (cf. Ghalyun, 1987B: 62–63). Again, as the Iranian case has proved, the support that the bazaris may give to an 'Islamic revolution' may not be long-lived either.

IS ISLAM 'THE SOLUTION'?

We have argued so far that political Islam has emerged as a moralist/
culturalist response to a severe developmental crisis that engulfs many
Arab societies. But can we deduce from this that political Islam
possesses a solution for the current social impasse? This is doubtful in
my view, except in a rather limited and indirect sense. We should not
confuse the fact that Islamic resurgence is a reaction to social and
political problems with the proposition that Islamism would offer the
solution to such problems.

We have repeatedly suggested in this work that Islam has no specific
theory of the State or of economics. Apart from a moral code and a
few 'fixations' related to dress, penalties, and *halal/haram* foods,
drinks and social practices, there is no well-defined comprehensive
social–political–economic totality that can be described as 'Islamic'.
The Islamism of any such social–political–economic programme can
only be deduced from the characterisation of its proponent as an
Islamist. Islamism therefore becomes an eclectic assembly of signs,
symbols and practices, believed to be Islamic by a person, a group or a
regime, that describes itself as being Islamic. Thus there is no such
thing as an Islamism that is there to be embraced or applied; as 'Aziz
al-'Azmah maintains, things become Islamic when they are identified
as being so, and this identification is normally done by way of contrast
with a few separate practices that are considered non-Islamic or anti-
Islamic, such as drinking alcohol, uncovering the head or mixing the
sexes. Islamism is then defined as the moral counterpart of each of
these practices, and – al-'Azmah suggests – it acquires a cohesion of its
own only inasmuch as it is repeated, orated and chanted (al-'Azmah,
1987: 53–59).

There is nothing, of course, to stop Islamists from incorporating
within their eclectically assembled construct a few economic and
political components. The earlier Islamic 'modernists' (Afghani,
'Abdu, etc.) did that, as also did some of the Salafis; thus, for example,
Qutb's celebrated *Social Justice in Islam*, and Siba'i's *The Socialism of
Islam*. Yet, the latter-day Sayyid Qutb, as well as Mawdudi, and the
whole range of fundamentalist trends that emerged from these two
'gurus' were to part company with this practice. This is indeed typical
of the fundamentalist intellectual and philosophical outlook.
Fundamentalists, regardless of their specific religion, tend to believe in
the limited ability of the human being in attaining knowledge –
fundamentalists are thus opposed to the humanist or the anthropocen-
tric concept. The ability of the human being to comprehend, and

subsequently to change, the World (i.e. 'progressivism') is believed to be extremely limited (and possibly undesirable). The Islamic fundamentalist version of this view is best illustrated by Mawdudi's and Qutb's concept of God's *hakimiyya*. The Islamic fundamentalist is not concerned with modernisation, development or progress but with more profound and total issues, indeed – as Qutb puts it – with no less than the emergence of God's kingdom on earth, and the removal of the human kingdom. Thus it seems that in their despair over a social and political order that they detest but cannot change, the fundamentalists are inclined simply to 'escape upwards', to the Heavens, by seeking solace in total and absolute submission to God, to nobody else, to nothing else.

It is in fact interesting to observe how the Islamists' attitude towards modernisation has changed over time. May I suggest here that, whereas the earlier 'Islamic reformers' such as Afghani and 'Abdu were striving to modernise Islam, the following generation of Islamists such as al-Banna and the Muslim Brothers were striving to Islamise modernity. The current generation of neo-Islamists (the Qutbians, Takfirists, Jihadists, etc.) appears, by contrast, to be largely anti-modernist.[6]

What is the contribution of the contemporary Islamists on matters pertaining to politics and the State? Hasan al-Turabi, one of the most sophisticated and influential leaders of Islamism in the Arab world, and one who moreover had the opportunity to influence political developments from a position of power in his country, the Sudan, was courageous enough to admit, in 1987, that the contribution of the Islamic revival movement to the debate on the State in the Arab world has been very limited:

> The [Islamic] Revival (*al-sahwa*) has started with a limited reserve, to which it has not added much . . . This is probably attributable to the fact that the early [Islamic] Revival in the Arab World was led by scholars who were not sufficiently knowledgeable about the intellectual reservoir [of ideas] or about international political realities, to be able to delve into the issue of the territorial state that was invoked by Western history. Another possible reason is that the Revival did not witness the evolution of this issue within contemporary Arab history – for the [Islamic] Revival had not emerged during the time of the secession from the Ottomans, and it was not strong enough during the time of decolonisation. (Al-Turabi, 1988: 316)

The contribution of the current generation of Islamists on socio-economic issues is even more limited. We should not confuse the

socio-economic factors that may give rise to fundamentalist movements on the one hand with the intellectual–philosophical tenets of
fundamentalism on the other. We cannot read the first, literally and
mechanically, into the second. The fact that political Islam has
emerged as an outcome to acute social and economic problems does
not necessarily mean that the discourse of political Islam addresses
such problems directly, or seeks concrete solutions to them. The real
concerns of the fundamentalists are quite different. Bruce Lawrence is
right in suggesting that:

> The major problem facing Muslim fundamentalists is not . . .
> simply one of identity formation. Rather, it is one of professing
> loyalty *at any cost*. They know their mission: to advocate a moral
> ideal of Qur'anic purity, a model of history linked to the prophet
> and the earliest companions . . . They are interlocked through a
> shared perception that Islam, with a capital I and in the singular
> case, matters more than the several alternative ideologies that
> compete with it, and more than the several state structures that
> attempt to define, and so control, it. (Lawrence, 1987: 31–34)

It is therefore strange to find someone like Eric Davis arguing that:

> as economic conditions for the lower classes have worsened,
> youthful Islamic radicals (in contrast to older Muslim Brothers)
> have felt an increasing need to incorporate a socio-economic
> program into their interpretation of Islam. This is evident in the
> increased impact of Socialist ideas, even if not articulated as such,
> upon radical Islamic doctrine. (Davis, 1987: 52)

This statement is inaccurate on practically every count. In fact the
older Muslim Brothers had more to say by way of a 'socio-economic
program' than do the younger Islamic radicals. And inasmuch as such
a programme existed at all, it has tended to be of a populist–
corporatist, rather than of a socialist, flavour. The main contemporary
Islamist with a socialist inclination is Hasan Hanafi, who is not, at
least in terms of age, particularly young! I wonder where such a
programme is to be found, since the writings (and trials) of the leading
Islamic radicals such as Shukri Mustafa, 'Abd al-Salam Faraj and
Khalid al-Islambuli (who are *not*, incidentally, of the lower classes),
are lamentably void of any such programme. The same applies to
other younger fundamentalists in other Arab countries, with the
possible exception of Tunisia.[7]

Indeed, Rashid al-Ghanushi's kind of 'self-criticism' of his Islamic
movement on this front represents an unusual departure from the

norm, and imparts a distinctive character to the Mouvement de la Tendance Islamique in Tunisia. With regard to the concerns of the working class, for example, al-Ghanushi observed that:

> This group [the workers] came to represent a huge problem for many capitalist regimes and even socialist ones . . . and yet the Islamists have . . . failed to mobilise it, leaving the door wide open for the proponents of leftist and rightist ideologies to dominate this sector by claiming to share its problems and to defend it. The reason behind the weakness of Islamist influence in this sector goes back to their [the Islamists'] ignorance and insensitivity regarding the political and social problems of the working class – problems which must be addressed before there can be [any kind of] moral ideology . . . The problem is that societies have evolved while the Islamists have not, and so it is as if they were calling to the people from a faraway place. (al-Ghannoushi, 1988: 23)

The same line of argument has been maintained by 'Abdalla al-Nafisi, a Kuwaiti who, again, is himself an Islamic sympathiser with admirers in a number of Gulf countries. Al-Nafisi has observed that:

> The follower of what the Islamic revival pens write would notice that [the movement] in general concentrates on the normative and moral dimension in Islam. Yet to emphasise this side and neglect others – especially in the future – will have no justification. If the Islamic revival wants to maintain the broad masses it will have to pay attention in the future to the importance of emphasising a social dimension to Islam and of taking the side of the needy and oppressed masses . . . The contradiction between us [Muslims] and capitalism . . . has not yet become clear to many proponents of the Islamic revival, and herein is a dangerous lacuna that should be filled, before it is too late. (al-Nafisi, 1987: 326–327)

The fundamentalists therefore have no solution to offer for the socio-economic crisis of their society. Their message is simple: 'Islam *is* the solution' (*al-islam huwa al-hall*). The implication seems to be that if true Islamists took over power and declared the full sovereignty of God, social, economic, constitutional, technological and cultural problems will all somehow find their own solution. As the Jordanian scholar Fahmi Jad'an, himself sympathetic to the Islamic revival, confirms:

> The 'revivalist project' has not presented itself at any time as aiming in essence to tackle the temporal or historical issues that the national . . . or progressive 'project' has failed to tackle. The

revivalists have not involved themselves, except by the way, in the actual struggle for achieving such objectives. For they have always seen that the solving of such problems is an outcome that will inevitably result from the establishment of an Islamic solution and an Islamic State as such. To say that the revivalist movement has come as an alternative to the national project is to suggest that the 'revivalist' project has come to solve the problems of independence, liberation, Arab unity, social progress, and to struggle against imperialism, exploitation and dependency, etc. In reality, however, all such does not represent in the manifestos of the Islamic movements central aims that legitimise the emergence and the activity of these movements. (Jad'an, 1989: 28–45)

We have suggested elsewhere in this work why the recent Islamists have remained silent over socio-economic questions – and the reasons range from the politically opportunistic to the philosophically necessary. For some, the vagueness of the doctrine is a guarantee for its appeal to the broadest audience possible. For others, however, the failure of various secular developmental formulas might have turned them against the very concept of progressivism. This is all the more so as one of the main experiments that did not seem to work has been the populist–corporatist model, previously favoured by many Islamists, but put on trial by mainly secularist national governments – usually of the 'bureaucratic authoritarian' type – in the fifties and sixties. The fundamentalists in particular seem to want to 'throw the baby out with the bathwater'. The failure of this or that developmental experiment is taken to mean the bankruptcy of progress and modernisation as such, even of humanism as an endeavour to understand and to influence the world. Ironically, the fundamentalists have not hesitated to use the products of human improvisation in propagating their cause: printing presses, loudspeakers, cassettes, and so forth form an important part of the fundamentalists' gadgetry.[8] Doctrinally, however, the fundamentalists remain largely anti-intellectual and anti-modernist:

Fundamentalism is anti-intellectual to the point that it denies the vigilant scrutiny which characterises aspects of the tradition that has evolved over all the intervening years [between the 'Golden Age' and the present time]; it is anti-modernist to the extent that it refuses to allow any durable contribution from either the scientific/ technological or the bureaucratic/military achievements of the contemporary era. In sum, fundamentalism is above all a kind of ideological formulation, affirming the modern world not only by opposing it, but also by using its means against its purposes. (Lawrence, 1987: 31–32)

There is no doubt that by transcending the precise details of the existing crisis, and by adopting an attitude of moral hauteur and superiority (*ta'ali* – an expression of which the current Islamists are quite fond) over the various secular developmental options, the Islamist discourse succeeds in imparting to itself a certain symbolic strength. Yet ironically, this kind of attitude 'in actuality reinforces and reproduces [the existing] blockages, by displacing the nature of the crisis onto the level of utopia' (Gilsenan, 1982B: 226). The energies that such an attitude may release among members of the lower middle class and the urban 'masses' are thus negated, by taking refuge merely in the power of the Word, and failing to confront effectively a Leviathan State that is busy strengthening itself politically and ideologically and a dependent capitalism that continues to wreak havoc with the national economy and with the native culture.

It is partly because of their lack of a social vision that the fundamentalists are rather unlikely to be able to strike deep or extensive roots among the popular masses (apart from the lower middle classes) and eventually to assume political power. If one judges by historical precedent, the militant (extremist) Islamic movements may face one of the following fates, depending on the social and political conditions surrounding them: they will be liquidated and/or contained by the State; they will mellow and establish themselves as fairly institutionalised sects or communities (as the Khawarij did historically in Oman and North Africa); or they will lose heart so that in the immediate future they will give up action, 'ignore' existing politics, and wait for the *mahdi* (messiah) to appear.

It is unlikely that the Islamists will succeed in taking over power in any of the Arab countries in the foreseeable future, with Egypt being a possible exception. In Egypt, not only is the social crisis likely to become more acute, but the Islamic movement is also more sizeable and entrenched. One aspect of its strength is that it is multi-layered, with the Muslim Brothers representing the largest mass organisation, and with a whole range of smaller, more radical organisations, and with fairly open lines of communications and exchanges of membership among the various groups. A second element of strength is that, although the authorities are wary of the infiltration of the Islamists into the armed forces, no one can be sure that a large army of conscripts could remain shielded from the influences of the Islamic movement. After all, Sadat was assassinated in a military parade, and news of the arrest of military personnel for membership in 'extremist religious organisations' surfaces from time to time under Mubarak. A third possible source of strength is that the Islamic movements could derive a certain amount of power from the alternative (parallel) economy and social welfare systems to which they appear to be linked. They would achieve this mainly through the Muslim philanthropic and charitable societies, the Islamic banks and investment companies, and through a whole range of 'Islamic' schools, clinics and welfare organisations. However, it is probably the Muslim Brothers (rather than the smaller, more radical organisations) who – as the most popular, and populist, of the movements – are most likely to benefit from networks such as these, and eventually to coalesce organically with a certain segment of the rising bourgeoisie. It will remain an open question as to whether an 'Islamic revolution' might take place in Egypt. In the meantime, however, there is little doubt that the emergence of a powerful Islamic movement in Egypt has created a situation where the secular State appears to be rather 'frightened' and seems to be deprived of a much-needed moral legitimacy.

But to say that the State is suffering from a decline in effectiveness and in legitimacy is not to suggest automatically – as do the fundamentalists – that the Islamic movement would do better. The Islamists are far from being ready, even on a purely intellectual and ideological level, with workable solutions for the major socio-economic or political problems of their societies. It would be risky to allow our understanding of the trying conditions that led to the rise of fundamentalist movements, or our sympathy with the agonies of the social groups that are attracted to the fundamentalist message, to oblige us to read into the fundamentalist discourse what is *not* there. The rise in fundamentalism is a symptom of a social crisis; it does not include a plan for solving it. Their ideology may console some souls and may camouflage some conflicts, but it cannot resolve the economic, the social or even the cultural crisis. As Burhan Ghalyun, who is quite understanding towards the Islamic trend, admits, 'there is no solution to the cultural crisis from within the culture itself – [it can be solved] only by changing the material and social reality and only through transforming it' (Ghalyun, 1987B: 112). The neo-fundamentalist attempt to negate modernity is not likely to succeed – to quote Ghalyun again — because 'modernity is not simply a few values and institutions that we can accept or reject as we wish, but a continuous process that has been with us for two centuries, and will continue in spite of us' (Ghalyun, 1987A: 302–304). Part of the problem may indeed be attributed not to the fact that the society has been modernising, but that this modernisation has remained 'alien' in terms of its cultural manifestation, and limited in terms of its social base.

The contemporary Islamist ideology may mediate certain contradictions, but it cannot resolve them. Different emphases and connotations are given to the same Islamist communicative code by various social groups. Even if one excludes the 'defensive Islamism' of several ruling elites, there are major intellectual differences between the fundamentalist Islamism of Sayyid Qutb and the Jihadists, the liberal–nationalist Islamism of M. Khalafalla and M. 'Imara, the cultural–historicist Islamism of Tariq al-Bishri and 'Adil Husain, and the Islamism claimed by owners of the so-called Islamic Investment Companies.

On an intellectual level, liberal–nationalist Islamism, cultural–historicist Islamism, and the broader circle of discourse revolving around the issue of authenticity (*asala*) may eventually translate themselves into a movement for cultural nationalism that is nativist, 'specifist', if not particularly secularist. Some of the Islamists' concepts pertaining to the establishment of an 'Islamic order' can be, and are being, gradually absorbed into a broader intellectual discourse that is partly traditional/salafi and partly communitarian/corporatist.[9] Several liberals, nationalists and even leftists, are starting to speak an 'Islamicate'[10] language which is really more nationalist (or nativist) than it is Islamist, and even the occasional Christian, such as Anwar 'Abd al-Malik, can sometimes sound as though he too is speaking the same language. Leonard Binder is not so far off the point in predicting that Tariq al-Bishri and his colleagues 'may produce a modified Nasserism – bureaucratic authoritarianism plus Islam' (Binder, 1988: 291–292). Even 'an Islamic ideology of the left' is a possibility, although this — as Maxime Rodinson observes – 'will perhaps be slow in coming' (Rodinson, 1979: 16).

The Islamic enterprises' may simply be the spearhead for an emerging native capitalism, using its own cultural idiom and following its own behavioural patterns. In the longer run, the Islamic 'cultural nationalists' and the Islamic 'native capitalists' may coalesce within a certain corporatist formula.

The expansion of 'Islamic companies' is governed by a similar logic to that governing the spread of 'Islamic dress'. A few doctrinaire actors may initiate the practice of non-usury business or of the Islamic dress (*al-zayy al-Islami*). The phenomenon is then adopted, in a milder, ameliorated form, by larger social segments, and is routinised as part of a general trend towards 'cultural nativisation'. The 'Islamic' business can then improvise, adopting new, innovative devices not known to the conventional jurists, and the all-enveloping *niqab* (total veil) can be modified into a face veil, a Turkish turban or Arabian kefiya, or even into a simple 'European' headscarf. There are already fashion houses that specialise in tailoring elegant 'Islamic' costumes for the design-conscious in various Muslim countries.

The society at large has thus partly absorbed and partly resisted the fundamentalist call. It has achieved this through things such as the routinisation of the veil and of the so-called Islamic dress, but also through the ritualisation of a few Islamic symbols such as starting letters 'In the Name of God', broadcasting the Quran through loudspeakers everywhere, and giving 'Islamic' names to shops, farms and factories.

There are also signs that the political energies of at least some of the Islamists may be on their way to 'routinisation' too. In addition to the traditional cases of Islamists standing for elections in Jordan and Kuwait, the Islamists have recently done the same and managed to win seats in Egypt, Sudan and Tunisia. It is quite possible that some of the heat (and some of the excitement) in the fundamentalist cause will be taken away once the Islamists are permitted to air their views in the open, and once they are allowed to compete, succeed *and* fail. The last point is particularly important, for the more Irans and Sudans you get, the less impressive and appealing the Islamists' call will become.[11]

In the meantime, the discourse of the political Islamists will not remain the only light on the horizon. We have seen that the Islamic liberals and the liberal Muslims have already started to answer back. The secularists have not all faded out either. Furthermore, once the confusing effects of the petroleum era have declined, and once its overwhelming impact on the oil-rich and the oil-poor countries has diminished, class realities are likely to take a more distinctive form, and class contradictions (and the socio-economic factors behind them) are likely to become much clearer. This in turn is likely to give rise to socially-, rather than to culturally-based, political struggles. A revival in the appeal of leftist movements should not be ruled out of hand, especially as several of these movements are becoming much more 'acclimatised' and sensitised to their social and cultural environments.

Notes

1 THE THEORY AND PRACTICE OF THE ISLAMIC STATE

1 Although some dates are specified and some Arabic terms approximately explained, this has not been done with the intention to instruct clearly and systematically those who are completely unfamiliar with the subject, for that would have seriously distracted from the main argument. Ideally, too, this chapter should be read in conjunction with a chapter on the 'Islamic State' appearing in my forthcoming book on *The Arab State*. Unfortunately, however, for practical reasons this latter book may not appear until some time after this one is published.

2 A similar phenomenon seems to exist today whereby the religio-political opposition resorts to metaphysical symbolism, whereas the State claims to be speaking the language of reason and 'rationality'. See Chapters 6, 7, and 10 of this book.

3 The issue of modes of production, and the patterns of their 'articulation', is discussed in detail in my forthcoming book on *The Arab State*.

4 Ira Lapidus has in fact suggested that by the middle of the 9th century AD the socio-religious opposition and the Sunni traditionalists 'had tested the boundaries of Caliphal authority in religion': the theological opposition to the caliph al-Ma'mun by the jurist Ibn Hanbal in the *mihnah* ('inquisition') over the 'creation of the Qur'an', was clearly linked to popular demonstrations, especially by Khurasanis, against the policy of the regime. In subsequent centuries, this initial differentiation of religious and communal institutions from the political institution of the caliphate grew more profound and more clearly defined, so that religious and political institutions were in fact – even though not in theory – separate from each other (Lapidus, 1975: 363–385).

2 THE POLITICS OF SEX AND THE FAMILY, OR THE 'COLLECTIVITY' OF ISLAMIC MORALITY

1 It is arguable, of course, that our distinction between social morals on the one hand and political matters on the other is based on a narrow, and possibly artificial, conception of politics that is too influenced by the individualistic (and/or class-based) analyses that dominate contemporary

political science. Ethics and culture do indeed figure more prominently in the writings of the Latin and Germanic 'organic' and historicist authors – but these seem to have been eclipsed with the demise of Fascism in the Second World War. About quarter of a century ago, David Apter drew attention, with discernment, to what he called the 'sacred-collectivity' model of politics (Apter, 1969: 31ff). The Islamist concept of public order may fall more comfortably within this category, which has been rather neglected by political scientists in recent years. Apter is right in reminding us that not all political values are instrumental, and not all legitimacy is concerned with the 'effectiveness of policy-making'. Some political values are 'consummatory', and their aspects of legitimacy are related to things such as identity and solidarity (ibid.: 266). It is perhaps due time for political scientists to reincorporate morals and culture into their major concerns, but without falling into the 'Fascist' trap of glorifying a specific moralist/culturalist set or else into the behaviouralist and/or functionalist trap of excessive relativism and of unilinear evolutionist analysis. The contribution of Antonio Gramsci would represent a good starting point in this respect. In the meantime, however, the 'narrow' definition of politics remains with us. As for the case of Muslim societies, perhaps the most distinguishing feature of the Islamic discourse is not its concern with matters of sex, the family and social morals, but its excessive (almost obsessive) emphasis on such matters, often *to the exclusion* of straightforward (narrow) political concerns such as the formation and management of governments, the representation of interests, and the rights of citizens, etc. These and other related issues will be dealt with in my book on *The Arab State.*

2 Richard Antoun corroborates Eugene Smith's theory that 'organic' societies, such as Muslim societies, are characterised by organic religious systems in which the primary expression of religion is found in 'societal' rather than in individual (i.e. purely 'religious') manifestations. Organic religious systems have, according to D.E. Smith, three defining attributes: an 'integralist' religious ideology, internal societal mechanisms of religious control, and a dominant political authority. Although this idea is not without merit, I do not agree – as will be clear throughout this book – with Antoun's more specific conclusion that 'the separation of religion and politics or religion and government has no traditional place in Muslim society, and still has no place, as recent events at the end of the twentieth century are making all too clear' (cf. Antoun, 1989: 187).

3 In reality, however, polygamy was practised by a relatively small percentage of well-to-do men, and nowadays even fewer take the permitted number of wives. Polygamy still has its supporters, though, who are capable of producing the strangest arguments in its favour. In a book published in Arabia in the second half of the seventies, the author claims that 'the way of God . . . has made polygamy unsuitable for women but suitable for men. This is clear from [the fact] that the woman has a womb . . . while man hasn't'! (quoted in Barakat, 1984: 211–212).

4 All generalisation with regard to cultural traits is extremely risky, but some attempt at 'characterisation' is often necessary. I try as much as possible to think in terms of an imagined 'social character' rather than a presumed

'modal personality' or 'basic personality'. If I miss the point, I beg forgiveness! For further discussion see: A-S. Yasin (1983), Zai'ur (1988), Ju'ait (1984), Barakat (1984), and Sharabi (1987).

5 This may partly explain the Western public's surprise at the attitude of Muslims in Britain who continued their demonstrations, burnings and condemnation of Salman Rushdie's book *The Satanic Verses* in 1989 even though India and Pakistan (where most of the demonstrators had originally come from) had banned the book and British politicians had said that the book was offensive. The normal (individualistic) attitude of the Western person was to say: do not read it if *you* find it offensive. But Islam is about the collective enforcement of public morals – and the Muslims wanted to see *public and official* condemnation and prosecution of the book and its author.

6 Veiling may be at least partly regarded as an ancient 'ecological' device that acquired, with the passage of time, a certain cultural fixedness. In symbolic terms, however, the significance of the veil is contingent upon a whole range of social, and in the current phase particularly political, considerations. Thus in the Egypt of the early eighties, for example, the campus police of the al-Azhar (Islamic) University were prohibiting unveiled girls from entering the university precincts, whereas at the same time the campus police in the national (secular) university were preventing veiled girls from going into the university grounds! Obviously in the first case, veiling was regarded as a measure for enforcing the traditional, conventional and overwhelmingly paternalistic concept of modesty (and hence discipline) on girls. In the second instance, veiling was viewed as an act of protest and as a symbol of defiance towards the authorities which had to be stopped if the government was to retain political credibility. New-style 'Islamic' veiling has also been regarded in the same light by the authorities in other countries, such as Tunisia.

3 THE VARIETY OF MODERN ISLAM: INTELLECTUAL EXPRESSIONS AND POLITICAL ROLES

1 One can of course argue that what makes the veil 'oppressive' is its obligatory nature; but are we not, after all, obliged to go to work dressed? The point, therefore, is that modernisation is a misleading paradigm because it can always lead to asking the wrong questions and dealing with irrelevant issues. 'Re-inventing' the veil, which is characteristic of the new 'Islamic gear' of various neo-fundamentalist movements, is, however, a different phenomenon and represents a sign of socio-political protest, as we argue elsewhere in this work. See also on this point Chapter 2, note 6.

2 Having read Arkoun's essay (1988) after writing practically my entire manuscript, I am pleased to see that his thesis corroborates what I have been arguing in Chapter 1 and in the rest of this book. Other *Islamic* writers have argued along similar, basically secularist, lines: Khalid Muhammad Khalid in the fifties and Muhammad Ahmad Khalafalla and Muhammad

'Imara (although not in so many words) in the seventies and eighties (see Chapter 9).

3 In September 1981 this new 'principle' was endorsed by a popular referendum, following extensive arrests of over 1500 Muslim and Christian leaders as well as numbers of secular intellectuals. No one understood, however, how this principle could be reconciled with the constitutional amendment of 1980 that made shari'a (religious law) *the* main source of legislation in the state. Sadat was, of course, assassinated shortly after this, in October 1981, by the brother of a detained militant Islamist.

4 'I testify that there is no god but God, and that Muhammad is his messenger.'

5 The theses of this culturalist/corporatist school are discussed in my forthcoming book on *The Arab State*. But for the time being, see, for example: Husain (1985); al-Bishri (1980); H. Amin (1985); 'Abd al-Malik (1983); Sahhab (1984). For a review and critique of some of these theses see: al-'Alim (1986: esp. 189–257); Vatikiotis (1987: Chs. 4 and 5) and Binder (1988: esp. Ch. 7).

4 THE ISLAMIC MOVEMENTS: SOME COUNTRY STUDIES – PART 1

1 Qadhdhafi's approach to Islam is fascinating and rather untypical. Belittling Hadith, discarding fiqh and excluding the ulama, he has tended to interpret Islam in a socially radical way, and has adopted a number of unorthodox practices (such as changing the Islamic calendar to start with Muhammad's death rather than with his hijra to Madina). 'Eclectic reliance on science, Islamic forms, and personal reflection typified Qaddafi's approach to religion in the second decade of the revolution' (L. Anderson, 1983: 144–145).

2 The town of Asyut in the harsh desert environment of Upper Egypt is of particular importance in this respect; the leader of Takfir and several of Jihad's leaders came from there, and the town witnessed some of the bloodiest of the armed confrontations between the militant Islamic groups and government security forces that followed Sadat's murder. Christians are numerically important and, since the mid-nineteenth century, have been in the ascendant economically, producing a situation that is liable to stimulate fascist-type reactions in times of socio-economic strain. Several strong institutions of Islamic education are located there, and, furthermore, the governorate (of which Asyut city is the capital) was entrusted by Sadat for many years to an official – known for his pro-Muslim Brothers sympathies and his anti-Christian views – who is said to have given serious support to the activities of the militant Islamic groups. For further details see the special study on Asyut in Chapter 7.

3 This is the more orthodox Ikhwan view, although some of those sympathetic to the Brothers, such as Ma'ruf al-Dawalibi who participated in the formation of al-Sha'b party in 1948, maintain that the umma is the

source of all authority, provided that it is guided by the shari'a (cf. al-Dawalibi, 1984: 45–48).

5 THE ISLAMIC MOVEMENTS: SOME COUNTRY STUDIES – PART 2

1 According to *Al-Thawra al-Islamiyya*, no. 84 (March 1987: 45), the Ministry of Awqaf and the Ministry of Information now prepare the texts of the Friday religious sermons that are delivered in all governmental mosques in Saudi Arabia, and impose penalties on any disgression from their content.

2 In the attempt to reunite Morocco at the end of the eighteenth century under the central authority of the royal state (*al-makhzan*), the 'Alawi sultanate was to adopt Wahhabism and ally itself with the ulamas against the 'popular Islam' of the sufi *zawiyas*. The claimed Sharifian descent of the king and the religious support he received from the jurists had enabled the king to project the monarchy as an institution that transcends, and stands above, the ethnic (Arab/Berber) and the tribal division of the society (cf. Darif, 1988; Aknush, 1987).

6 POLITICAL ISLAM: INTELLECTUAL SOURCES

1 'Aziz al-'Azmah refutes the salafi and fundamentalist thesis which maintains that the Islamic heritage (*turath*) is still alive and effective, and argues a case that maintains the total 'alienation' and 'alterity' of the past. He holds that what the Islamists are trying to do is to remove and 'empty' the present reality and to refill it with a 'retrieved' past that is to be installed in its place. In his view this attempt, and its discourse, are little more than the hiccups of a civil society that is being pushed from a declining, irrelevant ancestral culture into a ready-made universalist culture (cf. al-'Azmah, 1987: Chs. 1, 2 and 5).

2 According to most jurists, a person becomes, and remains, a Muslim once he/she utters the 'credo' or the 'two testimonies' (*al-shahadatain*): 'I witness that there is no god but God, and that Muhammad is his messenger'.

3 The word *siyasa* is, however, probably of older origin, though it was usually used in the sense of managing/manipulating/humouring animals and minors! (compare also Lewis, 1988).

4 Abu al-Hasan al-Nadwi, in a book first published in 1950, also refers to modern-day jahiliyya and similarly traces its origins to sources from within the historical Muslim states and sources coming from Western civilisation, and he then concludes that 'the whole world is moving towards *jahiliyya*' (al-Nadwi, 1984: 134ff, 258ff). He subsequently admitted, however, that this description was sometimes applied to other (less than perfect but by no means infidel) Muslims too easily, leading to counter-accusations of 'extremism' (in Hasana, 1988: 24).

5 There are reports that Qutb was of Indian origin (Diyab, 1988: 88). It is an

interesting, and still open, question as to whether this might have contributed to Qutb's attraction to the ideas of the 'Indian' Islamic school.

6 Hasan al-Hudaibi, the formal leader (*murshid*) of the Ikhwan at that time, was apparently opposed to the new Qutbian thesis. In his book *Du'atun la quda* (Callers, Not Judges) first published in 1969, he was obviously setting out to refute Qutb's thesis, without mentioning him by name. According to Hudaibi,the term *hakimiyya* has no mention in the Quran or Hadith. In his view, its recent coinage and current connotation, implying that humans who legislate for themselves are usurping one of God's exclusive prerogatives, is completely mistaken (cf. Umlil, 1985: 183–187).

7 According to Zuhair Mardini, in the early 1980s, older and/or more moderate groupings within the Ikhwan included a group of moderates, mainly intellectuals, revolving around 'Umar al-Tilmisani (in his eighties), and a group of Banna devotees, mainly professionals and artisans, represented by people such as Shaikh Salah Abu-Isma'il (in his fifties). This latter group, whose views were often represented by *Al-I'tisam* magazine, lies, in terms of militancy, half way between the moderate Tilmisanists on the one hand and the 'extremist' Qutbists on the other (Mardini, 1984: 139).

8 In comparison to our approach with regard to other intellectual sources of political Islam, we have not delved here into the social context of the Jihadist and other neo-fundamentalist ideas. This is mainly because much of the analysis in the book as a whole actually pertains to the relationship between the ideas of the neo-fundamentalists on the one hand, and the social context in which they have emerged on the other.

9 An indication of the 'populist' (but mainly middle strata) orientation of the Islamic revolution can be gleaned from an examination of the social groupings represented in its early institutions. Of the 19 members of cabinet appointed after the fall of the Provisional Revolutionary Government, 4 were *hojjatolislams* (clerics), 9 were professional men from bazaar-clerical families, one was a Tehran merchant, and 5 were professionals of 'new middle class' background. The composition of the first *Majles* (council) of the Islamic republic was equally significant. Out of 216 deputies elected by spring 1980, 98 were *hojjatolislams* and *modarresin* (lower clergy), 51 were from a bazaar background, 64 were lawyers, doctors, teachers and civil servants, 2 were wives and daughters of clerics, and one was a worker. The social background of the fathers of the deputies was as follows: 96 were born into rural families; 69 into clerical families; 51 into bazaar merchant families; 19 into bazari 'traditional working class' (artisan) families; and 8 into 'new middle class' families (civil servants and professionals) (Bashiriyeh, 1984: 173, 178 and refs quoted).

10 The powers of the jurisconsult are all the more sweeping as he seems to have no corresponding institutional responsibilities that would make him politically (rather than 'divinely') accountable. According to Khomeini,

> the religious leaders do not wish to be the government, but neither are they separate from the government. They do not wish to sit in the Prime Minister's residence and fulfil the duties of premiership, but at the same

time they will intervene to stop the Prime Minister if he takes a false step. (Khomeini, 1985: 343).

It is obvious that such an arrangement would enable the jurists both to exercise power *and* to blame anything that might go wrong on the administrators.

11 Khomeini, for example, reasserts in the *Wilayat* the Shi'i belief, contested by the Sunnis, that Prophet Muhammad had appointed 'Ali to replace him as the ruler of Muslims after his death (Khumaini, 1979: 131).

12 According to Khomeini, 'the imam has a praise-worthy status, a supreme rank, and an existential reign (*khilafa takwiniyya*) to whose guardianship and domination all atoms of this universe are subjugated' (Khumaini, 1979: 52).

13 It should be remembered that the most influential thinkers with regard to the doctrine of political Islam in Sunni societies have been civilians, not clerics. This applies to Mawdudi, al-Banna and Qutb as well as to most ideologues of the neo-fundamentalist movements.

7 POLITICAL ISLAM: SOCIO-ECONOMIC BASES

1 Unfortunately no comprehensive studies are available that try to trace the changes in the ideological and political inclinations of the Islamist youth as they mature in age. One study, pertaining to Morocco, suggests that members of 'secretive' Islamic groupings in Casablanca are overwhelmingly students in the 17–24 age group, and that most of these sever their relations with such movements as they reach the age of 25 or so and engage in employment and other public activities. It should be observed, however, that the Islamic movement in Morocco, as in several other 'traditional' monarchies, is relatively small and fairly integrated within the regime, and that it tends to direct most of its 'militant' activities against the leftist opposition rather than against the State as such (cf. al-Jabiri, 1987: 227–235).

2 This account of Upper Egypt is based on personal experiences and encounters, supplemented by historical and sociological readings. Some discussion of the case of Asyut is also to be found in Mahfuz (1988: 85–97 *et passim*), Huwaidi (1987: 212–227) and Hammuda (1987A: 137–139).

3 Hisham Ju'ait has argued the same point even with regard to the more ostensibly secularist model of Bourguibism. According to him, 'it may be possible to consider Bourguibism in some ways an outcome of the fundamentalist trend (*al-naz'a al-'usuliyya*), but without the faith (*bidun al-'aqida*)'. He also ranks Nasserism and Ba'thism within the same category. If these nationalist models have failed it is because they have 'isolated Islam from the political dialogue, and even belittled – in some cases – anything that has to do with Islam'. The Islamist trend is in some ways similar except that it represents, on the whole, a variety of 'moralist populism' (Ju'ait, 1982: 55–57).

4 Although the Islamic radicals have now placed themselves in a position of complete contradiction with the State, the initial surge of the Islamic trend

had in some ways emerged from within the dominant ideology itself. The writings of Sayyid Qutb and his brother Muhammad Qutb were published and distributed by the semi-governmental press during Nasser's time, and new editions of Ibn Taimiya's works were also printed during that period. Some of the ex-Ikhwan members (e.g. 'Abd al-'Aziz Kamil) continued to cooperate with the Nasserist regime to the end. This component in the dominant ideology was to acquire greater prominence after the 1967 defeat. It was Nasser in his first public speech after the defeat who proclaimed, to the enthusiastic roar of the audience, that 'religion' should from then on play a more important role in the affairs of the society. And still in Nasser's time, it was the official governmental and 'party' authorities which played up the claimed apparition of the Virgin Mary on top of a Coptic church in 1968. Sadat, of course, pushed the process much further, declaring himself the 'Believer-President', calling his regime a 'State of Science and Faith', and allowing the Islamists greater scope for intellectual and organisational action (see Ayubi, 1980B). For another, and stronger, statement that views 'the rise of Islamic discourse as an expansion and a reconstruction of an already present element of the dominant ideology, in the context of its intense crisis', see Shukrallah, (1989: 90ff).

5 Both Philip Khoury (1983) and Nadia Ramsis Farah (1986) have used the concept of 'State exhaustion' in their explanation of religious resurgence. The concept is presumably inspired by political economy analyses of the 'Latin American school' (e.g. Guillermo O'Donnell). It should be emphasised, however, that although the State in the post-populist stage may be structurally strained and exhausted in economic and financial terms, it is often still quite authoritarian (if not more so) in terms of its political and 'security' functions. These issues will be dealt with in more detail in my forthcoming book on *The Arab State*.

8 ISLAMIC BANKS, COMPANIES AND SERVICES, OR THE RISE OF A NATIVE COMMERCIAL BOURGEOISIE

1 The Faisal Islamic Bank of Sudan is often reputed to be the 'fundamentalists' bank', with a number of Muslim Brothers on its board, and with much of its business conducted with National Islamic Front supporters.

2 According to the *mudaraba* method an Islamic bank would lend money to a client to be invested in a certain activity, in return for the bank receiving a specified percentage of the profits of that activity for a certain designated period (in addition to periodical repayments of the principal). The bank's share of the profit (or the loss) is then distributed among the bank's depositors. According to the *musharaka* method the Islamic bank would enter into a partnership with a client in which both share the equity capital. The management is either shared or entrusted to the bank or to the client for a certain fee. The profits or losses incurred by the project would then be shared by the two sides according to their proportionate equity

shareholding. According to the *murabaha* method (mentioned below), the Islamic bank would buy for a client certain goods needed by him, then sell these goods to the client at an agreed mark-up. This method is used for financing the purchase of machinery and vehicles or the importation of commodities for trading purposes. The client then repays the price of the goods to the bank in instalments. The pre-determined margin of profit designated for the bank arouses some suspicions over the pure 'Islamic' nature of this transaction, but it is usually presented as a return for a real service performed by the bank, that includes a certain element of risk. For details cf. 'Uwais, 1986 and 'Atiyya 1987.

3 Thus, for example, the Egyptian Rayyan Islamic Investment Company that nearly went bankrupt in 1988 seems to have had at least one counterpart, run by a Christian in Lebanon, that suffered a similar fate during the same year. In a fascinating article entitled 'A New Rayyan in Lebanon', the story is told of an individual who ran one of these 'personal' financial concerns and managed to receive deposits from some 18,000 people, including several military personnel, and who used to pay his depositors returns that exceeded the interest paid by the banks at the time (cf. *Al-Sharq al-Awsat*, 13 December 1988).

4 As of late summer 1989 the Egyptian State was still unable to oblige the MUCs to conform to the new legal requirements, however minimal, that should govern their activities. Of 106 existing companies, only al-Sharif's company and three Al-Sa'd companies had adjusted their legal status, twelve companies had presented plans for re-scheduling their debts to depositors, while the remaining 90 companies, including the notorious Al-Rayyan, were still under investigation (Egyptian Minister of the Economy in *Al-'Arab*, 25 September 1989).

5 This term is due to Richard Sklar (1976: 85–87).

9 THE ISLAMIC LIBERALS ANSWER BACK

1 The main bulk of this book was written before I had access to Leonard Binder's valuable work on *Islamic Liberalism* (1988). It is perhaps because Binder regards liberalism as a process that he found it possible to include the wide variety of authors that he reviews (although the inclusion of S. Qutb among the liberals still baffles me). Many of his authors, however, are not 'Islamic' either in terms of their doctrinal orientation or even in terms of the subject-matter that they deal with. Indeed some of them are not even nominally Muslim (e.g. Samir Amin, a Christian by birth), and several are not even Arab or Middle Eastern. For example, practically all the authors reviewed in Chapter 6 on Islam and Capitalism are Westerners, although some Arabs such as Husain Muruwwa, Tayyib Tizini and Mahmud Isma'il have written extensively on this subject, and could gainfully have been reviewed by Binder. My definition of the Islamic liberals is much stricter than that of Binder, and it applies only to writers who are both Muslim and liberal, and who address specifically Islamic subjects.

2 For a comprehensive work on the Coptic debates see Yusuf (1987). For

other examples of the response by liberal Christians see Hanna (1980), Samir Amin (1985), and compare the rather unusual argument put forward by Farah (1986). Compare also the comments by F. al-Fanik and G. Salama in Ibrahim, 1988.

3 A similar idea is argued by Ahmad Kamal Abu al-Majd. According to him the fusion of religion and government is only peculiar to the special Prophetic era of Muhammad. Subsequent to him, authority has no religious derivation. He argues that political authority in Islam is based on popular acceptance (which may take the form of a 'selection contract' – *'aqd al-bay'a* – or any other form), not on any divine right or religious support (Abu al-Majd, 1988: 133–141).

4 According to Mahmud Mutawalli the issue is simple: Islam is a 'religion' (*din*) and not a 'state' (*dawla*). The concept of 'state' is not mentioned at all in the Quran, nor is the concept of 'government': the term *hukm* (as in the *Surat al-Ma'ida*) refers to adjudication among people, not to rule over them (M. Mutawalli, 1989: 15–20). See also along similar lines 'Abd al-Karim (1987).

5 In fact al-Sanhuri himself, in spite of his enthusiasm for Islamic tradition, could find very few stipulations directly inspired by shari'a that he could incorporate even into the civil law that he was entrusted with codifying in the thirties (cf. the debate between Tariq al-Bishri and Husain A. Amin in CAUS, 1985: 617–650). Over half a century after Sanhuri's observations, another Egyptian legalist observed that Muslim jurists still paid very little attention to constitutional (i.e. political) matters, except sometimes for the subject of the caliphate 'which today belongs to the antiquities museum of government systems' ('A. Mutawalli, 1985: 164–165).

6 There is already an established opinion among many Egyptian legalists that most of the laws that are of foreign derivation have already been 'acclimatised', both during the stage of formulation and as a result of the relatively long period of application and adjustment. At the very least, therefore, they could be regarded as *'urf* (custom) which is an admissible supplementary source of shari'a. (cf. N. 'Abd al-Fattah in Ibrahim, 1988: 293–294, and 'Abd al-Fattah, 1984: esp. 85–109).

7 Any intellectual or political trend that the Islamists do not like is often attributed to a conspiracy by the 'polytheists'. Thus 'deterministic' modern social science is blamed on the three 'Jewish devils', Durkheim, Marx and Freud. The termination of the Ottoman caliphate is blamed on the 'Dunama' Jews of the Balkans. And the emergence of Arab nationalism is blamed on Christian Arabs.

8 There are, of course, serious limitations to our ability to predict *individual* ideological inclinations on the basis of class affiliation, and this is particularly true of the elusive middle classes and strata (and more so of individual intellectuals within them). Brothers from the same family may adhere to different, and sometimes contradictory, intellectual/ideological positions. Thus, for example, from among personalities mentioned in this book: 'Abd al-Qadir 'Awda was a leading Muslim Brother 'fundamentalist', whereas his brother 'Abd al-Malik is a secularist Egyptian nationalist; Zainab al-Ghazali is the leader of the 'Muslim Sisters' whereas her brother

'Abd al-Mun'im is a Marxist; Ahmad Husain was an 'Islamic corporatist' whereas his brother 'Adil was a Marxist (and was imprisoned for several years on that account, although in recent years he has moved closer to a position somewhat similar to that of his older brother).

9 The divisionism of the modernist thesis is manifested by things such as the dichotomisation of the 'sacred' versus the 'profane', and of the 'subjective' versus the 'objective'. Such divisionism is rejected by the Islamic leftist thinker Hasan Hanafi (cf. Shimogaki, 1988), but also by other post-modernists such as the Christian-born Anwar 'Abd al-Malik (cf. 'Abd al-Malik, 1983).

10 POLITICAL ISLAM: WHY AND WHERE TO?

1 This term is due to Richard Sklar. He argues that it is difficult in many developing countries to draw distinct analytical boundaries between the bureaucratic and the entrepreneurial spheres of life. The concept of 'Managerial bourgeoisie' is suggested as a means 'to comprehend businessmen, members of the learned professions, leading politicians, and upper level bureaucrats as members of a single class' (Sklar, 1976: 81).

2 Another theory holds that the State in Egypt was sometimes behind the sectarian strife on the assumption that if the Islamists concentrated their fury on the Christians they would thus be distracted from attacking the Establishment itself. There is some circumstantial evidence to support this, such as the long-term appointment of Muhammad 'Uthman Isma'il as governor of Asyut (which has the highest percentage of Christians in Egypt) and some inflammatory circulars attributed to the Church and said by others to have been produced by the government. One commentator goes further by suggesting that the timing of sectarian conflicts usually corresponds to critical times from the point of view of the Egyptian regime (such as elections, for example) (cf. Huwaidi in *Al-Ahram*, 12 May 1987: 7; and compare Farah, 1986: 125–127).

3 Shenuda, who became Coptic Pope in 1971, was not only one of the youngest Patriarchs (b. 1923) ever to take office, but he is also a dynamic personality and a 'political' figure: a graduate in arts, he worked as a teacher and as a journalist, and even fought in the Palestine War of 1948 (cf. Pakhumius, 1971). He set about reorganising the Church, invigorating the clergy and reviving Coptic language and culture; much of this occurred at a time when the Islamic revival in Egypt was gathering momentum and worrying the authorities, and consequently resulted in a falling out between him and Sadat in 1981 (when Sadat removed him from the Patriarchate and banished him to monasterial seclusion). Shenuda was restored by President Mubarak in 1985.

4 *Fara'un* (Pharaoh) who, in the secularist culture, epitomises the national glory of Egypt, becomes in the Quranic rendering the epitome of the highest level of tyranny and despotism.

5 Significantly it was only after the defeat of 1967 and the arson in Al-Aqsa Mosque in Jerusalem that the first Islamic Summit was held in September

of that year. The Summit was followed by the creation of the Organisation of Islamic Conference, with forty two member states and headquarters in Jiddah, Saudi Arabia (cf. Kizilbash, 1982).

6 Bruno Etienne suggests that the Islamic movements of the seventies and eighties refuse to 'modernise Islam' and propose to 'Islamise modernity' (Etienne, 1987: 108ff). I think that such an attitude may apply to the main tendency within the Muslim Brothers. It does also apply to the so-called *al-turathiyyun al-judud* (the new upholders of the cultural heritage), and certainly to those that I have termed the Islamic liberals. By contrast, I find the thesis of the neo-fundamentalists openly anti-modernist, even though they are often prepared to make use of the *material* products of modern technology. I am more inclined to agree with the suggestion of Bruce B. Lawrence that the neo-fundamentalists are 'affirming the modern world not only by opposing it, but also by using its means against its purposes' (Lawrence, 1987: 31–32).

7 To judge by the 'Statement on the Islamic Revolution in Syria and its Method', issued in 1980 by the Islamic Revolutionary Command, IRC (*Qiyadat al-thawra al-islamiyya*), the radical offshoot of the Syrian Muslim Brothers seems also to show interest in socio-economic matters. However, it is difficult to know how representative this document is of the mainstream Islamist thinking, and also the extent to which the concern over socio-economic matters could be said to have been genuine and the extent to which it might have been a mere 'tactical response' necessitated by the emphasis that official state propaganda lays on such issues (cf. IRC, *Qiyadat*, 1980: 21ff; Janahani, 1987: 138ff).

8 The Islamists are, of course, obsessed with modern Western thought, but in a partly subconscious and partly negative way. This point has been made by Hisham Ju'ait who has aptly observed that although contemporary Islamists are launching the most rampant riposte against modern Western thought, they are in reality caught in its concepts and methods (cf. Ju'ait, 1988: 285–286). It is in fact interesting to see that several Islamists have adopted Arabic translations of the terms that were coined in the West to describe their movements, such as Islamic 'revival' (*sahwa*) and Islamic 'fundamentalism' (*'usuliyya*). For some detail see the glossary at the end of this book.

9 In spite of their Islamicist terminology, several of the fundamentalists – as Sami Zubaida observed – still operate within the 'Western-inspired political paradigms of the nation-state and "the people" and several of them espouse a kind of 'populist nationalism with "Islam" as the identifying emblem of the common people against the "alien" social sphere in their own country which had excluded and subordinated them' (Zubaida, 1989: 33).

10 The term 'Islamicate' is due to Marshall Hodgson (1974). Analogous with, for example, 'Italianate', it is meant here to imply 'in the Islamic style'.

11 As the Islamic writer Kamil al-Sharif admits, one of the factors that 'helped in giving currency to the [Islamist] idea is the fact that the Islamic movements have not practised government or contributed to it in any influential way. This has exempted the movements from any responsibility

for the catastrophes [that beset the Muslim community], and preserved its capability for dealing with them at a 'theoretical' level, that is not tested in real practice. *It is in this point in particular that a real danger for the Islamic movements lies – the danger of shifting from idealism to reality, from theory to practice, with all the challenges involved in such a shift* (al-Sharif, 1988: 248 – emphasis in the original).

Glossary

'Abbasids dynasty of caliphs ruling from Baghdad from AD 750 to 1258, although with little actual power after AD 945.

'Adl Islamic, 'apportionate' concept of justice – 'to give every one his due'.

Ahl al-Kitab 'People of the Book'. Followers of other monotheistic religions, mainly Jews and Christians. Later described by the jurists as *ahl al-dhimma* (or *dhimmis*): protected, non-Muslim subjects of the Islamic State.

'Asabiyya 'group solidarity', often based on 'tribal' ancestry.

Asala 'cultural authenticity' – the authentic or original (*'asil*) is often contrasted with the 'introduced' or 'imported' (*wafid; mustawrad*), and authenticity is often contrasted with 'modernity' (*al-mu'asara*).

Awqaf (sing. *Waqf*) religiously-endowed property, entrusted to the clerics. *Habus* in Maghrib countries. In modern states the administration of awqaf and of Islamic affairs in general is often assigned to one government ministry.

Bayan the 'revealing' of meaning through linguistic textual analysis.

Dar al-Islam 'the Abode, or Household, of Islam'. Islamdom, or lands where Islam reigns supreme.

Da'wa literally 'call'; signifies proselytisation and missionary and propaganda work with the intention of both spreading and confirming the Islamic message.

Dawla originally 'turn' or 'cycle', subsequently 'dynasty'; currently 'State' (in the European sense).

Diwan originally 'register', subsequently government administration or department.

Faqih (pl. *Fuqaha'*) jurisconsult. A man with good 'comprehension' of the technicalities of Islamic jurisprudence (*Fiqh*).

Fard; Farida (pl. *Furud*) religious obligation, duty or commandment of which there are two kinds, according to the jurists: *fard 'ain*, or a duty incumbent upon the individual (such as prayer), and *fard kifaya*, or a duty incumbent upon the community (such as holy war). The fulfilment of this last by a sufficient number of members of the community excuses other individuals from the duty of fulfilling it.

Fasad 'corruption'; and *mufsidun*: 'corruptors' – defined in a broad moral, social and political sense.

Fatwa (pl. *Fatawa*) a religio-juridic verdict or counsel, issued by a recognised scholar.

Firinja 'Franks', i.e. Europeans (*rum* or 'Romans' in the Maghrib). The Firinji (efrangi) or *rumi*, i.e. foreign, is often contrasted with the *baladi*:

'native', or *watani*: national. And the *gharbi* (Western) is often contrasted with the *sharqi* (Eastern). *Farnaja* (or *tafarnuj*) is acting or thinking like the 'Franks', i.e. Europeanisation and, by extension, Westernisation. *Gharbzadegi* (pers.): intoxicated with the West.

Fitna 'seduction' (as caused by a tempting female) and/or 'sedition' (as caused by misleading ideas that result in social disorder and strife).

Ghaiba 'occultation'; disappearance of a Shi'i imam from sight.

Hadith sayings attributed to Prophet Muhammad.

Hakimiyya a new coinage by the political Islamists. Derived from *hukm* which meant originally 'adjudication' but has gradually been extended to mean ruling or governing (hence, *hukuma*: government). Hakimiyya is the principle that maintains that absolute sovereignty and rulership should be for God alone, not for the people or for the law.

Halal/Haram religiously permitted and religiously prohibited, respectively.

Hanbali one of the four recognised juridic schools (cf. *madhahib*) of Sunni Islam, initiated by Ahmad Ibn Hanbal (d. AD 855) and known for its strict adherence to the Quran and the 'genuine' Hadith. It is the dominant school in Saudi Arabia.

Hijra emigration (or immigration). The main *hijra* in Islam is that of Prophet Muhammad from Mecca to Madina in AD 622.

Hudud Islamic penalties.

'Ibadat matters of 'devotion' within Islam (i.e. man/God relationship; often contrasted with *mu'amalat*.

Ijma' consensus (usually of the jurists).

Ijtihad independent reasoning with regard to religious issues. A gradual 'Closing of the Gate of Ijtihad' started to take place fairly early in the tenth century AD

'Ilmaniyya secularism. An established distortion of the original rendering *'alamaniyya* (this-worldliness), presumably from French *laïcité*. 'Secularism' is often mistakenly translated by the Islamists as 'non-religion-ness' (*la diniyya*).

Imam leader – religious (and sometimes political). *Imama*: leadership. It may range from casual leadership of collective prayers, to being a religious leader of an entire community. Has a much grander and more revered spiritual significance in Shi'ism.

Imara command, rule. *Amir*: Commander, chief, prince.

Iqta' the Eastern form of State-controlled landlordism (bureaucratic-feudalism may represent an approximate, but by no means perfect, translation).

Jahiliyya originally the total pagan ignorance that is supposed to have characterised pre-Islamic Arabia. Used by contemporary political Islamists (following S. Qutb and A. Mawdudi) to characterise all societies that are not genuinely and thoroughly Islamic.

Al-Jama'a al-Islamiyya 'the Islamic Society or Group'. Often used in this singular form by the Islamists to emphasise their doctrinal unity. Usually used by others in the plural (*Al-Jama'at al-Islamiyya*) to describe the various Islamic movements.

Jihad exertion, striving or struggling by all means, including military ones. In the most militant sense it is somewhat similar to a 'crusade'.

Kalam literally 'speech' or 'statement'; subsequently 'scholastic theology'

with a certain 'philosophical' touch (based originally on atomistic theory).

Khalifa (Caliph) 'successor' to Prophet Muhammad. *Khilafa* (Caliphate): the institution of Islamic government after Muhammad (and its theory).

Khawarij (Kharijites) 'exiters' or 'seceders', deviating from the 'consensus of the community'. Originally rebellious ultra-zealous religio-political movements that disagreed with, and revolted against, 'Ali and subsequent Muslim rulers.

Madhahib (sing. *madhhab*) recognised juridic schools, which flourished between the mid-eighth and the mid-tenth centuries AD, of which there are four major ones in Sunni Islam founded by Malik (d. AD 767), Abu Hanifa (d. AD 767), Shafi'i (d. AD 820), and Ibn Hanbal (d. AD 855).

Maslaha (pl. *masalih*) 'interests' of the community.

Milla religion or sect; taken by the Persians and Turks to mean 'nation'.

Mu'amalat matters pertaining to social 'dealings' within Islam (i.e. man/ man relationships); often contrasted with *'ibadat*.

Mulk 'personal monarchy', usually not derived from or based on the Shari'a.

Al-Mustad'afun (Pers. *mustazafin*) literally, 'those rendered weak, or forced into a position of weakness', i.e. the oppressed, or downtrodden.

Al-Mustakbirun (Pers. *mustakbirin*) literally, 'those who (undeservedly) claim for themselves a position of grandeur and haughtiness', i.e. the oppressors.

Al-Mutatarrifun 'the extremists' – the term usually given by the authorities (and some others) to the radical Islamists. Similar to *ghulat* in older treatises.

Mu'tazila (Mu'tazilites) a school of 'philosophical theology' (cf. *kalam*) that emphasises the importance of reason. Historically it was superseded by the more 'conservative' Ash'arite school, but is now reclaimed by a number of contemporary Islamic writers such as Rashid al-Ghanushi and Hasan Hanafi.

Ottomans a Turkish dynasty claiming to have inherited the caliphate from the 'Abbasids. Ruled the Muslim empire and parts of South East Europe, using Istanbul as the capital after AD 1453. The caliphate was abolished by the Turkish Republic in 1924.

Qawm people (currently 'nation'); *Qawmiyya*: nationalism.

Qiyas reasoning by analogy; deduction.

Rashidun the 'wise' and rightly-guided first four caliphs to succeed Muhammad (Abu Bakr, 'Umar, 'Uthman and 'Ali). Ruled from AD 632 to 661. Their era is regarded as the 'Golden Age' of Islam, from a *religious* point of view.

Riba 'usury' – describes most 'interest' charged by or received from modern (capitalist-style) banks.

Al-Sahwa al-islamiyya 'the Islamic Awakening' – a very recent translation of the English 'Islamic revival', used even by some of the Islamists themselves.

Salafi pertaining to the good 'ancestral' example and tradition of Prophet Muhammad, his companions, and the first four caliphs (with the possible addition of 'Umar ibn 'Abd al-'Aziz).

Al-Shahadatain the 'Credo' or testimony professing that 'there is no god but God and that Muhammad is His Messenger'. The first of the five 'pillars' of Islam.

Shari'a, also *Shar'* (adj. *shar'i*) originally 'path' or 'way'; subsequently the 'legislative' part of religion as stipulated in the Quran and Hadith.

Shi'a (adj. *Shi'i*) 'the Party of 'Ali', who believe that leadership of the

Muslim community after Muhammad should have gone to 'Ali (the Prophet's cousin and son-in-law) and his family.

Shura   usually unbinding consultation sought by the ruler from colleagues or scholars (or, in modern interpretations, from 'the people').

Siyasa   originally connoting the effective way to handle animals or minors, used in modern times to signify 'politics' or 'policy'.

Sufi   'mystic'.

Sultan   in the abstract sense, political power; more specifically the incumbent of the highest political position.

Sunna (adj. Sunni)   strictly, the sayings, ways and 'traditions' of Prophet Muhammad. By extension it is used to distinguish the mainstream majority Muslim 'sect' (*Sunnis*) from the *Shi'a*, or 'the party of 'Ali'.

Taba'iyya   dependency. Although used more typically by the Marxists, it is sometimes used (but with particular emphasis on cultural aspects) by Islamists with nationalistic and/or leftist tendencies (e.g. 'Adil Husain, Munir Shafiq).

Taghut   ungodly hegemony (and allegiance to it).

Takaful   a solidaristic notion, used by many Islamists to describe a populist–corporatist formula based on collaboration rather than conflict between classes, and on mandatory charity from the rich to the poor. Most writings on social justice in Islam and certainly the writings that claim a 'socialistic' character to Islam, are centred round this notion.

Takfir   to judge and pronounce someone as being infidel (somewhat similar to 'excommunication').

Taqiyya   strictly, caution; concealment of real religious beliefs in adverse conditions.

Tawhid   'one-ness', 'unification' – strictly signifying monotheism, but taken by some to signify a holistic world view or even, on occasion, used to urge for an integrated orderly community.

Turath   'cultural heritage', often – but not always – taken to revolve around Islam.

'Ulama (sing. *'Alim*)   'scholars' or people trained in the religious 'sciences'.

Umma   community, either in an ethno-cultural, or in a religious sense.

Ummayads   dynasty of caliphs ruling from Damascus from AD 661 to 750.

Usuliyyun   A term, less than a decade old, that represents a direct translation of the English word 'fundamentalists'. It is not a bad translation as there is actually a branch of Islamic studies known as *usul al-din* (fundamentals of the religion).

Wilaya   guardianship, 'being in charge', incumbency.

Zakat   obligatory alms-giving. One of the four ritualistic duties on Muslims (in addition to prayer, fasting and pilgrimage).

Al-Zayy al-islami   the 'Islamic costume'. Modern, made-up garb believed to meet the Islamic requirements for modesty. According to Islamic precepts the female is required to cover the whole body except for the face and the hands. Such a 'cover' is usually known as the *hijab* (veil). The ultra-zealous neo-fundamentalists frequently opt for a more extreme garb known as the *niqab*, which also covers the face (with a mask) and the hands (with gloves).

Bibliography

'Abd Al-Fadil, Mahmud (1988), *Al-Tashkilat al-ijtima'iyya wa al-takwinat al-tabaqiyya* . . . [Social Constellations and Class Formations in the Arab World], (Beirut: Centre for Arab Unity Studies and United Nations University).

'Abd Al-Fattah, Nabil (1984), *Al-Mushaf wa al-saif* . . . [The Book and the Sword: the Conflict of Religion and State in Egypt], (Cairo: Madbuli).

'Abd Al-Halim, Mahmud (1985), *Al-Ikhwan al-muslimun* . . . [The Muslim Brothers: Events that Made History], Vol. III, (Alexandria: Dar al-Da'wa).

'Abd Al-Karim, Khalil (1987), *Li tatbiq al-shari'a, la li al-hukm* [For the Application of Shari'a, Not for Government], (Cairo: Kitab al-Ahali).

'Abdalla, 'Abd al-Ghani B. (1986), *Nazariyyat al-dawla fi al-islam* [Theory of the State in Islam], (Beirut: Al-Dar al-Jami'iyya).

Abdalla, Ahmed (1985), *The Student Movement and National Politics in Egypt* (London: Al-Saqi Books).

'Abdalla, Isma'il-Sabri, *et al.* (1987), *Al-Harakat al-islamiyya fi al-watan al-'arabi* [Islamic Movements in the Arab World], (Beirut: Centre for Arab Unity Studies and United Nations University).

'Abd Al-Latif, Ahmad (1978), 'Al-infitah al-istihlaki w'al-akhlaq' [Ethics and the Consumerist 'Open Door'], *Al-Da'wa*, no. 26, July 1978.

'Abd Al-Latif, Kamal (1987), *Al-Ta'wil wa al-mufaraqa.* . . [Hermeneutics and Irony: Towards a Philosophical Inquiry into Arab Political Theory], (Casablanca: Al-Markaz al-Thaqafi al-'Arabi).

'Abd Al-Malik, Anwar (1983), *Rih al-sharq* [Wind of the East], (Cairo: Dar al-Mustaqbal al-'Arabi).

'Abd Al-Raziq, 'Ali, (1966), *Al-Islam wa 'usul al-hukm* [Islam and the Essentials of Government], new edn, (Beirut: Dar Maktabat al-Hayat).

'Abd Al-Salam, Ahmad (1985), *Mustalah al-siyasa 'ind al-'arab* [The Term 'Politics' Among the Arabs], (Tunis: Société Tunisienne de Diffusion).

Abir, Mordechai (1988), *Saudi Arabia in the Oil Era: Regime and Elites, Conflict and Collaboration* (London: Croom Helm).

Abrahamian, Ervand (1988), 'Ali Shari'ati: Ideologue of the Iranian Revolution', In E. Burke and I. Lapidus, eds, *Islam, Politics and Social Change* (Berkeley & Los Angeles: University of California Press).

Abu Al-Majd, Ahmad Kamal (1988), *Hiwar la muwajaha* [Dialogue, Not Confrontation], (Cairo: Dar al-Shuruq).

Abu Dharr (pseud.) (1980), *Thawra fi rihab makka* [Revolution in the Precinct of Mecca], (n.pl.: Dar Sawt al-Tali'a).

Adams, Charles J. (1983), 'Mawdudi and the Islamic State', in John L. Esposito, ed., *Voices of Resurgent Islam* (New York and Oxford: Oxford University Press).

Ahmed, O.B. (1988), 'Islamic Credit, Its Role and Significance; the Case of Faisal Islamic Bank (Sudan)', *Proceedings*, Annual Conference of the British Society for Middle East Studies, Leeds University, July 1988.

Ajami, Fouad (1982), *The Arab Predicament* (Cambridge: Cambridge University Press).

Akhavi, Shahrough (1980), *Religion and Politics in Contemporary Iran* (Albany: SUNY Press).

Aknush, 'Abd al-Latif (1987), *Tarikh al-mu'assasat wa al-waqa'i' al-ijtima'iyya bi al-Maghrib* [History of Social Institutions and Events in Morocco], (Casablanca: Ifriqiya al-Sharq).

Alavi, Hamza (1988), 'Pakistan and Islam: Ethnicity and Ideology', in F. Halliday and H. Alavi, eds, *State and Ideology in the Middle East and Pakistan* (London: Macmillan Education).

Algar, Hamid (1983), *The Roots of the Islamic Revolution* (London: The Open Press).

'Ali, Haidar Ibrahim (1987), 'Al-Intillijinsiya al-sudaniyya bain al-taqlidiyya wa al-hadatha' [Sudanese Intelligentsia between Traditionalism and Modernity], *Al-Mustaqbal al-'Arabi*, Vol. 10, no. 104, October 1987.

Al-'Alim, Mahmud Amin (1986), *Al-Wa'iy wa al-wa'iy al-za'if. . .* [Consciousness and False Consciousness in Contemporary Arab Thought], (Cairo Dar al-Thaqafa al-Jadida).

Amer, Hassan H. (1988), 'Islamic Activism and Religious Non-Governmental Societies', *mimeo.*, 1988.

Amin, Galal (1974), *The Modernisation of Poverty* (Leiden: Brill).

—— (1989), 'Migration, Inflation and Social Mobility', in Charles Tripp and Roger Owen, eds, *Egypt Under Mubarak* (London: Routledge).

Amin, Husain Ahmad (1985), *Dalil al-muslim al-hazin ila muqtada al-suluk fi al-qarn al-'ishrin* [The Sad Muslim's Guide to the Requirements of Conduct in the 20th Century], (Cairo and Beirut: Dar al-Shuruq).

—— (1987), *Tatbiq al-shari'a al-islamiyya* [Implementation of the Islamic Shari'a], (Cairo: Madbuli).

—— (1988), *Al-Islam fi 'alam mutaghayyir* [Islam in a Changing World], (Cairo: Madbuli).

Amin, Osman (1966), 'Some Aspects of Religious Reform in the Muslim Middle East', in Carl Leiden, ed., *The Conflict of Traditionalism and Modernism in the Muslim Middle East* (Austin: University of Texas Press).

Amin, Sadiq (1982), *Al-Da'wa al-islamiyya* [The Islamic Call], (Amman: Jam'iyyat 'Ummal al-Matabi' al-Ta'awuniyya).

Amin, Samir (1978), *The Arab Nation*, trans. M. Pallas (London: Zed Press).

—— (1985), *Azmat al-mujtama' al-'arabi* [The Crisis of Arab Society], (Cairo: Dar al-Mustaqbal al-'Arabi).

Anawati, Georges C. and Borrmans, Maurice (1982), *Tendances et courants de l'Islam arabe contemporain; Vol. I: Egypte et Afrique du Nord* (Munchen and Mainz: Kaiser-Grunewald).

Anderson, Lisa (1983), 'Qaddafi's Islam', in John L. Esposito, ed., *Voices of Resurgent Islam* (New York and Oxford: Oxford University Press).

Anderson, Perry (1980), *Lineages of the Absolutist State* (London: Verso).

Ansari, Hamied N. (1984A), 'The Islamic Militants in Egyptian Politics' *International Journal of Middle East Studies*, Vol. 16, no. 1, March 1984.

—— (1984B), 'Sectarian Conflict in Egypt and the Political Expediency of Religion', *The Middle East Journal*, Vol. 38, no. 3, Summer 1984.

Antoun, Richard (1989), *Muslim Preacher in the Modern World: A Jordanian Case Study in Comparative Perspective*, (Princeton, N.J.: Princeton University Press).

AOHR – Arab Organisation for Human Rights (Al-Munazzama al-'Arabiyya li Huquq al-Insan) (1984), *Al-Nashra*, no. 3 (27 August 1984).

Apter, David, ed. (1964), *Ideology and Discontent* (New York: Free Press of Glencoe).

—— (1969), *The Politics of Modernization* (Chicago and London: Chicago University Press).

Al-'Arawi, 'Abdallah (1981), *Mafhum al-dawla* [Concept of the State], (Casablanca: Al-Markaz al-Thaqafi al-'Arabi).

Arkoun, Mohammed (1988), 'The Concept of Authority in Islamic Thought' in Klaus Ferdinand and Mehdi Mozaffari, eds, *Islam: State and Society* (London: Curzon Press for the Scandinavian Institute of Asian Studies).

El-Ashker, Ahmed Abdel-Fattah (1987), *The Islamic Business Enterprise* (London: Croom Helm).

Al-'Ashmawi, Muhammad Sa'id, (1983A), *Ruh al-'adala* [The Spirit of Justice], (Beirut: Dar Iqra').

—— (1983B), *Usul al-shari'a* [The Fundamentals of Shari'a], (Cairo: Madbuli).

—— (1987), *Al-Islam al-siyasi* [Political Islam] (Cairo: Sina).

Al-Aswani, Ahmad (1985), *Hadith al-asdiqa' fi al-takfir wa al-jihad* [Friends' Talk on Excommunication and Crusade], (Cairo: Matba'at al-Ashraf).

'Atiyya, Jamal al-Din (1987), *Al-Bunuk al-islamiyya* [Islamic Banks], (Qatar: Kitab al-Umma).

'Awda, 'Abd al-Malik (1988), 'Al-Watan al-'arabi wa al-'alam al-thalith' [The Arab World and the Third World], in 'Aliy al-Din Hilal *et al.*, *Al-'Arab wa al-'alam* [Arabs and the World], (Beirut: Centre for Arab Unity Studies).

'Awda, 'Abd-al Qadir (1951), *Al-Islam wa awda 'una al-qanuniyya* [Islam and our Legal Situation], (Cairo: Dar al-Kitab al-'Arabi).

Ayubi, Nazih (1978), *Siyasat al-ta'lim. . .* [Education Policy in Egypt: A Political and Administrative Study], (Cairo: Centre for Political and Strategic Studies).

Ayubi, Nazih (1980A), *Bureaucracy and Politics in Contemporary Egypt* (London: Ithaca Press).

—— (1980B), 'The Political Revival of Islam: the Case of Egypt', *International Journal of Middle East Studies*, Vol. 12, no. 4, December 1980.

—— (1982), 'Implementation Capability and Political Feasibility of the Open Door Policy in Egypt', in Malcolm Kerr and El Sayed Yassin, eds, *Rich and Poor States in the Middle East* (Boulder, Colo.: Westview Press).

—— (1982/83), 'The Politics of Militant Islamic Movements in the Middle East', *Journal of International Affairs*, Vol. 36, no. 2, Fall/Winter, 1982/83.

—— (1984), 'OPEC and the Third World: the Case of Arab Aid', in Robert W. Stookey, ed., *The Arabian Peninsula: Contemporary Politics, Economics and International Relations* (Stanford, Calif.: The Hoover Institution).

—— (1988A), 'Adabiyyat dirasat al-mujtama' wa al-dawla' [Literature on the State/Society Inquiry], in Sa'd al-Din Ibrahim, ed., *Al-Mujtama' wa al-dawla fi al-watan al-'arabi* [State and Society in the Arab Homeland], (Beirut: Centre for Arab Unity Studies).

—— (1988B), 'Domestic Politics', in L.C. Harris, ed., *Egypt: Internal Challenges and Regional Stability* (London: Routledge and Kegan Paul for the Royal Institute of International Affairs).

Al-'Azmah, 'Aziz (1987), *Al-Turath bain al-sultan wa al-tarikh* [The Cultural Heritage Between the Ruler and History], (Casablanca: 'Uyun).

Al-Azmeh, Aziz (1982), *Ibn Khaldun; An Essay in Reinterpretation* (London: Frank Cass).

Badawi, Jamal (1980), *Al-Fitna al-ta'ifiyya fi misr* [The Sectarian Strife in Egypt], (Cairo: Al-Markaz al-'Arabi li al-Sahafa).

Al-Banna, Hasan (1954), *Al-Rasa'il al-thalath* [Three Tracts], (Cairo: Dar al-Kitab al-'Arabi).

Barakat, Halim (1984), *Al-mujtama' al-'arabi al-mu'asir* [Contemporary Arab Society], (Beirut: Centre for Arab Unity Studies).

Bashiriyeh, Hossein (1984), *The State and Revolution in Iran, 1962–1982* (London: Croom Helm).

Basyuni, Hasan A. (1985), *Al-Dawla wa nizam al-hukm fi al-islam* [The State and System of Government in Islam], (Cairo: 'Alam al-Kutub).

Batatu, Hanna (1988), 'Syria's Muslim Brethren', in F. Halliday and H. Alavi, eds, *State and Ideology in the Middle East and Pakistan* (London: Macmillan Education).

Bayat, Mangol (1983), 'Secularism and the Islamic Government in Iran', in Philip H. Stoddard, ed., *The Middle East in the 1980s: Problems and Prospects* (Washington DC: The Middle East Institute).

Baydun, Ibrahim (1983), *Al-hijaz wa al-dawla al-islamiyya* [The Hijaz and the Islamic State: A Study in the Problematic of Relationship with the Central Authority in the First Hijri Century], (Beirut: Al-Mu'assasa al-Jami'iyya)

Bayyumi, Zakariyya S. (1979), *Al-Ikhwan al-muslimun wa al-jama'at al-*

islamiyya . . . [The Muslim Brothers and the Islamic Groupings], (Cairo: Wahba).

Beinin, Joel and Lockman, Zachary (1987), *Workers on the Nile: Nationalism, Communism, Islam, and the Egyptian Working Class, 1882-1954* (Princeton NJ,: Princeton University Press).

Bensaid, Said (1987), '*Al-Watan* and *Al-Umma* in Contemporary Arab Use', in Ghassan Salame, ed., *The Foundations of the Arab State* (London: Croom Helm).

Bezirgan, Najm A. (1979) 'Critique of Religion in Modern Arabic Thought', *mimeo.* (University of Texas at Austin).

Bill, James A. (1982A), 'The Arab World and the Challenge of Iran', *Journal of Arab Affairs*, Vol. 2, no. 1, 1982.

—— (1982B), 'Power and Religion in Revolutionary Iran', *The Middle East Journal*, Vol. 36, no. 1, Winter 1982.

—— and Leiden, Carl (1984), *Politics in the Middle East*, 2nd edn, (Boston: Little Brown & Co.).

Binder, Leonard (1988), *Islamic Liberalism: A Critique of Development Ideologies* (Chicago and London: Chicago University Press).

Al-Bishri, Tariq (1980), *Al-Muslimun wa al-aqbat.* . . [Muslims and Copts in the Context of the National Community], (Cairo: Hai'at al-Kitab).

Boulby, Marion (1988), 'The Islamic Challenge: Tunisia since Independence' *Third World Quarterly*, Vol. 10, no. 2, April 1988 (issue on *Islam and Politics*).

Al-Buraey, M.A. (1985), *Administrative Development: an Islamic Perspective* (London: Kegan Paul International).

Butterworth, Charles E. (1987), 'State and Authority in Arabic Political Thought', in Ghassan Salame, ed., *The Foundations of the Arab State* (London: Croom Helm).

Carré, Olivier and Seurat, Michel (1982), 'L'utopie islamiste au Moyen-Orient arabe et particulièrement en Egypte et en Syrie', in Olivier Carré, ed., *L'Islam et l'État dans le Monde d'Aujourd'hui* (Paris: Presses Universitaires de France).

Carré, Olivier and Michaud, Gerard (1983), *Les Frères Musulmans (1928–1982)*, (Paris: Editions Gallimard).

CAUS - Centre for Arab Unity Studies (Markaz Dirasat al-Wahda al-'Arabiyya), (1985), *Al-Turath wa tahadiyat al-'asr fi al-watan al-'arabi (al-asala wa al-mu'asara)*, [The Cultural Heritage and Contemporary Challenges in the Arab 'Homeland' (Authenticity and Modernity)]; papers and discussions of a seminar, (Beirut: CAUS).

CPSS - Centre for Political and Strategic Studies (Markaz al-Dirasat al-Siyasiyya wa al-Istiratijiyya), (1988), *Al-Taqrir al-istiratiji al-'arabi* [The Arab Strategic Report for 1987], (Cairo: Al-Ahram).

Cudsi, Alexander S. (1986), 'Islam and Politics in the Sudan', in James P. Piscatori, ed., *Islam in the Political Process* (London: Cambridge University Press for the Royal Institute of International Affairs).

Dagnino, Evelina (1980), 'Cultural and Ideological Dependence; Building a Theoretical Framework', in Krishna Kumar, ed., *Transnational Enter-*

prises: Their Impact on Third World Societies and Cultures (Boulder, Colo.: Westview Press).

Darif, Muhammad (1988), *Mu'assasat al-sultan 'al-sharif' bi al-Maghrib* [The 'Sharifian' Sultanic Institution in Morocco], (Casablanca: Ifriqiya al-Sharq).

Davis, Eric (1987), 'The Concept of Revival and the Study of Islam and Politics', in Barbara Stowasser, ed., *The Islamic Impulse* (London: Croom Helm).

Al-Dawalibi, Muhammad Ma'ruf (1984), *Al-Dawla wa al-sultan*. . . [State and Authority in Islam], (Cairo: Dar al-Sahwa).

Dietl, Wilhelm (1984), *Holy War*, trans. (New York: Macmillan).

Diyab, Muhammad Hafiz (1988), *Sayyid Qutb* . . . [Sayyid Qutb: Discourse and Ideology], (Cairo: Dar al-Thaqafa al-Jadida).

Donohue, John and John Esposito, eds, (1982) *Islam in Transition: Muslim Perspectives* (New York: Oxford University Press).

Al-Duri, 'Abd al-'Aziz (1982), *Muqaddima fi al-tarikh al-iqtisadi al-'arabi* [An Introduction to Arab Economic History], (Beirut: Dar al-Tali'a).

—— (1984), *Al-takwin al-tarikhi li al-umma al-'arabiyya* [Historical Formation of the Arab Nation], (Beirut: Centre for Arab Unity Studies).

Ebeid, Mona Makram (1989), 'The Role of the Official Opposition', in Charles Tripp and Roger Owen, eds, *Egypt Under Mubarak* (London and New York: Routledge).

Eickelman, Dale F. (1981), *The Middle East: An Anthropological Approach* (Englewood Cliffs, NJ.: Prentice-Hall).

—— (1987), 'Changing Interpretations of Islamic Movements', in William R. Roff, ed., *Islam and the Political Economy of Meaning* (London: Croom Helm).

Eisenstadt, S.N. (1969), *The Political System of Empires* (New York: Free Press of Glencoe).

—— (1986), 'Comparative Analysis of the State in Historical Contexts', in A. Kazancigil, ed., *The State in Global Perspective* (Aldershot, Hants: Gower for UNESCO).

EIU – Economist Intelligence Unit (1987-88), *Country Reports: Sudan* (London: EIU).

Enayat, Hamid (1982), *Modern Islamic Political Thought* (Austin: Texas University Press).

—— (1986), 'Iran: Khumayni's Concept of the 'Guardianship of the Jurisconsult", in James P. Piscatori, ed., *Islam in the Political Process* (London: Cambridge University Press for Royal Institute of International Affairs).

Esposito, John L. (1987), *Islam and Politics*, 2nd rev. edn (New York: Syracuse University Press).

Etienne, Bruno (1987), *L'Islamism Radicale* (Paris: Hachette).

Farah, Nadia Ramsis (1986), *Religious Strife in Egypt: Crisis and Ideological Conflict in the Seventies* (New York and London: Gordon and Breach).

Faraj, Muhammad 'Abd al-Salam (1982), *Al-jihad: al-farida al-gha'iba* [Jihad: the Absent Commandment], (Jerusalem: Maktabat al-Batal).

Faruki, Kemal A. (1971), *The Evolution of Islamic Constitutional Theory and Practice from 610 to 1926* (Karachi-Dacca: National Publishing House Ltd).

Fawda, Faraj 'Ali (1985), *Qabl al-suqut . . .* [Before the Fall: a Quiet Dialogue on the Application of Islamic Shari'a], (Cairo: n.p.).

—— et al. (1987), *Al-Ta'ifiyya: ila ain?* [Sectarianism: Where To?], (Cairo: Dar al-Misri al-Jadid).

—— (1988), *Al-Haqiqa al-gha'iba* [The Absent Truth], (Cairo: Dar al-Fikr).

Fischer, Michael M.J. (1983), 'Imam Khomeini: Four Levels of Understanding', in John L. Esposito, ed., *Voices of Resurgent Islam* (New York and Oxford: Oxford University Press).

Flores, Alexander (1988), 'Egypt: A New Secularism?', *Middle East Report* Vol. 18, no. 4, July–August 1988.

Ghalyun, Burhan, (1979), *Al-Mas'ala al-ta'ifiyya wa mushkilat al-aqaliyyat* [The Sectarian Issue and the Problem of Minorities], (Beirut: Dar al-Tali'a).

—— (1987A), *Ightiyal al-'aql . . .* [Assassination of the Mind: the Agony of Arab Culture Between Salafiyya and Dependency], (Beirut: Dar al-Tanwir).

—— (1987B), *Al-Wa'iy al-dhati* [Self Consciousness], (Casablanca: 'Uyun).

Al-Ghannoushi, Rashid (1988), 'Deficiencies in the Islamic Movement', trans., in *Middle East Report*, no. 153, July–August 1988.

Al-Ghanushi, Rashid (1987), 'Tahlil li al-'anasir al-mukawwina li al-zahira al-islamiyya bi Tunis' [Analysis of the Component Elements of the Islamic Phenomenon in Tunisia], in I.S. 'Abdalla et al., *Al-Harakat al-islamiyya fi al-watan al-'arabi* (Beirut: Centre for Arab Unity Studies and United Nations University).

Al-Ghazali Al-Jubaili, Zainab (1988), 'Al-Sahwa al-islamiyya wa al-muwatana wa al-musawa' [The Islamic Revival and Citizenship and Equality], in Sa'd al-Din Ibrahim, ed., *Al-Sahwa al-islamiyya wa humum al-watan al-'arabi* [Amman: Arab Through Forum and Mu'assasat Al-al-Bait].

Ghunaim, 'Adil (1986), *Al-Namudhaj al-misri li ra'simaliyyat al-dawla al-tabi'a* [The Egyptian Model of Dependent State Capitalism], (Cairo: Dar al-Mustaqbal al-'Arabi).

Gilsenan, Michael (1982A), 'Approaching the Islamic Revolution', *MERIP Reports*, no. 102, January 1982.

—— (1982B), *Recognizing Islam: Religion and Society in the Modern Arab World* (New York: Pantheon Books).

Goldberg, Ellis (1988), 'Muslim Union Politics in Egypt: Two Cases', in E. Burke and I. Lapidus, eds, *Islam, Politics and Social Change* (Berkeley and Los Angeles: University of California Press).

Gran, Peter (1980), 'Political Economy as a Paradigm for the Study of Islamic History', *International Journal of Middle East Studies*, Vol. 11, no. 4, July 1980.

—— (1987), 'Intellectuals and the Syrian Revolution', in J.A. Allen, ed., *Politics and the Economy in Syria* (London: School of Oriental and African Studies).

Grandguillaume, Gilbert (1982), 'Islam et politique au Maghreb', in Olivier Carré, ed., *L'Islam et l'État* (Paris: Presses Universitaires de France).

El Guindi, Fadwa (1981), 'Veiling *Infitah* with Muslim Ethic: Egypt's Contemporary Islamic Movement', in *Social Problems*, Vol. 28, no. 4, April 1981.

Haddad, Yvonne Y. (1982), *Contemporary Islam and the Challenge of History* (Albany, NY: SUNY Press).

—— (1983), 'Sayyid Qutb: Ideologue of Islamic Revival', in John L. Esposito, ed., *Voices of Resurgent Islam* (New York and Oxford: Oxford University Press).

Haidar, Khalil 'Ali (1987), *Tayyarat al-sahwa al-islamiyya* [Currents in the Islamic Revival], (Kuwait: Kazima).

Halliday, Fred (1983), 'Year IV of the Islamic Republic', *MERIP Reports*, no. 113, March–April 1983.

—— (1988), 'The Iranian Revolution: Uneven Development and Religious Populism', in F. Halliday and H. Alavi, eds, *State and Ideology in the Middle East and Pakistan* (London: Macmillan Education).

—— and Alavi, H. eds, (1988), *State and Ideology in the Middle East and Pakistan* (London: Macmillan Education).

—— and Molyneux, F. (1989), on 'Tunisia', in the *Guardian*, 26 May 1989.

Hamdi, 'Abd al-Rahim (1989), 'Al-Masarif al-Islamiyya' [Islamic Banks], interview in *Al-Tadamun*, 20 March 1989.

Hammuda, 'Adil, (1985), *Qanabil wa masahif* [Bombs and Bibles: Story of the Jihad Organisation], (Cairo: Sina).

—— (1987A), *Al-Hijra ila al-'unf* . . . [Emigration to Violence: Religious Extremism from the June (1967) Defeat to the October (1981) Assassination], (Cairo: Sina).

—— (1987B), *Sayyid Qutb* . . . [Sayyid Qutb: from the Village to the Gallows; a Documentary Investigation], (Cairo: Sina).

Hanafi, Hassan, (1979), *Al-Hukuma al-islamiyya* . . . [Islamic Government: by Ruhullah al-Khumaini], edited with an introduction by H. Hanafi (Cairo: n.p.).

—— (1980), *Al-Turath wa al-tajdid* [Heritage and Renewal], (Cairo: Al-Markaz al-'Arabi).

—— (1982), 'The Relevance of the Islamic Alternative in Egypt', *Arab Studies Quarterly*, Vol. 4, nos. 1 and 2, Spring 1982.

—— (1988), *Min al-'aqida ila al-thawra*. . . [From Faith to Revolution; Vol. I: Theoretical Introduction], (Cairo: Madbuli).

Hanna, Milad (1978), *Uridu maskanan* . . . [I Need a Home! A Problem that has a Solution], (Cairo: Rose al-Yusuf).

—— (1980), *Na'am aqbat lakin misriyyun* [Yes, Copts; but Nonetheless Egyptians], (Cairo: Madbuli).

—— (1988), *Al-Iskan wa al-masyada* [The Housing Trap], (Cairo: Dar al-Mustaqbal al-'Arabi).

Al-Harawi, 'Abd al-Sami' (1986), *Lughat al-idara* . . . [The Language of Administration in Early Islam], (Cairo: Hai'at al-Kitab).

Al-Hasab, Fadil 'A. (1984), *Al-Mawardi fi nazariyyat al-idara al-islamiyya al-'amma* [Al-Mawardi on the Theory of Islamic Public Administration],

(Amman: Arab Organisation for Administrative Sciences).

Hasana, 'Umar 'Ubaid (1988), *Fiqh al-da'wa*. . . . [Jurisprudence of the Message: Interviews with Abul-Hasan al-Nadwi and others], Vol. I, April 1988 (Qatar: Kitab al-Umma).

Hawwa, Sa'id, (1979), *Al-Madkhal ila da'wat al-ikhwan al-muslimin* [Introduction to the Mission of the Muslim Brothers], (Amman: Dar al-Arqam).

—— (*c.* 1980), *Jund Allah* [God's Soldiers], (Cairo: n.p.).

Heikal, Mohamed (1983), *Autumn of Fury: The Assassination of Sadat* (London: André Deutsch).

Hinnebusch, Raymond A. (1982), 'The Islamic Movement in Syria', in Ali Dessouki, ed., *Islamic Resurgence in the Arab World* (New York: Praeger).

Al-Hirmasi, Muhammad 'Abd al-Baqi (1987), 'Al-Islam al-ihtijaji fi Tunis' [Protest Islam in Tunisia], in I.S. 'Abdalla *et al.*, *Al-Harakat al-islamiyya fi al-watan al-'arabi* (Beirut: Centre for Arab Unity Studies and United Nations University).

Hodgson, Marshall G.S. (1974), *The Venture of Islam: Conscience and History in a World Civilisation*, 3 vols.; I: *The Classical Age of Islam*; II: *The Expansion of Islam in the Middle Periods*; III: *The Gunpowder Empires and Modern Times* (Chicago: University of Chicago Press).

Hudson, Michael C. (1980), 'Islam and Political Development' in John L. Esposito, ed., *Islam and Development: Religion and Socio-Political Change* (Syracuse: Syracuse University Press).

—— (1986), 'The Islamic Factor in Syrian and Iraqi Politics', in James P. Piscatori, ed., *Islam in the Political Process* (Cambridge: Cambridge University Press for the Royal Institute of International Affairs).

Hunter, Shireen T. (1988), 'Iran and the Spread of Revolutionary Islam' in *Third World Quarterly*, Vol. 10, no. 2, April 1988 (special issue on *Islam and Politics*).

Husain, 'Adil (1985), *Nahwa fikr 'arabi jadid* [Towards a New Arab Thought], (Cairo: Dar al-Mustaqbal al-'Arabi).

Huwaidi, Fahmi (1985), *Muwatinun la dhimmiyyun* (Citizens, Not Protected Subjects), (Beirut and Cairo: Dar al-Shuruq).

—— (1987), *Al-Tadayyun al-manqus* [Incomplete Religiosity], (Cairo: Mu'assat al-Ahram).

—— (1988A), *Azmat al-wa'iy al-dini* [Crisis in Religious Consciousness], (San'a: Dar al-Hikma al-Yamaniyya).

—— (1988B), *Iran min al-dakhil* [Iran from the Inside], (Cairo: Markaz al-Ahram).

Ibn Khaldun (1978), *The Muqaddimah: An Introduction to History*, trans. F. Rosenthal, abridged and edited N.J. Dawood, (London: Routledge and Kegan Paul).

Ibn Taimiya, Taqiy al-Din (1965), *Al-Fatawa al-kubra* (Cairo: Al-Tahrir).

—— (1983), *Al-Siyasa al-shar'iyya* (Beirut: Al-Afaq al-Jadida).

Ibrahim, Saad Eddin (1980), 'Anatomy of Egypt's Militant Islamic Groups: Methodological Note and Preliminary Findings', *International Journal of Middle East Studies*, Vol. 12, no. 4, December 1980.

Ibrahim, Sa'd al-Din, ed. (1988), *Al-Sahwa al-islamiyya wa humum al-watan al-'arabi* [The Islamic Revival and Concerns of the Arab 'Homeland'] (Amman: Arab Though Forum and Mu'assasat Al-al-Bait).

ICO – The Islamic Conference Organisation (Munazzamat al-Mu'tamar al-Islami, Jidda), (1982), *Al-Islam wa al-nizam al-iqtisadi al-dawli al-jadid* [Islam and the New International Economic Order], (Tunis: Dar Siras li al-Nashr).

ILP – Islamic Liberation Party (1985), *Hizb al-tahrir* [The Liberation Party] (n.pl.: n.pub.).

Imam, 'Abdalla (1985), *Jihan* (Cairo: Rose al-Yusuf).

'Imara, Muhammad (1979), *Al-Islam wa al-sulta al-diniyya* [Islam and Religious Authority], (Cairo: Dar al-Thaqafa al-Jadida).

—— (1980), *Nazariyyat al-khilafa al-islamiyya* [Theory of the Islamic Caliphate], (Cairo: Dar al-Thaqafa al-Jadida).

—— (1982), *Al-Fikr al-qa'id li al-thawra al-iraniyya* [The Pioneering Thought of the Iranian Revolution], (Cairo: Dar Thabit).

—— (1983), *Al-Farida al-gha'iba: 'ard wa hiwar wa taqyim* [A Presentation, Discussion and Evaluation of 'The Absent Commandment'], (Beirut: Dar al-Wahda).

—— (1984), *Al-Islam wa al-'uruba wa al-'ilmaniyya* [Islam, Arabism and Secularism], (Beirut: Dar al-Wahda).

—— (1985), *Al-Sahwa al-islamiyya wa al-tahaddi al-hadari* [The Islamic Revival and the Civilisational Challenge], (Cairo: Dar al-Mustaqbal al-'Arabi).

—— (1987), *Abu al-A'la al-Mawdudi . . .* [Abu al-A'la al-Mawdudi and the Islamic Revival], (Cairo: Dar al-Shuruq).

IRC – The Islamic Revolutionary Command (Qiyadat al-thawra al-islamiyya, Syria), (1980), *Bayan al-thawra al-islamiyya fi suriyya wa minhajuha* [Statement on the Islamic Revolution in Syria and its Methodology], (Damascus: IRC).

IRO – Islamic Revolution Organisation of the Arabian Peninsula (Munazamat al-thawra al-islamiyya fi al-jazira al-'arabiyya), (1981A), *Intifadat al-haram* [Uprising in the Sanctuary], (London?: IRO).

—— (1981B), *Intifadat al-mantiqa al-sharqiyya* [Uprising of the Eastern Region], (London?: IRO).

'Isa, Salah (1986), *Muthaqqafun wa 'askar* [Intellectuals and Soldiers], (Cairo: Madbuli).

Islamic Republic of Iran (1979), *Al-Dustur al-islami li jumhuriyyat iran al-islamiyya* [The Islamic Constitution of the Islamic Republic of Iran], (Qum: Mu'assasat al-Shahid).

Isma'il, Mahmud (1980), *Susyulujiya al-fikr al-islami* [Sociology of Islamic Thought], 2 vols., (Casablanca: Dar al-Thaqafa).

Al-Jabiri, Muhammad 'Abid (1982A), *Al-'Asabiyya wa al-dawla* [Group Solidarity and the State: Khaldunian Theoretical Features on Islamic History], (Casablanca: Dar al-Nashr al-Maghribiyya).

—— (1982B), *Al-Khitab al-'arabi al-mu'asir* [Contemporary Arab Discourse], (Casablanca: Al-Markaz al-Thaqafi al-'Arabi).

—— (1985), *Takwin al-'aql al-'arabi* [Formation of the Arab Mind], (Beirut: Dar al-Tali'a).

—— (1986), *Binyat al-'aql al-'arabi* [Structure of the Arab Mind], (Beirut: Centre for Arab Unity Studies).

—— (1987), 'Al-Haraka al-salafiyya. . .' [The Salafi Movement and the Contemporary Islamic Society in Morocco], in I.S. 'Abdalla *et al.*, *Al-Harakat al-islamiyya fi al-watan al-'arabi* (Beirut: Centre for Arab Unity Studies and United Nations University).

Jadaane, Fahmi (1987), 'Notions of the State in Contemporary Arab-Islamic Writings', in Ghassan Salame, ed., *The Foundations of the Arab State* (London: Croom Helm).

Jad'an, Fahmi (1989), 'Al-Harakat al-islamiyya al-mu'asira fi al-watan al-'arabi' [The Contemporary Islamic Movements in the Arab 'Fatherland'], in *Majallat al-'Ulum al-Ijtima'iyya* (Kuwait), Vol. 17, no. 1, Spring 1989.

Al-Janahani, al-Habib (1987), 'Al-Sahwa al-islamiyya fi bilad al-sham. . .' [The Islamic Revival in Syria], in I.S. 'Abdalla *et al.*, *Al-Harakat al-islamiyya fi al-watan al-'arabi* (Beirut: Centre for Arab Unity Studies and United Nations University).

Jansen, Johannes J.G. (1986), *The Neglected Duty: the Creed of Sadat's Assassins and Islamic Resurgence in the Middle East* (New York: Macmillan Publishing).

Jazani, Bizhan (1980), *Capitalism and Revolution in Iran*, trans. (London: Zed Press).

Jones, Linda G. (1988), 'Portrait of Rashid al-Ghannoushi', *Middle East Report*, no. 153, July–August 1988.

Ju'ait, Hisham (1982), 'Min al-islah ila al-thawra al-islamiyya' [From Reform to the Islamic Revolution], in ICO, *Al-Islam wa al-nizam al-iqtisadi al-dawli al-jadid* (Tunis: Dar Siras li al-Nashr).

—— (1984), *Al-Shakhsiyya al-'arabiyya al-islamiyya. . .* [The Arab-Islamic Personality and the Arab Destiny], trans. (Beirut: Dar al-Tali'a).

—— (1988), 'Al-sahwa al-islamiyya wa al-thaqafa al-mu'asira' [The Islamic Revival and Contemporary Culture], in S. Ibrahim, ed., *Al-Sahwa al-islamiyya wa humum al-watan al-'arabi* (Amman: Arab Through Forum and Mu'assasat Al-al-Bait).

Junaina, Ni'matalla (1988), *Tanzim al-Jihad . . .* [The Jihad Organisation: Is it the Islamic Alternative in Egypt?], (Cairo: Dar al-Hurriyya).

Al-Kabbashi, Al-Makashifi Taha (1986), *Tatbiq al-shari'a al-islamiyya fi al-sudan, bain al-haqiqa wa al-ithara* [The Application of Islamic Shari'a in Sudan, between Reality and Sensationalism], (Cairo: Al-Zahra' li al-I'lam al-'Arabi).

Katouzian, Homa (1981), *The Political Economy of Modern Iran*, (London and New York: Macmillan and NYU Press).

—— (1989), 'Islamic Government and Politics: The Practice and Theory of the Absolute Guardianship of the Jurisconsult', *paper* at Symposium on the Post-War Arab Gulf, Centre for Arab Gulf Studies, Exeter University, 12–14 July 1989.

Keddie, Nikki R. (1968), *An Islamic Response to Imperialism: Political and*

Religious Writings of . . .'Al-Afghani' (Berkeley and Los Angeles: University of California Press).

—— (1981), *Roots of Revolution: an Interpretive History of Modern Iran* (New Haven and London: Yale University Press).

—— (1988A), 'Iranian Revolutions in Comparative Perspective', in E. Burke and I. Lapidus, eds, *Islam, Politics and Social Change* (Berkeley and Los Angeles: University of California Press).

—— (1988B), 'Ideology, Society and the State in Post-Colonial Muslim Societies', in F. Halliday and H. Alavi, eds, *State and Ideology in the Middle East and Pakistan* (London: Macmillan Education).

Kedourie, Elie (1966), *Afghani and 'Abduh: An Essay on Religious Unbelief and Political Activism in Modern Islam* (London: Frank Cass).

Kepel, Gilles (1985), *The Prophet and Pharaoh: Muslim Extremism in Egypt*, trans. (London: Al-Saqi Books).

Kerr, Malcolm H. (1966), *Islamic Reform: the Political and Legal Theories of Muhammad 'Abduh and Rashid Rida* (Berkeley and London: University of California Press and Cambridge University Press).

Keyder, Caglar (1986), 'The Rise and Decline of National Economies in the Periphery', *mimeo*.

Khalafalla, Muhammad Ahmad (1981), *Al-qur'an wa al-dawla* [The Quran and the State], (Beirut: Al-Mu'assasa al-'Arabiyya).

—— (1985), 'La ta'udu ila madhahib al-fuqaha' [Do Not Go Back to the Jurists' Schools], *Al-Yaqza al-'Arabiyya*, Vol. I, no. 5, July 1985.

—— (1987), 'Al-Sahwa al-islamiyya fi misr' [The Islamic Revival in Egypt], in I.S. 'Abdalla *et al.*, *Al-Harakat al-islamiyya fi al-watan al-'arabi* (Beirut: Centre for Arab Unity Studies and United Nations University).

Khalid, Khalid Muhammad (1950), *Min huna nabda'* [From Here We Start], 4th edn, (Cairo: Al-Khanji).

—— (1981), *Al-Dawla fi al-Islam* [The State in Islam], (Cairo: Dar Thabit).

—— (1982), interview in *Mayu*, 8 March 1982.

Khalid, Shawqi (1986), *Muhakamat Fir'awn* [The Trial of Pharaoh: Revelations about the Trial of Sadat's Assassins], (Cairo: Sina).

Khalil, Khalil Ahmad (1985), *Al-'Arab wa al-qiyada* [The Arabs and Leadership], (Beirut: Dar al-Hadatha).

Al-Khatib, Muhammad (1978), 'Ghazwat badr' [The Conquest of Badr], in *Al-Da'wa*, no. 27, December 1978.

Khomeini, Imam (1985), *Islam and Revolution: Writings and Declarations*, trans. and annotated by Hamid Algar, (London: KPI Ltd).

Khouri, Rami G. (1987), 'Islamic Banking: Knotting a New Network', *ARAMCO World Magazine*, Vol. 38, no. 3, May–June 1987.

Khoury, Philip S. (1983), 'Islamic Revivalism and the Crisis of the Secular State in the Arab World: an Historical Appraisal', in I. Ibrahim, ed., *Arab Resources: the Transformation of a Society* (London: Croom Helm).

Khumaini, Imam Ruhullah (1979), *Al-hukuma al-islamiyya* (Arabic trans. of Wilayat-i-faqih), (Cairo: n.p.).

—— (1986), 'Darurat tashkil al-hukuma al-islamiyya' [On the Necessity of

Forming an Islamic Government], *Al-Hiwar*, Vol. 5, no. 34, Autumn 1986.

Al-Khuri, Fu'ad (1988), *Imamat al-shahid wa imamat al-batal* [Leadership of the Martyr and Leadership of the Hero], (Beirut: Markaz Dar al-Jami'a).

Kizilbash, Hamid H. (1982), 'The Islamic Conference: Retrospect and Prospect', *Arab Studies Quarterly*, Vol. 4, nos. 1 & 2, Spring 1982.

Klower, Gerd Gunter (1982), *Islamic Banks and Strategies for Economic Cooperation; Report of an International Symposium* (Baden-Baden: Nomos Verlagsgesellschaft).

Lambton, Ann K.S. (1981), *State and Government in Mediaeval Islam* (Oxford: Oxford University Press).

Lapidus, Ira M. (1975), 'The Separation of State and Religion in the Development of Early Islamic Society', *International Journal of Middle East Studies*, Vol. 6, no. 4, October 1975.

Lawrence, Bruce (1987), 'Muslim Fundamentalist Movements', in Barbara F. Stowasser, ed., *The Islamic Impulse* (London: Croom Helm).

Lewis, Bernard (1982), 'The Question of Orientalism', *The New York Review*, 24 July 1982.

—— (1988), *The Political Language of Islam* (Chicago and London: University of Chicago Press).

McDonough, Sheila (1984), *Muslim Ethics and Modernity: a Comparative Study of the Ethical Thought of Sayyid Ahmad Khan and Mawlana Mawdudi: Vol. I of Comparative Ethics* (Waterloo, Ont.: Wilfrid Laurier Univ. Press for the Canadian Corporation for Studies in Religion).

Al-Mahdawi, Tariq (1986), *Al-Ikhwan al-muslimun 'ala madhbah al-munawara* [The Muslim Brothers on the Altar of Manoeuvre], (Beirut: Dar Azal).

Al-Mahdi, Al-Sadiq (1983), 'Islam – Society and Change', in John L. Esposito, ed., *Voices of Resurgent Islam* (New York and Oxford: Oxford University Press).

Mahfuz, Muhammad (1988), *Alladhin zulimu. . .* [The Wronged Ones: Islamic Organisations in Egypt], (London: Riad El-Rayyes).

Mahmud, Mustafa (1982), 'Islam vs. Marxism and Capitalism' in J. Donohue and J. Esposito, eds, *Islam in Transition: Muslim Perspectives* (New York: Oxford University Press).

Mann, Michael (1986), *The Sources of Social Power*, Vol. I (Cambridge: Cambridge University Press).

Mardini, Zuhair (1984), *Al-Ladudan . . .* [The Two Adversaries: the Wafd and the Ikhwan], (Beirut: Dar Iqra').

Al-Mawardi, Abi Al-Hasan (new edn, 1985), *Al-Akham al-sultaniyya. . .* [Government Rulings and Religious Incumbencies]. 450 AH (Beirut: Dar al-Kutub al-'Ilmiyya).

Al-Mawdudi, Abu al-A'la (1982), 'Political Theory of Islam', trans., in J. Donohue and J. Esposito, eds, *Islam in Transition: Muslim Perspectives* (New York: Oxford University Press).

—— (1984), *Al-Hukuma al-islamiyya*, trans. [Islamic Government], (Jidda: Al-Dar al-Sa'udiyya).

—— (1987), *Hawla al-din wa al-dawla* [On Religion and the State], (Jidda: Al-Dar al-Sa'udiyya).

Mazrui, Ali (1985), 'Is Modernization Reversible?', *paper* in the International Political Science Association's World Congress, Paris, July 1985.

Mernissi, Fatima (1985), *Beyond the Veil: Male–Female Dynamics in Muslim Society*, rev. edn, (London: Al-Saqi Books).

—— (1988), 'Muslim Women and Fundamentalism', *Middle East Report*, no. 153, July–August 1988.

Metcalf, Barbara D. (1987), 'Islamic Arguments in Contemporary Pakistan', in W. Roff, ed., *Islam and the Political Economy of Meaning* (London: Croom Helm).

Mitchell, Richard P. (1969), *The Society of the Muslim Brothers* (London: Oxford University Press).

Moghadam, Val (1988), 'Women, Work and Ideology in the Islamic Republic', *International Journal of Middle East Studies*, Vol. 20, no. 2, May 1988.

Al-Mubarak, Muhammad (1981), *Al-Nizam al-islami fi al-hukm wa al-dawla* [The Islamic System of Government and State], (Beirut: Dar al-Fikr)

Mujahidin Khalq Iran (1979), *Statement of the People's Mujahidin Organisation of Iran*, reprint (Washington DC: Muslim Students' Association).

Munson, Henry (1988), *Islam and Revolution in the Middle East* (New Haven and London: Yale University Press).

Muru, Muhammad (1985), 'Fath malaf hadith al-manshiyya' [Opening the File of the Manshiyya Event], in *Al-Mukhtar al-Islami*, Vol. 7, no. 37 September–October 1985.

Muruwwa, Husain (1981), *Al-naza'at al-madiyya fi al-falsafa al-'arabiyya al-islamiyya* [Materialist Tendencies in Arab–Islamic Philosophy], 2 vols (Beirut: Dar al-Farabi).

Mus'ad, Ra'uf (1985), "Ashrat ayyam fi al-sudan' [Ten Days in Sudan], in *Al-Manar*, Vol. I, no. 6, June 1985.

Musailihi, Fathi M. (1988), *Tatawwur al-'asima al-misriyya . . .* [Evolution of the Egyptian Capital City and the Greater Metropolis], (Cairo: Dar al-Madina al-Munawwara).

Musallam, Basim F. (1983), *Sex and Society in Islam* (Cambridge: Cambridge University Press).

Mutawalli, 'Abd al-Hamid (1985), *Azmat al-fikr al-siyasi al-islami* [The Crisis of Islamic Political Thought in Modern Times], (Cairo: Hai'at al-Kitab).

Mutawalli, Mahmud (1989), *Al-Ikhwan al-Muslimun wa al-'amal al-siyasi* [The Muslim Brothers and Political Action], (Cairo: Al-Fajr li al-Tiba'a).

Al-Nadwi, Abu al-Hasan (1977), *Al-Sira' bain al-fikra al-islamiyya wa al-fikra al-gharbiyya* [The Conflict Between the Islamic Idea and the Western Idea], (Cairo: Dar al-Ansar).

—— (1984), *Madha khasira al-'alam bi inhitat al-muslimin* [What the World has Lost by the Decline of Muslims], (Beirut: Dar al-Kitab al-'Arabi).

Al-Nafisi, 'Abdalla F. (c. 1980), *'Indama yahkum al-islam* [When Islam Rules], (London: Taha).

—— (1987), 'Mustaqbal al-sahwa al-islamiyya' [The Future of the Islamic Revival], in I.S. 'Aballa *et al.*, *Al-Harakat al-islamiyya fi al-watan al-'arabi* (Beirut: Centre for Arab Unity Studies and United Nations University).

Al-Najjar, Husain Fawzi (1985), *Al-Dawla wa al-hukm fi al-islam* [State and Government in Islam], (Cairo: Dar al-Hurriyya).

Nasr, Muhammad 'Abd al-Mu'izz (1963), *Fi al-dawla wa al-mujtama'* [On State and Society], (Alexandria: Alexandria University Press).

Nassar, Nasif (1983), *Mamfun al-umma bain al-din wa al-tarikh* [Concept of the Community Between Religion and History], (Beirut: Al-Tali'a)

Nienhaus, Volker (1986), 'Islamic Economics, Finance and Banking – Theory and Practice', in Butterworths Editorial Staff, *Islamic Banking and Finance* (London: Butterworths).

Numairi, Ja'far M. (1980), *Al-Nahj al-islami: limadha* [Why the Islamic Way], (Cairo: Al-Maktab al-Misri al-Hadith).

Owen, Roger (1982), *The Middle East in the World Economy 1800–1914* (London and New York: Methuen).

Pakhumius, Al-Anba (1971), *Al-Sijill al-tarikhi li qadasat al-baba Shinuda al-thalith* [The Historical Record of His Holiness Pope Shenuda the Third], (Cairo and Damanhur: Nasr Misr).

PDK – Protagonists of Democracy in Kuwait Ansar al-Dimuqratiyya fi al-Kuwait (1978), *Al-Ta'amur 'ala al-dimuqratiyya fi al-kuwait* [The Conspiracy on Democracy in Kuwait], (n.pl.: PDK, c.1978).

Pipes, Daniel (1982), 'Oil Wealth and Islamic Resurgence', in A. Dessouki, ed., *Islamic Resurgence in the Arab world* (New York: Praeger).

Piscatori, James P., (1980), 'The Roles of Islam in Saudi Arabia's Political Development', in John Esposito, ed., *Islam and Development: Religion and Socio-political Change* (Syracuse: Syracuse University Press).

—— (1986), *Islam in a World of Nation-States* (Cambridge: Cambridge University Press).

Al-Qa'id, Yusuf (1988), 'Iqtisad misr fi qabdat sharikat al-amwal' [The Egyptian Economy in the Fist of the Money Companies], in *Al-Mustaqbal*, 4 June 1988.

Al-Qardawi, Yusuf (1983), *Al-Hall al-islami . . .* [The Islamic Solution: A Duty and a Necessity], (Beirut: Mu'assasat al-Risala).

Qurban, Milhim (1984), *Khalduniyyat: al-siyasa al-'umraniyya* [Khaldunian Issues: The Politics of Urbanity and Civilisation], (Beirut: Al-Mu'assasa al-Jami'iyya).

Qutb, Sayyid (1951), *Ma'rakat al-islam wa al-ra'simaliyya* [The Battle of Islam and Capitalism], (Cairo: Dar al-Kitab al-'Arabi).

—— (1958), *Al-'Adala al-ijtima'iyya fi al-islam* [Social Justice in Islam], (Cairo: 'Isa al-Babi al-Halabi).

—— (1985), *Ma'alim 'fi al-tariq* [Signposts on the Road], new edn, (Damascus and Qum: Dar al-Nashr Qum).

Qutb, Muhammad (1981), *Jahiliyyat al-qarn al-'ishrin* [Twentieth Century 'Pagan Ignorance'], new edn, (Beirut and Cairo: Dar al-Shuruq).

Rabi', Hamid A. (1980; 1983), *Suluk al-malik fi tadbir al-mamalik: ta'lif al-'allamma Shihab al-Din ibn Abi al-Rubayyi'* [Suluk al-Malik fi tadbir al-mamalik: by the scholar Shihab al-Din ibn Abi al-Rubayyi'], Vol. I (1980); Vol. II (1983), (Cairo: Dar al-Sha'b).

Ra'if, Ahmad (1985), *Al-Bawwaba al-Sawda'*. . . [The Black Gate: Pages from the History of the Muslim Brothers], (Cairo: Al-Zahra').

Ramadan, 'Abd al-'Azim (1982), *Al-Ikhwan al-muslimun.* . . [The Muslim Brothers and the Secret Organisation], (Cairo: Rose al-Yusuf).

Rizq, Jabir (1981), 'Al-Wad' al-'arabi al-mumazzaq' [The Sundered Arab Situation], *Al-Da'wa*, no. 57, January 1981.

Rodinson, Maxime (1971), *Mohammed*, trans. A. Carter (Harmondsworth: Penguin Books).

—— (1978), *Islam and Capitalism*, trans. B. Pearce (Austin: University of Texas Press).

—— (1979), *Marxism and the Muslim World*, trans. Michael Pallis (London: Zed Books).

—— (1981), *The Arabs*, trans. A. Goldhammer (Chicago and London: Chicago University Press and Croom Helm).

Roff, William R. (1987), 'Islamic Movements: One or Many?', in W. Roff, ed., *Islam and the Political Economy of Meaning* (London: Croom Helm).

Rosenthal, Erwin I.J. (1958), *Political Thought in Mediaeval Islam: an Introductory Outline* (Cambridge: Cambridge University Press).

Runciman, W.G. (1989), *A Treatise on Social Theory* (Cambridge: Cambridge University Press).

El Saadawi, Nawal (1982), *The Hidden Face of Eve: Women in the Arab World* (Boston: Beacon Press).

Sa'd, Ahmad Sadiq (1988), *Dirasa fi al-mafahim al-iqtisadiyya lada al-mufakkirin al-islamiyyin: kitab al-Kharaj li Abi Yusuf* [A Study on Economic Concepts among Islamic Thinkers – al-Kharaj Book of Abu Yusuf], (Cairo: Dar al-Thaqafa al-Jadida).

Al-Sadr, Muhammad Baqir (1986), 'Hawla mashru' dustur al-jumhuriyya al-islamiyya' [On the Proposal for a Constitution of the Islamic Republi]), *Al-Hiwar*, Vol. 5, no. 34, Autumn 1986.

Sahhab, Victor (1984), *Darurat al-turath* [Necessity of the Heritage], (Beirut: Dar al-'Ilmli al-malayin).

Al-Sa'id, Rif'at (1977), *Hasan al-Banna.* . . [Hasan al-Banna: When, How and Why?], (Cairo: Madbuli, 1977)

Saif Al-Dawla, 'Ismat (1986), *'An al-'uruba wa al-islam* [On Arabism and Islam], (Beirut: Centre for Arab Unity Studies).

Salman, Magida, *et al.* (1987), *Women in the Middle East* (London: Zed).

Al-Sayyid, Radwan (1984A), *Mafahim al-jama'at fi al-islam* [The Concept of Groups in Islam], (Beirut: Dar al-Tanwir).

—— (1984B), *Al-'Umma wa al-jama' wa al-sulta* [Community, Group and Authority], (Beirut: Dar Iqra').

—— (1988), 'Al-Haraka al-islamiyya wa al-thaqafa al-mu'asira" [The Islamic Movement and Contemporary Culture], in S. Ibrahim, ed., *Al-*

Sahwa al-islamiyya wa humum al-watan al-'arabi (Amman: Arab Through Forum and Mu'assasat Al-al-Bait).

Sayyid-Ahmad, Rif'at, (1985), 'Ishkaliyyat al-sira' bain al-din wa al-dawla fi al-namudhaj al-nasiri' [The Problematic of Religion/State Conflict in the Nasserist Model], in *Al-Yaqza al-'Arabiyya*, Vol. I, no. 4, June 1985.

—— (1988A), *Al-Islambuli*. . . [Al-Islambuli: A New Perspective on the Jihad Organisation], (Cairo: Madbuli).

—— (1988B), *Rasa'il Juhaiman al-'Utaibi* [The Tracts of Juhaiman al-'Utaibi], (Cairo: Madbuli).

Schacht, Joseph (1964), *An Introduction to Islamic Law* (Oxford: Oxford University Press).

Shadid, Mohamed K. (1988), 'The Muslim Brotherhood Movement in the West Bank and Gaza', *Third World Quarterly*, Vol. 10, no. 2, April 1988 (on *Islam and Politics*).

Shafiq, Munir (1983), *Al-Islam wa tahadiyat al-inhitat al-mu'asir* [Islam and the Challenges of Contemporary Decline], (London: Taha).

—— (1985), *Rudud 'ala utruhat 'ilmaniyya* [(Responses to Secularist Theses], (Tunis: Dar al-Hikma).

—— (1986), *Qadaya al-tanmiya wa al-istiqlal fi al-sira' al-hadari* [Issues of Development and Independence within the Cultural/Civilisational Conflict], (Tunis: Dar al-Buraq).

Shalabi, Ahmad (1983), *Al-Siyasa fi al-fikr al-islami* [Politics in Islamic Thought], (Cairo: Al-Nahda al-Misriyya).

Shalaq, Al-Fadl (1988), 'Al-Kharaj wa al-iqta' wa al-dawla' [Tribute, Eastern Feudalism and the State], in *Al-Ijtihad*, special issue, Vol. I, no. 1, July–September 1988.

Shamuq, Ahmad M. (1981), *Kaifa yufakkir al-ikhwan al-muslimun* [How Do the Muslim Brothers Think?], (Beirut and Khartoum: Dar al-Jil and Dar al-Fikr).

Sharabi, Hisham (1987), *Al-binya al-batrakiyya* . . . [The Patriarchal Structure: a Study in Contemporary Arab Society], (Beirut: Dar al-Tali'a)

Sharara, Waddah (1981A), *Al-Ahl wa al-ghanima* [Kin and the Booty: The Foundations of Politics in the Kingdom of Saudi Arabia], (Beirut: Dar al-Tali'a).

—— (1981B), *Isti'naf al-bad'* [Resuming the Start: Essays on the Relationship Between Philosophy and History], (Beirut: Dar al-Hadatha).

—— (1985), *Al-Madina al-mawqufa* [The Suspended City: Beirut Between Kinship and Residence], (Beirut: Dar al-Matbu'at al-Sharqiyya).

Al-Sha'rawi, Shaikh Mutawalli (1982), interview in *Mayu*, 8 June 1982.

Al-Sharif, Kamil (1988), 'Al-Sahwa al-islamiyya wa al-musharaka al-siyasiyya [The Islamic Revival and Political Participation], in S. Ibrahim, ed., *Al-Sahwa al-islamiyya wa humum al-watan al-'arabi* (Amman: Arab Through Forum and Mu'assasat Al-al-Bait).

Al-Sharqawi, 'Abd al-Rahman (1982), 'Ibn Taimiya: al-faqih al-mu'adhdhab' [Ibn Taimiya: the Tormented Jurist], *Al-Ahram*, 23 June 1982, and subsequent weeks.

Shimogaki, Kazuo (1988), *Between Modernity and Post Modernity: the*

Islamic Left and Dr Hasan Hanafi's Thought; a Critical Reading Niigata, International University of Japan, Working Papers Series no. 14.

Shuhaib, 'Abd al-Qadir (1989), *Al-Ikhtiraq: qissat sharikat tawzif al-amwal* [The Penetration: Story of the Money Utilisation Companies], (Cairo: Sina).

Shukrallah, Hani (1989), 'Political Crisis/Conflict in post-1967 Egypt' in C. Tripp and R. Owen, eds, *Egypt Under Mubarak* (London and New York: Routledge).

Al-Siba'i, Mustafa (1962), *Ishtirakiyyat al-islam* [The Socialism of Islam], (Cairo: Dar al-Sha'b).

Sivan, Emmanuel (1985), *Radical Islam: Medieval Theology and Modern Politics* (New Haven and London: Yale University Press).

—— (1989), 'Sunni Radicalism in the Middle East and the the Iranian Revolution', *International Journal of Middle East Studies*, Vol. 21, no. 1, February 1989.

Sklar, Richard L. (1976), 'Post-imperialism; A Class Analysis of Multi-national Corporate Expansion', *Comparative Politics*, Vol. 9, no. 1, October 1976.

Tabliyya, Al-Qutb Muhammad (1985), *Nizam al-idara fi al-islam* [The System of Administration in Islam], (Cairo: Dar al-Fikr al-'Arabi).

Tachau, Frank (1985), 'States and Bureaucracies in the Middle East', *paper* presented at the 13th World Congress of the International Political Science Association, Paris, July 1985.

Taha, Taha 'Abd al-'Alim (1988), 'Al-Iqtisad al-islami bain al-mafahim wa al-mumarasat' [The Islamic Economy between Concepts and Practices], in S. Ibrahim, ed., *Al-Sahwa al-islamiyya wa humum al-watan al-'arabi* (Amman: Arab Through Forum and Mu'assasat Al-al-Bait).

Al-Tawati, Mustafa (c.1985), *Al-ta'bir al-dini 'an al-sira' al-ijtima'i fi al-islam* [Religious Expression of Social Conflict in Islam], (Tunis: Dar al-Nashr li al-Maghrib).

Tawfiq, Mamduh (1977), *Al-Ijram al-siyasi* [Political Criminality], (Cairo: Dar al-Jil).

Taylor, John G. (1979), *From Modernization to Modes of Production: A Critique of the Sociologies of Development and Underdevelopment* (London: Macmillan).

Thamir, Fadil (1988), 'Min sultat al-nass ila sultat al-qira'a' [From Authority of the Text to Authority of the Reading], in *Al-Fikr al-'Arabi al-Mu'asir*, no. 48–49, February 1988.

Al-Tilmisani, 'Umar (1984), *Hasan al-Banna: ustadh al-jil* [Hasan al-Banna: Teacher of the Generation], (Cairo: Dar al-Nasr li al-Tiba'a al-Islamiyya).

Tizini, Tayyib (1971), *Mashru' ru'ya jadida li al-fikr al-'arabi* [A Project for a New Perspective on Arabic Thought in the Mediaeval Era], (Damascus: Dar Dimashq).

Al-Turabi, Hassan (1983), 'The Islamic State', in John L. Esposito, ed., *Voices of Resurgent Islam* (New York and Oxford: Oxford University. Press).

—— (1988), 'Al-Sahwa al-islamiyya wa al-dawla al-qutriyya . . .' [The Islamic Revival and the Territorial State in the Arab World], in

S. Ibrahim, ed., *Al-Sahwa al-islamiyya wa humum al-watan al-'arabi* (Amman: Arab Through Forum and Mu'assasat Al-al Bait).

Turner, Bryan S. (1974), *Weber and Islam* (London: Routledge and Kegan Paul).

—— (1978), *Marx and the End of Orientalism* (London and Boston: Allen and Unwin).

Umlil, 'Ali (1985), *Al-Islahiyya al-'arabiyya wa al-dawla al-wataniyya* [Arab Reformism and the National State], (Casablanca: Al-Markaz al-Thaqafi al-'Arabi).

'Uthman, 'Uthman Ahmad (1981), *Tajribati* [My Experience], (Cairo: Al-Maktab al-Misri al-Hadith).

'Uwais, 'Abd al-Halim (*c*.1986), *Mushkilat al-iqtisad al-islami* [Problems of the Islamic Economy], (Jidda: Al-Sharika al-Sa'udiyya li al-Abhath wa al-Taswiq).

Vatikiotis, P.J. (1987), *Islam and the State* (London: Croom Helm).

Vatin, Jean-Claude (1982), 'Revival in the Maghreb', in A. Dessouki, ed., *Islamic Resurgence in the Arab World* (New York: Praeger).

Voll, John O. (1983), 'The Evolution of Islamic Fundamentalism in Twentieth Century Sudan', in Gabriel Warburg and Uri Kupferschmidt, eds, *Islam, Nationalism and Radicalism in Egypt and Sudan* (New York: Praeger).

Walz, Terence (1978), 'Asyut in the 1260's (1844–53)', *Journal of the American Research Center in Egypt*, Vol. 15, 1978.

Watt, W. Montgomery (1968), *Islamic Political Thought: the Basic Concepts* Islamic Surveys no. 6, (Edinburgh: Edinburgh University Press).

Wilson, Rodney (1983), *Banking and Finance in the Arab Middle East* (London: Macmillan).

Wolf, Eric R. (1982), *Europe and the People Without History* (Berkeley: University of California Press).

Woodward, Peter (1983), 'Islam, Radicalism, and Nationalism in Sudanese Politics Before Independence', in Gabriel Warburg and Uri Kupferschmidt, eds, *Islam, Nationalism, and Radicalism in Egypt and the Sudan* (New York: Praeger).

Yasin, 'Abd al-Jawwad (1986), *Muqaddima fi fiqh al-jahiliyya al-mu'asira* [An Introduction to the Jurisprudence of Contemporary 'Ignorance'], (Cairo: Al-Zahra' li al-I'lam al-'Arabi).

Yasin, Bu'Ali (1985), *Al-Thaluth al-muharram. . .* [The Forbidden Trinity: A Study on Religion, Sex and Class Struggle], (Beirut: Dar al-Tali'a).

Yasin, Al-Sayyid (1983), *Al-Shakhsiyya al-'arabiyya. . .* [The Arab Character: Between Self-Image and Perception by Others], (Beirut: Dar al-Tanwir).

Youssef, Michael (1985), *Revolt Against Modernity: Muslim Zealots and the West* (Leiden: Brill).

Yusuf, Abu Saif (1987), *Al-Aqbat wa al-qawmiyya al-'arabiyya* [The Copts and Arab Nationalism], (Beirut: Centre for Arab Unity Studies).

Zakariyya, Fu'ad (1986), *Al-Haqiqa wa al-wahm fi al-haraka al-islamiyya al-mu'asira* [Fact and Fiction in the Contemporary Islamic Movement], (Cairo: Dar al-Fikr li al-Dirasat).

—— (1987), *Al-Sahwa al-islamiyya fi mizan al-'aql* [The Islamic Revival in the Scales of Reason], (Cairo: Dar al-Fikr al-Mu'asir).

Zai'ur, 'Ali, (1988A), *Al-Hikma al-'amaliyya. . .* [Practical Wisdom: or Ethics, Politics and Dealings], (Beirut: Dar al-Tali'a).

—— (1988B), 'Nahwa nazariyya 'arabiya fi al-jasad wa al-insan' [Towards an Arab Theory for Body and the Human Being], *Al-Fikr al-'Arabi al-Mu'asir*, nos. 50–51, March–April 1988.

Zubaida, Sami (1988), 'An Islamic State? The Case of Iran', *Middle East Report*, no. 153, July–August 1988.

—— (1989), *Islam, the People and the State* (London: Routledge).

Journals, magazines and newspapers

Al-Ahram
Al-Ahram al-Iqtisadi
Al-Akhbar
Al-'Arab
Al-Da'wa
Al-Dawha
Al-Hiwar
Al-Iqtisadi al-Islami
Guardian
Al-Islah
Al-Jumhuriyya
Al-Liwa' al-Islami
Al-Manar
Mayu
Middle East Economic Survey (MEES)
Mid-East Mirror
Al-Musawwar
Al-Mustaqbal
Al-Nahar
Oxford Analytica
Al-Rayah
Al-Riyad
Rose al-Yusuf
Sabah al-Khair
Al-Safir
Al-Sharq al-Awsat
Al-Siyasa
Al-Tadamun
Al-Thawra al-Islamiyya
Al-Yaqza al-'Arabiyya

Index